KAZAKHSTAN

Stay in a traditional nomad's yurt on the shore of Aidarkul
pages 202–3

Admire the splendid gilt and mosaic tilework of Samarkand's picture-perfect Registan
pages 158–9

Eat *shashlik* and haggle for souvenirs in the mosaic trading domes of Tashkent's Chorsu Bazaar
page 100

KYRGYZSTAN

Gazalkent

TASHKENT Chirchik

Shardara Bgeni

Syr Darya

TAJIKISTAN

10

Tashkent International

Namangan Andijan

Angren

11

Almalyk

Kokand *Fergana Valley*

sert

Lake Aidarkul

Nurata

Gulistan

Kairakkum Reservoir

12

Fergana

13

Konibodom

Zarafshon

M39

9

UZBEKISTAN

Javoi

M37

Kattakurgan

M37

8

M39 Dzhizak

5

Samarkand

TAJIKISTAN

Urgut

Travel into the fertile Fergana Valley to appreciate Uzbekistan's linguistic, ethnic and cultural diversity
pages 125–47

Karshi

Shakhrisabz

TAJIKISTAN

DUSHANBE

6

Denau

Pamir

7

Wander through the turquoise and lapis lazuli blue tombs of the Shah-i Zinda
pages 160–2

Termez

H i n d u   K u s h

PAKISTAN

Get better acquainted with national hero Amir Timur in his hometown of Shakhrisabz
pages 171–7

Explore Uzbekistan's pre-Islamic history by visiting Buddhist Termez
pages 183–90

Indus

■ **KABUL**

Uzbekistan
Don't
miss...

Camel trekking
Get to know your
Bactrian camel whilst
riding through the sands
of the Kyzylkum Desert
(J/S) page 203

Islamic architecture
The Registan in Samarkand is one
of the world's greatest examples
of medieval Islamic architecture
(EA/D) pages 158–9

Museum City
The Ichon Qala – the central walled city of Khiva – is stuffed with mosques, madrassas and mausoleums
(DP/D) pages 240–50

Traditional style
Uzbekistan is famous for its wonderful silk carpets, with their tight weave, smooth finish and rich colours
(AS/D) pages 33–4

Khorezm fortresses
The Ayaz Qala fortress is part of UNESCO's Ring of Ancient Khorezm
(SI) pages 233–4

Uzbekistan in colour

above left   The gilded interior of the Tilla Kari Madrassa reveals the incredible wealth of these Islamic schools (GA/S) pages 158–9

above right   The founder of the Samanid dynasty is buried at this place of pilgrimage in Bukhara (AL/S) pages 222–3

left   The Mir-i Arab Madrassa has been an important Islamic educational institution for nearly 500 years (MEP) pages 220–1

below   The Gur-i Amir is the burial place of Amir Timur, though Timur never wanted to be buried here (AL/S) pages 162–3

above Few of Tashkent's historic buildings survived the 1966 earthquake, so this mosque is doubly important (Lp/S) page 103

right No trip to Samarkand is complete without visiting Shah-i Zinda, a magnificent collection of medieval tiled tombs (e/S) pages 160–2

below The khans of Kokands were great patrons of the arts, as shown by the Khudayar Khan Palace (EF/D) page 145

<table>
<tr><td>left</td><td>Carpets are for sale in most of Uzbekistan's cities, like here in Tashkent (SS) pages 33–4</td></tr>
<tr><td>above</td><td>Women still weave intricate carpets by hand in Uzbekistan's carpet workshops (AB) page 157</td></tr>
<tr><td>below</td><td>All manner of carpets, from handwoven silk masterpieces to factory-made rugs, are on sale in Uzbekistan's bazaars (A/D) page 71</td></tr>
</table>

AUTHORS

Sophie Ibbotson and Max Lovell-Hoare first arrived in central Asia in 2008 when their two auto-rickshaws (tuk-tuks) got snowed in *en route* from Darjeeling, India, to London. Forced to overwinter, they fell in love with the region and became excited by the opportunities it offered, opening the Kyrgyz office of their investment promotion company, Maximum Exposure Productions (MEP), the following year. Max continues to explore investment and development projects in central Asia and the Middle East; Sophie now runs Maximum Exposure Ltd, providing tourism and culture consultancy and PR services, and is the co-founder and managing editor of *Panorama: The Journal of Intelligent Travel*.

Sophie and Max are both members of the Royal Society for Asian Affairs (*www.rsaa.org.uk*), where Sophie is also a member of council. They have co-written Bradt guides to Kashmir, Tajikistan, Sudan and South Sudan, and updated guides to Kazakhstan and Kyrgyzstan.

AUTHORS' STORY

Normally when we tell a story that starts with getting the runs whilst travelling, it finishes either up to our ankles in a squat toilet (a particularly poignant scene from the film *Slumdog Millionaire* comes to mind) or lying face down on the marble floor of a toilet off the foyer of the nearest four-star hotel. Only once (so far) has it taken us to a wedding. Uzbekistan is nothing if not full of surprises.

It was a beautiful, bright day in November, cold but with an azure sky, and we were photographing every last inch of Bukhara. Standing in the Poi Kalyon, staring up at the Kalyon Minar, I was overcome by the architectural splendour, and Max was overcome with an attack of the runs. As he dropped his bags and started sprinting across the square towards hotels and their much-needed facilities, I called out directions to the nearest public loo. Clearly my directions were not up to scratch, as he ended up instead in Bukhara Silk Carpets, throwing himself on the mercy of Sabina and her staff. Thank God, they were very accommodating.

Half an hour later, Max re-materialised looking rather more relaxed than before, and indeed quite proud of himself, as the urgent bathroom visit had unexpectedly yielded no fewer than three invitations to Sabina's cousin's wedding. Neither Sabina nor the bride had ever met Max before, and he was hardly in the most sociably acceptable of states, but Uzbek hospitality is such that the hand of friendship was straightaway extended, and at 19.00 we were on our way to the party.

Uzbek weddings are riotous affairs, with hundreds of guests and a bottle of vodka on every table. Vodka and Fanta is a surprisingly good combination, and we danced until midnight, fuelled no doubt by the toasts and E numbers. We danced with the girls, and we danced with the boys, and we tucked in to mountains of cake. The family gave speeches, and the band played on, and the Imodium did exactly what it was intended to do.

PUBLISHER'S FOREWORD

Adrian Phillips, Managing Director

Reckon writing a guidebook to a country on the Silk Road must be the most romantic job around? Read Max and Sophie's authors' story on the first page and think again… It's typical of the warts and all approach they take to their guides. You mustn't miss a ride on a camel, of course, but be aware too that camels are 'invariably smelly and jolly uncomfortable to ride'. Explore Chorsu Bazaar, the 'first and only place we've seen the boot of a Lada stacked with decapitated cow heads'. Max and Sophie tell it how it is. But that means too that they tell of a country where spring brings a riot of colourful flowers in mountain pastures, where summer offers starry skies and nights spent in yurts, where traditional festivals are things of thrilling pomp and circumstance – and where a toilet stop in a carpet shop can lead to an invitation to a family wedding!

Second edition published August 2016
First edition published 2013
Bradt Travel Guides Ltd
IDC House, The Vale, Chalfont St Peter, Bucks SL9 9RZ, England
www.bradtguides.com
Print edition published in the USA by The Globe Pequot Press Inc,
PO Box 480, Guilford, Connecticut 06437-0480

Text copyright © 2016 Sophie Ibbotson and Max Lovell-Hoare
Maps copyright © 2016 Bradt Travel Guides Ltd; includes map data © OpenStreetMap contributors
Photographs copyright © 2016 Individual photographers (see below)
Project Managers: Claire Strange & Laura Pidgley
Cover research: Pepi Bluck, Perfect Picture

ISBN: 978 1 78477 017 4 (print)
e-ISBN: 978 1 78477 162 1 (e-pub)
e-ISBN: 978 1 78477 262 8 (mobi)

British Library Cataloguing in Publication Data
A catalogue record for this book is available from the British Library

Photographs Adam Balogh (AB); Alamy: Jorge Fernandez (JF/A); AWL Images: Jane Sweeney (JS/AWL); Dreamstime: Antonella865 (A/D), Alex Semenov (AS/D), Alexat25 (AX/D), Daniel Prudek (DP/D), Eduard Kim (EK/D), Evgeniy Agarkov (EA/D), Elizaveta Kharicheva (EK/D), Enrico Mariotti (EM/D), Mattiaath (M/D), Radist (R/D); Maximum Exposure Productions (MEP); Shutterstock: Anatolijs Laicans (AL/S), eFesenko (EF/S), Galyna Andrushk (GA/S), javarman (j/S), Limpopo (L/S), Milosz Maslanka (MM/S), posztos (p/S); Sitara International (SI); SuperStock (SS); Wikimedia Commons: ChanOJ (C/WC)
Front cover Mir-i Arab Madrassa, Bukhara (JF/A)
Back cover Bibi-Khanym Mosque (EK/D); local market seller (MEP)
Title page Islam Khoja Minaret (j/S); Tilla Kari Madrassa (GA/S); foothills of Uzbekistan (SS)

Maps David McCutcheon FBCart.S

Typeset by www.dataworks.co.in
Production managed by Jellyfish Print Solutions; printed in India
Digital conversion by www.dataworks.co.in

Acknowledgements

Writing a travel guide is always a team effort, and so there are a huge number of people to thank for their contributions to both editions of this book.

For the research, endless phone calls and embassy runs for the first edition, we're grateful to Jack Barkley-Smith, Ainura Temiralieva and Sam Caplat. Thank you to Rachel Fielding at Bradt for commissioning this guide in the first place, and to Maisie Fitzpatrick and Claire Strange for such patient handling of the manuscript and production process.

In Uzbekistan, John Newby, Bryn Kewley, Steve and Jo Dew-Jones, Jamie Lessor and Amanda Curley were first-rate travelling companions and co-drivers, and we're also hugely appreciative of the constructive input, beer, *shashlik* and good humour of Raphael, Tristan, Finn and Blaise in Tashkent.

To all the families storing Coca-Cola bottles full of black market petrol in your front rooms, kitchens and outside loos: though we don't endorse such practice, we couldn't have done it without you either.

There are a number of boxes in this guide written by people with far more detailed knowledge than us, and we're indebted to them for the time and thought that went into writing them. Worthy of particular mention in this regard are Bijan Omrani (*www.bijanomrani.com*), Ben Tavener (*www.bentavener.com*) and Lainie Mullen. Thank you.

Things have changed in Uzbekistan at great pace over the past few years, and so updating this second edition was no small task. Our main research trip coincided with the official tour to Uzbekistan of the Royal Society for Asian Affairs (*www.rsaa.org.uk*), the members of which gave invaluable feedback on the first edition of the guide, as well as new observations.

Super linguists Georgina Suttie and Stephanie Adams both did an incredible job fact checking and undertaking additional research for the practical information chapters. Svetlana Rakhimova significantly improved the *Language* appendix, ensuring that you can now express yourself using key phrases in Uzbek, and Steve Rooke (*www.sunbirdtours.co.uk*) enlightened us about Uzbekistan's wealth of birdlife. John Fry (*www.fryfilm.com*) rewrote the photography section, and also added tips on shooting video during your trip. Finally, Sharon Ibbotson provided invaluable input for the expanded history and culture sections, and she and Ed Day rescued the updated Tashkent chapter at the eleventh hour when the MacBook swallowed it in its entirety. Thank you all.

Contents

LIST OF MAPS

FEEDBACK REQUEST AND UPDATES WEBSITE

At Bradt Travel Guides we're aware that guidebooks start to go out of date on the day they're published – and that you, our readers, are out there in the field doing research of your own. You'll find out before us when a fine new family-run hotel opens or a favourite restaurant changes hands and goes downhill. So why not write and tell us about your experiences? Contact us on 01753 893444 or e info@bradtguides.com. We will forward emails to the author who may post updates on the Bradt website at www.bradtupdates. com/uzbekistan. Alternatively you can add a review of the book to www. bradtguides.com or Amazon.

Introduction

In his 1913 poem *The Golden Road to Samarkand*, each of James Elroy Flecker's characters describes in vivid detail moonlit cities, the heat of the winds, shadows cast on the sands, and the silent air of the desert. The reader is swept along in their timeless caravan, sharing in the atmospheric journey, and, like the merchants, gives scarcely a thought for the women left behind, ignored completely, as everyone's attention is utterly transfixed by the destination of which they dream.

Uzbekistan captures the imagination like almost nowhere else. The country is virtually synonymous with the Silk Road, and three of the greatest Silk Road cities – Samarkand, Bukhara and Khiva – all fall on Uzbek soil. The people, ideas and goods that travelled east to west, and, indeed, west to east, have left indelible marks on Uzbekistan's landscape, its culture and the genetic make-up of its people, creating a diverse destination with layer upon layer of competing (but entwined) identities.

It is a country with a rich, fascinating past, and its long settled history has left numerous physical remains, making it far more tangible than in neighbouring Kazakhstan or Kyrgyzstan where nomadism was the norm. The country has been continually inhabited since Neanderthal man first walked across the steppe and took refuge in the Gissar Mountains south of Samarkand. His Stone Age descendants carved their marks in caves, and by the first millennium BC Iranian nomads had settled the grassy plains, planted crops and built rudimentary irrigation channels. In their wake came wave after wave of invaders: Scythians, Achaemenids, Greeks, Arabs and Mongols. Each group built palaces, fortresses, and places of worship and of trade, attempting to eclipse both physically and in public memory whatever had been there before.

The constant cycle of construction and destruction has had a significant impact on what we see in Uzbekistan today. The buildings which survive, and which make the striking skylines of each and every city, are not necessarily the most modern or the mostly strongly constructed: they are the ones which, by dint of good fortune, have avoided both the attentions of marauding hordes and equally destructive natural disasters. Well into the 20th century the Soviets were levelling ancient buildings to make way for architecture that was, in its aesthetics and its function, better in keeping with their ideology. To a far lesser extent, the same is also true of the post-independence period. Restoration projects, some more sympathetic than others, have raised medieval buildings like phoenixes from the ashes, though how much of their appearance is original and how much should be attributed to artistic licence, a modern architect or a politician's idealised vision of the past, is always open to debate. City-wide beautification projects, such as the ongoing one in Shakhrisabz, are especially controversial.

Man's impact, past and present, on the natural environment as well as the urban landscape is clear in Uzbekistan, too. The taming of the Amu Darya and Syr Darya rivers, the construction of canals, dams and other irrigation methods, has made it possible to farm huge swathes of land that naturally could not support crops. The country's lucrative cotton crop especially depends on man's manipulation of nature. Interfering in this manner is not without its dangers, however, and in the race to cultivate more and more land, to produce ever greater quantities of cotton, the ecosystem has become disturbingly unbalanced: the Aral Sea has already retreated beyond the level from which it is thought to be recoverable; stretches of once fertile land are turning to desert; and even greater areas are increasingly saline and/or toxic, heavily polluted with industrial waste and chemical pesticides.

In many ways, Uzbekistan is at a crossroads. This applies, as it has always done, in a physical sense, as the country lies in the heart of Eurasia: Europe and Iran are to the west; Russia is to the north; China is to the east; and Afghanistan and the Indian subcontinent spread out southwards. But it is also true culturally, economically and politically. Two decades after the fall of the Soviet Union, Uzbekistan is no longer a bedfellow of Moscow, but neither has it been able to properly integrate with markets and potential allies in the West. If any country is the beneficiary of this economic and political power vacuum, it is China, who is now Uzbekistan's biggest investor, but even so, the Chinese are still viewed by the Uzbeks with suspicion. Unlike in Africa and other resource-rich regions, the Chinese have not had it all their way in Uzbekistan, with local firms, and government regulations, keeping them in check.

History has shown us that Uzbekistan is at its greatest when it has a symbiotic relationship with its neighbours, when people, ideas and goods flow back and forth, enriching every aspect of society. In this transitional period, when Uzbekistan is cautious of how to promote itself outside its borders, the world must come to Uzbekistan, visitors bringing with them the finest aspects of their own societies, and a willingness to share and learn.

Part One

GENERAL INFORMATION

Location Landlocked in the heart of central Asia

Neighbouring countries Afghanistan, Kazakhstan, Kyrgyzstan, Tajikistan and Turkmenistan

Area 447,400km²

Climate Extreme continental

Status Republic

Population 29.2 million (July 2015)

Life expectancy 73.5 years

Capital Tashkent (population 2.5 million)

Other main towns Andijan, Bukhara, Nukus, Samarkand

Major exports Cotton, jute, minerals (notably copper, lead, zinc, tung, uranium and gold), chemicals, fertiliser, leather and natural gas

GDP (PPP) US$172.3 billion; GDP (PPP) per capita US$5,600 (2014)

Official language Uzbek. Russian and Tajik are also widely used.

Religion Islam (90% of the population), Russian Orthodox

Currency Uzbek som (UZS)

Exchange rate £1 = UZS4,200; US$1 = UZS2,900 (official); £1 = UZS5,000; US$1 = UZS3,800 (unofficial) (June 2016)

National airline Uzbekistan Airways

International telephone code +998

Time UTC (GMT) +5

Electric voltage 220AC (50Hz)

Weights and measures Metric

Flag Three vertical stripes of light blue, white and green, with thin red stripes in between each colour. There is a crescent moon and 12 stars in the top left-hand corner.

National anthem 'O'zbekiston Respublikasining Davlat Madhiyasi'

National sports *Kupkari* (a game played between two teams, using a goat's carcass to score points), *kurash* (traditional wrestling), football, judo, boxing and tae kwon do

Public holidays 1–2 January (New Year's Day), 14 January (Day of Defenders of the Motherland), 8 March (International Women's Day), 21 March (*Navruz*, the Persian New Year), 9 May (Remembrance Day), 1 September (Independence Day), 1 October (Teachers' Day), 8 December (Constitution Day)

1

Background Information

GEOGRAPHY AND CLIMATE

Viewed from the air, Uzbekistan is a striking patchwork of colours, with vast stretches of arid desert in the west giving way to jade green stripes along rivers and in the fertile Fergana Valley. The seams of snow-capped Tian Shan Mountains denote the country's southern and eastern borders, their glacial meltwater the lifeblood of the plains.

CLIMATE Uzbekistan has an extreme continental climate due to its location at the centre of the Eurasian landmass. In the north of the country summer temperatures usually surpass 40°C, and winters are as cold as the summers are hot, with lows of 20°C or even 30°C below freezing not uncommon. Winter begins in late October on the plateau, and in late December in the south. January is the coldest month, and the winter generally lasts until April. The average snowfall nationwide is 5cm, rising to 10–12cm in the foothills.

Much of Uzbekistan is arid and has little rainfall. Humidity is generally low and annual rainfall is typically 100–200mm, stunting the growth of crops and other flora during the summer months. There is some regional variation, however, as the far south of Uzbekistan has a more tropical climate (complete with higher levels of humidity and rainfall), and the annual rainfall in the mountains can be as much as 900mm.

THE SYR DARYA

Known to the ancient Greeks as the Jaxartes on account of its colour (from the Persian *yakhsha arta*, meaning 'great pearly river'), the Syr Darya became famous in the classical world as the site where Alexander the Great fought the Scythians in 329BC at the Battle of Jaxartes. Subsequent Islamic writings from the medieval period suggest that the Syr Darya is one of four rivers whose common source lies in paradise. The others are the Amu Darya (the Oxus), the Nile and the Euphrates.

In reality, the Syr Darya rises from headstreams in the Tian Shan Mountains of Kyrgyzstan and flows 2,212km (1,374 miles) west through Uzbekistan and Kazakhstan, and would naturally finally drain out into the Aral Sea. Its water flow is around 37km³ a year.

The diversion of the Syr Darya's water into a network of canals is one of the main reasons for the environmental disaster that is the shrinking of the Aral Sea (see box, page 4). So much water is used for cotton irrigation (and lost due to evaporation and leakage from poorly maintained channels) that the river runs dry long before reaching its natural end.

GEOGRAPHY At 447,400km² in size, Uzbekistan is equivalent in area to Spain or California. The country measures 1,425km from its western to eastern borders, and 930km from north to south. Uzbekistan is one of only two double-landlocked countries (ie: landlocked countries completely surrounded by other landlocked countries) in the world, the other being Liechtenstein.

The physical environment of Uzbekistan is diverse, ranging from the flat, arid deserts that cover almost 80% of the country's territory, to the eastern mountain peaks that rise up to 4,500m (14,800ft) above sea level.

Water resources are unevenly distributed in Uzbekistan. The two largest rivers are the Amu Darya (known to the ancient Greeks as the Oxus) and the Syr Darya (the Jaxartes; see box, page 3), both of which originate in the mountains of Kyrgyzstan and Tajikistan. The shallow Sarygamysh Lake sits on the border with Turkmenistan, and much of the ill-fated Aral Sea (see below) was once within Uzbek territory.

THE ARAL SEA

The Aral Sea, which means 'Sea of Islands' in reference to the 1,534 islands it once contained, was previously one of the four largest lakes in the world with an area of 68,000km² (26,300 square miles). It straddled the border between Kazakhstan and Uzbekistan and was clearly visible from space.

In a period of just 50 years, however, it has declined to just 10% of its former size, with the remaining waters toxic and extremely saline. The retreat of the sea has also caused noticeable localised climate change, and those who once depended on the sea for their livelihood have quite literally been left high and dry. Scientists have called the shrinking of the Aral Sea 'one of the planet's worst environmental disasters'.

The sea's decline began in the 1960s when Soviet bureaucrats decided to divert the waters of the Amu Darya and Syr Darya rivers to irrigate water-intensive crops such as cotton and melons. The irrigation canals were poorly constructed, however, with as much as 75% of the water leaking out or evaporating before it reached the crops. Even today, only 12% of Uzbekistan's irrigation canals are waterproofed.

Deprived of its water supply, the Aral Sea began to shrink. In the 1960s the water level fell at a rate of 20cm a year. This rate tripled in the 1970s, and by the 1980s the water dropped, on average, by 90cm annually. The quantity of water being diverted for irrigation continued to increase too, despite its obvious impact on the sea.

Following independence, Uzbekistan continued the Soviet irrigation policies and the agricultural focus on cotton production, despite its unsustainability. Monoculture and soil depletion required ever higher quantities of artificial fertiliser to be used, with the run-off further increasing the chemical levels in the sea.

The increase in salinity and pollution had wiped out most of the sea's flora and fauna by the early 2000s, and the rate of evaporation was faster than expected. The decline of the North Aral Sea, now separated from the southern part by desert, was partially reversed by the construction of a dam by the Kazakh government, but the South Aral continues to shrink. The desert formed on its former seabed is called the Aralkum.

ENVIRONMENTAL POLICY Uzbekistan's government has recognised the country's environmental problems and created a 'Biodiversity Action Plan'. However, the implementation of environmental policy is poor, with numerous competing agencies and no one direction or set of objectives being followed. Inconsistency and corruption are the biggest factors holding back progress.

International donors and grass-roots NGOs have devised programmes and endeavoured to implement them, but as the environmental problems are largely the result of abuse and mismanagement of resources to fulfil certain economic goals, they are fighting an uphill battle. In what is naturally a desert state, cotton production is not sustainable, and neither is growing watermelons. Until the government accepts this and diversifies its economy into other areas, desertification will continue, and the land will increasingly become saline and toxic. The nation's forests are also under threat. Between 1990 and 1995, deforestation occurred at an average annual rate of 2.65%. However, since the

NATURAL GAS

Chief amongst Uzbekistan's natural resources, from a strategic and commercial perspective, is natural gas. The country has 1.84 trillion cubic metres of proven reserves, which places it 18th in the world (ahead of Kuwait), and annual production of 60 billion cubic metres (in the top ten of worldwide producers). The sale of natural gas generates approximately 40% of the direct foreign earnings that the state receives. The reserves are primarily concentrated in the Bukhara-Khiva region.

This hydrocarbon legacy is the result of decomposing flora and fauna deposited on the seabed millions of years ago then trapped under a layer of impermeable rock and subjected to immense pressure and heat. During the Soviet era there was some development of the hydrocarbon industries but it was never fully exploited, in part because beyond the domestic market there was little external demand. This marketplace picture has changed significantly with the economic and political growth of China to the east.

China became the fourth-largest natural gas user in the world in 2010 and is set to double that demand again by 2020. The Chinese plan to source at least 80 billion cubic metres a year from central Asia. Consequently, 2008 saw the start of the construction of the 7,000km, 1,076mm-diameter central Asia–China gas pipeline, designed to transport gas east from Uzbekistan, Kazakhstan and Turkmenistan. The US$2.2 billion Uzbekistan–China section, which has a capacity of 25 billion cubic metres and is financed by loans from China Development Bank and direct investment from China National Petroleum Corporation, started transporting gas to China in August 2012.

Though projects such as this help ensure regional energy security, there is some evidence that Uzbekistan is already exporting too much of its gas, leavings its own citizens short of supplies. In the winter of 2012, homes and businesses around Tashkent, including farmers using gas to heat their greenhouses, had their gas disconnected, driving up food prices and the cost of alternative heating fuels beyond the reach of poorer families. There are known to be natural gas shortages in the Samarkand, Fergana, Syr Darya and Andijan provinces as well, as testified to by the queues of 200+ cars we often see outside gas stations.

late 1990s reforestation efforts have begun. Shrinking forest habitats not only threaten the land but also the livelihoods of the people living on it.

Biodiversity conservation and rural development often confront each other in Uzbekistan. Major threats to biodiversity include the destruction of flora and fauna, unsustainable natural resource use, and expansion of land occupied for agriculture at the expense of wildlife. The government of Uzbekistan has been working on research to improve the situation since 1993, and in 2000 approval was received for the Global Environment Facility proposal to establish the Nuratau-Kyzylkum Biosphere Reserve (pages 198–9). Due to political constraints, the biosphere has yet to be fully implemented. Nevertheless, in co-operation with the German Society for Nature Protection and various local bodies, progress towards the project's conservation aims is being made.

POLLUTION Large-scale use of chemical fertilisers and pesticides in cotton cultivation, inefficient irrigation and poor drainage have led to highly saline and contaminated water being pumped back into the soil. The use of chemicals in agriculture is now up to eight times higher than it was in the Soviet period, and

MINING IN UZBEKISTAN

Uzbekistan has a relatively well-educated population, but since independence has suffered a notable 'brain drain' of skilled professionals leaving the country to work in better-paid jobs elsewhere. It is particularly noticeable in the extractive mineral industries, which, given their economic value, one would expect to be far more developed than they actually are.

The extraction of high-profile metals, specifically gold and uranium, has taken priority, and their extraction, processing and export contribute significantly to the economy. Uzbekistan produced 90,000kg of gold in 2011, making it the world's tenth-largest producer, and this commodity was the country's second-largest earner of foreign currency. Production is expected to increase to 120,000kg per year by 2020 as old mines are reconditioned and brought back online, and new sites start pouring. Uzbekistan's proven gold reserves are the fourth largest in the world.

The size of metal reserves, including gold, is such that they could one day dominate the economy, reducing Uzbekistan's need to produce relatively low-value items such as cotton. What stands in the way of growth, however, is sovereign risk: investors require a long-term, stable political outlook and a national government that they trust to protect their assets. The US-based Newmont Mining Corporation developed the Muruntau gold mine in the Kyzylkum Desert for more than a decade, only to be forced to write off its investment and accept a settlement of US$80m (a fraction of its worth) from the Uzbek government for 50% of the venture. In 2011, the London-based Oxus Gold had one of its metallurgists imprisoned for alleged spying.

Such cases, regardless of where blame lies, damage potential investors' confidence, with a resulting fall or stagnation in inward investment. In a bid to overturn this and to seek new investment, infrastructure development and efficient technologies, representatives from the State Committee for Geology and Mineral Resources have approached corporate and state bodies in China, Japan and Korea for partnership in joint ventures. We wait to see what degree of success such new relationships will enjoy.

high levels of industrial pollutants (including oil and phenol) are also pumped into the Amu Darya. An official report from the Uzbek government suggested that half of the country's population resided in areas suffering from severe water pollution, and that only a quarter of houses outside Tashkent have proper sewers.

Environmental mismanagement has also caused significant levels of air pollution. Salt and dust storms and the spraying of pesticides have led to severe degradation of air quality in rural areas, whilst in the cities factories and cars are belching out fumes. Fewer than half of factory smokestacks have adequate filtration devices, and none has the capacity to filter gaseous emissions. In addition, a high percentage of existing filters are defective or out of operation. Air pollution data for Tashkent, Fergana and Olmaliq show all three cities exceeding recommended levels of nitrous dioxide and particulates. High levels of heavy metals have also been recorded, particularly around Tashkent.

NATURAL HISTORY AND CONSERVATION

GEOLOGY Uzbekistan lies on several geological fault lines. Its proximity to the Tian Shan and Pamir-Alay ranges, the Kyzylkum and Karakum deserts, and the Kazakh steppe has given the country rich and diverse geological resources, but also made it prone to earthquakes. Uzbekistan's mineral wealth was first comprehensively surveyed during the Soviet period. The country is known to have significant deposits of precious metals and rare and ferrous metals (see box, page 6), as well as coal and hydrocarbons, construction materials and radioactive raw materials. Of more than 3,000 large (and potentially commercially viable) deposits discovered prior to 2007, less than half have been explored.

The down-side of Uzbekistan's geology is the constant threat of earthquakes, many of which emanate from the densely populated Fergana Valley. Although the 7.5-magnitude 1966 Tashkent earthquake (see box, page 111) is the best known, it is by no means an isolated incident. A 6.1-magnitude quake was recorded on the Uzbek–Kyrgyz border in July 2011 and killed 13 people. Smaller quakes (4.0–5.0 on the Richter scale) hit parts of the country on an almost monthly basis.

PALEONTOLOGY Uzbekistan has a rich fossil record, both of plant life and of dinosaurs. The most important specimens to date come from the Cretaceous Period (145–66 million years ago) and have been uncovered at the Dzharakuduk site in the Kyzylkum Desert.

Excavations at the site, which first began in the 1970s, have revealed abundant remains of a very diverse biota including both mammals and dinosaurs. Large vertebrate remains were collected, as was sediment that could then be processed for microvertebrate remains. Well-preserved dinosaur bones and teeth have all been unearthed, from sauropods and even central Asia's first known ceratopsid. The discoveries at Dzharakuduk significantly contribute to our understanding of faunal evolution in the northern hemisphere during the Cretaceous Period.

Hominid remains were discovered in the Teshik Tash Cave in the Gissar Mountains south of Samarkand in 1938. The remains of a young male, known as the Teshik Tash Boy, were found buried with five pairs of ibex horns, possibly in an early funeral rite. Though assumed to be Neanderthal, there was little hope of telling as the bones were in such poor condition. It was not until the advent of DNA testing (and this too is tricky as fossils don't contain much DNA) that scientists were able to confirm that the genetic material was 98% the same as Neanderthal material discovered elsewhere. When combined with a similar discovery in Siberia,

1

Uzbekistan has two major national parks, both of which are legally protected biospheres with a wealth of indigenous wildlife and glorious, untouched landscapes.

The **Ugam-Chatkal National Park** is situated close to Tashkent and lies on the spurs of the Western Tian Shan Mountains. Contained within its 570km² of territory are mountain steppe and forest, alpine meadow, river valleys and floodplains. The park was founded in 1947 and designated a UNESCO biosphere reserve in 1978.

Ugam-Chatkal supports more than 1,100 species of plant including grasses, wild fruit trees and juniper forests. They provide food for 230 species of birds, of which wild turkeys and mountain partridges are particularly numerous. The rarer golden eagles and bearded vultures soar periodically overhead.

The park also has 44 species of mammal. Patient visitors (preferably armed with binoculars) can expect to see wild rams, mountain goats and Siberian roe; wild boar, stone marten and red marmots are also present in large numbers. White-claw bears and wolves are found in the Pskem Valley, and there are Turkestan lynx and even snow leopards in the river basins.

The oldest nature reserve in Uzbekistan is the **Zaamin National Park**, created in 1926 as the Guralsh Nature Preserve. It encompasses 156km² of rolling hills and mountains in the Kulsoy, Guralsh, Baikungur and Aldashmansoy river valleys near Dzhizak.

The park was created to preserve unique mountain-pines ecosystems. The main asset of the reserve is the *archa* (also known as the Central Asian juniper), which reaches 18m in height. Some of the junipers in the reserve are nearly 1,000 years old. In addition to juniper there are rowan, currant, dog rose, barberry, St John's wort and origanum amongst the park's 700+ plant species.

Fauna in the park include 150 species of birds and reptiles and 40 species of mammal, the highlights of which are white-claw bears, lynxes, wild boars and porcupines.

the Teshik Tash Boy has helped to prove Neanderthal man stretched far further east than previously expected.

FLORA It is said that the green of Uzbekistan's flag represents nature, and the state emblem depicts the bright sun shining above a valley in bloom, with wheat and cotton crops clearly visible.

Given that Uzbekistan has more than 3,700 species of plants, 20% of which are endemic, it's unsurprising they've been unable to select a single national flower. Rosa eglantaria, Juno irises, hollyhock, filipendula, forget-me-not, patchouli, Salvia sclarea, safflower, helianthus and petunia violacea all grow in large numbers, creating a riot of colour in spring and summertime. Flowers native to Uzbekistan include *Tulipa batalinii* and *Tulipa clusiana*.

The majority of the plants occurring in Uzbekistan grow in the **mountains**, although only 30% of the high mountains are covered with plants and this is mainly tipchak, a plant which is somewhere between a grass and a herb, which is common across central Asia. In the middle ranges dog-rose and other bushes grow, but it is in the lower mountains where a wide variety of deciduous trees and bushes may be found. The main plants in this area are fir trees, the timber of which is highly valued – some of which are more than a thousand years old. Beside these, deciduous trees like maple, hawthorn, wild apple, pistachio, walnut, birch, poplar and cherry are widespread here, as are honeysuckle, barberry, dog-rose, meadow-sweet and bushes of wild grape.

Grasses are also diverse. Herbs such as Muscat sage, rhubarb, tulip and Pskem onion (a precious herb used for medical purposes) grow profusely. Also in the lower mountains is the most valuable wood species –*archa*, the Central Asian juniper. In the vast, low plains along the river valleys, wooden, bushy, grassy plants, such as sedges and hawthorn, are well developed. On the sub-mountainous plains, the landscape is characterised by grass; there are no trees, but barberry bushes, dog roses, and honeysuckle grow along water courses. There are a significant number of vascular plants unique to Uzbekistan, of which the most notable are *Iris hippolyti, Iris Capnoides, Tulipa butkovii, Tulipa uzbekistanica, Allium haneltii* and *Dianthus uzbekistanicus.* The high foothills feature dry steppes with sparse grass on bare earth.

The **desert plants** are particularly interesting as they protect the soil from being blown away by constant desert winds, and are well adjusted to poor soil and conditions of drought by being having no leaves (or only very tiny ones). Much of the Ustyurt Plateau is covered with saxaul (small, dry shrubs found in southwest and central Asia). The black saxaul is the only plant that can grow in saline areas, and although it grows quickly, it is short-lived, but it is a source of food for desert animals like sheep and camels.

FAUNA Uzbekistan's diverse natural habitats host all manner of wildlife, many species of which are indigenous or endemic. The most iconic of these is surely the rare snow leopards.

In desert areas, common **mammals** include wolves, jackals and foxes. Here, animals need to be quick to survive, and have therefore evolved with longer legs than their counterparts in Europe and elsewhere. This is particularly true of the deer. In the mountains bordering Kyrgyzstan and Tajikistan you'll see wild goat and boar, mountain sheep, lynx, Bukhara deer, Alpine ibex, and maybe even the endangered saiga antelope or elusive snow leopard. The Western Tian Shan is one of the most ecologically clean regions of the world, and its fauna remains as abundant as it was thousands of years ago with up to 44 species of mammals, including the white-claw bear in the River Pskem Valley.

Reptiles are also abundant in deserts, such as such as the roundhead lizard, steppe agama and the 1.6m-long monitor lizard. The threatened Central Asian cobra is still found in the Karshi Desert, and the saygak and four-striped runner (an eastern rat snake) can be seen across the Ustyurt Plateau.

Insects found only in Uzbekistan include the butterflies *Hyponephele murzini* and *Melitaea permuta*, the grasshopper *Conophyma turkestanicum*, a long-horned beetle *Psilotarsus turkestanicus* and a chalcidoid wasp *Entedon tobiasi.* Other endemic invertebrates include the jumping spiders *Yllenus tamdybulak* and *Yllenus bucharensis*, the tree-trunk spider *Hersiliola esyunini* and the 4cm-long scorpion *Orthochirus feti.*

Almost as diverse are the species of **fish**. There are more than 60 types of river fish in Uzbekistan, including Amudarya trout, European perch, northern pike, Turkestan sculpin roach and barbel, as well as a species of loach (*Dzihunia ilan*) found only in Uzbekistan. Sadly, due to the destruction of the Aral Sea, the once common Aral salmon is now extinct in Uzbekistan.

According to the International Union for Conservation of Nature and Natural Resources (IUCN) in 2006, Uzbekistan is home to several **threatened species** including Strauch's toad, the slender-billed curlew and the Asiatic wild dog.

The rich variety of habitats found within Uzbekistan make it a wonderful country for birdwatching, a pastime now made a lot easier with the recent publication of the field guide *The Birds of Central Asia* by Christopher Helm in 2012. The birds one encounters vary according to the time of year, with May perhaps the best time to see breeding and migrant species. However, even the winter months have their rewards with flocks of waxwings and black-throated thrushes visiting from their breeding ground further afield.

Even among the parks and wooded areas of verdant Tashkent you can find hobby, European nightjar, white-winged woodpecker and golden orioles, and at night hear the distinctive sonar-like 'ping' of the Eurasian scops owl. The ubiquitous common myna is a relatively recent colonist to the region but can now be found everywhere throughout the country. During spring migration almost anything can turn up in the city parks with species such as Blyth's reed warbler, and scarlet rosefinch particularly common.

The hills and mountains of Uzbekistan are rich in birds and those looking for a day excursion from Tashkent should visit the area around Chimgan. Here among the juniper you can find species such as Hume's lesser whitethroat, Hume's leaf warbler, greenish warbler, nightingale, yellow-breasted tit, rock and white-capped buntings. One special feature of the birdlife in Uzbekistan is the sprinkling of Himalayan species that creep into the Tian Shan Mountains, and around Chimgan you can see three of these – the large blue whistling thrush which, along with brown dipper, is always found near fast-running water, and rufous-naped tit, which favours mature juniper. Large raptors often seen here and in other hilly areas include both Himalayan and Eurasian griffon vultures, cinereous (black) vulture, and the mighty lammergeier, while in May it's not unusual to see large migrating flocks of both European and Oriental honey buzzards.

HISTORY

ANCIENT HISTORY Though Stone Age man carved his mark on Uzbekistan's caves as far back as 100,000 years ago, the country's better-understood history begins when Iranian nomads first settled the northern grasslands around the turn of the first millennium BC. They lived predominantly along the region's river valleys and made good use of the fertile land for agriculture, even building irrigation channels in the more drought-prone areas.

Their descendants, **the Scythians** (or Sakas in Persian sources) formed a loosely controlled empire stretching from Khorezm in the west to the Fergana Valley in the east. They were skilled raiders with fast, strong horses and formidable iron weapons, and their incursions struck fear into the hearts of neighbouring tribes.

Cyrus the Great, the Achemenid king of Persia, finally put down the Scythians shortly before his death in battle near the Aral Sea in 530BC, and his successors divided their territory into what became the Bactrian, Sogdian and Tokharian states. Silk Road trade between Persia and China began to flourish, and the populations of central Asia urbanised and fully participated in it. The Sogdians became particularly wealthy, and their capital Marakanda (today's Samarkand) became rich. The religions of Zoroastrianism and Buddhism, both of which

The rocky hills to the south of Samarkand on the road to Timur's birthplace, Shakhrisabz, are covered in scrub and hawthorn bushes and offer some fantastic birding. Red-headed buntings are everywhere, and special birds up here include white-throated robin and Upcher's, eastern Orphean, and barred warblers, with lesser grey and isabelline shrikes common. Fanatical birders will seek out the monotone Hume's short-toed lark, but perhaps more obvious will be European bee-eaters, flocks of pink-and-black rose-coloured starlings, and dapper pied wheatears. Although Samarkand city is not as green as Tashkent, it still has its birds and particularly obvious are the large brown-and-white alpine swifts screaming around the old buildings such as Bibi Khanum. This species, along with the smaller common swift, has become scarcer in recent years as better restoration removes its nesting holes.

In and around Bukhara you will find Eurasian collared and laughing doves throughout the city, while smaller birds include tree Sparrow and pied bushchat. A short ride from the town takes you to the wetlands surrounding the huge Lake Tadykol, where reed beds are alive with clamourous reed warblers, bearded tits and citrine wagtails, while careful searching of the bushes may reveal bluethroats. Travelling east from Bukhara across the Kyzylkum Desert, roadside birds include beautiful Wedgewood-blue European rollers and vivid blue-cheeked bee-eaters, which can be very common in places, while the shy Maqueen's bustard can be very hard to find despite its size. This vast expanse is home to the 'poster bird' for Uzbekistan, the remarkable Pander's ground jay. One of four species of ground jay in the world, it is found only here and in some very remote parts of Kazakhstan, and the road to Khiva is without doubt the best place on the planet to see it. A striking thrush-sized pale grey bird with distinctive black-and-white wings, it can often be spotted perched up on a saxual bush or telegraph pole, or racing over a sand dune.

travelled to Uzbekistan along the Silk Road with merchants and missionaries, were in the ascendency.

Alexander the Great seized Samarkand in 329BC and married Roxana, the daughter of a local Bactrian chief. He continued down the Oxus, founding the easternmost of many Alexandrias in the Fergana Valley before continuing on towards the Indian subcontinent. Though Alexander himself did not stay in central Asia, many of his troops also married local women and remained, one general establishing the Seleucid Empire. Graeco-Bactrian kingdoms would exert influence in Uzbekistan and the surrounding countries for centuries to come.

In the early centuries AD Zoroastrianism remained the dominant religion, but Buddhism was still present, and Manichaeism and Christianity were both on the rise. Uzbekistan was a cultural and ethnic melting pot due to its central position on the Silk Road, and its cities were known for their intellectuals and artisans as well as for trade.

Uzbekistan was about to enter a politically turbulent period, however. Though the Sogdian state persisted, it was ravaged in turn by the nomadic Khidarites and Khionites, and Turkish raiders from Mongolia. The Sogdians were exhausted and fatally weakened by internal divisions.

ARAB INVASION Arab forces first entered central Asia in AD649, during their conquest of Persia, but it was the crusading **General Qutaybah ibn Muslim** who entered the area of Mwarannahr, a deeply divided land with poor indigenous leadership, who would finally seize Uzbekistan for Islam, easily subduing its people. The new religion spread gradually into the region, replacing the native religious identity with Persian influences. In just seven years he conquered Bukhara, Khorezm, Samarkand and Tashkent, but rather than being lauded as a hero, he was assassinated by his own troops in Fergana in 715. Though the Sogdians resisted, they would never again control Uzbekistan, and Arab pre-eminence was guaranteed when they drove out the Chinese forces of the Tang emperor Xuanzong at the Battle of Talas (now in western Kyrgyzstan) in 751. Central Asia as an Islamic region was now firmly established and the result of the Arab invasion was to totally change the way of life of the region. Architecture, art and science declined under the pressures of war and arose again only in the middle of the 9th century.

Though Uzbekistan's culture did continue to be influenced by its Persian past, the Arab conquest made its presence felt too. Islam replaced Zoroastrianism and other faiths; Arabic became the primary language for government, literature and commerce. The relationship was not one-way, however, as the Abbasid Caliphate, which would rule the Arab world for five centuries, defeated the ruling Umayyads in part due to central Asian support.

The 8th and 9th centuries were a golden age for Uzbekistan. Bukhara grew to become one of the wealthiest and most important centres in the Islamic world, a fitting rival to Baghdad, Cordoba and Cairo. The city's elite patronised some of the greatest artists and intellectuals of the day, the scientist and medic Abu ibn Sina (known as Avicenna in the West) and the Persian poet Rudaki among them. The Samanids and Buyids grew increasingly powerful, and Ismail ibn Ahmad, ruler of Bukhara, united the independent provinces under his Samanid Empire.

The Karakhanids, Turkic nomads from the northern steppes, overran Uzbekistan in AD999 and, joining forces with the Turkic slave soldiers who had served in the Samanid army, they formed their own state. At the same time, the Afghan Ghaznavids took control of lands south of the Amu Darya, and slowly expanded their territories into Iran and even as far south as India.

The dominance of these groups was short-lived, however, as another Turkic group was on the rise: the Seljuks. From their capital of Merv (now in Turkmenistan) they established an empire stretching from Asia Minor to the western reaches of modern China. The Seljuks in turn fell to the Mongol Karakhitai, and Khorezmshah Muhammad, a self-proclaimed second Alexander, marched on Samarkand to liberate it from these infidels in 1212.

GENGHIS AND THE MONGOLS The Mongol invasion was a turning point for central Asia in numerous ways: it broke Islamic hegemony, replacing it with a Turkic identity; it razed cities to the ground, destroying any pre 13th-century architecture; and it gave the region's population much of the genetic make-up it has today.

Mongol forces marched on the Kara-Khitan Khanate and by 1218 controlled territory as far west as Lake Balkhash in the southeast of what is now Kazakhstan. **Genghis Khan** initially looked towards the Khwarezmid Empire as a trading partner, but when his mercantile caravan was slaughtered and a subsequent envoy killed, battle lines were drawn. With 200,000 troops under his command, he marched across the Tian Shan Mountains and into the heart of Uzbekistan.

It's a name that instilled fear in the hearts of the medieval world from Mongolia to Moscow and Europe to the Indian subcontinent, and one that echoes to the present day, still associated with rape, pillage and brutality. But just who was this great khan, and how did a nomad from the Mongolian steppe establish an empire covering 24,000,000km² (9,300,000 square miles) in little more than a generation?

Genghis Khan (an honorific title) was born around 1162 in Deluun Boldog, not far from the modern Mongolian capital of Ulaanbaatar. The first son of a Mongol chief, he was named Temüjin, and legend has it that he was born grasping a clot of blood, a sure-fire sign that he would become a powerful leader in later life.

Temüjin's father was murdered by a rival clan while Temüjin was still a child and, too young to take over leadership of his clan, he was cast out by older, more powerful rivals. Along with his mother and younger siblings he lived in poverty, and was for a while enslaved by his father's former allies.

At the age of 16, Temüjin was married to Borte to cement an alliance between their two families. She was almost immediately kidnapped by Merkits, a rival clan, and though she was ultimately rescued, when their first child, Jochi, was born nine months later, his parentage was thus distinctly cloudy. They went on to have three other sons, Chagatai, Ögedei and Tolui, and it's amongst these four legitimate offspring he would ultimately divide his empire.

Temüjin rose to power through a series of careful alliances, first with Toghrul, the khan of the Kerait. Unlike other Mongol chiefs, however, he delegated authority based on merit and loyalty rather than family ties, and he motivated his followers with a share of the spoils of war. Conquered peoples were integrated into his tribe, inspiring loyalty and reducing the likelihood of future rebellion. Temüjin was a great innovator and inspired confidence in his men.

When the Keraits opposed Temüjin, he took advantage of their internal divisions to defeat them. He then turned his attentions to the Naimans, many of whom followed him voluntarily. Together they defeated the Merkits, leaving Temüjin as the sole ruler of the Mongol plains. In 1206, at a council of Mongol chiefs, he took the new title 'Genghis Khan'. All the armies of the Mongolian steppe were now willingly at his command.

The Mongols first seized Otrar, murdering many of its inhabitants and enslaving the rest. Inalchuq, the governor responsible for the previous envoy's demise, had molten silver poured into his eyes and ears as punishment. In quick succession, Mongol forces seized and decimated Samarkand and Bukhara, leaving them as virtual ghost towns. Thousands of people perished – in Samarkand only 50,000 out of around a million people survived. Pyramids of severed heads were raised as a sign of victory. In Termez the entire population was killed, and perhaps a million people were slaughtered in a similar bloodbath in Urgench.

Genghis Khan died in 1227 and his empire was divided among his four sons. From the ashes of central Asia came the Pax Mongolica, a century or so of relative peace in which merchants and travellers could journey the length of the Mongol Empire without harassment.

THE TIMURIDS As the constituent parts of the Mongol Empire began to separate in the early 14th century, various tribes competed for regional influence. Among them, **Timur** (see box, below) was ultimately victorious. Like Genghis Khan before him, Timur would conquer an empire stretching from Asia Minor to Delhi, even venturing up into southern Russia before his death in 1405.

The Timurids did not call themselves Timurids: contemporary chroniclers refer to them as the Gurkanis, meaning 'son-in-law', a reference to the fact that it was Timur's wife, Saray Mulk Khanum, who was the direct descendant of Genghis Khan, not Timur himself. Her title, Khanum, means the daughter of the khan, or a princess.

In the earliest period of the Timurid Empire (1360–80), the bulk of territorial expansion was achieved through forming alliances with neighbouring tribes. Among these alliances, those with Samarkand (1366) and Balk (1369) were most significant. As an *emir* (a military commander or local chieftain) Timur was nominally subordinate to the Chagatai (Mongol) khans, but as he was able to select these khans, they were in reality no more than puppet rulers. The real power was wielded by Timur.

The Timurids' most aggressive period of military expansion began in 1380 when Timur began to seize the deteriorating Ilkhanate states, fragments of the

TIMUR-I LENG

Let he who doubts Our power and munificence look upon Our buildings.
Amir Timur, 1379

Amir Timur, Uzbekistan's national hero and one of the most accomplished warriors, rulers and patrons the world has ever seen, was born the son of a minor chief in Shakhrisabz in 1336. As with Genghis Khan, it is said he came into the world grasping a clot of blood, an omen of what was to come.

The young Timur (who you may be more familiar with as Christopher Marlowe's Tamerlane) excelled in horsemanship, sword fighting and archery, as well as raiding caravans and rustling horses. He became chief of the Barlas clan in 1360 and steadily increased his influence from the Amu Darya to the Syr Darya. In the process he incurred various injuries including one to his leg, which earned him his nickname: Timur-i Leng (Timur the lame).

In 1370 Timur conquered the last surviving Mongol khanate and made Samarkand his capital. For the next 35 years he ruthlessly expanded his territories across central Asia, Iran, Turkey and northern India. He even attempted to conquer China, but succumbed to a fever in 1405 and died with this ambition unrealised.

Historians estimate that Timur's conquests may have been responsible for the deaths of as many as 15 million people. And yet, ever the raider, he made little attempt to consolidate his conquests, smashing, grabbing and then moving on. Consequentially, the Timurid dynasty was short-lived.

Timur's personality was a dichotomy. On one side he was brutal and ruthless on the battlefield; on the other he was highly cultured, thirsted for knowledge and enjoyed debating history, medicine and astronomy. He was a passionate supporter of the arts, and plundered cities such as Damascus, Baghdad, Isfahan and Delhi not only for their financial assets but also for their skilled artisans, whom he brought back to build and beautify Samarkand.

Mongol Empire in what is now Iran, Azerbaijan and eastern Turkey. In quick succession, Timur took control of Herat, Esfahan, Shiraz and Baghdad – once the Ilkhanate heartland – and he then turned his attentions to defeating the Golden Horde in the Caucasus. By the end of the 14th century, these lands were firmly under Timurid control, and the Timurids had also made substantial territorial gains in Afghanistan, Pakistan, and in India as far east as Delhi. Timur put his own governor, Khizr Khan, on the Delhi throne, and the Delhi Sultanate became a vassal state. Before his death in 1405, Timur had made further gains in Syria, Iraq and Turkey, and was the most powerful ruler in the Islamic world.

Timur made Samarkand his capital, and he rebuilt and expanded it with the finest artisans and materials his empire could offer. He patronised scientists and other scholars, and Samarkand became a centre for intellectuals and for religion. Its architecture was the envy of the Islamic world.

The Timurid Empire did not survive long after Timur's death: his sons and grandsons had been appointed to governorships in different parts of the empire, but they lacked the diplomatic and military skills of Timur. The family members were also prone to infighting, so civil wars were rife and many of the territories again became independent states. Timur's grandson, Ulug Beg, clung on to Samarkand but prioritised scholarship and, in particular, his personal pursuit of astronomy, over matters of state. Uzbek tribes, led by Muhammad Shaybani (see below), were therefore able to seize much of central Asia, and Uzbekistan entered into a new era: that of the khanates.

THE KHANATES AND EMIRATES The khanates were regional kingdoms controlled by a khan, self-proclaimed successors to Genghis Khan, and the most powerful of these was the Khanate of Bukhara, ruled by the **Shaybanid dynasty**. A second khanate was established at Khiva, and a third in the Fergana Valley at Kokand.

The Shaybanids were Turko-Mongols and claimed patrilineal descent from Genghis Khan through his grandson Shiban. The Shaybanid horde were the Timurids main rivals – they believed their claim to be heirs of Genghis was far stronger than that of Timur – but it was not until the mid 15th century that they were able to start consolidating their power, first in Siberia and then in central Asia. Muhammad Shaybanid (r1500–10) was able to take advantage of the disintegration of the Timurid Empire to seize Balkh, Bukhara, Herat and Samarkand, and his descendants went on to found and rule not only the Khanate of Bukhara, but also the Khanate of Khiva.

Under Shaybanid rule, Bukhara was a major centre of the arts and Islamic learning. Many of the finest surviving buildings date from this period of wealth and patronage. The city was packed with poets and calligraphers, dervishes and physicians, theologians and mathematicians. The library of Abd al-Aziz Khan was said to have no equal anywhere in the world. Public education was introduced for boys from the age of six, and the curriculum in the madrassas was expanded to include logic, jurisprudence, mathematics, music, and poetry, as well as traditional classes in theology and Qu'ranic Arabic.

The Shaybanids retained control of Bukhara for a century, after which power passed to the **Janids**, descendants of the son-in-law of the last Shaybanid ruler, Pir Muhammad Khan.

The Janids, like the later Timurids, were plagued by infighting. There was no clear line of succession – any brother could inherit, regardless of age – and so fratricide and scheming were rife at court. Vali Muhammad Khan (r1605–11), for example, came to power after the death of his brother. Hearing of a coming assassination attempt, he fled to the Safavid court of Shah Abbas I to garner support, and returned home with an army, but it was not enough: Vali Muhammad Khan was killed during the insurgency.

The 17th and 18th centuries were a difficult period for Uzbekistan: Silk Road trade was in decline, and the strength of the Shi'ite Safavids in Iran had isolated central Asia from other Sunni territories in the Middle East. Bandits and slave traders plagued those caravans that did brave the steppe; the Persian Nadir Shah marched through almost unopposed in 1740, medieval weaponry no match for his modern artillery; and Russian generals were starting to take a serious interest in the lands beyond their southern border.

Central Asia's khanates had become emirates: this was not out of respect for Amir Timur, however, but rather to show that their allegiances and culture lay with the Islamic world – the dominant power block at the time – rather than with their Mongol past. The **Emirate of Bukhara** (1785–20) remained the most powerful of the three and was ruled by a succession of colourful emirs. Though some of them were undoubtedly competent, others lived up to the European stereotype of the eastern despots, and tales of their excesses and cruelty spread to Russia and beyond.

When **Peter the Great** sent an expedition to Khiva in 1717, it was the first time tsarist forces had officially set foot on Uzbek soil. They were slaughtered to a man, but would certainly be back, first invited in as allies and protectors against rival khanates, and later as invading forces. Russian forces entered Tashkent (1865), Bukhara (1867) and Samarkand (1868); they all became Russian protectorates.

The expansion of Russia into central Asia caused great concern for the British, who saw it as a stepping stone *en route* to British India, the jewel in the imperial crown. The Great Game (see box, page 17) ensued, each side vying for influence and territory.

Modernity came to Uzbekistan with the arrival of the Trans-Caspian railway in the 1890s. Large numbers of Russian émigrés began to arrive, and they started to industrialise the country and introduce more intensive forms of agriculture, including irrigated cotton production. Rather than look to the Islamic or Mongol worlds for trade and influence, Uzbekistan was now looking due northward to Russia.

THE SOVIET UNION The Bolshevik Revolution took place in 1917, and communism emerged as the dominant ideology from the melting pot of socialism, pan-Islamism and pan-Turkism, all of which were poised to guide the next generation of central Asia's rulers. It was not a smooth transition, however, as White Russians, the Basmachi (see box, page 18), British agents and a host of other resistance fighters opposed the Red Army.

An independent Jadist state was briefly established in Kokand (pages 142–7) but the matter was really settled in 1920 when **General Mikhail Frunze** stormed through and established the Soviet Republic of Turkestan. The People's Republic of Khorezm was set up in parallel in Khiva. These gave way to the Uzbek SSR in 1924, and with them went any real hope of political or economic autonomy in the region. Controversially, Stalin created his new states on the basis of perceived ethnicity (thus reducing the likelihood of an opposition united on the basis of shared Islamic identity), but included the Tajik-majority cities of Bukhara and Samarkand in the Uzbek state. The Uzbek-majority Khujand was given to the

When two mighty empires meet, there will always be blood and intrigue. As the Russian Empire spread south into the Kazakh steppe and the frontier of British India pushed across the subcontinent and up into Afghanistan, the no man's land in between became the jousting ground in a 19th-century 'Tournament of Shadows'. The British were keen to gain new markets here for their exported goods, and the Russians exploited the fierce rivalries of the khans of Bukhara, Khiva and Kokand, playing them off against one another to ensure protective alliances with Moscow were actively sought.

Agents, explorers and spies from both sides infiltrated courts across central Asia, Afghanistan and Pakistan to seek information and gain influence; they sought out unmapped wildernesses, surveying and recording everything they saw. Rudyard Kipling's protagonist, Kim, and his real-life equivalents, men like George Curzon (later the Viceroy of India), Francis Younghusband and the Russian Bronislav Grombchevsky, played hide-and-seek across mountains and deserts, adopting a veritable prop cupboard full of disguises in the hope that gaining a better understanding of the lie of the land (literal and metaphorical) would give their side a strategic advantage. Neither open warfare nor simply innocent exploration of the unknown, Rudyard Kipling declared their acts 'the Great Game'. It encompassed espionage in all its intricate, innovative forms.

The central tenet of the Great Game was suspicion: lack of knowledge about what lay in this central Asian hinterland led to doubts about where the imperial frontier might lie; and both sides jealously coveted the other's colonial possessions. Britain and Russia were frequently at loggerheads in Europe too, and by frightening each other into wrongly thinking that a full-scale military incursion was being planned in Uzbekistan or Tajikistan, it tied up resources and wealth, preventing them from being deployed elsewhere.

That is not to say that actual war did not feature in the Great Game. Britain's primary strategic interest in the 19th century was to establish a frontier that could be securely defended against Russia. Britain invaded Afghanistan in the First and Second Afghan Wars (1838–42 and 1878–80), fearing that if they did not take control of the country first then it would almost certainly fall to the Russians; envoys sent to the Afghan court had raised this concern. When Dost Muhammad, the then ruler of Afghanistan, was defeated by the British in 1839, he fled across Afghanistan's northern border to Uzbekistan and sought refuge in Bukhara at the court of Nasrullah Khan.

Though many players of the Great Game were murdered in central Asia (see box, page 220), either by each other or by the locals, or simply disappeared, those who did survive often returned to London and Moscow as national heroes. The British spoke to packed lecture halls at the Royal Geographic Society (www.rgs.org) and the Royal Society for Asian Affairs (founded in 1901 as the Central Asian Society; www.rsaa.org.uk), both of which came into their own at the height of the Great Game and exist to the present day, and accounts of daring exploits enraptured newspaper readers. Paranoia about what Imperial Russia could be up to made newspapers sell like hot cakes, much as fear of Communist Russia did 50 or so years later. Indeed, the Great Game could be interpreted as a forerunner to the Cold War as definite continuity is in evidence in the two powers' fight for influence in satellite states.

Tajik SSR, and a large number of Uzbeks were cut off inside the new Kyrgyz SSR, deliberately or otherwise creating long-term instability in the region.

The 1930s brought Stalinist purges to Uzbekistan. Religion, tolerated for the first few years of Soviet rule, was seen as a threat that must be eradicated. Imams were killed, going on hajj was banned, and those determined to keep their faith had to do so in the strictest secrecy. Madrassas (Islamic schools) and mosques were closed wholesale, many of them converted into warehouses or social clubs.

It was not all doom and gloom, however. Uzbekistan's economy modernised and grew rapidly as part of the USSR. For the first time the entire population had access to a secular education, and men and women studied and worked together. Uzbekistan's cities became increasingly cosmopolitan, with immigrés from across the Soviet Union coming to live and work. Though many of these foreigners were originally exiled to central Asia, they became well integrated, bound together by a shared Soviet identity and by the Russian language.

Under **Nikita Khrushchev** (in office 1953–64), some Russified Uzbek nationalists, formerly purged as subversive elements, were allowed to rejoin the Communist Party and rose to government positions. The most notable of these was **Sharaf Rashidov** (see box, page 169), First Secretary of the Communist Party of Uzbekistan from 1959 to 1982. Rashidov was closely aligned with Leonid Brezhnev (leader of the Soviet Union 1964–82), which gave him a certain amount of autonomy, often paying little more than lip service to Soviet policies. After Rashidov's death, however, Uzbekistan's political elite were brought sharply back into line with purges, corruption trials and the posthumous villification of Rashidov. The backlash was a strengthening of Uzbek nationalism.

Violence flared in the Fergana Valley in 1989 on both sides of the Uzbek–Kyrgyz border. **Islam Karimov** (see box, page 21), a political outsider, was appointed by Moscow to the position of first secretary in a hope that it would calm the troubles.

THE BASMACHI

The roots of the Basmachi lay in the forced conscription of central Asian Muslims by the Russian army towards the end of World War I. Horribly treated, the potential conscripts resisted, attacking Russian civilians as well as militias. The Russian response was brutal: whole villages were massacred and their property burned to prevent any survivors' return. Many more families died fleeing across the mountains to China.

The Basmachi developed largely as a Muslim resistance force against the 'godless' Bolsheviks. Their numbers comprised both peasants and intellectuals, and they were supported by White Russians and even British agents keen to stem the rise of Russian influence in central Asia.

The Basmachi fought under the leadership of the Turkish World War I general Enver Pasha, and for many this was a *jihad* against the infidels. The deposed Emir of Bukhara, Mohammed Alim Khan, provided the movement with funds, no doubt in the hope that if they were successful then they would invite him to return.

The resistance was most successful in the Fergana Valley, where raids inflicted significant casualties amongst Red Army troops, but by the early 1920s the battle was already lost and many of the movement's leaders had fled to relative safety in Afghanistan.

UZBEKISTAN SINCE INDEPENDENCE When there was an attempted coup against Mikhail Gorbachev in 1991, Uzbekistan was initially hesitant to back it: the country's economy and its status on the world stage depended on being part of the Soviet Union. Sensing which way the winds were blowing, however, the Uzbek SSR's leaders began making changes: the Communist Party of Uzbekistan (CPU) cut its ties with the central Communist Party in Moscow and changed its name to the **People's Democratic Party of Uzbekistan** (PDPU) in anticipation that elections would be forthcoming.

On 21 December 1991, Karimov agreed with the leaders of the other SSRs to dissolve the Soviet Union, and he declared Uzbekistan to be an independent republic and a founding member of the Commonwealth of Independent States (CIS). Karimov was elected as Uzbekistan's first president, with 86% of the vote, and the PDPU dominated the new parliament, in part because the main opposition party, Birlik, was refused electoral registration until it was too late.

Politically, there was a great deal of continuity between the 1980s and 1990s, not only in terms of key personnel. Early elections could be contested by only two parties, the PDPU and the pro-government Progress of the Fatherland Party; opposition figures were frequently arrested on fabricated charges, as were those who criticised the government in the press; and there was severe repression of anyone suspected of Islamic extremism. Some 6,000 supposed members of Hiz ut-Tahrir were incarcerated, and torture and abuse of these inmates was rife.

There was, quite rightly, international criticism of the government's human rights abuses, but the invasion of Afghanistan in 2001 meant that western governments needed allies in central Asia. Military goals took priority, as the US wanted to open an air base on Uzbek soil. The base, known as the **Karshi-Khanabad Airbase**, or K2, opened in 2001 and remained operational until 2005 when it was moved to neighbouring Kyrgyzstan. The reason for the move is that after the Andijan Massacre (see box, page 132) it became more difficult for foreign governments to turn a blind eye to Uzbekistan's flouting of international human rights law, and they were more vocal in their criticism. In response, the Uzbek government asked the Americans to vacate the base, and gave them just six months to do so.

Today, relations between Uzbekistan and the West are generally good. The global economic downturn has meant that many of the business deals which would have been done with European and American companies have instead been picked up by Chinese, state-backed firms, but there is still a sizeable expat population in Tashkent, and foreign embassies are gently backing, and supporting, reform. Support is being given in particular to the training and modernisation of the Uzbek armed forces so that they can better control their borders and participate in regional peace keeping missions.

GOVERNMENT AND POLITICS

The 1992 constitution of Uzbekistan describes a presidential republic in which the president is both head of state and head of government. Executive power is exercised by the government, and legislative power is divided between the government and a bicameral parliament. The president should be elected for a seven-year term by popular vote. The president also appoints the prime minister, deputy prime ministers and regional governors, and together this executive holds almost all power in the country, the judiciary only being nominally independent.

The legislative branch of government is the Supreme Assembly or National Assembly (Oliy Majlis). There are 150 elected members in the Legislative Chamber (the lower house) and 100 members in the Senate, some of whom are elected and others who are appointed by the president. The parliament can be dissolved by the president providing he has the support of the Constitutional Court, members of which are selected by the president.

Politics in Uzbekistan is very much a one-horse race. President Karimov officially received more than 90% of the vote in each of the last two presidential elections (2007 and 2015), and his party, now called the Uzbekistan Liberal Democratic Party, also has the largest number of seats in parliament.

Since 2003, the Prime Minister of Uzbekistan has been Shavkat Mirziyoyev, former governor of Dzhizak and Samarkand. Mirziyoyev has played an important role in Uzbekistan's foreign affairs, forging new diplomatic and economic relationships for the country, especially with South Korea and other states in east Asia. His deputies are Ergash Shoismatov and Kuvandik Sanakulov, who each hold different portfolios. Sanakulov is responsible for mining and metallurgy, giving him great economic clout.

Opposition parties in Uzbekistan are typically opposition in name only and have policies closely allied to those of the government; genuine opposition figures have been incarcerated, assaulted and generally harassed even when outside the country; and external observers generally consider Uzbekistan's elections to be no more than political charades. Only four parties are currently allowed to contest parliamentary elections.

ECONOMY

In 2014, the most recent year for which full data is available, Uzbekistan's economy looked to be in reasonable shape. GDP (PPP) stood at US$172.3 billion, 67th in the world and an increase of over US$12 billion from the previous year. Per capita GDP was at US$5,600, second only to Kazakhstan in the region, and the unemployment figure was relatively low at just 4.8%, though another 20% of the population is thought to be under employed.

Though much of the economy has been privatised since independence, economic reform has been gradual. The state still controls around a quarter of the economy and artificially manipulates the official exchange rate so the currency appears stronger than it really is. Imports of foreign goods are restricted and heavily taxed so as to protect domestic production.

The strength of Uzbekistan's economy in recent years has been thanks to the high international prices of gold, oil, gas and cotton, all of which Uzbekistan exports. For information on Uzbekistan's natural resources, see pages 5 and 6.

The agricultural sector employs around 30% of Uzbekistan's population and contributes 20–30% of GDP. The most important crop is cotton, the so-called white gold, of which Uzbekistan is the world's seventh-largest producer and fifth-largest exporter. Cotton production is extremely water intensive and requires significant levels of chemical fertiliser, both of which have had a detrimental impact on Uzbekistan's environment (pages 5–7). Controversially, Uzbekistan has a history of using forced labour during the cotton harvest, leading many international brands to boycott Uzbek cotton. The government has attempted to circumnavigate such restrictions by first exporting the cotton to neighbouring countries (in particular Kyrgyzstan) and then re-exporting it from there.

When we first started working in central Asia in 2008, Russia was the dominant foreign power in the region (as it had been since the late 19th century), followed

The public face of modern Uzbekistan is the country's first (and so far only) president, Islam Karimov. Born on 30 January 1938 (making him the elder statesman of the central Asian leaders), he survived the spartan privations of a Soviet orphanage and went on to study engineering and then economics. After spells in an agricultural machinery factory and the Chkalov Tashkent aviation production complex, he moved into the state apparatus, starting in the state planning office.

His move to become minister of finance in 1983 allowed a better understanding of the statesmanship required to concentrate power, and three years later he became Deputy Chairman of the Council of Ministers and Chairman of the State Planning Office. His trajectory to power was set and in quick succession he was promoted to First Secretary and then President of the Uzbek SSR.

After initial hesitancy, Karimov embraced the break-up of the USSR and consequently benefited considerably from it. He was voted in as President of the Republic of Uzbekistan in December 1991, four months after independence. This election and subsequent ones have garnered considerable international criticism, but though he's frequently vilified in the international press, many political leaders of international standing have found it necessary to compromise with him in order to achieve their own geopolitical aims.

Despite a constitutional restriction on presidents running for more than two terms, Karimov is essentially president for life: he won a landslide victory in 2015, though the election was widely criticised by western media and elections monitors. At the age of 78, he is not in the best of health but battles on in power nevertheless and shows no sign of retiring. He has no clear successor either within his own party or amongst the opposition. Tony Blair has purportedly been advising him (as well, more famously, as the Kazakh president Nazarbayev) on succession planning, as the power vacuum likely to follow his demise could easily destabilise the whole region.

Karimov has been married twice and has three children, his son Rustam and two daughters, Gulnara (see box, page 30) and Lola.

by the US. Since then, however, there has been a dramatic shift. The crash in the Russian rouble – caused by a combination of falling energy prices and sanctions – has meant that Russian companies have had little spare capital to invest. The Uzbek economy has contracted further because migrant workers in Russia, who used to send remittances home, have lost their jobs and returned to Uzbekistan seeking work. There is therefore less liquid capital in circulation.

The beneficiary of this situation has been China, however. The country has an economic interest, certainly, but intimately connected to this is its geo-strategic interest.

In 2012, China became Uzbekistan's single largest investor, and in 2014 Chinese President Xi Jinping committed US$40 billion to developing infrastructure in the region. Uzbekistan is considered a key component in the Beijing-led Silk Road Economic Belt (which is expected to ultimately usurp the Russian-dominated Eurasian Economic Union), and the Chinese and Uzbek governments have

COTTON

Cotton fibre is almost pure cellulose and it grows in a boll, a protective capsule around the plant's seeds. It is native to tropical and subtropical zones, and is found growing wild in Mexico, Australia and parts of Africa.

Successful cotton cultivation requires moderate temperatures and rainfall, and plenty of sunshine. The crop is reasonably drought and salt tolerant, but in arid and semi-arid conditions artificial irrigation is required to provide the requisite level of water. Genetically modified cotton has been developed to reduce reliance on chemical pesticides, but it is still not resistant to plant bugs, stink bugs and aphids.

World cotton production is around 25 million tonnes a year, and 2.5% of all arable land is given over to cotton. It is predominantly used for clothing production, but also in book binding, fishing nets and explosives (in the form of nitrocellulose). Cottonseed oil can be refined and used in cooking as if it were vegetable oil, and cottonseed meal can be fed to ruminant livestock.

In the next five years, Uzbekistan is looking to cut its cotton production by around 10% as the international cotton price is relatively low, and more money can be made from agricultural diversification.

already agreed a number of oil, gas and uranium deals. With a struggling Russian economy due to falling commodity prices and sanctions, it looks as though China will continue expanding into Russia's shoes in Uzbekistan, at least for the foreseeable future.

Other major agricultural products are raw silk, fruits (notably grapes and melons) and vegetables, which are consumed domestically and exported to neighbouring countries. Some 11% of Uzbekistan is artificially irrigated, and the most fertile agricultural land is in the Fergana Valley and in the south of the country around Surkhan Darya and Qashqa Darya.

Uzbekistan also has a strong industrial base, which includes chemical industries and oil and gas refineries. Coca-Cola has bottling plants in Namangan, Samarkand and Tashkent; Texaco produces lubricants in Uzbekistan for the central Asian market; and GM-Dat, the Korean subsidiary of car giant General Motors, assembles Korean-made cars at Asaka in the Fergana Valley in a joint venture with UzDaewoo. These are sold primarily in Uzbekistan, and to a lesser extent in the surrounding countries.

Uzbekistan is a member of the International Monetary Fund (IMF), the World Bank, the Asian Development Bank and the European Bank for Reconstruction and Development. It has observer status at the World Trade Organization (WTO).

PEOPLE

With a population fast approaching 30 million, Uzbekistan is by far the most populous country in central Asia. As much as 35% of the population is under 18, and though it has grown rapidly in recent decades, growth is now slowing due to economic outward migration and much smaller family sizes. The average number of children per woman is now 1.89, as opposed to 2.92 in 2002.

Uzbekistan is ethnically diverse, though ethnic **Uzbeks** may make up as much as 80% of the population. The Uzbeks are a Turkic people who originated in southern Siberia and the Altai Mountains and came south with the Mongols in the early medieval period. There are significant Uzbek populations in Afghanistan (2.7 million), Kyrgyzstan (800,000) and Tajikistan (1.6 million) as well as in Uzbekistan. The majority of Uzbeks follow the Hanafi school of Sunni Islam, though atheism is also widespread amongst those who grew up under the Soviet Union.

Uzbekistan also has a large **Tajik** population. Although census data suggest they make up only around 5% of the population, some observers believe the real figure to be far larger as there is a tendency for some Tajiks to declare themselves as Uzbek on official paperwork. Tajiks are essentially central Asian Persians, the division between the two groups being the result of Stalin's border creation in the 1920s. They consider themselves to be the oldest ethnic group in central Asia and trace their ancestry right back to the Bactrians and Sogdians (pages 10–11). The Tajiks are not a homogeneous group, however, and are deeply divided along clan-based lines with strong regional affiliations and blood ties. The cities of Bukhara and Samarkand both have large Tajik populations, and many feel they should have been given the opportunity to join Tajikistan rather than being part of Uzbekistan.

Around 5% of the population is **ethnic Russian**. This figure was significantly higher during the Soviet period, peaking at just under 15% in the late 1950s, but many Russians chose to leave Uzbekistan for Russia following independence, regardless of whether or not they had been born in the country. Significant numbers of Russians came to Uzbekistan from the 19th century onwards to take advantage of the economic opportunities the country offered. Others were intellectuals, petty bourgeoisie and political opponents forcibly exiled here during the purges. The Russian community tends to follow the Eastern Orthodox faith and large numbers of them reside in Tashkent.

The Soviet policy of deporting subversive and other undesirable elements to central Asia (the alternative place of exile to Siberia), mixed with a few self-orchestrated migrations, has left Uzbekistan with notable populations of **Kazakhs**, **Tatars**, **Volga Germans**, **Poles**, **Ukrainians** and even **Koreans**. **Afghans** have also fled across the border to escape the violence and to seek work. Though these groups have frequently intermarried, and many have now re-emigrated, it is still possible to hear snatches of their languages and, more importantly for those fed up with the ubiquitous *shashlik*, to feast on their various cuisines.

LANGUAGE

The main languages spoken in Uzbekistan are Uzbek (74.3%), Russian (14.2%) and Tajik (officially 4.4% but potentially far higher), with other langauges spoken including Kyrgyz, English and German. Karakalpak has official status in the Karakalpakstan Autonomous Republic. Almost all road signs and other public notices are written in Uzbek, in the Latin script.

UZBEK Worldwide Uzbek has more than 35 million speakers, and it has been the official language of Uzbekistan since independence. Nationalists in the late 1980s campaigned strongly for Uzbek to replace Russian as the language of state in the hope it would reverse the process of Russification and in its place promote Uzbek culture. In 1995 the government went one step further and introduced the Law of the Republic of Uzbekistan on State Language, which demands Uzbek be used in all public spheres and official jobs. Some have seen this as a move that discriminates against non-Uzbek speakers in the country.

Uzbek belongs to the Karluk family of Turkic languages, from which it gets its lexicon and grammar, and it also contains many loan words from Persian, Arabic and Russian, all of which have influenced its development. It is considered to be the direct descendant of Chagatai Turkish, the language of the Timurid court, and it is from this era of linguistic development that the influence of Persian is seen most clearly.

Over its history, Uzbek has been written in all manner of scripts. As late as 1928, all literate Uzbeks wrote using the Perso-Arabic script, but there was then a brief period of 12 years during which the Turkic languages were typically written using the Latin alphabet. In 1940 it was all change again as Stalin decided Cyrillic was the way forward. This Russian script continued to be the primary alphabet used until 1992, when the Latin script was reintroduced. Today you will see Uzbek written in both Latin and Cyrillic scripts, often on the same billboard or page.

Grammatically, Uzbek shares many features with other Turkic languages. Words are ordered subject–object–verb, there is no grammatical gender and no definite or indefinite article. Relative clauses are replaced by various participles, gerunds and verbal nouns and the language is agglutinative (combines word elements to express compound ideas). Most word roots are monosyllabic, and suffixes are added in a fixed order.

For pronunciation and helpful phrases, see pages 258–61.

RUSSIAN Russian remains the language of inter-ethnic communication, science, business and advertising. It is the *lingua franca* of central Asia. It is the most

UZBEK SCRIPT COMPARISON

Uzbek in Latin script
Barcha odamlar erkin, qadr-qimmat va huquqlarda teng bo'lib tug'iladilar. Ular aql va vijdon sohibidirlar va bir-birlari ila birodarlarcha muomala qilishlari zarur.

Uzbek in Cyrillic script
Барча одамлар эркин, қадр-қиммат ва ҳуқуқларда тенг бўлиб туғиладилар. Улар ақл ва виждон соҳибидирлар ва бир-бирлари ила биродарларча муомала қилишлари зарур.

Uzbek in Perso-Arabic script
برچہ آدملر ایرکین، قدر-قیمتی و
حقوقلرده تنگ بولیب توغیلہ
دیلر. اولر عقل و وجدان
صاحبدیدیلر و بیر-بیرلریا یله
برادرلرچہ معاملہ قیلیشیلری
ضرور.

English translation
All human beings are born free and equal in dignity and rights. They are endowed with reason and conscience and should act towards one another in a spirit of brotherhood.

The text used here is Article 1 of the Universal Declaration of Human Rights

widely spoken of the Slavic languages and has an estimated 155 million native speakers worldwide. A further 110 million people speak Russian as a second or additional language. It is one of the six official languages of the UN. In Uzbekistan, most people speak and understand some Russian, even if they cannot write it. It was the main language of education during the Soviet period, and so those who were schooled prior to 1991 are likely to speak Russian more fluently than younger people.

TAJIK Tajik is an Indo-European language closely linked to Persian and Dari, and hence these three languages have a shared literary heritage. Unlike most central Asian languages, it is not related to Turkish. From the 9th century, Tajik was written in a modified version of the Perso-Arabic script (it had previously been written in Sogdian), and the Arab invasions of this time account for its Arabic loan words. It was only with Stalin's division of central Asia in the 1920s that Tajik began to be seen as a linguistic entity distinct from Persian.

For the first decade of being promoted as a distinct language (starting in 1929 when it was designated the official language of the Tajik SSR) it was written in a modified Latin script, but in 1939 the alphabet was again replaced, this time by Cyrillic. You will find Tajik mostly spoken in Samarkand and Bukhara, both of

PROVERBS

Zabon Doni Jahon Doni (Know Language, Know The World)

Tajik proverb

Proverbs give you an important insight into a country and how its people think. What is more, learning just a few and being able to use them in conversation shows your host that you are taking an active interest in their culture, their country and their language. Here are a few of our favourites from the different communities in Uzbekistan.

Uzbek
Don't choose a house, choose neighbours.
A word said is a shot fired.
Verboseness is a load even for a donkey.
When everything you have at home is on the table, your guest will never say he has not seen anything.

Russian
It is easier for the mare when a woman gets off the cart.
The thief who stole an altyn (3 kopecks) is hung, and the one who stole a poltinnik (50 kopecks) is praised.
Your elbow is close, yet you can't bite it.
A beard doesn't make a philosopher.

Tajik
One who is always laughing is a fool, but the one who does not laugh is unhappy.
The walls have mice, and the mice have ears.
If you sit with the moon you become the moon. If you sit in a deg (cooking pot) you become black.

which are ethnically and culturally Tajik cities, even though they are within the borders of modern Uzbekistan. The majority of Uzbekistan's medieval literature, and poems in particular, is in Tajik rather than in Uzbek.

KARAKALPAK This is a Tukic language from the Kypchak family to which Kazakh and Tatar also belong. There are just over 400,000 native speakers in Uzbekistan, and an estimated 2,000 speakers in Afghanistan. It is an agglutinative language with vowel harmony but no grammatical gender. The word order, as with Uzbek, is subject–object–verb. Although it can be written in either Latin or Cyrillic script, the latter is most common.

RELIGION

Communism was supposed to supplant religion during the Soviet period, but attempts to secularise Uzbek society were less successful than in other parts of the USSR. Many people retained their faith in private even if they publicly claimed to be atheist, and the post-independence years have seen a rise in religious practice, including mosque building, which has caused some concern amongst the political elite lest it provide cover for religious extremism and challenges to the state.

ISLAM Some 90% of Uzbekistan's population is nominally Muslim, though there is great breadth in both the degree of religiosity and in the form of Islam practised.

Islam arrived in Uzbekistan with Arab invaders in the 8th century. It spread through the work of missionaries, and was popularised following the conversion of the ruling elite. Bukhara, and later Samarkand, became important regional centres of Islamic learning, their mosques and madrassas heavily patronised by the likes of Timur (page 14).

There was a severe clampdown on all religious practice during the Soviet period, but particularly on Islam as it was feared that pan-Islamism, if allowed to develop, could challenge communism and even the USSR. The 65 registered mosques that were allowed to continue were overseen by the Muslim Board of Central Asia, and those working within them were screened for their political reliability. Other mosques were closed, many Muslims were victims of mass deportation, and the government sponsored numerous anti-religious campaigns.

Islam returned to the public sphere following independence in 1991, and though adherence is growing, particularly amongst the young, surveys suggest that personal understanding of what it means to be a Muslim remains limited or distorted. Self-defining as Muslim appears to be more of an attempt to align oneself with Uzbekistan's cultural heritage than a confirmation of belief in Islamic doctrine.

There has also been a rise, albeit relatively small, in militant Islam in Uzbekistan. Fomented primarily in the Fergana Valley and amongst politically and economically disenfranchised youth, groups such as the IMU (Islamic Movement of Uzbekistan, see box, page 27) and Hizb ut-Tahrir (Party of Islamic Liberation) have found support, though this probably has more to do with poverty than ideology. The label 'Islamic extremist groups' has been used extensively by the government in recent years to describe all manner of political opponents, and fear of Islamic militancy (justified or otherwise) has been used to legitimise political and religious repression. Although there are a number of Uzbeks fighting with militant groups in Syria and Iraq, it is thought that they were radicalised and recruited outside of Uzbekistan, not in the country itself.

CHRISTIANITY Around 5% of Uzbekistan's population are Christians, the vast majority of them being members of the Eastern (or Russian) Orthodox Church, with small numbers of Roman Catholics, Protestants and other groups. Prior to the arrival of Islam the country had a sizeable population of Nestorians and Jacobites, though these were largely killed or converted by Timur. Christianity returned with the arrival of the Russians in the 1860s.

There is significant concern amongst the international community about the persecution of Christians in Uzbekistan, despite a constitutional right of freedom of religion. New parishes cannot register themselves, the printing of unauthorised

THE ISLAMIC MOVEMENT OF UZBEKISTAN

The Islamic Movement of Uzbekistan (IMU) is a banned militant organisation formed in the 1990s by two natives of the Fergana Valley, Tahir Yuldashev and Juma Namangani, who aimed to overthrow President Karimov and create a sharia state in Uzbekistan. They initially fought from bases in Tajikistan and Taliban-controlled Afghanistan, and Namangani in particular was active during the Tajik civil war as a field commander for the Islamic Renaissance Party of Tajikistan (IRPT). Yuldashev, meanwhile, spent much of the late 1990s in Peshawar in Pakistan, where he was allegedly in contact with Osama bin Laden.

After the end of the civil war in Tajikistan, Yuldashev and Namangani turned their attention back to Karimov and Uzbekistan. They received funding from Pakistan's Inter Services Intelligence Agency (ISI) and became ideologically aligned with extremist groups including the Taliban. They found recruits amongst the Fergana Valley's impoverished and politically disaffected youth, and set to work.

The year 1999 saw a series of explosions in Tashkent in failed attempts to assassinate Karimov. There is some doubt as to whether the IMU was actually responsible, but they were blamed nonetheless, and the attacks were used as a justification to crack down on Islamic groups generally. The IMU kidnapped the mayor of Osh, Kyrgyzstan, the same year, and also abducted a group of Japanese geologists.

The IMU established training camps in Afghanistan, having offered the Taliban their alliance to help defeat the Northern Alliance, the main opposition to the Taliban during Afghanistan's civil war. The IMU was equipped with advanced weaponry (including two transport helicopters) and continued to make raids and kidnap foreigners, leading to international pressure on Karimov to fix the problem.

In the end it was the US invasion of Afghanistan that destroyed most of the IMU, as their militants were killed alongside the Taliban. Namangani was killed in 2001, and Yuldashev fled once again to Pakistan. Although occasional attacks in central Asia are still, correctly or otherwise, attributed to the IMU, Yuldashev himself was likely killed in a US drone strike in 2009. Those IMU militants who have survived have either reintegrated into civilian society, or left central Asia and joined ISIS groups in Syria and Iraq as mercenaries. They are valued for their technical skills (particularly building improvised explosive devices) and long experience of guerrilla warfare, and it is thought that the militants behind ISIS's very successful social media network and websites are probably of Uzbek origin.

religious books (including the Bible) has been prohibited since 2006, participants in unregistered services have been detained and beaten, and Jehovah's Witnesses have been imprisoned for teaching religion.

JUDAISM Uzbekistan once had more than 90,000 Jews, most of them living in Bukhara, though now only a fraction of these remain. Ancient texts imply they may have come to Uzbekistan as far back as the 10th century BC, though most trace their ancestry to exiles from the Assyrian Empire in the 7th to 5th centuries BC. In any case, they have been cut off from the rest of the Jewish world for around 2,500 years. The German eccentric Josef Wolff (see box, page 208) visited the Bukharan Jews in 1843 while searching for the lost tribes of Israel.

The 20th century saw several significant Jewish migrations. Some Bukharan Jews fled Uzbekistan for Palestine during the purges of the 1920s and 30s, but the population then swelled with Ashkenazi Jews fleeing the Holocaust. The third wave of migration took place following independence: almost all of Bukhara's Jewish community emigrated then to Israel or the USA. Daniel Metcalfe's *Out of Steppe* contains a fascinating account of those few Jewish families who remain.

EDUCATION

Uzbekistan has nine years of free and compulsory education, starting from the age of seven. The official literacy rate in the country is 99%, a legacy of the comprehensive Soviet education system, though as primary school enrolment in 2009 had fallen to 90%, there is a real likelihood that the current school-age generation will be less literate than their parents.

The vast majority of primary and secondary schools are state run and teach the national curriculum. The exceptions are a handful of international schools in Tashkent. At 1:25 the teacher:pupil ratio in primary schools is reasonably good, but teaching methods and materials tend to be outdated. The medium of instruction is Uzbek (having replaced Russian at independence) and the broad school curriculum includes languages, mathematics and science.

Uzbekistan has 65 universities and higher education institutes, the largest of which are in Nukus, Samarkand and Tashkent. In the first decade of independence, university admissions dropped sharply from 19.4% of the college-age population, to just 6.4%. There are currently thought to be around 300,000 students studying for bachelors' degrees, and between 15,000 and 20,000 studying postgraduate courses.

Higher education is predominantly funded and co-ordinated by the Ministry of Higher and Secondary Specialised Education (MHSSE). The MHSSE also sets the curriculum. In the first two years of an undergraduate degree students take general courses; subject specialisation begins in the third year. It takes four years to obtain a bachelor's degree, and the language of instruction can be either Uzbek or Russian.

Although the quality of higher education in Uzbekistan is reasonable (a fine legacy of the Soviet education system), in recent years the government has encouraged foreign institutions to open campuses, bringing much-needed investment for infrastructure and also updating teaching methods and curriculums. The most successful of these new institutions is **Westminster International University in Tashkent** (*www.westminster.uz*), which opened in 2002 in the historic buildings of what used to be the second Women's Gymnasium. Today, Westminster is considered to be among the most respected universities in central Asia. It has around 3,000 students, most of whom are studying degree courses in business and economics.

CULTURE

MUSIC Uzbekistan is widely considered to have the most diverse range of musical styles in central Asia. The classical style of *shashmaqam*, now widespread across the region, is believed to have developed in the cities of Bukhara and Samarkand in the late 16th century. The term refers to the structure of music with six sections in different musical modes. This style is similar to classical Persian music and is often interspersed with devotional Sufi poetry. This lyrical, deeply spiritual music is usually accompanied by stringed instruments like the dutor, rubber and the ghizhzhak.

Ethnomusicologists first began recording Uzbek folk music in the late 19th century, and as a means of recording songs and tunes for posterity they also introduced written notation. Though banned from radio station playlists during the Soviet period, folk music continued to be enjoyed at weddings and other festivals, surviving long enough to be revived on the back of Uzbek nationalism. Nowadays Uzbek television and radio stations regularly play folk music, and singers of traditional music, such as Sherali Jo'rayev, Yulduz Usmonova and Sevara Nazarkhan, have gained a wide following both in Uzbekistan and on the world music circuit.

Pop music has flourished in Uzbekistan since the early 1990s, with Uzbek, Russian and Turkish artists dominating the charts. Several Uzbek singers, most notably Shahzoda and Sogdiana Fedorinskaya, have achieved commercial success in Russia, though Uzbek artists are not really known outside the former USSR. The exception to this rule is Googoosha (aka Gulnara Karimov); see box, page 30.

The following of other contemporary music styles is harder to judge, as much of it is underground. A few pop-rock bands have emerged (specifically Bolalar and Sahar), but the lifestyles stereotypically associated with heavy rock music are generally disapproved of, and Tashkent's tiny population of goths has reported

RUDAKI

It is sometimes said that Rudaki is to the Tajik language as Shakespeare is to English: despite the passing of centuries, many know a few lines, and allusions to his work still permeate modern poetry and prose.

Abu Abdullah was born in the village of Rudak (hence his moniker) in Transoxiana (now the area surrounding Penjikent in Tajikistan), in AD857. Many of his biographers believe him to have been blind, but doubt is cast over this assertion by the vivid descriptions of colour in his poems, around 2,000 lines of which survive.

At the height of his career, Rudaki was appointed as court poet to Nasr II, the Samanid ruler of Bukhara, and it was here that Rudaki produced his greatest works. His lyrical poems were philosophical in nature and included messages of patriotism (popular with the ruler) and messages of freedom (popular with the ordinary people but somewhat less popular with the ruler).

A refusal to stop preaching liberty to the masses ultimately ended Rudaki's life at court; he fell from favour and, without the support of a wealthy patron, he died in poverty at the remarkable age of 84.

Gulnara Karimova (stage name Googoosha), the eldest daughter of President Karimov, released her first music video 'Unutma Meni' (Don't Forget Me) in 2006. Cynics suggest it may have been a ploy to show the fluffier side of Uzbekistan's first family, and it's certainly brought publicity if not critical acclaim and platinum record sales. She went on to duet with Julio Iglesias, and in 2012 released her first single, 'Round Run', and an album that was given international release.

Karimova is no star-struck show-child, however. Born in July 1972, she has a fist-full of academic qualifications from various Uzbek institutions, but also a masters degree in regional studies from Harvard. In 1998 and from 2000 to 2003 she was consul at Uzbekistan's Mission to the United Nations in New York, then minister-consul at the Uzbek embassy in Moscow. She advised the Ministry of Foreign Affairs, became the Permanent Representative of Uzbekistan to the United Nations in Geneva in 2008, and in January 2010 she was named Uzbek Ambassador to Spain. She has significant business interests, allegedly in everything from retail to telecoms, with some commentators speculating she has assets worth in excess of US$600m.

In the last couple of years, however, Karimova seems to have fallen from favour, and has disappeared from the society scene at home as well as internationally. Letters purportedly written by Karimova and released by her lawyer allege that she is being held under house arrest against her will, though no official comment has been made. Credible sources have suggested that the reason for her imprisonment is that her business activities were too corrupt. Believing she was immune from prosecution, she went too far, embarrassing her father. This is his attempt to bring her back under control.

being harassed by both the state and the community at large for their musical and fashion tastes. The Uzbek government censors rap music because it believes it is not complementary to Uzbek culture.

LITERATURE Uzbekistan's literary canon is a reflection of its diverse linguistic and cultural heritage. In addition to writings in Uzbek, some of the finest works of Persian/Tajik literature were written in Samarkand and Bukhara, and in the 20th century writers seeking a Soviet Union-wide audience for their work were compelled to write in Russian.

Early literature in Uzbekistan developed as an oral medium: travelling bards and local storytellers were important figures in local communities, their heroic tales an essential part of weddings, funerals and other festivals. The genre includes epic poems, known as *dastan*, in which the protagonist must protect his tribe and homeland from foreign invaders. Famous epic poems in this style include *Kyor-ogly* and *Alpamysh*, a celebration of the bravery of Uzbek warriors.

A significant proportion of Uzbekistan's classical literature dates from the medieval period. The writer and philosopher **Abu Abdullah Rudaki** (see box, page 29) is considered to be the father of Tajik literature. Along with **Ferdowsi** (934–1020), author of the epic poem *Shahnameh* (The Book of Kings), and the scientist **Hussayn ibn Abu Ali ibn Sina** (980–1037), known in the West as Avicenna, he is a pillar of classical Tajik literature, and rightly commemorated with street names and monuments across both Uzbekistan and beyond.

Lainie Mullen

The Ilkhom Theatre, a company now based in Tashkent, began with a group of young artists and thinkers led by artistic director Mark Weil in 1976. They staged bold performances about current issues and gained notoriety in the USSR by presenting material not approved by the censorship board.

Weil worked by the philosophy that theatre is a spiritual search. 'We were not a political theatre,' he wrote, 'we did not try to change anyone's thinking with our performances, we did not moralize ... We just reproduced unedited life and real people on our stage.' The theatre faced ongoing opposition but survived through the country's transition to independence. It continued to present plays on contemporary and controversial themes and often pulled from Uzbek literature and traditions. Weil formed many foreign partnerships and toured the company through Russia, Europe, Asia and North America.

Weil also developed a training programme for young actors in the 1990s that continues every several years to take in new local and foreign actors.

With the opening of the theatre's 32nd season in 2007, it suffered an irreparable blow: Mark Weil was murdered. The theatre continued to work, however. Actors collaborated with local and Russian artists to stage a stunning music-based production of Alisher Navoi's *Seven Moons* in 2010. In 2011, the theatre won the Prince Claus Award for its contribution to culture and development.

The theatre's current artistic director is Boris Gafurov, a leading actor of the theatre. Ovlyakuli Khodjakuli, a guest director, has staged some of the most recent performances. The theatre remains the only professional non-state-sponsored theatre in Uzbekistan. Plays are usually performed in Russian with some Uzbek. A few shows per month have English subtitles.

Background Information CULTURE

1

The 11th century also produced didactic works based on religious norms of Islamic morality. Well-known poems include *Knowledge, Providing Happiness* (1069) by **Yusuf Balasaguni** and *The Gift of Truths* by Akhmad Yugnaki, and especially *The Dictionary of Turkic Dialects* (1072–74), composed by **Makhmud Kashgari**. The first dictionaries and grammars also date from this era.

With vast sums spent on patronising the arts, and Samarkand serving as the imperial centre, it is of little surprise that the golden age of literature was under the Timurids. Both religious and secular works were produced in large numbers, the latter category encompassing everything from fiction to medical treatises and astronomical observations. The language of court, and therefore of much of the literature, was Chagatai Turkish, and the most famous writer and cultural figure to emerge from these years is undoubtedly **Alisher Navoi**, though **Zakhiriddin Babur**, the founder of the Mughal Empire in India, also wrote his autobiography in the Chagatai language during this period.

The 20th century gave birth to a wide number of important authors writing in Russian as well as local languages. **Khamza Khakimzade Niyazi**, **Sadriddin Aini**, **Abdulla Kadiri** and **Gafur Gulyam** all rose to prominence during this period, with organisations such as the Uzbekistan Writers Union actively promoting their work. Many of their homes and collected papers are preserved in house museums around the country; these are well worth visiting if you have an interest in Soviet literature.

Ikat is a word from Indonesian and Javan languages, and it is used to refer to a dyeing technique similar to tie-dye in which either the warp or weft fibres are tied in a specific pattern before being dyed. Alternating the patterns of bindings and the use of several colours produces elaborate, multi-coloured patterns. At the points where the different dyed sections meet, carefully controlled amounts of colour merge with one another randomly creating subtle, slightly blurred patterns that are unique: every dyeing will result in a slightly different appearance, even if the same colours are used. The dyed threads can then be woven. The difference between tie-dye and ikat is that in ikat the dyeing takes place before the fabric is woven.

Uzbekistan has a number of contemporary writers, though few of these are known outside Uzbekistan as their works are rarely available in translation. Electronic publishing may, of course, change this. **Salomat Vafo**, a young woman from Khorezm, has had some critical acclaim overseas for her 2004 novel *The Empire of Mystery*, though due to its discussion of intimate relationships, the Uzbekistan Writers Union initially tried to prevent its publication.

THEATRE An appreciation of theatre and formalised performance arrived in Uzbekistan with the Russians in the late 19th century. For the first time designated performance spaces were built, the most attractive of which is surely the Alisher Navoi Opera and Ballet Theatre in Tashkent, though several other companies have played more active roles in promoting and developing drama in Uzbekistan. The critically acclaimed theatre company of Uzbekistan is the Ilkhom Theatre of Mark Weil (see box, page 31).

DANCE There are two main types of dance in the Uzbek tradition: folk and classical. Some folk dances are reserved for special occasions, while others are impromptu expressions of joy. Classical dance is primarily the domain of women; lyrical upper body movement, facial expressions and empathy with the music characterise these performances. The three main schools are found in the Fergana Valley, Khiva, and Bukhara.

ARTS AND CRAFTS For centuries Uzbekistan has been known for its artistic output: from glazed tiles to the finest silks, finely worked jewellery set with precious and semi-precious stones, to handwoven and knotted carpets.

Uzbekistan is home to some of the most spectacular architecture not only in the Islamic world but worldwide, and several sites are justifiably recognised by UNESCO as being of international cultural importance. Monuments to both God and man incorporate influences from ancient Greece to the Buddhist temples of the Indian subcontinent, a riotous fusion of ideologies, tastes and techniques. The lack of stone and timber available locally pushed forward advances in brick and tile making and there was significant medieval innovation in the design and engineering of domes (including ribbed domes and double domes).

Architectural decorative art holds a prominent place in the arts and crafts of Uzbekistan. The world famous architectural monuments of Bukhara, Samarkand, Khiva and other cities testify to the mastery of medieval artists and

TILE MAKING

Tiles must be the most impressive of Uzbekistan's decorative mediums, and tile making reached its peak during the Timurid era. Soft clay tiles were individually carved, painted, fired and glazed, their colours derived from ground lapis lazuli and turquoise, yellow ochre and burnt sienna, terra verde and red iron oxide. Similar techniques have been used to produce a variety of plates, bowls and other homeware items, which are popular and affordable souvenirs for visitors.

architects, ornamental designers and calligraphers, engravers and ceramicists. Wall painting, sculptural carving and ornamental carving and painting have been practised since before the medieval period – in the 8th and 9th centuries there was a period of intensive development of ornamental, floral-vegetal polychromatic painting and relief carving. Carved wood also played a large part in architectural décor and is still used in the production of household goods and furniture.

Other crafts include engraving on copper and wood, ornamental embroidery using gold thread, decoration of tanned leather and inlaid work on musical instruments. The silk carpets of Uzbekistan, with their tight weave, smooth finish and rich colours are made in Dzhizak, Syr Darya, Qashqa Darya, Karakalpakstan, and Samarkand. The weaving and embroidery of silks and cotton into wonderful, shimmering cloth is famously the passion and occupation of women in Samarkand, Bukhara, Shakhrisabz, Surkhan Darya, Fergana, Kokand, Margilan, and Namangan.

Throughout the centuries, the handing down of artistic traditions from one generation to the next has continued. The skills and knowledge imparted by the various ethnic groups that eventually came together to constitute the Uzbek nation created a true diversity of artistic traditions, which is the distinguishing feature in works of art of all genres.

Of ever increasing popularity are the art galleries and workshops that showcase Uzbek modern, classical and folk art. Tashkent, with about a dozen major galleries, hosts regular exhibitions of fine art, folk pieces and antiques. Art studios and galleries in Samarkand, Bukhara and Khiva are also enjoying success among both Uzbek and international tourists. As well as buying these products, it is also possible to attend masterclasses where the process of producing unique items is shown.

Many say Islam prohibits the depiction of living things in art, but this is scarcely evident in Uzbekistan. Though ornate calligraphy, colourful geometric patterns and nature-inspired motifs (the usual alternatives) are all in evidence, so too are tiles painted with animals, flowers and human faces and beautifully illustrated manuscripts depicting men, beasts and even the occasional prophet or angel.

The most noted masters of wall painting in the last century were from Bukhara, and the art of master painters from Samarkand, Tashkent and Khiva is also renowned. Even today, the work of Saidmakhmud Narkuziev, an outstanding painter based in Kokand, is much admired and his sons and grandsons continue his tradition.

Natural pigments are also important for Uzbekistan's carpet-making industry. Though most carpets are now produced by machine, and Turkmen and Afghan carpets often labelled as Uzbek, some small workshops do still

Background Information CULTURE

1

produce carpets by hand. The revival of traditional carpet making in Khiva is the subject of the fascinating and very readable *Carpet Ride to Khiva* by Chris Alexander, and you can also see carpets being made on looms in Bukhara and Samarkand.

Uzbekistan was one of the earliest producers of silk after the secrets of production escaped from China, and the country's farmers and artisans continue to raise silkworms and weave high-quality silks. Some of the most attractive silk designs are dyed and woven using a method known as *ikat* (see box, page 32).

SPORT

A diverse range of sports are practised in Uzbekistan, from traditional wrestling and horse games, to judo and freestyle skiing. Rugby union is on the rise, and President Karimov is a big fan of tennis.

Uzbekistan has competed as an independent nation in every Olympic and Winter Olympic Games since 1994 (prior to this Uzbek athletes competed on behalf of the Soviet Union), and has won medals in a variety of combat sports as well as gymnastics. At the London Olympics in 2012 Uzbekistan's Artur Taymazov took the gold medal in the wrestling (men's freestyle 120kg), and his teammates took bronze medals in judo (men's 60kg) and boxing (men's middleweight).

FOOTBALL Nicknamed the 'White Wolves', the national football team of Uzbekistan played its first competitive match, against Tajikistan, on 17 June 17 1992. Despite having played international matches for only two decades, the Uzbekistan Football Federation (UFF) has actually been in charge of the national team since 1964. In 1994, FIFA and the Asian Football Confederation (AFC) officially recognised the country as an independent football-playing nation after its split from the USSR.

The country's relatively short football history has produced surprisingly good results. They won the Asian Games Tournament in 1994 (hosted in Hiroshima, Japan) at their first attempt, and reached the quarter-finals at the next competition in 1998. Since 2002, however, football at the Asian Games has been an under-23s tournament. Uzbekistan has yet to qualify for any World Cup despite six attempts but does hope to qualify for Russia in 2018.

Uzbekistan's biggest win came against Mongolia in 1998, when they won 15–0, and their biggest defeat was at the hands of Japan in 2000 when they lost 8–1. Their record goalscorer is Maksim Aleksandrovich Shatskikh, who is now retired. Born on 18 August 1978, Shatskikh has scored an extremely impressive 34 goals in only 59 appearances for his country.

The UFF currently presides over, and organises, the Uzbekistan National League, the second tier (Uzbekistan 1-Division) and the Uzbekistan Women's Football Championship. Unlike many other Islamic countries, Uzbekistan has actively promoted the growth of women's football, with ten clubs competing annually in the national league. The two dominant women's teams are Andijanka Andijon and Sevinch Qarshi, and between them they have won every single title since the league's inauguration in 1996.

The men's National League consists of 14 teams and was founded in 1992. Much like the women's competition, there are two teams that dominate the league, both of which are from the capital (Paxtakor Tashkent and Bunyodkor

Uzbekistan's most famous international sports star is Djamolidine Abdoujaparov, 'The Tashkent Terror'. He was a professional road cyclist, best known for his explosive finishes in races, and sometimes unorthodox and erratic approach towards winning them.

Born on 28 February 1964, 'Abdou' graduated from the Soviet Sports Programme just prior to Uzbek independence. After initial difficulties arising from Uzbekistan not being affiliated with the Union Cycliste Internationale (UCI), Djamolidine eventually turned professional in 1990, and raced for several European teams (including Carrera, Novell and Lotti) in his seven-year professional career.

Despite his many successes, Djamolidine is perhaps best known for his tussles with fellow sprinter Laurent Jalabert for the green sprinter's jersey in various stages of the Tour de France in the early 1990s. Between the two men, they won five consecutive green jerseys between 1991 and 1995, with Jalabert claiming two of those titles, and Abdou claiming three.

Abdou's first victory came in 1991, despite an unbelievable crash on the Champs-Elysées (the traditional finishing point of the Tour de France since 1975), which saw the Uzbek cyclist clash with a giant promotional drinks can with just 100m left in the race. Abdou was sent spiralling into the air and was seriously injured, but the rules of the competition stipulated that despite already holding enough points to win the green jersey for that year, the cyclist must cross the finish line unaided. As a result of this rule, members of his Carrera team subsequently picked him up, helped him back onto his bike and he rode gingerly to the finish line where he was greeted by paramedics and his newly claimed title.

Sadly for the sport, and despite a glittering career, the end of the Uzbek's career was overshadowed by his failing of an anti-doping test during the early stages of the Tour de France in 1997. However, as one of only four men to have won the points competition in all three Grand Tours (the Tour de France, Giro d'Italia and Vuelta a Espana), he remains one of the greatest sprint cyclists of all time.

Tashkent). Between them they have won the trophy for 13 years in succession. The Uzbekistan 1-Division is split into two zones (east and west), with each league featuring 12 teams. In order to reach the top division of Uzbek football, teams must first finish top of their respective zonal league, and then compete in the top tier the following season.

RUGBY UNION Rugby union was introduced to the Russian Empire in 1908, and the Soviet Union hosted championships in Moscow from 1936 onwards. The sport began to be actively promoted in Uzbekistan in the early 1960s, and regional teams were founded in addition to the national team.

Today, the sport is mainly played in Uzbekistan's universities and by the military. The fact that Kazakhstan has achieved notable success on the world stage, especially with its women's team, has led the Uzbeks to up their game (excuse the pun). The Rugby Federation in Uzbekistan was established in 2001, and though an Uzbek side is yet to play in the Rugby World Cup, they do compete in the Asia Rugby Championship.

Background Information SPORT

1

TENNIS Walk around any Uzbek city and you will quickly come across tennis courts and tennis academies. The sport has been heavily promoted by President Karimov, and is hugely popular. The Uzbekistan Tennis Federation (UTF) became a full member of the International Tennis Federation (ITF) in 1993, and it organises championships within Uzbekistan as well as sending the national team to major international competitions, including the Davis Cup and the Fed Cup.

Uzbekistan's #1 seed is Denis Istomin (b1986), who was born in Russia to Uzbek parents and moved to Tashkent as a child. He stepped onto the international circuit in 2006 when he received the Asian wildcard to play in Australian Open, losing gracefully to Roger Federer. The same thing happened at the 2008 Australian Open, though this time it was Lleyton Hewitt who knocked him out.

Istomin has been growing in profile in the last few years. In 2012 he reached a worldwide singles ranking of #33, and in 2013, 2014 and 2015 he won the doubles title at the ATP World Tour 250 Series. 2015 was an especially good year, as he also took the singles title. With several years of his professional tennis career left to play, Istomin is well worth watching.

2

Practical
Information

WHEN TO VISIT

Uzbekistan is a year-round tourism destination, though most people choose to visit between May and October, as the winter months can be bitingly cold both in the desert and in the mountain foothills.

Spring breaks in March and April (slightly later in the mountains) and brings with it a riot of colourful flowers in the mountain pastures. The rivers are in full spate with the glacial meltwater, and the country comes swiftly back to life. If you visit in springtime, you may also be able to join in celebrations for Navruz, the Persian New Year (celebrated in Uzbekistan on 21 March). During this two-day festival, which is a national holiday, families feast, watch traditional sports including *kopkari* (horse racing) and *kurash* (wrestling), and there's plenty of musical entertainment. You'll invariably be asked to join in the fun.

The **summer** can be bakingly hot on the plains, particularly in July and August, but this is the best time to trek in the mountains and to try a night or two sleeping in a yurt. It's also the time of some of Uzbekistan's biggest festivals, including the UNESCO-backed Festival of Traditional Culture and Samarkand's International Music Festival. Expect plenty of pomp and circumstance if you're in Uzbekistan for Independence Day (1 September).

When **autumn** comes, Uzbekistan turns terracotta red and gold almost overnight. It's one of the most beautiful times to visit. Late September and early October is the ideal time to visit the big three, Samarkand, Bukhara and Khiva, as temperatures are still warm but many of the crowds have gone. By early November, the warmly dressed can have Khiva in particular almost entirely to themselves, though many restaurants and shops will be closing up at the end of their season.

In the **winter** months few tourists come to Uzbekistan, but that means you can negotiate favourable rates for hotels and tours. It's also the time for skiing: the resorts of Chimgan and Beldersoy have excellent snow from January to March, and you can even risk your neck heli-skiing for descents up to 10km in length.

HIGHLIGHTS

It's clichéd but true to say that Uzbekistan offers a little something for everyone. Whether your idea of a trip of a lifetime is wandering amongst the medieval tombs of Samarkand, shopping in Tashkent's vast Chorsu Bazaar or trekking across the Kyzylkum Desert by camel and sleeping in a nomad's yurt, you won't be disappointed. The challenge is how to pack everything into the time available. If you're in need of a little guidance, here are our must-see sights and experiences:

CAMEL TREKKING We have sadly found that camels are invariably smelly, bad-tempered and jolly uncomfortable to ride. However, the Silk Road would never have got going without them, and so you will need to saddle up and take at least a short journey on camelback if you want the full, authentic experience. The best camel treks are around Nurata in the Kyzylkum Desert (pages 202–3), where you can ride across the dunes well away from roads and human habitation. Make Aidarkul Lake (pages 198–9) your destination, and tie your camel on the shore while you have a swim in the slightly salty waters or try your hand at fishing. Come nightfall, you can stay with nomadic families in a traditional yurt (albeit with the added advantage of a toilet block), sit around the fire listening to stories and music, and engage in some splendid star-gazing.

CHORSU BAZAAR This bazaar is the first and only place where we have seen the boot and back seat of a Lada stacked to the gunwales with decapitated cow heads. The sight was truly gruesome. Quite what they were doing there, we can only dread to think, but in Chorsu Bazaar (page 100) they didn't look a bit out of place. The modern incarnation of Silk Road trading posts now long gone, the market buzzes with energy and everything conceivable (and, like the cow heads, a few things normally inconceivable) is for sale. You can of course buy a trailer-load of watermelons and 300 plastic buckets, but the real delight comes in spending an hour or three exploring the trading domes, drinking bowls of fragrant black tea, smelling the *shashlik* grilling and engaging in an animated, good-natured haggle for a bag of salted pistachios and a fresh, pink pomegranate. Come here for some well-placed souvenirs, including a wide selection of ceramics, and the best people-watching in Tashkent.

HOTEL ORIENT STAR A single hotel wouldn't normally feature in the highlights section of our guide, but then the Hotel Orient Star (page 238) is no ordinary hotel. The Muhammad Amin Khan Madrassa, in the heart of Khiva's Ichon Qala, has been sensitively converted so that all mod cons are hidden behind the elaborately tiled 19th-century façade. Each room is inside a former *hujra* (student's cell), though with considerably more creature comforts, and the hotel courtyard once housed the city's Supreme Court. When you step outside your door in the mornings, you can look up in wonder at the jewel-like Kalta Minar.

IGOR SAVITSKY MUSEUM There would be little reason to come to Nukus at all if it weren't for the Igor Savitsky Museum (pages 255–7), an unexpected treasure trove of Soviet avant-garde art from the 1920s and 30s. The 2010 documentary *Desert of Forbidden Art* provides an informative and moving account of Savitsky's life and work and will certainly whet your appetite and motivate you to make the trek out to what feels like the other side of the moon. In addition to the striking, and in many cases controversial, paintings Savitsky collected, you will also find galleries of folk art and archaeological finds illustrating Khorezm's rich past. When the two new museum buildings open (hopefully during the lifespan of this edition), an even greater part of the collection will finally be on show.

KHOREZM FORTRESSES It is of course possible to come to Khorezm and only visit Khiva, but you would sadly be missing out. Not far away, on the edge of the Kyzylkum Desert, are a string of fortresses (pages 232–4) dating from the early centuries BC. Listed by UNESCO as the Golden Ring of Ancient Khorezm, the most impressive are the mud-brick Toprak Kala and the Koi Krylgan Kala, but there are plenty of smaller sites if you want to explore on your own. You will need your own transport to get here, but it is well worth hiring a car for a couple of days and staying on site in the yurt camp beside the Ayaz Kala to be able to appreciate the site at both sunset and sunrise. You can take a camel ride from the yurt camp here, too.

KHUDAYAR KHAN'S PALACE The 19th-century palace of Khudayar Khan (page 145), ruler of Kokand, once had more than 100 rooms and was described as the most magnificent in central Asia: its nickname is the Pearl of Kokand. Though a shadow of its former self, 19 of its rooms survive today and in them are displayed an eclectic collection of jewellery, stuffed animals, fine woodcarvings and *objects d'art*. Here, you will have a sense of the exorbitant wealth and excesses of the khans, and how they were able to dazzle foreign visitors. The palace is said to have been built by 80 master builders and 16,000 conscripted labourers, the descendants of whom still live in and around Kokand today.

POI KALYON The entirety of Bukhara probably deserves mentioning as a highlight, but it is the Poi Kalyon (pages 219–20) that particularly caught our eye. This simple square is framed by some of the most spectacular buildings on earth: the Mir-i Arab Madrassa, the Kalyon Juma Mosque and the majestic 11th-century Kalyon Minar. The Kalyon Minar is one of the few buildings in the city to pre-date the invasion by Genghis Khan: he saw its elegant silhouette from a great distance away as he rode across the steppe, found it beautiful, and when he arrived in Bukhara, he could not bear to see it destroyed. Everything else, however, was razed to the ground, and the population of Bukhara was butchered.

SHAH-I ZINDA Most people come to Samarkand for the Registan but, though it is undoubtedly impressive, the city's real gem is the collection of medieval tiled tombs known as the Shah-i Zinda (the Living King) (pages 160–2). Approaching through the back entrance (accessed through the parallel cemetery, watching out for the resident marmots) at dusk, the experience is magical. The tour groups have retreated to their hotels for dinner, as have the schoolchildren, and if you're lucky you'll have the place to yourself. You can expect to see every variety of turquoise- and lapis lazuli-coloured glazed tiles attached to the façades of the tombs of female members of the Timurid dynasty, as well as senior advisors and holy figures. Work is underway to properly conserve and restore the tiles after an earlier, rushed restoration.

SUGGESTED ITINERARIES

How much you can see in Uzbekistan is very much dictated by the length of your stay and your modes of transport. Travelling by camel may sound romantic, but it's still rather faster to go by plane. These itineraries give an idea of what you can hope to accomplish in different amounts of time, and which sites you should endeavour to squeeze into your trip. With just a **weekend** at your disposal, you have two options: focus on Tashkent and see most of what the city has to offer, or hire a car and driver, leave early for Samarkand and write-off the four hours' drive in each direction as the price you have to pay to see one of central Asia's most remarkable cities.

If you choose to stay in Tashkent, start in the Old Town with the Khast Imam Square, the world's oldest Qu'ran in the Muyie Muborak Library, and the 15th-century tombs of the Sheikhantaur Cemetery. Have a late lunch at one of the *plov* stalls in Chorsu Bazaar and explore the stalls in the afternoon before taking in a performance at either the Alisher Navoi Opera and Ballet Theatre or the Ilkhom Theatre in the evening. The following morning you should visit Amir Timur Square for a view of post-independence Uzbekistan before going to the State Fine Arts Museum, the core of whose collection was confiscated from Grand Duke Romanov, who in turn had stolen many of the items from the Hermitage in St Petersburg. We also like the Tamara Khanum Museum with its collection of theatrical and dance costumes, photos and posters, and the Railway Museum where you're still allowed to climb on and inside many of the exhibits.

In a **week** you can comfortably expect to see Tashkent, Samarkand and Bukhara. The roads between these three locations are well maintained and relatively fast, and you can also take the train. In Samarkand, book into the Antica B&B a stone's throw away from the Gur-i Amir, Timur's gilded mausoleum, and explore the heart of the city on foot. The Registan, Shah-i Zinda and Ulug Beg's astronomical observatory should not be missed, and neither should the ancient ruins of Afrosiab.

Travelling on to Bukhara, you should stay in a hotel close to Lyabi Hauz or the Kalyon Minar and pace yourself as you explore the bewildering selection of beautifully decorated mosques, madrassas and tombs. The Ark, Bolo Hauz Mosque and the Chor Minor are all best seen from the outside, Lyabi Hauz should be appreciated whilst relaxing with a bowl of tea by the water, and if your legs will carry you up the winding staircase to the top of the Kalyon Minaret, you'll get breathtaking views across the city.

With **two weeks** to spare, you can do all this and take in the highlights of Khorezm. Visiting Khiva's Ichon Qala goes without saying, but don't miss the Khorezm fortresses in the Kyzylkum Desert, or the chance to sleep in a nomad's yurt beneath the endless sky. Make sure you go to Nukus for the Igor Savitsky Museum and then continue through Karakalpakstan as far as Moynaq for the graveyard of ships left behind by the retreating Aral Sea.

A **month** is ample time to take in everything Uzbekistan has to offer. Consider travelling part of the way on the Trans-Caspian railway for a taste of travel in a bygone age, and allow at least a week to explore the little-visited Fergana Valley. Kokand is famous for its ornate 18th- and 19th-century architecture and also its craft workshops, Margilan has fascinating silk factories, and the base camp at Nanay is an ideal point from which to explore Kapchugai Gorge and the Chatkal Mountains.

TOUR OPERATORS

Though it is possible, and indeed relatively straightforward, to travel independently within Uzbekistan, many first-time visitors choose to go with a recognised tour operator as it generally reduces the hassles of bureaucracy, arranging internal transport and the language barrier. The companies below, all of which offer specialist, small-group tours, also provide knowledgeable guides, helping you to get the most out of the country.

All of the companies listed here are based outside of Uzbekistan, and their group itineraries visit either Uzbekistan alone or Uzbekistan and one or more of the other central Asian republics. Uzbekistan-based tour operators, of which there are a number of experienced, professional outfits, are listed under the *Tour operators*, *Travel agents* or *Tourist information* section of the city in which their offices are located.

UK

Audley Travel New Mill, New Mill Lane, Witney, Oxon OX29 9SX; ☎ 01993 838 205; www. audleytravel.com. Offers high-end, tailor-made trips to Uzbekistan, taking in the key sights of Tashkent, Samarkand, Bukhara & Khiva. Trips are arranged on a private basis, with a professional, English-speaking guide & driver throughout. Prices for the 11-day 'Uzbekistan Discovered' tour start from £2,395.

Exodus 9 Weir Rd, London SW12 0NE; ☎ 0845 805 5322; e sales@exodus.co.uk; www.exodus. co.uk. Their 'Uzbekistan Uncovered' trip is a 12-day excursion to the main cities, & also includes camel trekking & visits to the desert castles of Toprak Qala, Qavat Qala & Ayaz Qala.

Explore Nelson Hse, 55 Victoria Rd, Farnborough, Hants GU14 7PA; ☎ 01252 883 747; e sales@ explore.co.uk; www.explore.co.uk. Explore's 'Golden Road to Samarkand' trip is a small group adventure that takes in Uzbekistan's highlights over 11 days, including a yurt stay. The tour runs on fixed departure dates from Mar–Oct.

Golden Eagle Luxury Trains Denzell Hse, Denzell Gdns, Dunham Rd, Altrincham, Cheshire WA14 4QF; ☎ 0161 928 9410; www. goldeneagletrains.org. Luxury journeys by private train. The 'Silk Road', 'Taste of the Silk Road', 'Caspian Odyssey' & 'Persia & the Silk Road' trips all make stops in Uzbekistan.

Go Russia Boundary Hse, Boston Hotel, London W7 2QE; ☎ 020 3355 7717; e info@justgorussia. co.uk; www.justgorussia.co.uk. Offers 2 trips per year to Uzbekistan, the 26-day 'Silk Road Odyssey', which also takes in Kyrgyzstan & China, & an 8-day tour solely in Uzbekistan.

Indus Experiences Avanta Harrow, 79 College Rd, Harrow HA1 1BD; ☎ 020 8901 7320; e holidays@ indusexperiences.co.uk; www.indusexperiences. co.uk. Tailor-made itineraries & occasional group tours across Asia, including Uzbekistan. Focus is on exploring culture & unique local experiences.

Into Russia 7 Wellington Terrace, Notting Hill, London W11 4TR; ☎ 0207 603 5045; e reservations@into-russia.co.uk; www.into-russia. co.uk. 'Legends of the Great Silk Road' is an 8-day tour of Uzbekistan, & can be booked either on its own or with a 3-day extension in Moscow.

Intrepid Travel 1 Cross & Pillory Hse, Cross & Pillory Ln, Alton, Hants GU34 1HL; ☎ 0808 274 5111; www.intrepidtravel.com/uk. Intrepid offers a number of scheduled groups tours to Uzbekistan,

including the 12-day 'Classic Uzbekistan', which includes not only the big Silk Road cities but also the Khorezm fortresses and the Nuratau Mountains. Prices start from £1,365. Other itineraries include Uzbekistan as part of a longer central Asian journey.

Martin Randall Travel Voysey Hse, Barley Mow Passage, London W4 4GF; ☎ 020 8742 3355; e info@martinrandall.co.uk; www.martinrandall. com. Organises 11-day, expert-led tours between Apr–Sep. Itineraries include all the main cultural sites & in-country travel is by coach. 'Samarkand & the Silk Road Cities' is escorted by an expert lecturer.

Regent Holidays 6th Fl, Colston Tower, Colston St, Bristol BS1 4XE; ☎ 0203 553 0208; e regent@ regentholidays.co.uk; www.regentholidays.co.uk; see ad, inside front cover. Numerous imaginative, top-end itineraries including a 14-day private train ride from the Caspian Sea to the Tian Shan Mountains & a 'Monuments and Mountains of the Silk Road,' tour' which combines the sites of Uzbekistan & Tajikistan.

Steppes Travel 51 Castle St, Cirencester, Gloucs GL7 1QD; ☎ 01285 601 638; e enquiry@ steppestravel.co.uk; www.steppestravel.co.uk. Specialises in private holidays based on personal specifications & wants, ranging from a couple of days to a couple of months. Steppes currently has 3 expert-led group tours in Uzbekistan, including the 12-day 'Uzbekistan: Beyond the Oxus' from £2,145.

Sunbird 26B Market Sq, Potton, Sandy, Beds SG19 2NP; ☎ 01767 262 522; e sunbird@ sunbirdtours.co.uk; www.sunbirdtours.co.uk. Specialists in birding tours, with expert guides. 'Central Asia: Birding the Silk Road' combines Uzbekistan & Kazakhstan & is the foremost birding tour in the region.

Voyages Jules Vernes 21 Dorset Sq, London NW1 6QE; ☎ 020 3553 3326; e sales@vjv.co.uk; www.vjv.com. Choose from 1 of 2 upmarket tours: a week-long highlights tour of Tashkent, Bukhara & Samarkand, or the longer 'Golden Road to Samarkand', which includes an Uzbek cookery class.

Wild Frontiers 78 Glentham Rd, London SW13 9JJ; ☎ 020 7736 3968; e info@wildfrontiers.co.uk; www. wildfrontiers.co.uk. Winner of *The Guardian's* Best Ethical Travel Award, Wild Frontiers has numerous tailor-made & group itineraries including Uzbekistan, some of which are quite extraordinary. For the trip of a lifetime, pick the 47-day 'Great Silk Road Adventure', from £9,500.

USA AND CANADA

Bestway Tours and Safaris Suite #206, 8678 Greenall Av, Burnaby, BC V5J 3M6, Canada; ☎ +1 800 663 0844; e bestway@bestway.com; www. bestway.com. Regular group departures for tours lasting 9–25 days. Uzbekistan can be visited alone or combined with tours to Russia, China & Iran amongst others. Programmes often have a specific focus, such as sacred architecture, caravan routes or train travel.

MIR Corporation Suite 210, 85 Washington St, Seattle, WA 98102, USA; ☎ +1 800 424 7289; e info@mircorp.com; www.mircorp.com; see ad, 2nd colour section. The USA's Russia & central Asia experts offers exceptional tours of Uzbekistan, including not only multi-country Silk Road tours but also one-off art, dance & cultural tours. Uzbekistan can be combined with neighbouring republics & also with Iran. Highly recommended.

AUSTRALIA AND NEW ZEALAND

Odyssey Travel 36 Young St, Wollongong, NSW 2500, Australia; ☎ +61 1300 888 225; e info@ odysseytravel.com.au; www.odysseytravel.com. Offers several trips based solely in Uzbekistan, including country-wide archaeological tours & guided city tours. They also arrange a 'Silk Road Odyssey' tour that puts Uzbekistan in context with its historic trading partners. Prices for the specialist 'Archaeology in Central Asia' tour start from AUD\$5,950.

Peregrine Adventures Level 4, 380 Lonsdale St, Melbourne, Victoria 3000, Australia; ☎ +61 1300 854 445; e sales@peregrineadventures. com; www.peregrineadventures.com. Ranging from 12–36 days in length, Peregrine's accompanied tours blend Uzbekistan's cultural heritage & architecture with shopping in the bazaars, local food & good accommodation.

Silk Road Adventures 415 Main South Rd, Greymouth 7805, New Zealand; ☎ +64 3 762 6673; e enquiries@silkroad.co.nz; www.silkroad.co.nz. Group overland tours to Uzbekistan. The 'Persian Trilogy' tour combines Uzbekistan, Turkmenistan & Iran, while the 'Uzbekistan Silk Roads' trip is a comprehensive tour of the country, including the Fergana Valley.

Sundowners Overland Level 1, 51 Queen St, Melbourne 3000, Australia; ☎ +61 1300 559 860; e travel@sundownersoverland.com; www. sundownersoverland.com. Wide selection of fully escorted & independent tours, as well as tailor-made experiences. Luxury train travel is a speciality. Check out in particular the 30-day 'Silk Road Railway' & the 41-day 'Grand Asia Caravan' trips.

RED TAPE

Uzbekistan is a bureaucrat's dream. Much of the Soviet-era red tape persists, topped up with a few additional measures aimed at counter-terrorism or just making life difficult. Irregularities (real or actual) in paperwork are guaranteed to complicate your journey at some stage, and a fine or bribe may be demanded to fix the problem. If in doubt, be patient, be polite and hold your ground; you will get through it eventually.

LETTERS OF INVITATION The majority of visitors, including the passport holders of the UK, USA, Austria, Belgium, France, Germany, Italy, Japan, Spain or Switzerland, no longer require a letter of invitation in order to get a 30-day tourist visa for Uzbekistan. However, if you are one of the unfortunate nationalities that still do, or indeed if the regulations change, you will need to budget around US\$40 and request a letter of invitation (LOI) from Stantours (*www.stantours.com*), Travcour (*www.travcour.com*) or another travel agent able to provide visa support. You will need the LOI prior to making your visa application and should allow at least 10 days for the LOI to be processed.

VISAS All non-CIS nationals require a visa to visit Uzbekistan, and even CIS nationals may have difficulty entering if they do not have proof of onward travel. If Uzbekistan has an embassy or consulate in your country of residence (page 44) you will need the visa stuck into your passport before you fly; you may be prevented from boarding the plane if you do not have a valid visa.

To apply for the visa, fill out the online application form at www.evisa.mfa.uz and print it. Make sure you sign it in black ink as this box is frequently overlooked. Submit the form with two passport photos, a photocopy of your passport and your passport itself to the embassy.

The cost of a visa is dictated by your nationality, where you are applying, the length of your stay and whether it is for single, double or multiple entry. At the time of going to print, a UK national applying in London will pay £57 for a single-entry, 30-day visa, and US nationals applying for the same visa at the same embassy will pay £114. Visas typically take five working days to process, but it is possible to fast-track your application if you pay a 50% surcharge.

If Uzbekistan does not have diplomatic representation in your country of residence, it is sometimes possible to arrange in advance for a visa to be issued on arrival in Tashkent. You should contact a travel agent to arrange this, and you will need both your LOI and approval letter in hand before you board the plane.

It is theoretically possible to extend your visa for up to seven days once you are in Uzbekistan, but in practice people often prefer to leave for a neighbouring country and apply for a new Uzbek visa there. If you are feeling optimistic (or have run out of other options), you can obtain a seven-day extension from the Office of Visa and Registration (OVIR) at Tashkent International Airport for US$40, a big smile and a lot of persistence. Tashkent-based travel agents (pages 90–1) may also be able to smooth the way for an additional fee.

For nationals who do not require a LOI (page 42), the process for obtaining a business visa is the same as for a tourist visa. If you do require a LOI, your inviting partner will have to gain written authorisation from the Ministry of Foreign Affairs (MFA) in Tashkent before you apply for the visa. The visa costs are the same.

No exit visa or stamp is required for Uzbekistan: just make sure your visa is in date and you have the requisite registration slips (see below).

REGISTRATION The requirement for foreigners to register within three days of arriving in any given place is an irritating overhang from the Soviet period and, even more irritatingly, it is often enforced by the authorities.

If you check into a hotel authorised to take foreigners, the hotel will automatically register you. You are responsible for collecting the small slip they give you as proof of registration, and keeping hold of it until you have left Uzbekistan as you may be required to show it on departure. If you take an overnight train journey, keep the ticket stub or booking confirmation as proof of your whereabouts. If you are camping or staying with friends or at a homestay for more than three nights, you should register at the local OVIR to ensure you (and your hosts) are in the clear.

Punishments for failing to register are applied arbitrarily and you never know if you'll be the unlucky one. Whilst most people will get away with a few missing registration slips (and may not have them checked at all), we've also met a couple who were detained with their children for two days and fined US$1,500 each for failing to register, having arrived overland by train from Turkmenistan. Unless you have plenty of time and money to throw at extricating yourself from the problem, play it safe.

ADDITIONAL PERMITS Uzbekistan requires foreigners visiting sensitive border areas and some areas of military or special scientific interest to have a travel permit in addition to their visa. If you intend to mountaineer in Uzbekistan, or to visit either the Ugam-Chatkal or Zaamin national parks, then you may be affected. Check with a Tashkent-based travel agent (pages 90–1) for the latest information. They will also be able to apply for a permit on your behalf, often prior to your arrival in Uzbekistan.

EMBASSIES

A comprehensive and regularly updated list is available from the Ministry of Foreign Affairs website (*www.mfa.uz/en*). For a list of those in Tashkent, see http://embassy.goabroad.com/embassies-in/uzbekistan.

GETTING THERE AND AWAY

For somewhere so centrally located geographically, Uzbekistan can be surprisingly challenging to reach. There is a shortage of direct flights from Europe and the US, land borders open and close on a whim, and arriving by train requires you to have a passport full of transit visas and the patience of a saint.

BY AIR The vast majority of visitors arrive in Uzbekistan on a flight to Tashkent and this is, on balance, the easiest way to travel. Unless there are extenuating circumstances, you will need to have a visa before boarding the plane (pages 42–3) and may be prevented from flying if you do not.

Though it is improving, the safety record of many of central Asia's airlines (including some national carriers) is such that they are prevented from flying in European airspace. Aircraft are typically far older than those in service elsewhere, and they have not always been maintained to international standards. It is likely, therefore, that if you take a flight originating in Europe or the US you will need to get a connection in one of the regional hubs (Almaty, Istanbul or Moscow). With the exception of Uzbekistan Airways flights, direct flights to Uzbekistan tend to come only from the Middle East, Russia and the other CIS countries.

The arrivals procedure is relatively straightforward. When you enter the terminal building collect an immigration form, fill it in and then wait in the interminably long immigration queue. Keep a sense of humour and be prepared to use your elbows and hand luggage strategically to avoid getting shoved to the back of the crowd. The baggage hall is the usual scrum, and there is a bottleneck near the exit as you have to submit your customs form and have it stamped. Be sure to declare all your foreign currency. You will need to keep the stamped form for when you leave. All your baggage then has to pass through the X-ray machine.

At the time of going to print, all of the below-listed airlines had regular scheduled flights to Uzbekistan.

✈ **Aeroflot** \(071) 120 0555; e tastosu@ aeroflot.ru; www.aeroflot.ru. Daily flights to & from Moscow Sheremetyevo. Direct flight takes 4½hrs & is useful for onward connections to Europe & the US.

✈ **Air Astana** m 090 936 2533; e tas.airport@ airastana.com; www.airastana.com. Kazakh national carrier. Daily flights to Almaty, with connections to Europe, the Middle East & domestic destinations within Kazakhstan. Efficient.

✈ **Air Baltic** \(071) 120 9012; www. airbaltic.com. Latvian national carrier. Budget airline providing European connections via Riga 2–4 times a week depending on the season.

✈ **Asiana Airlines** \(071) 140 0900; www. flyasiana.com. 5 flights a week to Seoul.

✈ **China Southern Airlines** \(071) 231 8880; www.csair.com. Daily flights to Beijing with onward connections to the Far East, Australia & domestic destinations within China.

✈ **Iran Air** ✆(071) 233 5082; www.iranair.com. Flights once a week to Tehran.

✈ **Korean Air** ✆(071) 254 2001; www. koreanair.com. 3 flights a week to Seoul with onward connections across the Far East.

✈ **Malaysia Airlines** www.malaysiaairlines. com. 3 flights a week between Tashkent & Kuala Lumpur with onward connections across southeast Asia & Australia.

✈ **Rossiya** ✆(071) 255 5815; www.rossiya-airlines.com. 4 flights a week to St Petersburg with onward connections across Europe & Russia.

✈ **S7** ✆(071) 252 7871; www.s7.ru/en. Russian airline S7 has flights from Moscow to both Tashkent & Urgench.

✈ **Turkish Airlines** ✆(071) 147 0849; e info-uz@thy.com; www.thy.com. Daily flights to Istanbul with onward connections to Europe & the US. Also handles cargo.

✈ **Ural Airlines** www.uralairlines.ru/en. Direct flights to Ekaterinburg (Mon) & Krasnodar (Thu) with onward connections across Russia & the CIS.

✈ **UTair** www.utair.ru/en. 6 flights a week from Moscow.

✈ **Uzbekistan Airlines** 41✆(071) 140 0200; e info@uzairways.com; www.uzairways.com. Uzbekistan's national carrier serves Almaty (5 a week), Baku (3 a week), Beijing (2 a week), Bishkek (4 a week), Delhi (7 a week), Dubai (2 a week), Istanbul (daily), London (2 a week), Moscow (daily), Paris (2 a week), Seoul (2 a week) & others. Domestic routes connect Tashkent to Andijan, Bukhara, Fergana, Karshi, Namangan, Navoi, Nukus, Samarkand, Termez & Urgench. Also at 9 Usman Nosir (*✆(071) 256 3837*).

BY TRAIN There is a certain romance attached to train travel, and if you have the time to sit and watch the world pass by at a leisurely pace (very leisurely in the case of the old Soviet rail network), it is still a viable way to reach Uzbekistan. Regardless of where the train originates, you will need to ensure you have a valid transit visa for every country *en route*, as well as a visa for Uzbekistan.

Ticket classes are categorised in the Russian style. First-class or deluxe accommodation (*spets vagon*) buys you an upholstered seat in a two-berth cabin. The seat turns into a bed at night. Second class (*kupe*) is slightly less plush, and there are four passengers to a compartment. Third class (*platskartny*) has open bunks (ie: not in a compartment) and, if you are really on a very tight budget indeed, a fourth-class ticket (*obshchiy*) gets you an unreserved and very hard seat. Bring plenty of food for the journey, and keep an eye on your luggage, particularly at night, as theft is sadly commonplace.

There are four trains a week between Moscow and Tashkent, and an irregular service between Almaty and Tashkent. The Moscow service, train No 6 or 5 depending on the direction of travel, takes 66 hours and tickets start from around US$270 one way.

The train timetable for the whole Russian rail network (including central Asia) is online at www.poezda.net. The Uzbek Railways site, parts of which are in English, is www.uzrailpass.uz. The Man in seat Sixty-One (*www.seat61.com/silkroute.htm*) also has detailed information, including personal observations, about train travel in the former USSR.

If you are coming to Uzbekistan from China, it is possible to take the new train line from Urumqi to Almaty, and change there for Tashkent. We have not personally taken this route, but the intel from Caravanistan (*www.caravanistan.com*) is that the Urumqi–Almaty train goes twice a week, and costs US$110. It is, however, exceptionally slow: the bus is 10 hours faster.

If you love the romance of train travel, but the thought of having to deal with all the bureaucracy and then slumming it onboard fills you with dread, there is another option. Golden Eagle Luxury Trains (*www.goldeneagletrains.org*) runs scheduled departures onboard the Golden Eagle Express, a private train with creature comforts to rival those of the Orient Express. Uzbekistan is included on both their Caspian Odyssey and Silk Road itineraries, so you can pick the route which most appeals, and then just sit back and enjoy the ride.

BY ROAD Our preferred way to enter Uzbekistan is through a land border, not because customs and immigration make it a particularly easy or pleasant experience, but because of the freedom having your own transport gives you once you finally make it inside.

The information given below was correct at the time of going to print, and more detailed information about each border, including its times of operation, is given in *Part 2* of the guide. Be aware that border crossings open and close regularly, often with little warning, and some crossings are open only to locals and not to foreigners. Keep your ear to the ground and, if in doubt, contact a tour operator or Uzbek consulate before confirming your travel plans. We have previously ignored our own advice and been stuck for 12 hours in the no man's land between Uzbekistan and Kyrgyzstan. We do not recommend you follow suit.

Reaching Uzbekistan from **Afghanistan** tends to be fairly straightforward as diplomatic relations between the two countries are generally good. The main border crossing is at Hairatan between Mazar-i Sharif and Termez. Theoretically the border is open 24/7, but you may have to wait if the relevant official is at dinner or sleeping. Shared taxis from Hairatan to Mazar take an hour and cost US$4 per person.

There are several crossing points between **Kazakhstan** and Uzbekistan. The main crossing at Chernayevka (between Shymkent and Tashkent) is open 24/7 but there are often long queues. If you are travelling by public transport you will need to ride to the border, cross on foot, and then pick up another vehicle on the other side. For some reason, you are not supposed to cross this border in your own, foreign vehicle: you need to go to Konysbayeva.

We have also used the Konysbayeva (also known as Yalama) crossing north of Chinaz, which is considerably faster but only usable if you have your own transport in Uzbekistan. There are share taxis on the Kazakh side only. Further west, you can cross from Kazakhstan at Tajen on the Beyneu–Kungrad road.

Diplomatic relations with **Kyrgyzstan** are volatile, with border crossings opened and closed seemingly on a whim. The main border post is at Dostyk on the road between Osh and Andijan. Though relatively straightforward, you should note that the Kyrgyz and Uzbek sides have different opening times: the Uzbek post operates more or less around the clock, while the Kyrgyz side closes around 19.00 and reopens at 07.00. There are no facilities in no man's land if you have to stay the night, though you may be offered floor space to put down a sleeping bag.

Potentially more useful due to being closer to both Tashkent and Bishkek is the Uch-Kurgan crossing near Namangan. This has reopened to foreigners, though there is no public transport on either side. The border is open from 08.00 to 20.00. There are minibuses and taxis on the Uzbek side to take you to Uch-Kurgan town, and plenty of public transport heading to either Bishkek or Osh which you can hail on the main road when you cross into Kyrgyzstan.

Note that minibuses and trains between Bishkek and Tashkent all pass through Kazakhstan, for which you will need a Kazakh transit visa.

Relations with **Tajikistan** are also a little erratic, and hence at the time of going to print one of the most useful border crossings between the two countries, between Samarkand and Penjikent, was closed. There is unfortunately no rumour of it reopening any time soon.

The Tursunzoda–Denau crossing west of Dushanbe remains open, and this is currently the best option if you are going to or from anywhere other than Tashkent and the northeast of Uzbekistan. It is well served by minibuses and taxis running in both directions, and providing you're not stuck behind a busload of returning migrant workers carrying all their worldly possessions, processing is fairly quick. The border is open until late every evening, and sometimes 24/7.

Travelling **to or from Tashkent** you need the Oybek crossing 60km north of Khujand. The closest settlement on the Tajik side is the town of Buston. This crossing is open 24/7 for foreigners (locals have to camp outside the gates if they arrive at night) and it is relatively well organised on the Tajik side. Uzbek customs are utterly paranoid, want to X-ray every last sock (we saw one elderly gentleman even having to remove his car bumper and mud flaps to put them through the machine) and allow their admittedly very cute sniffer dog (a spaniel) to jump over everything. It also got overly excited and peed on our picnic. Taxi and minibus drivers hover on both sides of the border.

The border crossing at Bekhobod, just to the south of Oybek, is currently closed to foreigners.

You can cross to the **Fergana Valley** from Konibodom, northwest of Isfara. This border is little-used by foreigners and the onward transport is not as well organised as at the other border posts; try to arrange a taxi to meet you on the Uzbek side as there is a severe shortage of these. On the Tajik side, minibus #144 shuttles between the border and Konibodom town, from where you can pick up buses and taxis to Khujand.

Crossing to or from **Turkmenistan** takes around 2 hours and you must pay a US$12 entry tax (payable in US dollars only) when you arrive. Most foreigners use the Farap–Alat crossing between Turkmenabat and Bukhara, though the Shavat–Dashoguz border near Khiva and the Hojali–Konye-Urgench crossing near Nukus are also well used. Farap–Alat is open from 09.00 to 20.00. All three of these border posts close for an hour or so's lunch at 13.00, and there are plenty of shared taxis and minibuses. A taxi ride from Farap–Alat to Bukhara takes around 3 hours and should cost you no more than US$25 by taxi. Shared taxis and minibuses are, of course, much cheaper.

If you are bringing your own vehicle into Uzbekistan (regardless of the entry point) you will have to declare it on the usual customs form, plus fill in additional paperwork to be entered onto the computer system. Theoretically at least you will not be allowed to leave the country unless you take the vehicle with you. You may be told that right-hand-drive vehicles cannot enter Uzbekistan; this is not true so hold your ground. Expect to have the vehicle thoroughly inspected, sluiced with disinfectant, and to have all of its contents (sometimes right down to the jack and spare wheel) passed through the X-ray machine.

> **NOTE**
>
> That vehicles with Tajik registration plates cannot enter Uzbekistan, and those with Uzbek plates must pay import duty if they enter Tajikistan. This applies to taxis as well as private vehicles, so if you are travelling by taxi you should get dropped off at the border and pick up a second vehicle on the other side.

BEFORE YOU GO Comprehensive **travel insurance** should be high on your list when you contemplate travelling to Uzbekistan. Choose a policy that includes medical evacuation (Medevac) and make sure you fully understand any restrictions: it is not uncommon for insurance companies to exclude certain activities (including mountaineering and skiing) from cover. Leave a copy of the policy documents at home with someone you trust, and keep a copy of your policy number and the emergency contact number on you at all times.

Your GP or a specialised travel clinic (see below) will be able to check your immunisation status and advise you on any additional inoculations you might need. It is wise to be up to date on **tetanus, polio** and **diphtheria** (now given as an all-in-one vaccine, Revaxis, that lasts for ten years), and **hepatitis A**.

Hepatitis A vaccine (Havrix Monodose or Avaxim) comprises two injections given about a year apart, though you will have cover from the time of the first injection. The course typically costs £100 and, once completed, gives you protection for 25 years. The vaccine is sometimes available on the NHS. **Hepatitis B** vaccination should be considered for longer trips (two months or more) and by those working in a medical setting or with children for any length of time. The vaccine schedule comprises three doses taken over a six-month period, but for those aged 16 or over it can be given over a period of 21 days if time is short. The rapid course needs to be boosted after one year. A combined hepatitis A and B vaccine, 'Twinrix', is available, though at least three doses are needed for it to be fully effective. For those under 16, the minimum time is over 8 weeks.

The newer injectable **typhoid** vaccines (eg: Typhim Vi) last for three years and are about 75% effective. Oral capsules (such as Vivotif) may also be available for those aged six and over. Three capsules taken over five days last for approximately three years but may be less effective than the injectable version. Typhoid vaccines are particularly advised for those travelling in rural areas and when there may be difficulty in ensuring safe water supplies and food.

Rabies is prevalent throughout Uzbekistan and vaccination is highly recommended for those travelling more than 24 hours from medical help or who will be coming into contact with animals as there is unlikely to be treatment available within the country.

Crimean Congo Haemorrhagic fever is a viral illness spread by ticks. The animal reservoirs are cattle, sheep and goats or through contact with infected animal blood. The peak season is during the summer months and the mortality can be high. That said, the risk for most travellers is low but is higher for those in contact with animals or for those at increased risk of tick bites.

Precautions against tick bites should be taken by inspecting the skin daily for ticks and removing promptly by using tick tweezers or by grasping the tick as near to the skin surface as possible and pulling gently without twisting. The risk of **malaria** is low in Uzbekistan, so there is no need to take antimalarials.

While pharmacies in Uzbekistan are numerous, especially in the main cities, and some are well equipped, you should still pack a **first-aid kit** (a comprehensive kit is essential for trekkers and others visiting remote areas) and any prescription medicines you require.

TRAVEL CLINICS AND HEALTH INFORMATION A full list of current travel clinic websites worldwide is available on www.istm.org. For other journey preparation information, consult http://travelhealthpro.org.uk (UK) or http://wwwnc.cdc.

It is highly advisable to prepare your own first-aid kit and to carry it with you wherever you travel in Uzbekistan. A minimal kit should contain:

- A good drying antiseptic, eg: iodine or potassium permanganate
- A few small dressings (Band-Aids)
- Suncream
- Insect repellent ideally containing around 50% DEET
- Aspirin or paracetamol
- Imodium and rehydration salts
- Ciprofloxacin or norfloxacin (for severe diarrhoea)
- A pair of fine-pointed tweezers (to remove thorns, splinters, ticks, etc)
- Alcohol-based hand sanitiser or bar of soap in plastic box
- Clingfilm or condoms for covering burns (for anyone with a camping stove)
- A small needle and syringe kit

gov/travel/ (US). Information about various medications may be found on www. netdoctor.co.uk/travel. All advice found online should be used in conjunction with expert advice received prior to or during travel.

IN UZBEKISTAN The medical system in Uzbekistan is seriously overstretched. The quality of medical training has fallen since the end of the USSR era, many doctors have left to find work abroad, hospitals are run-down and equipment is out of date. Outside of the major cities there is also a shortage of drugs and other medical supplies. If you are ill or have an accident, you will be able to receive emergency treatment at one of the good private hospitals in Tashkent or at a more basic regional hospital but will then require Medevac to a country with more developed medical infrastructure for ongoing care.

Most towns in Uzbekistan have a number of **Apteka**, small pharmacies selling a range of generic drugs. You do not need a prescription to purchase medication, but should read the instructions carefully or get someone to explain them to you.

Potential medical problems

Altitude sickness Acute mountain sickness can affect everyone – even really fit people – during a rapid ascent and staying more than 12 hours above 2,500m (8,203ft). In the mountainous east of Uzbekistan, and, in particular, in the upper reaches of the Pskem and Gissar mountain ranges, where there are a number of peaks over 4,000m, it is important to be aware of the possibility of altitude sickness. Altitude sickness is caused by acute exposure to low partial pressure of oxygen: in layman's terms this means that the amount of available oxygen decreases as you ascend, to the point that the body has insufficient oxygen in the blood to continue functioning normally. Symptoms of mild altitude sickness include headaches, nausea, anorexia, insomnia and confusion and can be minimised by taking time to acclimatise to the altitude. Many people recommend taking acetazolamide (Diamox) prophylactically to assist in acclimatising. Discuss this with your doctor or other healthcare professional before you go. Even if you are taking Diamox, developing any symptoms which might be AMS means that you should descend at least 500m as soon as possible.

LONG-HAUL FLIGHTS, CLOTS AND DVT
Dr Felicity Nicholson

Any prolonged immobility, including travel by land or air, can result in deep-vein thrombosis (DVT) with the risk of embolus to the lungs. Certain factors can increase the risk and these include:

- Having a previous clot or a close relative with a history
- Being over 40, with increased risk in over 80s
- Recent major operation or varicose-veins surgery
- Cancer
- Stroke
- Heart disease
- Obesity
- Pregnancy
- Hormone therapy
- Heavy smoking
- Severe varicose veins
- Being tall (over 6ft/1.8m) or short (under 5ft/1.5m)

A deep-vein thrombosis causes painful swelling and redness of the calf or sometimes the thigh. It is only dangerous if a clot travels to the lungs (pulmonary embolus). Symptoms of a pulmonary embolus (PE) – which commonly start three to ten days after a long flight – include chest pain, shortness of breath, and sometimes coughing up small amounts of blood. Anyone who thinks that they might have a DVT needs to see a doctor immediately.

Prevention of DVT
- Keep mobile before and during the flight; move around every couple of hours
- Drink plenty of fluids during the flight
- Avoid taking sleeping pills and excessive tea, coffee and alcohol
- Consider wearing flight socks or support stockings (see www.legshealth.com)

If you think you are at increased risk of a clot, ask your doctor if it is safe to travel.

More serious forms of mountain sickness include pulmonary oedema also known as HAPE (fluid on the lungs) and cerebral oedema also known as HACE (swelling of the brain). The first is characterised by a shortness of breath, dry cough and fever and the latter by a persistent headache, unsteady gait, confusion, delirium and loss of consciousness. These are both serious medical emergencies and need immediate evacuation and treatment by qualified professionals.

A useful free download on altitude sickness can be found at www.medex.org.uk.

Travellers' diarrhoea Diarrhoeal diseases and other gastrointestinal infections are fairly common, and perhaps half of all visitors will suffer in this way. Travellers' diarrhoea, as well as more serious conditions such as typhoid, comes from getting bacteria in your mouth. To avoid getting ill you should ensure that you observe good hygiene practices, such as regular hand washing, using bottled water (including for cleaning teeth), and avoiding foods of doubtful provenance. Many travellers use the following maxim to remind them what is safe:

PEEL IT, BOIL IT, COOK IT OR FORGET IT

This means that fruit you have washed and peeled yourself, and hot foods, should be safe, but raw foods, cold cooked foods, salads, ice cream and ice are all risky, and foods kept lukewarm in hotel buffets often harbour numerous bugs. That said, plenty of travellers and expatriates enjoy fruit and vegetables, so do keep a sense of perspective: food served in a fairly decent hotel in a large town or a place regularly frequented by expatriates is likely to be safe.

If you are struck down with diarrhoea in spite of your precautions, remember that dehydration is your greatest concern. Drink lots of clear fluids. Sachets of oral rehydration salts give the perfect biochemical mix to replace all fluids you are losing. If you don't have rehydration salts, or can't stand the taste, any dilute mixture of sugar and salt in water will do you good: try Coke or orange squash with a three-finger pinch of salt added to each glass (if you are salt-depleted you won't taste the salt). Or add eight level teaspoons of sugar (18g) and one level teaspoon of salt (3g) to one litre (five cups) of safe water. A squeeze of lemon or orange juice improves the taste and adds potassium, which is also lost in diarrhoea. Drink two large glasses after every bowel action, and more if you are thirsty. These solutions are still absorbed well if you are vomiting, but you will need to take sips at a time. If you are not eating you need to drink three litres a day plus whatever is pouring into the toilet. If you feel like eating, take a bland, high-carbohydrate diet. Plain rice, dry bread or digestive biscuits are ideal.

If the diarrhoea is bad, or you are passing blood or slime, or you have a fever, you will probably need antibiotics in addition to fluid replacement. Consult a doctor as soon as possible. A dose of norfloxacin or ciprofloxacin repeated twice a day until better may be appropriate (if you are planning to take an antibiotic with you, note that both norfloxacin and ciprofloxacin are available only on prescription in the UK).

Prickly heat Uzbekistan can become exceptionally hot in summer: temperatures above 45°C are common. A fine pimply rash on the chest or forearms is likely to be heat rash; it is caused by sweat becoming trapped beneath the skin and causing

AVOIDING INSECT BITES

Although Uzbekistan is not an area with a high risk of malaria, mosquitoes can carry other diseases and their bites are, in any case, uncomfortable. As the sun is going down, don long clothes and apply repellent on any exposed flesh. Pack a DEET-based insect repellent (roll-ons or stick are the least messy preparations for travelling). Repellents should contain between 50–55% DEET and can be used by children and pregnant women. Insect coils and fans reduce rather than eliminate bites. Travel clinics usually sell a good range of nets, treatment kits and repellents.

Mosquitoes and many other insects are attracted to light. If you are camping, never put a lamp near the opening of your tent, or you will have a swarm of biters waiting to join you when you retire. In hotel rooms, be aware that the longer your light is on, the greater the number of insects will be sharing your accommodation.

a histamine reaction. Cool showers, dabbing dry, and talc will help. Treat the problem by wearing only loose, 100%-cotton clothes and sleeping naked under a fan. An antihistamine tablet may help reduce the itching, as will hydrocortisone cream or Sudocrem.

Sunstroke and dehydration The sun in Uzbekistan can be very harsh, even in the mountains where the lower temperatures may suggest otherwise. Sunstroke and dehydration are serious risks.

Wearing a hat, long loose sleeves and sunscreen helps to avoid sunburn. Prolonged unprotected exposure can result in heatstroke, which is potentially fatal. Stay out of the sun between noon and 15.00.

In the heat you sweat more, so dehydration is likely. Don't rely on feeling thirsty to tell you to drink – if your urine is anything other than colourless then you aren't drinking enough. Carry bottled water with you at all times and make sure you stop to drink it.

Rabies Rabies can be carried by all warm-blooded mammals and the disease is transmitted to humans through contact with an infected animal's saliva. If you are bitten, scratched or simply licked, you must assume that the animal has rabies. Scrub the area with soap under a running tap for around ten to 15 minutes or while pouring water from a bottle, then pour on antiseptic (or alcohol if none is available). This helps stop the rabies virus entering the body and will guard against wound infections, including tetanus.

Uzbekistan is classified as a high risk rabies country. Vaccination before travel is strongly recommended as there is almost certainly going to be a shortage of the specific post-exposure treatment in Uzbekistan. If you have not had a course of pre-exposure vaccine then you are likely to require a blood product Rabies Immunoglobulin (RIG) and definitely five doses of vaccine given over 30 days. The RIG and first dose of vaccine should be given as soon as possible and ideally within the first 24 hours. Neither RIG nor rabies vaccine is available at the time of writing in Uzbekistan and so evacuation would be the only recourse. Having three doses of the vaccine before travel over a minimum of 21 days, but ideally 28 days, simplifies the post-exposure treatment by removing the need for RIG and reducing the post-exposure treatment to two doses of vaccine given three days apart. Whilst evacuation may still be necessary, it is less of an emergency. Three doses of vaccine cost around £160 in the UK and last for at least ten years, unless you are planning to work as a vet abroad when boosters are recommended annually. Without the correct treatment for rabies following exposure the mortality is almost 100%.

Tetanus Tetanus is caused by the *Clostridium tetani* bacterium and though it can accumulate on a variety of surfaces, it is most commonly associated with rusty objects such as nails. Cutting yourself or otherwise puncturing the skin brings the bacteria inside the body, where it will thrive. Clean any cuts thoroughly with a strong antiseptic.

Immunisation against tetanus gives good protection for ten years, and it is standard care practice in many places to give a booster injection to any patient with a puncture wound. Symptoms of tetanus may include lockjaw, spasms in any part of the body, excessive sweating, drooling and incontinence and the disease results in death if left untreated. Mild cases of tetanus will be treated with the antibiotic metronidazole and tetanus immunoglobulin whilst more severe cases will require admission to intensive care, tetanus immunoglobulin injected into the spinal cord, a tracheotomy and mechanical ventilation, intravenous magnesium and diazepam.

SAFETY

The UK's Foreign and Commonwealth Office (FCO) generally considers Uzbekistan to be a safe place for foreigners to travel. They regularly update their travel guidance, and the latest advice for Uzbekistan is available online at www.fco.gov.uk.

The FCO advises caution when travelling to border areas, in particular the border between Uzbekistan and Afghanistan, as there is a threat of land mines. These regions can also be flashpoints for inter-ethnic violence, as was seen in the Fergana Valley in July 2010. Such violence is not typically targeted at tourists, but there is a risk of being caught up in the upheaval.

There is also an underlying threat from terrorism. Attacks could be indiscriminate, including in places visited by tourists. Security has been increased at airports and railway and metro stations as a result of the bombing at Moscow Airport in January 2011, with an increased police presence and the introduction of X-ray machines. You are expected to show your passport when entering metro stations, and the use of cameras (including camera phones) is prohibited.

Some visitors have been victims of petty crime, particularly mugging and pickpocketing, and a high number of visitors experience low-level corruption from traffic police and other officials. The latter is irritating more than dangerous, and can often be averted by requesting a receipt or refusing to hand over documents or cash on the street. Ask to be taken to the police station instead.

Uzbekistan is seismically active, and there is therefore a risk of earthquakes. On 20 July 2011 an earthquake measuring 6.2 on the Richter scale hit Batken, just across the Uzbek border with Kyrgyzstan, and tremors were felt in Tashkent. A number of deaths and injuries were reported.

ROAD SAFETY Driving standards in Uzbekistan are generally poor, and the motorists in Tashkent are some of the most boorish we've encountered anywhere in the world. The wide variety of vehicles on the roads, from decrepit Soviet-era makes to large modern 4×4s, makes for traffic travelling at different speeds. Overtaking on the inside, and illegal U-turns, are among many common infringements in the cities. The poor state of repair of many roads, with pot-holes and often inadequate or non-existent street lighting, adds to the difficulties. In rural areas, animals and pedestrians wandering into the road present a considerable risk.

If you are driving in Uzbekistan, you will need to be careful and cautious, always wear a seat belt and never drink and drive. Try to avoid driving outside cities after dark as roads are poorly lit and other vehicles may not have working lights. Bad driving also creates a risk to pedestrians.

When on foot, you should avoid the local practice of crossing busy roads by walking out to the centre of the road and waiting for a gap in the oncoming traffic, even if this means taking a detour to cross the road at the next set of traffic lights. Do not expect cars to stop for you, even if you are on a zebra crossing.

WOMEN TRAVELLERS Uzbekistan is generally a safe country for women to travel in, and there are no specific legal or cultural restrictions imposed on women (either locals or foreigners). The social conditions of women improved significantly during the Soviet period, and the enrolment of women in education and in the workplace remains high.

Women should, however, exercise the usual personal safety precautions. Particular caution should be taken when hailing taxis: in Tashkent, phoning for a cab, or getting the establishment you are in to do this for you, is probably a safer option.

Unaccompanied women may receive unwanted attention in bars and clubs but this is usually deflected with a few terse words. If the harassment continues, alert the management or leave the premises and find a more pleasant alternative. Try to avoid physical confrontation, as alcohol-fuelled violence and being tailed home are not uncommon. Domestic violence is high in Uzbekistan, as it is across central Asia. There have been suspected cases where 'date rape' drugs have been used; keep a close eye on your drink, and do not accept drinks from strangers.

You should dress modestly, especially in conservative rural areas and in the Fergana Valley where religious sentiments often run high.

GAY TRAVELLERS Homosexuality is illegal in Uzbekistan and Article 120 of the country's penal code punishes voluntary sexual intercourse between two men with up to three years in prison. Sexual intercourse between two women is not mentioned in the code.

Many people in Uzbekistan are deeply conservative, especially when it comes to the issue of sexuality, and homosexuality is still often seen as a mental illness (a hangover from the Soviet period). Muhammad Salih, leader of the People's Movement of Uzbekistan, said publicly in 2012: 'I support a civilised way of isolating gays and other sick members of society so that they could not infect healthy people with their disease.' Sadly, his views are widely shared. Homosexuals in Uzbekistan regularly experience harassment, including from the police; gay-friendly establishments are heavily monitored by the police and are often forced to close; and police detention and the threat of prosecution are regularly reported.

If you are travelling with a same-sex partner, you should refrain from public displays of affection and be exceptionally cautious when discussing your relationship with others: it is often simplest to allow others to assume you are simply travelling with a friend. Double rooms frequently have twin beds, so asking for one room is unlikely to raise eyebrows in any case.

TRAVELLERS WITH DISABILITIES Travellers with disabilities will experience difficulty travelling in Uzbekistan. Public transport is rarely able to carry wheelchairs, few buildings have disabled access, and streets are littered with trip hazards such as broken paving, uncovered manholes and utility pipes. Hotel rooms are often spread over multiple floors without lifts and assistance from staff is not guaranteed. If you have a disability and are travelling to Uzbekistan, you would be advised to travel with a companion who can help you when the country's infrastructure and customer service fall short.

TRAVELLING WITH CHILDREN This is relatively easy given Uzbeks' focus on family life. Children are welcomed in restaurants and shops but you may have difficulty manoeuvring pushchairs in and out of buildings and along broken pavements. Nappies, baby food and other similar items are available in supermarkets and larger stores, but you are unlikely to find European brands. There have been a number of scandals in recent years relating to the potentially toxic content of Chinese-made baby milk powder and, as many of the brands involved are for sale on shop shelves in Uzbekistan, you should stay on the safe(r) side and purchase Russian or European-made brands instead. The quality control is slightly higher.

Journeys by car and public transport are often long and uncomfortable, and food supplies erratic, which may deter families with younger children travelling beyond Tashkent and the main tourist sites. Ensure you stock up with plenty of snacks before leaving a town, and take plenty of entertainment options along for the ride.

WHAT TO TAKE

You may wish to consider the following, in addition to the usual holiday packing.

- **Plug adaptors** Sockets in Uzbekistan are the twin round pin, continental European type. The voltage is 220V.
- **A torch** Many parts of Uzbekistan, including city streets, are unlit at night, and pavements may conceal dangers such as uncovered manholes. Power cuts are not uncommon. If you are planning to camp, or use homestays in rural areas, you'll need a torch to navigate to the latrine at night.
- **Mosquito repellent** Uzbekistan may not be a malarial country, but the swarms of mosquitoes you may encounter in summer amongst its lakes and forests can still

SUITABLE CLOTHING

Exactly what you need to pack for your trip to Uzbekistan will depend on the time of year that you are travelling, the duration of your trip, where you are going, and the types of activities you intend to undertake. On the assumption that you are travelling in high season (page 37) and will be moderately active, perhaps taking a day trek or spending a night in a yurt in addition to city sightseeing, the following items would stand you in good stead. They can all be ordered online or purchased in-store from Mountain Warehouse (*www.mountainwarehouse.com*) who produce affordable, well-made travel and outdoor gear.

- Sturdy walking boots or shoes with a closed toe and a good grip on the sole
- Natural fibre socks that allow your feet to breathe
- Light-weight trekking sandals, again with a good rubber grip
- Crease-free, easy-dry travel trousers or capri pants (not shorts)
- Light, long-sleeved cotton shirts
- Light sweater or jacket for cooler evenings
- Sun hat with a brim that protects your neck as well as your face
- Cotton scarf or wrap
- UV sunglasses to protect your eyes from the intense sunlight

Although most hotels in Uzbekistan do offer a laundry service, there will be occasions when it is faster, easier and cheaper to hand wash a few things in the sink. You can get both dry and liquid travel wash (the former being lighter and less likely to spill), and Eagle Creek's Pack-It series (*www.eaglecreek.com*) is superb for keeping your packing organised and your clean and dirty clothes separate.

damage your enjoyment of your holiday. Make sure you also pack long-sleeved shirts (you'll also need these for visiting conservative areas and religious places).

- **Warm clothing** If you are planning a trip to Uzbekistan in the winter months (which in the north of the country means November to April), or plan to head up into the mountains or spend a night in the desert, you need to treat its cold temperatures with respect, with good warm clothing minimising areas of exposed skin. The locals often wrap themselves in fox or wolf furs, but if you do not want to wear fur clothing, outdoor adventure shops are probably the best source of suitably warm garments. Dress in several layers, with particularly warm (and preferably wind- and waterproof) outer garments.
- **Good footwear** In winter, wear strong, rubber-soled boots, preferably lined with fleece. If you are trekking, good hiking boots are essential.
- **Flip-flops** You'll need these inside homestay accommodation (shoes are left at the front door in Uzbek homes). They also come in useful in less than savoury bathrooms.
- If you will be staying in bottom-range accommodation, a **sheet sleeping bag,** of the kind used by youth hostellers, can help save you from unsavoury bedding. A **universal sink plug** is also worth packing.
- Good **suncream**, a **lip salve, sunglasses** and a spare set of any **prescription glasses.**
- **Toilet paper, wet wipes** and **hand sanitiser gel** are highly advisable and will make staying clean infinitely easier.
- **Dental floss** and a **needle,** a roll of **gaffer tape** and a packet of **cable ties** will enable you to fix almost anything while you're on the go.
- Small **gift items** related to your home country make ideal presents for hosts. Chocolates often melt, but photographs and souvenir items (think snow globes with castles or tea towels featuring cathedrals) go down a treat. Pictures of your home, family and friends are also popular.

MONEY AND BUDGETING

The unit of currency in Uzbekistan is the Uzbek som (UZS). It was first issued in 1993, and the current version in 1994. Notes are printed in denominations of one, three, five, ten, 25, 50, 100, 200, 500, 1,000 and 5,000 som, though you are unlikely to see the smaller denominations due to their virtual worthlessness. Change, in fact, is often given in small sweets or packets of matches.

Inflation (a sensitive subject for the Uzbek government) is such that the largest-value bill, the 5,000 som note, is worth just US$1.70 by the official exchange rate, and significantly less on the black market. In Uzbekistan you'll feel like a billionaire (or a mafia don), but traipsing round with a briefcase or rucksack full of cash soon gets tiresome.

WHAT TO CARRY The standard advice for travellers in the developing world used to be to carry most of their money in travellers' cheques. With the advent of ATMs, that is no longer the case, and in Uzbekistan it is almost impossible to change travellers cheques outside the largest banks in Tashkent. Even there you'll get an unfavourable rate.

You will need to carry most of your money in cash. US dollars are the easiest to exchange and transport, though someone can usually be found to exchange euros, roubles or, at a push, sterling. It is wise to divide your money between multiple locations about your person and carry a dummy wallet with just a few

1 litre petrol (at the pump)	2,500 som
1 litre petrol (black market)	4,500 som
½ litre beer	4,000 som
Postcard	1,000 som
Postcard stamp (international)	1,000 som
Loaf of bread	800 som
Mars bar	1,500 som

dollars and some old supermarket loyalty cards as a decoy for pickpockets and anyone attempting to extract a bribe.

Uzbekistan has very few **ATM**s, and almost none outside of Tashkent, probably due to the logistical challenge of restocking them after every other transaction. Those that do exist are often in the lobbies of larger hotels and dispense either dollars or som. Some banks have a relationship with Visa, others with MasterCard. You'll need to look at the logo on the machine to see if your particular card will work.

If you run out of cash in a smaller town, banks will often advance you cash on a Visa or MasterCard, or you can receive Western Union, MoneyGram and other money transfers. If you are stuck, look for a branch of the National Bank of Uzbekistan as they most often perform this service.

CHANGING MONEY Uzbekistan has two exchange rates: the official, government-controlled rate used by banks and businesses who have to report their currency exchange transactions; and the much better street (or black market) rate used by everyone else.

Banks are now more or less everywhere in Uzbekistan and, providing they have sufficient cash behind the counter, all of them will change dollars, euros and roubles at the official rate. You will need to show your passport and sometimes the customs declaration confirming you brought the currency into the country in the first place. The cashier will stamp the declaration and list the amount of money changed. If you need to change less common currencies (including the Swiss Franc, CHF), you will need to take them to a branch of the National Bank of Uzbekistan.

Most currency exchange in Uzbekistan is done by unofficial money changers. This is generally ignored by the authorities, and the rate is as much as 30% better than you will find in the banks. You are not required to show any paperwork, which comes particularly in handy if you have left your passport with an embassy or at the hotel. In touristy areas the money changers will often find you, but if not you should ask taxi drivers, hotel staff or stalls in the bazaar. Agree the rate before handing over your cash, and have a quick tot up of the bundles of som you receive in return. You're unlikely to have the time or inclination to count every note, but you'll swiftly become adept at calculating how many inches of som there are to US$100.

Uzbekistan's money changers are less fussy than others in the region, but to avoid hassle at an inconvenient moment you should keep your foreign notes clean, unfolded and uncreased. Flattening them inside a book may help. If there are any marks on the notes, including ink stamps from where they have been counted in a bank, they may be rejected. High-denomination bills are preferred, as are US dollars printed since 2006.

BUDGETING Uzbekistan is, on the whole, a cheap country in which to travel. Yes, it is possible in Tashkent to spend upwards of US$500 a night in a hotel, eat in expensive restaurants, and a hire a car and driver to escort you to every last lamp post, but fortunately this is a lifestyle choice only, and in many parts of the country it would be an impossibility in any case as top-end facilities with top-end prices are simply not there.

In Tashkent it is possible to get a dormitory bed for US$10–15, a clean budget double room for US$40 and a mid-range room with breakfast included will set you back between US$60–80. Upwards of US$200 a night is not uncommon for the top-end hotels. The price of meals is similarly varied: café snacks start at around US$1.50, and for a meal in a hotel restaurant with wine you can easily be looking at US$70.

Outside of Tashkent your money will go noticeably further. This is particularly true out of the tourist season when room rates fall significantly. Other than accommodation, transport and meals will be your greatest expenditures. If you are travelling on a budget you will survive on US$25 a day but this will restrict your sleeping options and require you to travel solely by public transport. A budget of US$50 would give you far greater flexibility.

Prices start rising dramatically when you make special arrangements. Car and driver hire is particularly expensive if you only plan to travel in one direction as you may end up paying for the driver's return journey too. Guides, trekking guides and pack animals are reasonably cheap by international standards, but the costs quickly add up if you are trekking for a protracted period or are part of a very small group.

Museum and theatre tickets are an absolute steal in Uzbekistan, so even budget travellers should be able to enjoy plenty of culture and entertainment. You will rarely pay more than US$2 to visit a museum or cultural site, and seats at theatrical performances, including the opera and ballet, typically also start at around US$2.

GETTING AROUND

Uzbekistan is a large country, and though road infrastructure between the main cities is steadily improving, travelling from A to B by road can still take up a significant proportion of your time. This is particularly true if you plan to travel from Tashkent to Khiva, Nukus or other sites in Karakalpakstan. If you are short on time, consider a domestic flight or overnight train journey. However you choose to travel, look out of the window and try to enjoy the views. It's all part of the big adventure.

BY AIR Uzbekistan Airways (*www.uzairways.com*) has domestic flights covering various destinations in Uzbekistan, though not all of the routes are flown on a daily basis. Cities with regular scheduled flights include Andijan, Bukhara, Fergana, Karshi, Namangan, Navoi, Nukus, Samarkand, Termez, Urgench and, of course, Tashkent. Flights are liable to be changed or cancelled at short notice, especially if the weather is poor or if only a small number of reservations have been made.

You should be aware that many of the planes in use in central Asia are old (often from the Soviet period) and have not always been maintained in accordance with international standards. The terrain and unpredictable weather conditions also make for challenging flying conditions. Weigh up the pros and cons of flying, sit next to the emergency exit if you have the choice, and if you are walking across the runway to the plane, do not walk in front of the propellers. Even at a distance of 20m it is possible for things to get sucked into the blades.

BY TRAIN Uzbekistan has a limited and largely out of date railway network, but there are a few routes that are of use to tourists, and the most important of these, the Afrosiab service between Tashkent and Samarkand, has even benefited from a recent investment in modern rolling stock.

Uzbekistan follows the Soviet model of ticket classes and the trains, though typically rather old and painfully slow, tend to run more or less to timetable. Tickets are purchased from the railway station, though local travel agents are usually able to assist if you lack the requisite language skills, time or patience. Caravanistan (*www.caravanistan.com*) can also book tickets on certain routes and deliver them to your hotel. The Uzbekistan Railways website (*www.uzrailpass.uz*) has an up-to-date schedule for the entire network and updates ticket prices on a regular basis.

The most useful train route in Uzbekistan is the high-speed **Afrosiab** service, which links Tashkent and Samarkand and is targeted at tourists, though locals make use of it as well. It is slightly more expensive than the slower trains operating the same route, but makes a day trip to Samarkand possible. Train 161 leaves Tashkent daily at 08.00, and 162 departs Samarkand to make the return journey at 17.00. Full details of this train route are given on page 88.

Also helpful are the train services between Tashkent and Bukhara. The **Sharq** (train 9 or 10) leaves in the mornings and takes 7 hours; the slower, overnight train is 661 or 662 and takes around 9 hours. Full details of both these services are on page 88.

HITCHHIKING IN UZBEKISTAN

With thanks to our hitchhiking guru, Steve Dew-Jones (author of The Rule of Thumb)

It is never possible to recommend hitchhiking without a word of caution, due to the inherent risks involved, but I know from experience that it is both possible and a lot of fun, wherever you are in the world.

Uzbekistan is no exception, although – as with much of central Asia – the Western concept of hitchhiking does not exist in quite the same way, as the bulk of vehicles double up as taxi services. As such, it is important to proceed with caution, both in terms of choosing which driver/vehicle you trust to brave the winding (and in some cases nausea-inducing) mountain roads, and clarifying whether you are willing to pay a small sum for the privilege.

Beyond this, the same rules and advice apply to Uzbekistan as to anywhere else in the world. Top tips include standing in a visible position (but not the middle of the road), making sure there is space for drivers to pull in on either side of where you are standing, and having a few words of the native language under your belt (20 words can get you a surprisingly long way) to ease with negotiations over direction and any monetary contribution you do (or do not) wish to make.

Patience, as ever, is a virtue when hitchhiking, and this is not helped by the noticeably decreased volume of traffic in remote areas. Try to make sure your driver takes you to a helpful spot, although this may be hard to communicate. Where possible, aim for petrol stations or main roads leading out of town (in the direction you wish to travel), and make sure you have a map.

When it comes to longer rail journeys in Uzbekistan, it's questionable as to whether the train is the best way to travel: buses, minibuses and shared taxis tend to be cheaper (or at least no more expensive) and are often faster. Flights are, of course, more expensive, but definitely the fastest and most comfortable option. If you are committed to travelling by train, however, there are regular services from Tashkent to Nukus, Termez, Urgench and various other cities. Details of these are in the cities' respective chapters, and also on the Uzbekistan Railways' website. If you are going to travel long-distance, pay the extra for a berth and be sure to take plenty of food and drink onboard with you as the options available on the train and at stations will be decidedly limited.

BY ROAD Wherever you want to go in Uzbekistan, getting there is half the fun. Hitchhiking and riding around in the back of a truck are still distinct possibilities in remoter areas, but in general things are getting easier: the new multi-lane highway under construction between Bukhara and Khiva should be completed during the lifespan of this edition, greatly decreasing cross-country driving times. It is, however, a big project and progress is slow.

However close your destination, you should allow plenty of time to get there. Taxi and minibus drivers may appear to be in a rush, but they're also the most likely to get flat tyres or to break down entirely. Snowfall and avalanches stop even the most determined of drivers in mountainous areas, and it's not uncommon for vehicles to run out of fuel. The journey may take a while but you will get there eventually, *inshallah* (God willing). Bad roads and cramped buses can be physically very wearing, so make sure you factor in as much time as you can between long trips for recharging your batteries.

One thing to bear in mind when travelling by road is dust. Even on predominantly paved roads there is plenty of sand and grit. Keep a scarf or bandana handy to protect your nose and mouth and keep anything that might get damaged (specifically electronics) inside the vehicle with you, as any bags on the roof will look like they've been through a dust storm.

By bus and minibus Uzbekistan's buses fall into two categories: the relatively modern, usually Chinese-made buses that serve set, inner-city routes and take approximately as many passengers as they have seats, and the *mashrutka*, overcrowded minibuses in varying stages of decay that are driven by devils on

BUS AND MINIBUS ROUTES AT A GLANCE

Prices and durations of bus journeys are given first, followed by those for minibus journeys.

Bukhara–Urgench	US$9/US$10	9hrs/6hrs
Samarkand–Bukhara	US$5/US$5	8hrs/5hrs
Samarkand–Termez	US$8/US$8	10hrs/7hrs
Tashkent–Samarkand	US$5/US$5	7hrs/5½hrs
Tashkent–Bukhara	US$9/US$10	14hrs/10hrs
Tashkent–Urgench		
(for Khiva)	US$18/US$20	25hrs/18hrs
Urgench–Nukus	US$3/US$4	3hrs/2½hrs
Urgench–Khiva	US$0.30/US$0.50	1½hrs/1hr

speed. These minibuses, sadly, are by far the most common, and if you are travelling between smaller cities in Uzbekistan they'll be the most frequent form of transport. You are not guaranteed a seat, and will likely spend much of your journey with someone else's shopping on your lap and their elbow in your face. The majority of minibuses run on gas.

If you are going on a long journey, try to get a minibus that leaves early in the morning. There are two reasons for this. Firstly, it will maximise the hours of daylight driving; your minibus may or may not have all its lights working (the same goes for other vehicles on the road) and the driver will have a better chance of seeing where the bends are. Secondly, it is not uncommon for minibus drivers to have a cheeky drink (or three), so starting out early maximises your chances of a sober drive.

Buses and minibuses operate between all of the major cities and towns in Uzbekistan. As a rule of thumb, you will pay around US$0.50 per hour of bus travel, and US$0.70 per hour of minibus travel. The minibuses drive much faster, so the cost of a ticket tends to be roughly the same. Each city or town has a bus station or stand where the buses, minibuses and shared taxis congregate, and in the case of larger cities, there may be more than one stand, with vehicles to different destinations departing from different places. Be sure to check the name of the correct bus station in the *Getting there and away* section of the relevant chapter.

By taxi Most towns have taxis. Drivers instantly mark up their fares for a foreigner, so be prepared to haggle. There are two types of taxis: professional taxis, which may even have a taxi sign on the roof and can sometimes be summoned by calling a central taxi dispatch office, and general motorists who are happy to pick up passengers and drop them at their destination for a few thousand som. In both cases you will need to agree a fare at the start of your journey and be prepared to stop and ask directions *en route*. Having a map and the name of any landmarks close to your destination will certainly help, as will writing down the address in Uzbek.

For longer drives it is often possible to hire a car and driver. Again you will need to confirm the price in advance, though remember the final price may depend on the distance driven. Ordinary taxi drivers may consent to being hired for several days, otherwise approach a travel agent.

In Uzbekistan, it is common to share a taxi with strangers, especially on the inter-city routes. Shared taxis tend to be found close to the bus stations, have their destination in the window, and will leave when all the seats are full. If you want to leave earlier, you can pay for the remaining seats. Men should aim to get the front seat as you'll have the most leg room and avoid any sharp elbows, but women should sit in the back or risk giving the wrong signal to fellow passengers. Shared taxis are one of the fastest ways to get around, normally completing a journey in half the time that it would take a bus, but fares are correspondingly higher.

Self-drive Having your own vehicle gives you the ultimate freedom to travel where you want, and we would thoroughly recommend it. Officially it is not permitted to bring a right-hand vehicle into Uzbekistan, or to drive it on Uzbek roads, but we have done so on a number of occasions and had no difficulty doing it. There is no fee for bringing in a foreign-registered vehicle temporarily (so stand your ground if you are asked for a bribe) and the third-party motor insurance which you may be offered is optional.

You need to be well prepared and do your research beforehand (the encyclopaedic *Vehicle-dependent Expedition Guide* by Tom Sheppard and *The Adventure Motorcycling Handbook* by Chris Scott stand out) but Uzbekistan has both some spectacular drives and some out-of-the-way destinations it would be a pity to miss out on just because of lack of transport.

A **4×4** is not essential for overlanding in Uzbekistan, but it certainly makes for a more comfortable ride on bad roads. In more remote areas, particularly in the mountains, you can frequently find yourself driving over mud and rock and through riverbeds, particularly in the spring, and will need the extra power to keep yourself from getting stuck. The Land Rover is still the vehicle of choice for most overlanders, but getting parts in Uzbekistan is nigh on impossible: you'll need to bring your own spares, or compromise and get a Toyota Hilux, which local mechanics will be more familiar with. If you do need spares, the best bet is to contact Sanar Motors (*6 Borovsky;* ✆ *(071) 1320353*) in Tashkent.

Whatever your vehicle, you will almost certainly have a big headache getting **fuel** in Uzbekistan. The government has slashed fuel imports in a bid to push local motorists to convert their vehicles to domestically produced local gas, but as you'll see from the mile upon mile of gas-station queues, even this is in short supply.

Tashkent is the first place to receive any diesel or petrol delivery, so fill your tank to the brim before leaving the city. If you have jerry cans, you may or may not be allowed to fill them on the forecourt. If staff will not let you fill them, take your vehicle away from the station, siphon the fuel from the tank into the cans (carefully) and then go back to the fuel station to top up the main tank. A plastic funnel and a length of hosepipe will come in very handy.

Away from Tashkent, fuel stations are numerous, particularly on the edge of towns, but few of them have any fuel. If there is a barrier across the entrance way or a cover over the pump, you're out of luck. If in doubt, look for the queue: if there is a mile-long tailback then they have supplies. Whether or not they will still have fuel by the time you reach the front of that queue is a different matter entirely.

If all the fuel stations in town are empty (not an uncommon occurrence), you will need to look out for the roadside stalls selling what looks like apple juice in old plastic drinks bottles lined up on trestle tables. It's petrol. Entrepreneurial sorts fill up every container to hand when fuel is available, stockpile it in their houses and outbuildings (ignoring the considerable safety implications) and then sell it to motorists at an inflated price when the petrol stations run dry. For price comparison, in the winter of 2015/16 the pump price was around 2,500 som per litre, and the black market price was a minimum of 4,500 som per litre. During the cotton harvest, this rate can double, and there may be no fuel available at all.

When buying fuel like this, you cannot be sure of the quality. It's worth filtering the fuel through a specialised filter or piece of gauze to prevent the crud blocking the fuel lines. Keep your glasses or sunglasses on and point your head away from the fuel as you pour it to avoid it splashing back into your eyes. Even better, let the vendor pour it and just stand back and count the containers as they go in.

Petrol (*benzene*) in Uzbekistan is sold by the litre and is usually available as 91 or 92 octane. The 95 is much harder to come by. The locals can tell the octane of a fuel just by sniffing it and will take a quick sniff to check what they're buying if they're filling up by the side of the road. If you follow suit, don't breathe too deeply as you'll make yourself light-headed. Diesel (80) is significantly cheaper and has the added advantage that you can always siphon some off a truck

- Drive a car that is common in the local area: you won't stand out and if you break down, the parts and expertise to repair it are more likely to be available.
- Check you have a spare tyre, jack, handle and wheel wrench. Spare oil and water, a tow rope, a jerry can of fuel and a shovel are also highly advisable.
- If you have the option, get central locking, electric windows and air conditioning: they give you greater control over what (and, indeed, who) comes into the vehicle with you.
- Make sure you know the rules of the road and have a good idea about where you are going. Tell someone you trust your route and your expected time of arrival.
- Carry your driving licence and any vehicle documentation with you at all times. Photocopies are useful for handing to police and other interested parties.
- Ensure there is a first-aid kit, food and plenty of drinking water in the boot in case of emergencies.
- A mobile phone (or a satellite phone in remote locations) is essential in the event of an accident or a breakdown you can't fix by the side of the road.

(with the driver's permission) if you run low in the middle of nowhere. Along with fuel, carry as much water as possible, both for yourself and to cool your engine in case of overheating.

Other essentials to carry are a comprehensive toolkit and manual for your vehicle, key spare parts and tyres (the locals often carry two) and a first-aid kit. If you plan on doing any off-road driving either in the mountains or in the desert, sand mats or tracks and a tow rope are strongly recommended.

Road surfaces vary greatly. Throughout the book we have attempted to give a guide to the general quality of road surfaces, but local conditions can vary greatly, with a gravel surface suddenly giving way to a kilometre of deeply rutted tracks. Mud and landslips can be a challenge in some areas in spring; rocks, pot-holes and random obstacles can blow a tyre at any time of year.

Last but not least, the **speed limits**. Uzbekistan has two speed limits: in built up areas it is 50km/h and on intercity roads it is 100km/h. There may not be signs to this effect, so use your own judgement and be aware that there are often police speed checks in force.

By bike Uzbekistan is a popular destination for cyclists, and many choose the country as a warm-up exercise before pitting themselves against the challenges of the Pamir Highway in neighbouring Tajikistan. It is not unusual to see Lycra-clad foreigners sweating their way up long and lonely hills, and they inspire both curiosity and confusion in the local population. Cycling is not widespread amongst locals in Uzbekistan, despite the high profile of the Tashkent Terror (see box, page 35).

Uzbekistan's roads are hard on both cyclists and their bikes. Replacement parts are not generally available locally, necessitating a wait in Tashkent while DHL delivers whatever is needed from home.

You wake up in a tent, under a bridge or in a bush and think, 'Where shall I go today?' Mounting your steed, bags loaded behind you and only a map in front, all you have to do is choose. Overland travel by motorbike is quite possibly the most liberating form of travel: there's something about being able to reach out and touch what's around you.

Uzbekistan is, by regional standards, a relatively sedate place to bike, but head into the mountains or desert and it's definitely a more serious undertaking. What appear to be major roads on the map can still have large stretches of broken rock or dirt track. The seasons should also be taken into account as high passes are likely to be snowy (not much fun on four wheels, let alone on two) and riding conditions are often quite literally freezing. That said, the views along these routes are unsurpassed, with a rugged, harsh beauty and that tingling feeling of being on roads a stone's throw from Afghanistan should bring some warmth back to your toes.

If you think you are ready for the challenge, source a suitable bike and fly it (or, even better, ride it) to Uzbekistan. Look for something with long suspension, a front disc brake, a big front wheel and a rack or other way of carrying your kit, as keeping it on your back is far from advisable. Before you leave make sure you check the lights and horn (the louder the better), the front and back brakes (it's a long way down those precipices), the suspension (you're going to need it), and that the chain is in good condition with plenty of oil. Make sure the wheels are round (seriously) and the tyres have a good amount of tread left in them. If the bike looks too old, is making particularly odd noises or rattles on tarmac, find something better. Traffic is rare and mechanics are only to be found in big towns. There are more fulfilling things than finishing an epic journey with your bike in the back of a truck.

Before you leave ask yourself lots of questions. What's my fuel range? Do I know how to repair a puncture? How will I navigate? Do people know where I'm going and what time I'll check in with them? Do I have enough clothes to be warm and dry? Will I need a sleeping bag?

Tashkent to Nukus is only around 1,250km but can easily take a motorcyclist two, or even three, days to travel safely. *En route* you can be struck by anything from dust storms to a herd of camels. If that sort of thing excites you, get to it.

MAPS Uzbekistan has been fairly well mapped, first by the Soviets for military and geological purposes, and more recently thanks to the influx of information-hungry tourists. If you are buying maps before you go, then Stanfords in London or Bristol has the most comprehensive selection, and they also sell maps online at www.stanfords.co.uk.

Our most used country map is the 1:1,500,000 *Uzbekistan* published by the Russian company Roskartografia. It includes the country's road and rail networks, and has larger-scale coverage of the Fergana Valley (1:750,000) and Tashkent (1:22,000). The map comes with a separate index of place names and notes on history, geography and economic development. Its only downside is that place names are written in Cyrillic. Another reasonable option, this time in English, is the slightly newer (2008) 1:1,700,00 *Uzbekistan Tourist Map* produced by the state-run Cartographiya. It's in full colour, illustrated around the edges with a few good photographs, and the reverse side has street plans of Tashkent (1:33,000) and Samarkand (1:14,000). You may also like ITMB's

Essential equipment
Spare key
Puncture repair kit
Engine oil
Covers for baggage rack
Basic tools (spanners, pliers, screwdrivers)
Emergency food and water
Reliable map and compass (1:500,000 or less)

Exceptionally useful equipment

Wire	Spare throttle and clutch cables
Duct tape	Spark plugs
WD40 and grease	Spare bulbs

Clothing

Helmet with visor, goggles or sunglasses (for dust)	Jeans (or similar) with over-trousers
	Sturdy walking boots or biker boots
Thick bike gloves	Thermal layer
Hardwearing jacket	Fleece jacket

The kit listed here is the absolute minimum for a short ride. Anyone wishing to go a long distance should read *The Adventure Motorcycling Handbook* by Chris Scott for practical information on bikes, preparation and maintenance as well as known trips and overland adventure stories. The website www.horizonsunlimited.com is an unparalleled resource for up-to-date overland information, and www.advrider.com gives plenty of inspiration.

Don't drive after dark, and keep it rubber-side down.

Bryn Kewley travelled with us on our first trip across Uzbekistan, caught the overland bug, then started motorcycling all the way from the UK to Singapore.

(International Travel Maps and Books) *Uzbekistan*, which is the most up to date of these three.

City maps of the main tourist sites are easy to come by and are often given away for free at the larger hotels. The locally produced *Tashkent Pocket Guide* has a fold-out map useful for getting your bearings, and also a metro map.

ACCOMMODATION

Uzbekistan has hotels for all budgets, and types of accommodation range from large, Western-style hotels to a converted madrassa, and family-run guesthouses to desert yurt stays.

At the **top-end** of the market (luxury and upmarket), Tashkent has hotels with marble bathrooms, quality restaurants and hot and cold running 'flunkies'. They typically fall into the four-star bracket, though the prices they charge might suggest otherwise. Prices are always advertised in US$ (to protect them against inflation) but government regulation requires them to bill guests in som at the official exchange rate. This has the fortunate upside that if you have changed your money at the unofficial rate, you will effectively get a 30% discount on the cost of your stay.

Mid-range hotels are a mixed bag, with some charging excessive sums for fairly basic facilities. The Soviet-era hotels often fall into this bracket, and are generally to be given a wide berth, but there are also an increasing number of pleasant, affordable choices. The best options are in Bukhara, Khiva and Samarkand, where competition has led to an improvement in quality but kept prices low. The mid-range bracket also includes a small number of boutique or heritage hotels, where historic buildings have been restored and converted into atmospheric places to stay. In addition to an attractive exterior, you can expect your room and public spaces to have ornately plastered or hand-painted ceilings, antique or hand-crafted furniture, and colourful, locally produced textiles.

Uzbekistan has plenty of **budget** rooms. Family-run guesthouses are frequently the best option (and ideal for meeting other travellers), and many of them offer beds in shared dorms as well as simple doubles. The room rate typically includes breakfast, and hosts may be able to arrange evening meals as well. Uzbekistan has a small number of homestays, all of which fall into the budget bracket, though in the accommodation listings we have typically not differentiated between these and guesthouses, as in the latter the family still tends to live on-site and frequently will share meals with visitors. The purest

PRICE CODES

ACCOMMODATION The price codes used in this guide indicate the approximate price of a standard double room, per night. The price codes below exclude the cost of any booking fee. They are given in dollars only because hotels and guesthouses typically quote their prices in dollars; if you are paying in som (compulsory in some larger hotels), the price will be calculated using either the official or unofficial exchange rate, with a resulting difference in price of around 30%.

Luxury	$$$$$	US$200+
Upmarket	$$$$	US$100–200
Mid-range	$$$	US$50–100
Budget	$$	US$20–50
Shoestring	$	up to US$20

RESTAURANTS The price codes used in this guide indicate the average price of a meat-based main dish, excluding vegetables and service charge. The price of a full meal is likely to be several times higher. Restaurants typically quote their prices in som and, other than in the large hotels, will not accept other currencies for payment. The prices, therefore, are given below in som only.

Expensive	$$$$$	25,000+ som
Above average	$$$$	12,500–25,000 som
Mid-range	$$$	8,000–12,500 som
Cheap & cheerful	$$	4,000–8,000 som
Rock bottom	$	up to 4,000 som

homestays are the yurt stays around Aidarkul where you will stay with a family in their traditional tent and see how they really live: tourists bring additional (and much-needed) income but host families do not lay on facilities over and above what the family already requires.

Shoestring options typically provide accommodation in dormitories; you may have a basic single bed or, more likely, a mattress and blankets on the floor. The bathrooms, as you might expect at this end of the market, are a little bit hit and miss, so prepare yourself for the occasional squat toilet and cold water in a jug.

Campsites are relatively uncommon in Uzbekistan and those informal sites that do exist are frequented almost entirely by foreigners. While it is permitted to camp in the national parks and in the deserts (for example at the camel camps), setting up a tent in other public places is generally frowned upon. If you wish to put up a tent on private land, you will need to ask the owner and will usually be expected to pay a few dollars for the privilege.

Note that many hotels in Uzbekistan, especially older, Soviet-built accommodation, offer a wide variety of room permutations and rates, so the rates given can only serve as a rough guide. The number of rooms has been listed where possible, though there are some instances where an establishment either could not or would not confirm the number of rooms on offer.

EATING AND DRINKING

Bread, noodles and mutton all feature heavily in Uzbek cuisine, and vegetarians are in for a tough time: the concept is little understood, and even less frequently catered for.

Uzbekistan's national dish is *plov* (also known as *osh*), an oily rice-based dish with pieces of meat, grated carrots, onions and, if you are particularly fortunate, roasted garlic and hard-boiled egg. It is typically only available at lunchtime, and is popular at weddings and other large celebrations when huge quantities are cooked in a single dish. Plov invariably is accompanied by *obi non* (flat bread) and is washed down with green tea, the astringency of which helps to cut through the mutton fat.

Other notable national dishes include *shurpa*, a soup with fatty mutton and vegetables; *norin* and *lagman*, two mutton-broth soups with noodles that may also be topped with a piece of horse meat, and the ubiquitous *shashlik*, grilled kebabs with cubes of mutton or beef and fat, which is considered to add to the flavour. For a quick snack, consider either *manti* (also called *qasqoni*), a steamed dumpling containing minced mutton, or *somsa*, a fried or baked pastry parcel that contains either mutton or, occasionally, mashed potato.

Every meal is accompanied by the flat, round loaves of bread known as *non*. The most common form, *obi non*, is cooked in a clay tandoor oven. The bread's rim rises, the centre is decorated with a pattern or dots imprinted in the dough. Non is generally torn into chunks rather than sliced, and you should show respect by not placing it upside down on the table.

If you are in Uzbekistan in late summer and early autumn, the country is bursting with fresh fruits. Roadsides stalls sell **watermelons** the size of beach balls; the sweet, juicy **pomegranates** are a glorious shade of pink; and you can also enjoy **grapes**, **apricots**, **apples**, **figs** and **peaches**.

An Uzbek's veins run with tea as much as blood, and the *chaikhana* (tea house) is central to any community: people go to do business as much as to gossip and relax. **Green tea** (*zilloniy chai*) is most common in the provinces, but **black tea** (*chorniy chai*) is preferred in Tashkent. Both are available wherever you go, but expect a

2

funny look if you want your tea with milk. Tea with sugar is fine. In summer you may also be offered *ayran*, a chilled yoghurt drink.

Alcohol is consumed in Uzbekistan, though less so than in the other central Asian republics, and both **beer** and **spirits** are widely available in shops and larger restaurants. The Russian beer Baltica is affordable and very drinkable: it's quite gassy and comes in large bottles so is ideal for sharing between two. Uzbekistan has a number of vineyards, some quite well established, and if you're offered the

HOW TO MAKE PLOV

It sometimes seems that Uzbekistan runs on plov, the heavy, calorie-laden dish that is the nation's undisputed favourite.

Serves 8

INGREDIENTS
1kg of lamb shoulder separated from the bone and cubed
1kg paella rice
250ml sunflower oil
1kg peeled carrots cut into 1cm lengths
3 whole garlic bulbs
3 medium-sized onions sliced thinly
1 tbsp cumin
pinch of salt
2 chillies (optional)

You will also need a 5-litre cooking pot.

METHOD
1. Wash and soak the rice in cold tap water.
2. Heat the oil in the cooking pot over a high flame and deep fry the meat until it is golden brown. Take the meat out and put to one side.
3. Fry the onions until they are golden and then add the meat again, as well as the carrots. Heat for 20 minutes (stirring frequently) or until the carrots are soft and slightly caramelised. Add the cumin.
4 Reduce heat and add water to cover the carrots and meat. Leave it to gently simmer for one hour or until most of the water has evaporated.
5. Place the whole bulbs of garlic on the top of the meat and carrots.
6. Add the rice that has been soaking on top of the meat and carrot layer in the cooking pot, and then cover contents with 2cm depth of boiling water. Boil it gently until the rice has completely absorbed the water. Be careful it doesn't burn on the bottom.
7. Reduce the heat and cover the pot with a lid. Allow the plov to steam for 20 minutes. If you think it might be catching, remove it from the heat entirely.
8. Remove the garlic bulbs and chillies and put them to one side. Gently mix the contents of the cooking pot and serve on a large serving plate, the garlic bulbs decorating it.

Enjoy with a tomato and onion salad, flat bread and a pot of freshly brewed black tea.

opportunity to try a glass or two, you should take it. The best Uzbek **wines** are produced around Samarkand from local varieties of grapes.

EATING OUT Uzbekistan does not have a long tradition of eating in restaurants: finding a restaurant was nigh on impossible during the Soviet period due to food shortages and the fact that people were encouraged to eat collectively in the work canteen. This is slowly changing in urban centres, particularly those with a significant tourist footfall, though you will not find the density nor quality of restaurants typical in some other parts of Asia.

The restaurants that do exist (particularly outside of Tashkent) tend to cater primarily to wedding parties, and this is where they make their money. If the restaurant is not fully booked for a celebration, you won't need a reservation, nor to wait for a table. Expect a fairly limited menu of Russian and Uzbek dishes and beware that it's unlikely that everything listed will be available. If you have any doubt about what to order, look around at what the other diners are eating and physically point a dish out to the waitress. Service may be chaotic, but it is generally good-natured. You'll be expected to leave a tip: 10% is standard. If you're lucky you may be invited to join a bride and groom at their dinner table and will spend the next few hours drinking the requisite toasts!

More common than restaurants and cafés are street-side food stalls: from American fast-food stands with burgers and fries, to smoking grills and the vinegary smell of shashlik and onions wafting down the road, making your stomach rumble. Women with trays piled high with savoury pastries saunter through markets and the lobbies of office buildings; trestle tables nearly buckle beneath the weight of freshly baked bread.

NIGHTLIFE

Nightclubs, in their western sense, are illegal in Uzbekistan, but entrepreneurs get around this by opening bars and hosting DJs or live music. There are, however, very few such establishments, and they are in Tashkent and the larger cities. They tend to be frequented predominantly by businessmen (both locals and foreign nationals); it's unusual to see unaccompanied women in bars unless they're working. Single women should therefore not go to a bar alone unless they want to be hassled.

Champagne and expensive vodka brands such as Beluga are the status drinks of choice, and cocktails are increasingly popular. Drinking to excess is common, as is drink driving home. Face control is often in place, so dress up smartly and don't wear trainers or jeans.

For the latest list of what's on in Tashkent, check out www.tashkent-events. info/newsletters/events.html. Mainly aimed at expats, it is nevertheless useful for tourists, too, as the newsletter is produced monthly and includes details on concerts, exhibitions, theatrical performances and sporting events. There is also a section on parties and happy hours.

PUBLIC HOLIDAYS AND FESTIVALS

1–2 January	Yangi Yil Bayrami	New Year
14 January	Vatan himoyachilari kuni	Day of Defenders of the Motherland
8 March	Xalqaro Xotin-Qizlar Kuni	International Women's Day

2

21 March	Navro'z Bayrami	Navruz (Persian New Year)
9 May	Xotira va Qadirlash Kuni	Remembrance Day
1 September	Mustaqillik Kuni	Independence Day
1 October	O'qituvchi va Murabbiylar Kuni	Teachers' Day
8 December	Konstitutsiya Kuni	Constitution Day

The Islamic festivals of Eid ul-Fitr and Eid al-Adha are also celebrated, but as they are based on the lunar calendar their dates change from one year to the next. For the lifespan of this edition, the likely dates are as follows: 6 July/11 September 2016; 26 June/3 September 2017; 15 June/22 August 2018.

SHOPPING

Shopping in Uzbekistan encompasses a complete range of experiences, from rummaging in workshops and warehouses akin to Aladdin's caves of carpets, silks and antique jewellery, to standing befuddled in a neon-lit supermarket attempting to work out quite which of the 101 different dairy products labelled in Russian might actually be milk. These experiences can be exhilarating and they can be infuriating, and sometimes both at once.

Souvenirs in Uzbekistan fall loosely into two categories: the mass-produced items (often manufactured in China) that the Uzbeks think foreign tourists want to buy and that are on sale outside every museum, mosque and madrassa; and the handmade, vintage or otherwise more individual pieces that you'll actually treasure once you get them home. Finding the latter can be slightly harder, but they're often competitively priced, particularly if they've originally been produced for the domestic market.

Uzbekistan has always been known for its **textiles,** and though during the Soviet period mass production rather than quality was the focus, in recent years smaller, independent workshops have once again sprung up. Many of them produce carpets, silks and embroideries in traditional styles and using long-established techniques, and buying directly from them supports the artisans and their families.

There are also some beautiful **ceramics** thrown, painted and fired in Uzbekistan. Gijduvan is particularly famous for its painted plates, as you can see from the numerous ornate façades, though the manufacture of tiles and other ceramics was once a major industry nationwide. We're particularly pleased with our giant teapot and handle-less tea bowls (drinking from them is an art, but one that you quickly get used to), and the small tiles, often painted with replica designs from the Registan and other major tourist sites, work well as coasters, heatproof mats or, as their predecessors were intended, simply to decorate your wall.

If you visit Uzbekistan on a package tour, or have the budget to eat predominantly in restaurants, **food shopping** in the country will be of little concern. You might decide to pick up the odd half kilo of pistachios or pomegranates in the bazaar (highly recommended when the latter are in season), but this is a charming novelty rather than the hard-fought prelude to every budget meal.

If your budget requires regular picnics or cooking for yourself, however, life becomes rather harder. The bazaars are a reliable source of bread and fresh produce, but there's often little on sale beyond this, even in the small convenience stores that brand themselves, misleadingly, as supermarkets. The market for pre-prepared and processed foods is still in its relative infancy in Uzbekistan; as you

UZBEK CARPETS

Every house in Uzbekistan is decorated with carpets. Though these days they will often be factory-made synthetic rugs from China, traditionally they would have been handwoven locally. Each community would have produced carpets in a distinctive style, and they were valued as much for their artistic qualities as for their functional properties. The largest single collection of carpets is thought to have belonged to the Emir of Bukhara: he had over 10,000 examples in his palace.

There are three main types of carpet produced in Uzbekistan: felt mats, flat-woven carpets and pile or tufted carpets. The first of these is the most ancient form, and would have first been produced by nomadic herders with surplus wool from their sheep. When wool is kneaded with soap and water, it becomes a thick, heavy felt that is not only warm but, as local legend has it, cannot be walked upon by a spider, nor crawled upon by a snake. It is either left in its natural colour (usually a cream or grey), or dyed with natural pigments such as indigo (for blue), moraine (red) and pomegranate bark (yellow). In desert areas, women also made similar rugs with camel hair.

It's not known exactly how long carpets have been woven in Uzbekistan, but archaeologists have found spindles in Stone Age sites that are similar to the wooden spindles still used in some rural areas of the country today. On the spindles you can spin a thick, coarse yarn that is required for *julhirs*, the loosely woven carpets still produced around Dzhizak and Nurata. Such carpets are often woven with a pattern of longitudinal stripes, edged with a chain of rhombuses and triangles. Modern flat-weave carpets can be woven from either woollen or cotton threads. The smooth surface is created by interlocking the warp (vertical) and weft (horizontal) threads. They are produced on a simple loom made from narrow, wooden beams. The width of the carpet strip is dictated by the width of the loom, but typically does not exceed 50cm. To make a wider carpet, therefore, several strips must be stitched together. The flat-weave carpets produced in Bukhara are considered to be the finest in the country; those from Surkhan Darya are unique in that the base threads are in two colours.

The most valuable carpets, however, are the tufted carpets. The finest fleece is used to produce their thread, and a thread count of 100 or more knots per centimetre is not uncommon. This makes the production process exceptionally time-intensive, and it requires an exceptionally high level of attention to detail; a single knot of the wrong colour in the wrong place will ruin months of work.

Though men do sometimes produce knotted carpets, it is generally considered a job for women as it helps to have small, deft hands. Women pass carpet-making techniques from mother to daughter, and it is still commonplace to see young girls working away at a loom. The warp threads are stretched on the loom, and onto these the weaver knots individual threads, hitting each one down with a metal hook so that it sits tightly alongside the previous knot.

Historically a small number of carpets were woven with golden thread and silk. Produced in Bukhara, Samarkand and Khiva for their respective courts, they became famous well beyond Uzbekistan and were prized as diplomatic gifts. Without imperial patronage, such carpets are increasingly rare.

survey aisle after aisle of tinned fish and jars of pickled vegetables, the merest thought of a deli counter or ready meal may well cause feelings of longing.

ARTS AND ENTERTAINMENT

Uzbekistan does not have a long tradition of going out in the evening: entertainment typically came to you. At weddings and other festivities, such as Navruz (the Persian New Year, celebrated in Uzbekistan on 21 March), families and friends would come together at home, and poets, musicians and singers would come to the house to perform. If the entertainment was particularly good, the guests would be inspired to dance and sing themselves.

This slowly began to change during the Soviet period, when theatres and concert halls were built across Uzbekistan, and a professional class of entertainer emerged, some of them performing traditional Uzbek works, but the majority spreading high culture from Russia such as academic works of drama, ballet and opera. Tickets were cheap (and remain so) in order to democratise access to the arts, and new works were commissioned that praised the worker and explored his/her life and experience, rather than focusing on kings, queens and fairy tales that had been popular before. Every town, however small, had its own performance space, and the populace was actively encouraged to attend.

Today Uzbekistan's **theatres** are a mixed bag. Often housed in striking, Neoclassical buildings, they have suffered since independence due to funding cuts and the cessation of movement of companies, directors and artists from other parts of the Soviet Union. Whereas once an Uzbek ballerina could have hoped to travel to Moscow or St Petersburg to train, and would have enjoyed an illustrious and peripatetic career, now such opportunities are few and far between. That said, there are companies that are thriving: the Ilkhom Theatre in Tashkent (see box, page 31) continues to put on challenging, world-class productions, including many new plays, and a night at the ballet at Tashkent's Alisher Navoi Opera is a highlight of any trip to Uzbekistan, particularly if you dress up and enjoy the sweet half-time Georgian champagne.

Uzbekistan's larger cities all have **cinemas** showing the latest Russian and Hollywood blockbusters. The latter are almost always dubbed or subtitled in Russian, though you can usually follow the plot of action films and thrillers. Art-house films are a little more challenging, even if you understand the language. Cinema tickets tend to be slightly more expensive than theatre tickets, though still rarely more than a few dollars a head.

In recent years Uzbekistan has started to host several annual **festivals** designed to showcase the country's artistic heritage to the world. The Silk and Spice Festival takes place for a week each year in Bukhara (page 213), and singers and storytellers perform at Chimgan's Echo Festival of Bards. In Samarkand, the Sharq Taronalari International Museum Festival (*www.en.sharqtaronalari.uz*) happens in the main Registan Square, and is very impressive indeed.

PHOTOGRAPHY   *With thanks to John E Fry (www.fryfilm.com)*

Uzbekistan is a photographer's dream, with everything from picturesque landscapes and medieval architecture, to flora and fauna and folk dancers in indigenous dress. Taking pictures in Uzbekistan throws up quite a number of important considerations when it comes to choosing the right gear and looking after it while you embark on your Silk Road adventure. I hope my tips below help you capture your experience fully, the way you want to, and come home with some great photographs!

ETIQUETTE As in any country, it is always polite to ask before taking someone's photo, and Uzbekistan is no exception. If you are using a long lens this may not be necessary because they may not notice you taking the picture from a distance. But if you can, it's still wise to ask permission first, then take a few shots quickly to be sure of capturing a good expression, and giving yourself options later. Do not worry excessively about photographing children in Uzbekistan, as they are usually happy to pose and there is absolutely no risk to them or you in you doing so.

Again, as in most countries of the world, pointing any sort of camera in the direction of anything military, border crossings or governmental buildings is to be avoided. It is not worth having your camera kit seized just for the sake of an otherwise useless picture of a typical border post or concrete bridge across the Amu Darya.

ADVERSE CONDITIONS The most common problem in hot countries is humidity. Humidity and temperature changes can cause condensation on and inside your lenses and camera almost instantly when going into the heat from an air-conditioned room or vehicle. If you can, try to slow down transitions between hot and cold areas, and wrap up your gear to insulate it against temperature and moisture. In most cases, if your lens or viewfinder has become misty with **condensation,** all you need to do is leave it to acclimatise for a few minutes, then give them a wipe with a lens cloth. Should the worst happen and condensation get inside your lens, one thing to try is leaving it in front of a hairdryer for 10 minutes or so, allowing the warm flow of air to push the moisture out.

Another particular problem for cameras, lenses and other equipment in Uzbekistan is **dust, sand** and other **dirt**. Keeping a close eye on your lens caps, changing lenses as little as possible and keeping all your gear in a bag or camera case when not in use will all help to minimise the ingress of potentially damaging grains. Sand and grit is of course pretty abrasive, and can easily scratch your lenses and LCD screens. Always carry a small air blower, lens pen and cotton buds to clean your kit whenever you can, for if particles are left they can work their way into lens gears, between elements and into connectors while moving around in the bag.

If you are heading up the mountains, either walking or skiing, taking pictures in the **snow** can confuse cameras occasionally. Due to the way automatic exposure systems measure the amount of light they are faced with, they see light colours such as snow incorrectly, as if the scene itself has more light in it, and consequently underexposes the image.

RECOMMENDED EQUIPMENT

Compact cameras The advantage of small compact cameras such as Canon's popular Ixus range or Nikon's Coolpix, is that they are very small, easy to use, produce stunningly good results in most conditions, and are easy on the budget. The disadvantages are mainly when it comes to controlling the picture, as many functions are automatic only. This can lead to under- or overexposure and even out-of-focus pictures in difficult or unusual conditions, such as high-contrast situations in strong desert sunlight. Read reviews in photography magazines or online, but remember the best camera for you is the one you can happily use most easily!

SLR cameras The big advantages of SLRs are an optical viewfinder and mirror, showing you exactly the view that will be captured through the lens, a larger and more sensitive image sensor, a very wide variety of lenses, and fully manual controls. Certain types now offer additional clever features, but to be honest a lot of these are fairly gimmicky and will end up being used very little or not at all.

To make best use of these cameras you will need at least a few good lenses, so your camera bag may end up feeling rather heavy. Ideally you want to change lenses as little as possible to avoid particles of dust and dirt getting into the body of the camera and ending up on the sensor.

Lenses Should you be fortunate enough to own an SLR system, there are ways to minimise what you take with you and the amount of lens changing you need to do. For example, some of the new compact high-zoom lenses can replace an entire bag full of f2.8 ones. For smaller chip SLRs (DX) there are a few very good 18–200mm lenses. For full-frame (35mm sized) sensors, my favourite is the Nikon 28–300mm AFS VR, which replaces my 28–70mm f2.8 AFS, my 80–200mm f2.8 AFS, and a 300mm, so that's at least three large, expensive lenses field of views covered by just one!

The trade-off is the maximum aperture and arguably build quality, but if you have a full-frame sensor the difference in depth of field is minimal, and as there is a lot of light around in the subcontinent it is unlikely you will miss the couple of stops of extra light an f2.8 or faster lens would give you.

If you are into wildlife or particularly enjoy 'sniping' candid shots from a distance, a longer zoom such as Nikon's 80–400mm VR is an excellent choice, although you can't add a teleconverter. There is a Canon 100–400mm but it's bigger and heavier than the Nikon.

I would probably still take a 50mm f1.8 as well because it's very small and inexpensive, and can offer you that tiny depth of field if desired, plus a few extra stops of light if you need them. It's always a good idea to have at least one spare lens anyway and you can get away with a 50mm for most things if you have to.

An ultrawide would also be a useful addition, but not essential. An 18mm on DX, or 28mm on full frame is wide enough for most things, but if you like wide angles and if you have the space in your bag, an ultrawide would be your third lens; something like a 14mm prime for FX, or a nice compact and surprisingly excellent Tokina 11–16mm for DX, or maybe a 16–35mm or 18–35mm depending on your budget. The trick is not to overuse wide-angle lenses; you should always be trying to mix close-ups, mid-shots and wides to tell a full and interesting story of where you have been.

Remember not to get too caught up with shallow depth of field and maximum apertures. Firstly because in such a beautiful place as Uzbekistan you want to see most things in focus anyway, and secondly because all lenses produce their optimum results in the middle of their aperture range, at least a couple of stops from either end. On an f2.8–22 lens, for example, it's sharpest images will be captured from about f4 to f11.

Flash Using flash creatively and artistically can be a real art. Luckily in Uzbekistan there is a lot of ambient sunlight around so you shouldn't need much flash (which will drain your batteries), but if you do, here are a few tips.

Generally, turn the automatic flash off unless it's really dark or you need to see a specific detail, such as a carving or painting, but be aware of the reflection of the flash back off the subject – you may need to take the picture from a different angle.

Try to avoid direct flash if you can; it is very unflattering to faces particularly, and results in harsh exposure drop-off leaving backgrounds very dark, sometimes to the point of invisible.

Batteries Low temperatures will also drain your batteries more quickly than usual, so make sure you have at least one spare.

LITTLE THINGS One thing to keep in mind: take pictures of the little things. It's often the small details that get missed in the wide expansive views and colourful scenes in Uzbekistan, but the things that jog your memory most effectively are often the little things, such a bright piece of clothing, an unusual door handle or an especially beautiful carving. Don't forget to capture some of these details, as well as the big, more typical holiday pictures.

DON'T GET TOO CAUGHT UP IN THE PHOTOGRAPHY! Enjoy yourself taking pictures, but do remember to put the camera down and enjoy the experience too. You are going to an amazing place, full of beautiful sights to photograph, but also tastes, smells, sounds, people to meet, new experiences and unusual places to explore. It is easy to want to record everything so you don't forget it, but sometimes putting the camera away and concentrating more on where you are and all the things the camera cannot capture, commits those things to memory even more effectively than taking a photograph. Have a fantastic time and bring back some great photos!

MEDIA AND COMMUNICATIONS

A government decree officially ended state censorship of the media in 2002. In reality, however, all forms of media in the country remain strictly controlled,

2

and this includes access to foreign news sites. Criticism has been made of the Uzbek government for imprisoning opposition journalists and for banning a number of foreign news agencies, including the BBC, from operating in the country. Foreigners wishing to report from the country require a press visa; the application process is rigorous and visas are regularly refused without a specific reason being given.

NEWS The readership of newspapers in Uzbekistan is low, with figures estimated to be not more than 50,000 people countrywide. The state controls newspaper distribution and materials supply, and hence the market is dominated by the three state-owned papers *Halq Sozi*, *Narodnoye Slovo* and *Pravda Vostoka*. Popular privately owned papers include *Novosti Uzbekistan* and *Noviy Vek*, though even they cannot be considered independent.

Uzbekistan's national news agency, the imaginatively named Uzbekistan News Agency, is state-controlled. Reuters and the Associated Press (AP) both have offices in the country, though they are only able to work within strictly enforced confines. The BBC was told to leave Uzbekistan following its coverage of the Andijan Massacre (see box, page 132) in 2005.

The four state-owned television channels dominate the television market, though there are a large number of small, private channels in existence. The State Press Committee and the Inter-Agency Coordination Committee issue broadcast licences to such channels, and withdraw licences swiftly from those organisations pursuing too independent a line. Live broadcasts are prohibited.

The most balanced news sources for Uzbekistan are to be found online. The Russian-language Uz News (*www.uznews.net*) has recently been shut down, but you can still read the latest stories from the Bishkek-based Times of Central Asia (*www.timesca.com*) and respected Eurasianet (*www.eurasianet.org*).

PHONE The country code for Uzbekistan is +998. To call abroad from inside Uzbekistan, dial 810 and then the country code. To make long-distance domestic calls, dial 8, wait for the tone, then dial 3, followed by the city or area code.

Area codes in this guide are typically listed at the start of each city section. They are between two and four digits long. Tashkent, for example, is 71. When a business has an alternative area or dialing codes, it is given in brackets at the start of the phone number. Mobiles numbers begin with 09 (drop the 0 when calling from abroad) and do not need to be prefixed with an area code.

Like so many other developing countries, Uzbekistan has jumped from having almost no communications infrastructure to having around 60% of the population connected by mobile phone. With fewer than two million landlines, and most of those used by businesses, they're simply not a consideration for individuals wanting to keep in touch.

Uzbekistan's most popular mobile service providers are UCell, Beeline and UzMobile. Regulations have changed to enable foreigners to buy SIM cards, though this fact has been slow to filter down to some of the smaller vendors. To get a SIM card you will need to take your passport and a current registration slip confirming your hotel or other address to one of the providers' offices or branded stores. Filling out the various forms and processing them takes about 15 minutes. Depending on the network you'll either pay around US$3, or the SIM will be free when you top-up by a certain amount.

Topping up your phone is easy. You can do it in store, anywhere showing your network's logo and at any Paynet machine. The machines (which are frequently in convenience stores or other places with high foot traffic) allow you to type in your phone number, feed in bank notes and *voila!* You've topped up.

Though the coverage of phone networks is improving, it is still by no means universal and large sections of the country (particularly remote and mountainous areas) are black holes for reception. If you are travelling to such areas and may need to keep in contact, you may want to rent, buy or borrow a satellite phone.

INTERNET Uzbeks have taken to the internet like ducks to water, and as of 2015 the country had more than 12 million regular internet users. The remaining population would probably like to get online but is held back by lack of electricity and communications infrastructure. Wi-Fi and internet cafés are increasingly common in the larger cities. Local SIM cards now include data packages, and it is also possible to buy an internet dongle for your laptop, enabling you to get online wherever there is 3G.

When you're surfing the web, you may find sites you normally looked at are blocked. VPN access is required for most foreign media sites, and even the BBC Uzbek service is only accessibly via VPN or a proxy server. The internet is tightly controlled by the Uzbek authorities and there are regular outages of Skype, Viber and YouTube.

POST Uzbekistan does have a domestic postal service with a central post office in most large towns, but you are likely to arrive home before your postcards, if indeed they arrive at all. Letters and parcels are generally transported internally by hand (you may be asked to carry a gift to your next destination for so and so's relative) and couriers and diplomatic bags are the preferred method to send and receive anything overseas. DHL and FedEx both have agents in Tashkent (pages 101–2), as do a number of smaller courier firms.

BUSINESS

Uzbekistan is a tough place to do business, for both locals and foreign investors. The country ranks 87th out of 185 countries for ease of doing business in 2016 (*www.doingbusiness.org/rankings*), a significant improvement from 2013 when the country was in 154th position, with the biggest causes for concern being cross-border trade, taxes, access to electricity and dealing with permits. That said, the government is seeking foreign investment and has recently taken steps

SATELLITE PHONES

A reliable communication link is always a concern while travelling in Uzbekistan, especially if you are likely to be travelling or trekking in the mountains and beyond the coverage of the mobile phone networks.

The portable Thuraya satellite phone (*www.thuraya.com*) is becoming cheaper and is the ideal option. The new version of the phone is as small as a normal GSM handset and you can even get a pay-as-you-go account; however, its battery life is not as long as the older versions – an important consideration in an environment with unreliable power supplies. A new feature is a facility where a credit card is linked to the account and when a secret code is SMS messaged to Thuraya, your account is topped up by a predetermined amount.

to simplify business procedures. Credit is much more readily available than it was a few years ago.

Any legal entity, be it an individual or an organisation, may invest in Uzbekistan. Foreigners can both establish companies and buy shares in existing companies. A company will be considered a foreign investment if its fund capital exceeds US$150,000 and 30% of the share value is held by foreign entities. Investments can be made into all economic sectors. Investment into some preferred sectors is tax exempt (see below).

Under Uzbek law foreign investors have the right to make contracts, acquire, own and dispose of their investments at will, freely dispose of revenue and attract credit or loans; inventions and designs can be patented abroad as well as in Uzbekistan. They are entitled to receive compensation in case of the requisition of assets and also to receive indemnification for damages caused as a result of the illegal actions (or inaction) and decisions taken by state bodies. Foreign investments and other assets of foreign investors in Uzbekistan are protected by law from nationalisation. Enforcing such regulation may, however, be difficult.

Any individual who resides in Uzbekistan for 183 days or more during a financial year is considered as a tax resident of the Republic of Uzbekistan. Legal entities (specifically companies) are considered tax resident if they are registered in Uzbekistan or registered abroad but have their headquarters in Uzbekistan. Non-residents and foreign legal entities doing business in Uzbekistan are only taxed on their income from activities performed in Uzbekistan. Reciprocal tax arrangements are in place with some foreign governments.

Tax exemptions of up to seven years are available for companies investing in the manufacturing of electronic components, light industry, silk production, construction materials, food production (in particular poultry, meat and dairy products), chemicals and pharmaceuticals. To qualify for these tax breaks enterprises must be located in regions with a labour surplus, have at least 50% foreign ownership, and the investments must be made in hard cash and/or modern equipment. It is expected that the tax savings will be reinvested into the business to ensure long-term growth. Foreigners are able to participate in the privatisation of state assets and industries. Depending on the investment proposal, it's sometimes possible to acquire unplaced state assets at zero cost.

Investment in Uzbekistan is promoted through the 'UzInfoInvest' Informational Support and Foreign Investments Promotion Agency. The agency is responsible for providing potential and existing foreign investors with information on prospective projects and investment legislation, including on guarantees and incentives. Their website, which includes additional information on the investment climate, investment legislation and the activity of the agency, is www.investuzbekistan.uz.

Doing business in Uzbekistan is strongly dependent on personal relationships. You will be expected to spend significant time getting to know potential business partners or clients and how they work, and this may include socialising and spending time with their family as well as more formal business meetings. If you are pitching for a contract, your bid will be considered not solely in terms of cost or quality; how the client feels about you and your colleagues will often be a contributing factor too.

The overlap between personal relationships and business often wrong-foots foreign business people working in Uzbekistan, and indeed across central Asia. Whereas Westerners may consider getting drunk on vodka and even sharing a naked *banya* (sauna) session with prospective business partners to be unprofessional, in Uzbekistan it is completely normal and you may be commercially disadvantaged if you are unwilling to participate since such activities are considered part of the process of building up trust. That said, there are Uzbeks who do not drink heavily on health or religious grounds, and if you decline offers politely and with a good reason, your hosts are unlikely to push you. Consider offering an alternative leisure activity that you can do together and that you are more comfortable with.

Problems also occur from mis-matched expectations; though Uzbekistan is now nominally capitalist, central planning and state ownership still dominate many people's thinking, and intricacies of concepts that Western companies take for granted, such as investment and shares, may have to be carefully explained. Understanding of what does and does not constitute corruption are often wildly different, as is the extent to which fast-tracking, the payment of fees, good-will gestures and even all-out extortion are acceptable. You will need to maintain good lines of communication, explain everything clearly (even if you think it is obvious) and ask plenty of questions.

OPENING TIMES

Companies in Uzbekistan do not typically keep to set opening times: restaurants, shops and other businesses will open in the morning when they are ready, will frequently close early if things are quiet, or they may not open at all. As a general guide, however, the working week runs from Monday to Friday; although it is the Muslim holy day, businesses still work on Friday as they did during the Soviet period. Shops will typically be open on Saturday as well, though offices will be closed. Museums tend to be open six days a week, taking their day off either on Sunday or Monday; check individual entries for which day they are closed.

Banks, shops and museums tend to keep standard office hours: they open around 09.00 and close at 17.00, often with an hour's lunch break between 13.00 and 14.00. Unless they are serving breakfast, cafés and restaurants open late morning and keep serving until the last customer has left; in larger places this may not be until 23.00, though shashlik stands and other local cafés will usually be finished around 19.00.

BUYING PROPERTY

Uzbekistan's 1998 Land Code and Law on Land is ambiguous about the legality of both private ownership and foreign ownership, leaving the door open for the government to potentially seize assets in the future. In practice, foreigners do buy property in Uzbekistan and are permitted to do so providing they have residency in the country. The government is attempting to make it easier for foreigners to invest, though you will still need a reputable local lawyer to help you navigate the extensive red tape. The process is relatively straightforward, but often frustratingly slow.

Before signing a purchase agreement you need to check the land registry (ideally several times) to ensure that the property being bought is legally owned by the seller. You pay a deposit to secure the property, then the purchase agreement and all supporting documents are sent to the local registry for the title to be signed over to the buyer. You then settle the balance of the purchase price, along with applicable taxes and notary costs.

There are no restrictions on foreigners leasing property in Uzbekistan. Rents are typically inflated by three to five times for expats, though you can always bargain with the owner for a fairer deal.

Residents of Uzbekistan are taxed on their worldwide income, from 9–22%. Rental income earned by non-residents is taxed at a flat rate of 20% and capital gains are taxed at a standard rate of 20% for non-residents.

CULTURAL ETIQUETTE

Hospitality towards guests is an important part of Uzbek culture. If you are invited to an Uzbek home, you should take a small gift for your hosts. A souvenir item, like a picture book, from your home country is ideal, but if you have brought nothing suitable with you a gift such as a bouquet of flowers (get an odd number) or box of chocolates is fine. Note that an invitation to go to someone's house for 'a cup of tea' invariably means something more substantial: often a full meal. If you bring biscuits, dried fruit and nuts, or chocolates, they might well be added to the spread.

On entering a home in Uzbekistan (regardless of whether it is a flat or a house in the country) you should remove your shoes at the door. There is usually a mixture of assorted slippers and flip-flops available to wear around the house.

In more traditional households you may find that men and women are entertained separately, often in different rooms. Although there is little concern about women being seen by non-family members, they often feel more comfortable sitting and talking with their own sex. There is a general assumption that women will be happier talking to other women in the kitchen or dining room, and that men will do their own thing outside, or elsewhere in the house.

At the end of the meal, thanks are given by the act of bringing the hands together in front of the face, then moving them down in an action symbolising a washing gesture. This is the signal for everyone to get up from the table. You shouldn't continue to pick at food after this point.

Mosques, shrines and other holy places often have their own sets of rules and you should endeavour to observe these. If in doubt, ask the guardian or someone else who appears to work or worship there, as it is better to appear naïve than disrespectful. Requirements are likely to include removing your shoes, covering your head (women only) and wearing long trousers or a skirt which covers the knees. Clothing which is revealing is unacceptable. You may be expected to wash your hands and face and in active mosques, and occasionally only men, or practising Muslims, are permitted to enter. Whatever your personal opinion about this, you should respect the local community's wishes.

TRAVELLING POSITIVELY

Uzbekistan needs foreign investment, foreign recognition and foreign scrutiny. Responsible tourists can contribute in all these areas by becoming both observers and ambassadors. Think about where and how you spend your money, remembering that family-run guesthouses, local restaurants and co-operative craft workshops are the best way to put your money into the local community.

If you want to volunteer in Uzbekistan, an internet search will reveal a small number of NGOs working within the country, most of which are in the environmental and social sector. Most western NGOs were expelled from the country in 2005–06 following international criticism of the Andijan Massacre (page 132). The work of the remaining NGOs is strictly controlled and their workers are often viewed with suspicion by the authorities. It is not uncommon for NGO workers to have their visas terminated suddenly.

Counterpart (*www.counterpart.org*) works with local NGOs around the world. In Uzbekistan it is involved in disaster response, humanitarian commodities distribution, leadership and enterprise development, and small reconstruction projects. It seeks donors, volunteers and corporate partners.

Medical Teams International (*www.medicalteams.org*) has a field office in Uzbekistan. It works primarily in two areas: emergency medical service training, and outreach and rehabilitation programmes for disabled children. It also provides medical supplies to under-stocked hospitals and clinics. Volunteers with professional backgrounds in medicine and dentistry are particularly sought, though there are also volunteering openings for non-medical support staff.

SOS Children's Village has an office in Tashkent (*79A Nukus;* \ *(071) 120 3783;* e *sos-na@sos-kd.uz; www.soschildrensvillages.org.uk*) and works with orphans throughout the country. It is always in need of extra hands and donations of spare cash, toys and children's clothing.

SEND US YOUR SNAPS!

We'd love to follow your adventures using our *Uzbekistan* guide – why not send us your photos and stories via Twitter (@BradtGuides) and Instagram (@bradtguides) using the hashtag #uzbekistan. Alternatively, you can upload your photos directly to the gallery on the Uzbekistan destination page via our website (*www.bradtguides.com/uzbek*).

Part Two

THE GUIDE

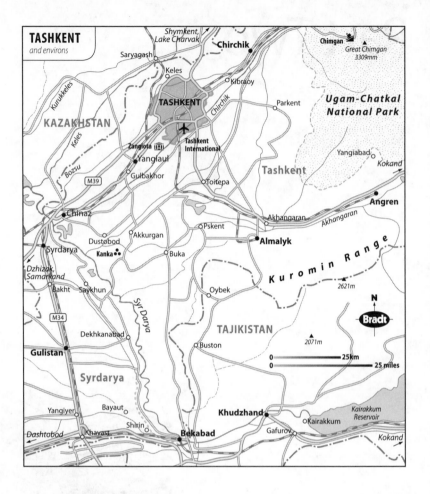

TASHKENT
and environs

Shymkent,
Lake Charvak

Chirchik

Chimgan
Great Chimgan
3309mm

Saryagash

Keles

Kibraoy

Kurukkeles

TASHKENT

Parkent

Ugam-Chatkal
National Park

KAZAKHSTAN

Keles

Chirchik

Bozsu

Zangiota

Yanglaul

Tashkent
International

Tashkent

Yangiabad

Kokand

M39

Gulbakhor

Toitepa

Angren

Chinaz

Akkurgan

Pskent

Akhangaran

Akhangaran

Dustobod

Dzhizak,
Samarkand

Syrdarya

Kanka

Buka

Almalyk

K u r o m i n   R a n g e

Bakht

Saykhun

Oybek

2621m

N

Syr Darya

Bradt

M34

TAJIKISTAN

2071m

Dekhkanabad

Buston

Gulistan

0   25km
0   25 miles

Syrdarya

Yangiyer

Bayaut

Shirin

Khudzhand

Kairakkum
Reservoir

Dashtobod

Khavast

Bekabad

Gafurov

Kairakkum

Kokand

3

Tashkent and Environs

Too frequently passed over in favour of the Silk Road's UNESCO stars, Tashkent is a vibrant crucible of historic architecture and Islam, Soviet town planning and propaganda, and 21st-century nation building. The varying, often seemingly incompatible strands of modern Uzbek identity are all entwined in Tashkent, and to understand both where Uzbekistan has come from and where it is going, you need to come here. A stone's throw from the capital in Tashkent and Syr Darya viloyati (provinces), the Syr Darya River carves up the steppe and cultivated lands. To the northeast of the city, the Chatkal National Park, with its alpine meadows and mountain forests, is a welcome natural haven amongst the mines, factories and infrastructure projects that are driving the Uzbek economy forwards.

TASHKENT *Telephone code: 71*

The capital of numerous incarnations of Uzbekistan, including the present republic, Tashkent morphs and expands with every new generation. With a population that by some estimates is as high as 4.45 million (though more likely around 2.5 million), Tashkent is by far and away the largest city in central Asia: only Kabul comes anywhere close. A stroll through any bazaar reveals the ethnic diversity of the people, with not only Uzbeks, Tajiks and Russians but also Crimean Tartars, Koreans, Bukharan Jews and other unexpected minorities each contributing to Tashkent's cultural smorgasbord. Though first impressions may be of chaos, concrete and cars, a stroll through the backstreets of the Old City or a rummage in Chorsu Bazaar reveals an older, slower way of life that continues to underpin modern life.

HISTORY An oasis on the Chirchik River, Tashkent began its life as a staging post for Silk Road merchants, missionaries and mercenaries *en route* between the Tian Shan Mountains in the east and the Kyzylkum Desert to the west. The archaeological site of Kanka (pages 120–2), 80km southwest of the modern city, was already thriving in the 4th century BC, so much so that it can be identified even in ancient Greek sources (recorded there as Antihiey Zayaksartskoy). It was the capital of the principality of Chach and, for the next thousand years, its citadel flourished as the centrepiece of a network of more than 30 towns, 50 irrigation canals and numerous caravanserais. The Battle of Talas in AD 751 ushered in a new era for Tashkent: the Arab Abbasid Caliphate conclusively defeated the forces of Tang emperor Xuanzong, halting Chinese expansion in central Asia and instead putting the whole Syr Darya region firmly under Arab (and therefore Islamic) control. The Samanids (AD819–AD999) called their new capital Binkath; the name Tashkent (meaning stone city) did not come into use until the time of the Karakhanid Khanate in the 10th century.

Tashkent became a wealthy and cosmopolitan city on the back of the trade passing through between Kashgar, Samarkand and Bukhara. Its wealth made it an inevitable target for looters, however: the city was sacked in 1214 by the Khwarazmian ruler Ala ad-Din Muhammad, and then again just five years later by Genghis Khan and his Mongol horde. Tashkent was utterly destroyed, and it would not recover until the time of Timur in the mid 15th century. The city's oldest remaining buildings (found in the Sheikhantaur Mausoleum Complex, page 106) date from this period, but it was still not a time of stability: Tashkent fell time and again to violent invaders – Kazakhs and Kalmyks, Persians and Uzbeks, Mongols and Oirots. They frequently levelled parts of the city, resulting in a fragmented architectural legacy from the period.

The history of modern Tashkent really starts in the late 18th century, again with a rise in trade, but this time from tsarist Russia. Drawn by the city's wealth and size (it is thought to have had over 100,000 inhabitants at the time), the Khan of Kokand annexed Tashkent in 1809, adding it to his ample territories in the East. When the Russians advanced on Kokand 60 years later, Tashkent was still the jewel in Kokand's crown, and therefore the first major target for General Chernyayev and his troops. The Russians seized Tashkent on their second attempt in 1865, a remarkable feat given that their 1,900-strong attack force was outnumbered 15 times over. For once the city was not levelled: the locals chose to surrender and in doing so saved both their lives and their homes.

Kokand became a vassal state of Russia, and in 1867 General Konstantin Petrovich von Kaufmann became its first governor general. He constructed a military cantonment across the Ankhor Canal from Tashkent's Old City, and this became the centre of the city's Russian community. Initially the population comprised military men, merchants and the occasional diplomat or spy (the number of which would increase exponentially with the Great Game; page 17) but the arrival of the Trans-Caspian railway in 1889 brought with it railway workers and their families who, a long way from home and with little money, decided to settle in Tashkent.

The early years after the Russian Revolution hit Tashkent hard. Although the city became the capital of the newly formed Turkestan Autonomous Soviet Socialist Republic in 1918, it was far from secure: White Russians fought with the Bolsheviks, the Bolsheviks then fought with the Basmachis (page 18), and Soviet purges followed. When Turkestan was further divided and the Uzbek Autonomous SSR was created, Tashkent initially lost out on capital status, but the honour was restored in 1930 and the city has remained Uzbekistan's political centre ever since.

As a Soviet capital, huge sums of money were invested into Tashkent's growth and industrialisation, a process which rapidly increased with the relocation of factories away from the Nazi advance in western Russia during World War II. The city's population swelled with migrant workers, evacuees and exiles: Tashkent would ultimately become the fourth-largest city in the Soviet Union, and more than half of its population was of Russian or Ukrainian origin. Many of these immigrants were housed in swiftly erected buildings, and they were consequently badly hit by the 1966 earthquake (see box, page 111) which ravaged the city.

Since independence in 1991, the face of Tashkent has continued to change. The demographics of the city have shifted notably with the mass exodus of ethnic Russians, Ukrainians, Germans and Poles, and an influx of Tajiks and Afghans fleeing their respective civil wars. President Karimov has actively encouraged ambitious building schemes, and Soviet symbols and statuary, notably what was once the world's largest statue of Lenin, have been slowly replaced with images more closely aligned with the identity of the modern, independent republic.

GETTING THERE AND AWAY

By air Tashkent International Airport (`\ 140 2801`), the main aviation hub for Uzbekistan, is situated 12km southeast of Tashkent. It has two terminals, international and domestic, next door to one another. Facilities are somewhat dated, despite the main terminal having been rebuilt in 2001, and both check-in and immigration tend to get overrun if more than one flight is scheduled. It is still, however, the most efficient way to enter and leave Uzbekistan, and the network of domestic flights from Tashkent is particularly good.

Airlines The following airlines served Tashkent at the time of going to print. For their contact details in Uzbekistan, pages 44–5.

- ✈ Aeroflot
- ✈ Air Astana
- ✈ Air Baltic
- ✈ Asiana Airlines
- ✈ China Southern Airlines
- ✈ Iran Air
- ✈ Korean Air
- ✈ Malaysia Airlines
- ✈ Rossiya
- ✈ S7 Airlines
- ✈ Turkish Airlines
- ✈ Ural Airlines
- ✈ UTair Aviation
- ✈ Uzbekistan Airways

Airport transfers As you would expect, the airport arrivals hall is plagued with the usual selection of aggressive taxi drivers demanding upwards of US$10 for the 20-minute drive into the city. If you have not pre-arranged a hotel taxi to collect you, simply walking out of the airport onto the main road will reduce your taxi fare to US$3. Be prepared in any case to haggle hard. If you are travelling on a budget, buses 11 and 76 go from the airport to Chorsu Bazaar, and bus 67 travels along Shakhrisabz to Amir Timur. Pay the driver for your ticket as you board the bus.

By rail Tashkent's main railway station (*zheleznodorozhny vokzal;* `\ 299 1873`) is situated to the south of the city centre on Turkiston. Whilst it is possible to arrive in Uzbekistan by rail from Russia, Kazakhstan, Tajikistan or Turkmenistan (pages 45–6), it is not a journey for the faint-hearted or time-poor.

Far more useful are Uzbekistan's domestic rail links, the latest fares and timetables for which are detailed at www.uzrailpass.uz.

Attempting to buy the ticket is likely to be the most stressful part of your rail journey. There are two ticket booths: one inside the main station to the right as you enter, and a second in the foreigners' ticket office behind the station. Sadly, the latter is often closed.

You will need your passport to buy a train ticket and it is helpful if you write down both your destination and the six-digit date you wish to travel so as to avoid confusion.

These ticket boots are your best bet if you want to buy a ticket on the day of travel, or 1–2 days beforehand. If you know your travel plans further in advance, and want to be relieved of the hassle for a small fee, Caravanistan (*www.caravanistan.com*) offer a reliable reservations service, and the tickets will be delivered to your hotel.

The following services are likely to be the most useful on your travels:

161/162 (Afrosiab) Tashkent–Samarkand; departs 08.00 daily, returns 17.00; 2½hrs; ticket start at 50,000 som. High-speed service with restaurant car & AC.
8/7 (Nasaf) Tashkent–Samarkand; departs 08.05 daily, returns 18.15; 3½hrs; tickets start from 38,885 som
50/49 & 662/661 Tashkent–Samarkand; tickets start from 20,075 som
10/9 (Sharq) Tashkent–Samarkand–Bukhara; departs 08.30 daily, returns 08.00; 3–4hrs between Tashkent & Samarkand, 6–9hrs between Tashkent & Bukhara; tickets start from 43,816 som. A good option for Bukhara as it has AC & reaches its destination mid-afternoon.
662/661 Tashkent–Bukhara; departs 20.55 daily; 9hrs; beds in 2- & 4-berth cabins cost 96,454 som and 65,924 som respectively.
56/58 Tashkent–Samarkand–Urgench 56 departs Tashkent 19.30 Tue, Fri & Sun, 58 leaves 19.30 Mon, Thu & Sat, both 56 & 58 return 15.20 daily except Wed; 17½hrs (4½hrs to Samarkand); seats start from 44,909 som, cabin bunks from 105,122 som

By road Tashkent is well-connected to all of Uzbekistan's main road transport arteries, and within easy reach of the borders with both Kazakhstan and Tajikistan. The road surfaces around the capital are generally well maintained and, unusually for Uzbekistan, well signposted, making navigation relatively straightforward. If you are approaching the city from the opposite side to your destination, taking the ring road is preferable to driving through the city centre, even if the route is a little longer. This especially applies at rush hour.

If you are driving your **own vehicle** and approaching or leaving Tashkent via the M39 (the main road southwest of the capital towards Samarkand), note that it passes briefly through Kazakhstan. If you do not have a Kazakhstan transit visa, you

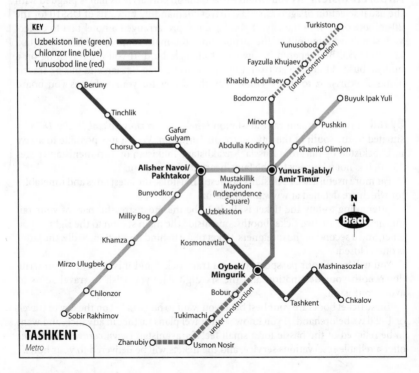

will need to travel instead on the M34 via Gulistan; take the A376 east of Dzhizak as far as the village of Hovos, then the M34 north of Hovos to Gulistan and Tashkent. It is a reasonably good road and well marked. However, due to the increased distance and travel time, we prefer to take the smaller and rougher but more direct road due west of Gulistan. This road passes through the villages of Alkaltyn, Yangiaul and Katta-Chuybek and joins the M39 about 8km south of the border. Signposts along this route are few and far between; expect to stop and ask for directions to Gulistan and to rely heavily on your sense of direction.

Tashkent has a number of **bus stations**, and the one you require will depend on your destination and choice of transport. For long-distance services it is advisable to book a day in advance as the scheduled buses fill up quickly.

The public bus station (*Tashkent Avtovokzal;* ✆ *279 3929*) is near to the Sobiz Rakhimov metro station on Bunyodkor, as is the Sobir Rakhimov private bus station, and it's from here that the majority of long-distance bus and Daewoo minibus services leave. From here you can take the bus/minibus to Samarkand (*US$5/US$5; 7hrs/5½hrs*), Bukhara (*US$9/US$10; 14hrs/10hrs*) or Urgench (*US$18/US$20; 25hrs/18hrs*). Shared taxis typically hover outside the bus station and will complete the same journeys in half the time of the buses but are approximately twice the price. If you are in a hurry or want to stretch out, you can always pay for the additional seats in the car rather than waiting for it to fill up.

To reach Karshi and Termez, use the private bus station at Ippodrom Bazaar 2km further along Bunyodkor. The bus to Termez takes about 16 hours (*US$17*) and the minibus 12 hours (*US$18*). There are currently no buses east to Fergana from Tashkent, but share taxis leave from Kuyluk Bazaar on the Fergana Highway (*5hrs; US$10–12*). If you are going elsewhere in the Fergana Valley, you will need to travel first to Fergana, and then get an onward connection from there.

GETTING AROUND

By car Soviet planners may have laid out much of Tashkent on a grid, but they didn't anticipate the boom in car ownership and resultant gridlock. Navigating Tashkent in your **own vehicle** is a challenging affair due to the lack of street signs, and drivers in the capital seem to be a needlessly aggressive bunch. You'll require a reasonable scale map, plenty of patience, and more importantly, to understand the reply. None of the major international car-hire firms have offices in Tashkent, but you can rent a vehicle (with or without a driver) from by Advantour and Sambuh (both page 90). Note that hiring a car and driver is frequently cheaper than self-drive.

Parking in the city is a perpetual hassle; there are few planned parking areas and drivers typically park two or even three cars deep along the edge of the road, causing chaos. Outside popular restaurants and other premises where there is competition for space, you may be asked for a semi-official parking charge by an attendant. Although you can usually get out of paying this, it is easier to hand over 1,000 som or thereabouts. Do not, however, part with your keys even if they claim valet parking is available; there's a real chance you'll never see your car again.

By public transport Most cars serve as **impromptu taxis**, so if you need a ride simply stand by the curb and put your hand out. Fares are typically US$3–4 depending on the length of the trip, but make sure you agree a price in advance. If you prefer a pre-booked **taxi**, O'zbegim Taxis (✆ *220 0300*), Tashkent Taxi Service (✆ *200 5151*) and Millennium Taxi (✆ *129 5555*) are all reputable firms.

Tashkent has a large number of buses, minibuses and trams; the minibuses tend to be far newer and more frequent than the other options. **Minibuses** are significantly cheaper than taxis (typically 1,000 som per ride) but still at the mercy of the traffic jams. The destination and route number (if applicable) are written on the front of the bus or on a card in the window. Pay the driver as you board. In terms of helpful **bus** routes, Bus 67 starts at the airport and has stops on Sh Rustaveli, Afrosiab, Sh Rashidova, Uzbekistan and A Timur, terminating at Yunusabad. Bus tickets cost 1,000 som. Bus 94 also has the airport as its terminus and runs to Karavanbazar. Buses generally run from around 05.00 until late evening, at approximately 15-minute intervals.

The best way to get across Tashkent, particularly at rush hour, is undoubtedly by **metro** (map, page 88). Opened in 1977 with one line and 12 stations, the system has since been expanded to take in all parts of the city you're likely to want to visit, with a fourth, partially overland line (the Sergeli Line) due to open by 2020. Tokens cost 1,000 som, the trains run from 05.00 to midnight and, as well as being theoretically earthquake-proof, many of the stations are elaborately decorated with golden domes, chandeliers, mosaics and other delightful frippery.

TOURIST INFORMATION AND TOUR OPERATORS There is no official tourist information centre in Tashkent; the national tourism company Uzbektourism (page 91) is the closest thing you will find. Hotel staff, fellow travellers and the below-listed tour operators are typically the best sources of tourist information in the city. Every other street corner seems to have an office selling airline tickets, largely because credit card sales and online booking are still limited in Tashkent. The following companies can sell you tickets and are sometimes able to accept card payment for their services. If not, dollars are preferred. In addition to making bookings, their English-speaking staff can also advise you on things to do and see, whether or not you require a personal guide.

Abda Travel 56 Buyuk Turon; ✆ 232 2256; e abdatravel@yahoo.com; www.abdatravel.uz. A joint Malaysian–Uzbek venture, Abda specialises in all-inclusive package tours within Uzbekistan. Prices are determined by the duration of your itinerary & number of people in your party. When planning your trip, ask for the English-speaking Robert Shin.
Advantour [108 C6] 47A Mirobod; ✆ 150 3020; e tashkent@advantour.com; www.advantour. com. Central Asia specialist offering a wide range of tours, from a single day's sightseeing in Tashkent to 3-week Silk Road odysseys. Their helpful staff can arrange guides, hotels, flights & car rental.
Asia Adventures [108 D6] 27/10 Mirobod; ✆ 150 6280; e info@centralasia-adventures. com; www.centralasia-adventures.com. Tour specialist with a range of programmes from horse trekking & mountaineering to escorting VIP business trips around Tashkent's cultural sites. Also make hotel bookings.

Marco Polo 20 Usman Nosir; ✆ 252 7641; e info@marcopolo.uz; www.marcopolo.uz. Specialist cultural tours with knowledgeable, multi-lingual guides. Translation services also available.
Novo Tours [109 E1] 14/49 Center-5; ✆ 235 4548; e info@novotours.uz; www.novotours.uz. Tour operator with English-, French- & Russian-speaking guides. Also provide visa support, airline ticketing & hotel reservations.
Sambuh 104A Kichik Beshgach; ✆ 120 8883; e info@sambuh.com; www.sambuh.com. Also known as Dolores Travel. Offers car & mini van rental (with or without driver), hotel reservations, &, in addition to the standard sightseeing packages, also has more unusual options such as camel trekking, long-distance cycle rides & railway tours.
✳ **Sitara Travel** 45/42 Sh Rustaveli; ✆ 281 4148; e sales.tashkent@sitara.com; www.sitara.com. Exceptionally helpful & professionally run tour operator with offices across the 'Stans, as well as in Canada and China. Sitara has some of the best

Sometimes great adversity can present the opportunity to implement great solutions, and so the Tashkent metro, the city's most important transport artery, was born out of the destruction caused by the 7.5 Richter-scale earthquake that levelled much of the Old Town in April 1966. Planners, architects and workers came from across the USSR to build a new model Soviet city, installing sewerage systems, wide boulevards and parks and, as a centrepiece, a metro system whose design and architectural beauty drew considerable inspiration from the jewel-like Moscow metro.

Tashkent metro has 29 stations on three principle lines; a fourth line has been proposed and approved, but there is as yet no estimated completion date. There is a total of 36km of track. As the city sprawls out ever further (an urban planner's response to having a conurbation in a seismically active area), so does the metro. The system is exceptionally clean, safe and runs reliably until late at night. The carriages are wide and the stations marked up in Latin script, a boon to English-speaking travellers. A typical travelling experience might begin with consulting the metro map (posted at the entrance to each metro station), a relatively courteous inquiry by a policeman to see your ID (always carry your passport or a copy if planning to travel on the metro), the purchase of a small, translucent blue plastic token (1,000 som) and then descending into the station to join some of the 400,000 commuters who use the Tashkent metro each day.

What you first notice is the space: it's not something normally associated with the economics of creating a subterranean complex. The platforms are wide and the ceilings are high. Each station is unique in its décor and is generally themed on some aspect of Uzbek life or culture. For instance, the first station to be built was the Mustakillik Maydoni in which Ulug Beg, grandson of Timur and historical astronomer of note, is acknowledged with the star patterns in the marble floor of the platform. The beautiful mosaics of cotton found on the walls of Pakhtakor station acknowledge the impact this crop has had on life in Uzbekistan. See map, page 88.

English-speaking guides in Uzbekistan, & their prices are very competitive. Highly recommended. **Uzbektourism** [109 E3] 47 Istiklol; ☏ 233 5414; e info@uzbektourism.uz; www.uzbektourism.uz. State-run tourism company with head office close to Hotel Uzbekistan. Staff are generally helpful & English is spoken. Tours are competitively priced, though less imaginative than those offered by the likes of Asia Adventures & Sambuh.

WHERE TO STAY Like any large Soviet city, Tashkent has a vast number of places you could stay, but remarkably few where you'd actually want to. Star ratings seem to be decidedly creative (certainly not comparable to international standards), and price is no guarantee of quality. Check out a number of rooms in your chosen establishment before parting with your cash, and always haggle hard on price.

Contrary to what the staff may tell you, Tashkent is not overrun with tourists, meaning you're well placed to get a discount if you ask. Expect to pay cash: outside of the top-end hotels, few businesses have the capacity to take credit or debit card payments. The majority of accommodation options are centrally located within the city, and few are more than 10 minutes' walk from a metro station. Most of top-end hotels are predictably clustered around Amir Timur

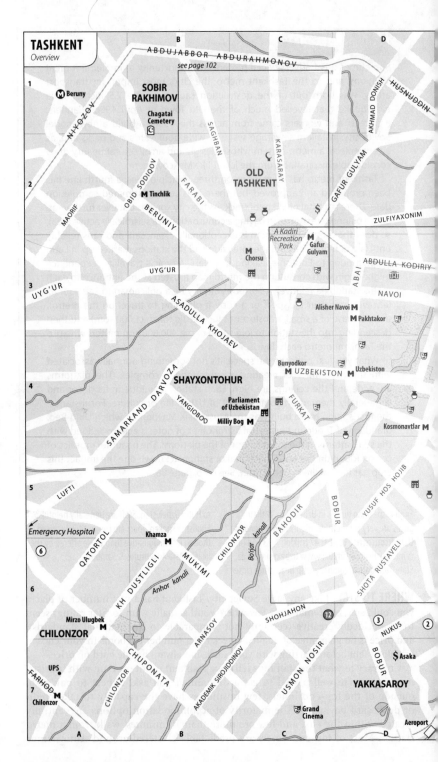

TASHKENT
Overview

see page 102

ABDUJABBOR ABDURAHMONOV

SOBIR RAKHIMOV

Beruny

Chagatai Cemetery

OLD TASHKENT

SAGHBAN

FARABI

KARASARAY

GAFUR GULYAM

AKHMAD DONISH

HUSNUDDIN

NIYOZOY

MAORIF

OBID SODIQOV

Tinchlik

BERUNIY

ZULFIYAXONIM

UYG'UR

UYG'UR

A Kadiri Recreation Park

Chorsu

Gafur Gulyam

ABDULLA KODIRIY

ABAI

NAVOI

ASADULLA KHOJAEV

Alisher Navoi

Pakhtakor

SHAYXONTOHUR

Bunyodkor

UZBEKISTON

Uzbekiston

SAMARKAND DARVOZA

YANGIOBOD

Parliament of Uzbekistan

FURKAT

Milliy Bog

Kosmonavtlar

LUFTI

Emergency Hospital

QATORTOL

Khamza

MUKIMI

CHILONZOR

Bo'rjar kanali

BAHODIR

BOBUR

YUSUF HOS HOJIB

SHOTA RUSTAVELI

KH DUSTLIGLI

Anhor kanali

ARNASOY

CHUPONATA

SHOHJAHON

CHILONZOR

Mirzo Ulugbek

CHILONZOR

AKADEMIK SIROJIDDINOV

USMON NOSIR

NUKUS

BOBUR

Asaka

UPS

FARHOD

Chilonzor

YAKKASAROY

Grand Cinema

Aeroport

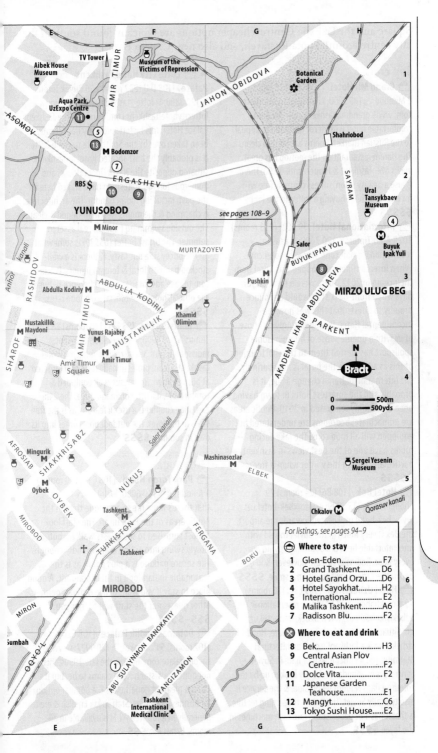

For listings, see pages 94–9

Where to stay

1	Glen-Eden	F7
2	Grand Tashkent	D6
3	Hotel Grand Orzu	D6
4	Hotel Sayokhat	H2
5	International	E2
6	Malika Tashkent	A6
7	Radisson Blu	F2

Where to eat and drink

8	Bek	H3
9	Central Asian Plov Centre	F2
10	Dolce Vita	F2
11	Japanese Garden Teahouse	E1
12	Mangyt	C6
13	Tokyo Sushi House	E2

see pages 108–9

Square and the UzExpo Centre; cheaper options are typically found south of the city centre around Shota Rustaveli, and also near Chorsu Bazaar.

Top end

⌂ **Grand Mir Hotel** [108 C6] (126 rooms) 2 Mirobod; ☎ 140 2000; e info@grandmorhotel.com; www.grandmirtashkent.com. Modern, comfortable hotel with décor designed to appeal to the Russian market. Rooms are large & clean. The Harem restaurant on the rooftop has great views over Tashkent & is open until 02.00. There is also a beauty salon, fitness centre & free Wi-Fi for guests & those buying a coffee in the lobby. **$$$$$**

⌂ **International Hotel** [93 E2] (233 rooms) 107A Amir Timur; ☎ 120 7000; e i.tasha.reservation@gmail.com; www.ihthotel.com. When InterContinental dropped this hotel from their chain in 2012, there were a few halcyon days when front-desk staff would announce proudly to guests that this was now the Incontinental Hotel. Disappointingly for those of us with a puerile sense of humour, some spoilsport has alerted them to the shortcomings of this as a brand, & the hotel is now boringly the International. Name change aside, it is probably still the smartest hotel in town having been thoroughly renovated in 2010. Public areas are immaculate; bedrooms are understated but equipped will all mod cons. The lake-facing rooms have one of the best views in Tashkent, particularly during the winter when it freezes. **$$$$$**

⌂ **Hotel Bek** [108 B6] (24 rooms) 29 Shohjahon; ☎ 215 5999; e info@bek-hotel.uz; www.bek-hotel.uz. Located towards the airport, the Bek is very much in the Soviet mould with uncomfortable beds & a *babushka* spying on every floor. Rooms are clean, however, & in good decorative order. Don't count on a smile. **$$$$**

⌂ **Hotel Uzbekistan** [109 E3] (120 rooms) 45 Musakhanov; ☎ 113 1111; e reservation@uzbekistanhotel.uz; www.uzbekistanhotel.uz/en. Situated right on Amir Timur Square, Hotel Uzbekistan is a Tashkent icon & architectural Marmite: you'll either love it or hate it. Soviet concrete is in abundance, barely broken up by the colourful flags & fountain outside, & the service is also typically Soviet. The hotel's redeeming feature is that it has 1 of Uzbekistan's rare cash machines in the foyer. **$$$$**

✳ ⌂ **Lotte City Hotel Tashkent Palace** [108 D4] (232 rooms) 56 Buyok Turon; ☎ 120 5800; e lotte_tashkent@mail.uz; www.lottecityhoteltashkent.com. Formerly the Tashkent Palace Hotel, this historic property has recently been taken over by the South Korean chain Lotte. It is probably the best-located hotel in Tashkent, situated opposite the Navoi Opera House, and numerous foreign statesmen have stayed here in the past, including Indira Gandhi. The architecture is charming & the rooms well maintained & clean. The outside swimming pool is a real asset in summer. The b/fast buffet (*US$20*) is somewhat on the pricey side but tasty, & there is a well-stocked bar with local & foreign liquors. Pay in som to take advantage of the difference between the official/hotel & unofficial exchange rates. **$$$$$**

⌂ **Radisson Blu** [93 F2] (110 rooms) 88 Amir Timur; ☎ 120 4900; e reservation.tashkent@radissonblu.com; www.radissonblu.com/hotel-tashkent. Clean, professionally run hotel targeted at businessmen. Rooms are well equipped & comfortable, if a little unimaginative. The 24hr exchange counter is a useful feature, as is the free Wi-Fi in the foyer. The outdoor pool comes into its own in summer. **$$$$**

Mid range

⌂ **Park Turon Hotel** [108 C1] (120 rooms) 1 A Kodiriy; ☎ 140 6000. We're sorry to say that there's more life in a morgue than in the public areas of the Park Turon. The staff look almost surprised to see guests walk in, but slowly swing into action & are friendly enough. The secure parking is a plus point, as is the reasonable Indian food in the restaurant. A good place to stay if you want peace & quiet; neither other guests nor the staff will bother you. **$$$–$$$$**

⌂ **Domina Shodlik Palace** [108 C2] (107 rooms) 5 Pakhtakor; ☎ 120 9977; www.shodlikpalace.com. Built in the late 1990s, this is not quite the 4-star hotel it claims to be, but it's clean & pleasant nonetheless & a popular option for business travellers. Staff speak English & are generally helpful. Free Wi-Fi is available in all rooms. B/fast inc. **$$$**

🏠 **Grand Nur Hotel** [102 B1] (37 rooms) 83 Guruch Arik; ✆ 230 0074; www.grandnur.uz. Fairly characterless hotel with large, clean rooms, AC & Wi-Fi. Front desk staff speak English. **$$$**

🏠 **Hotel Grand Orzu** [92 D6] (50 rooms) 27 M Tarobi; ✆ 120 8877; e info@grandorzu.com; www.grandorzu.com. Surprisingly friendly & well-run hotel with helpful staff & clean rooms. The outside pool is a bonus in summer. **$$$**

🏠 **Hotel Grand Raddus** [108 D7] (29 rooms) 11 Mirobod; ✆ 120 4477; e office@elenahotel.uz. Small rooms with reasonably new bathrooms. Soft furnishings can be tatty so ask to see several rooms before you decide. **$$$**

🏠 **Hotel Sayokhat** [93 H2] (81 rooms) 115 Buyuk Ipak Yoli; ✆ 268 1971; e info@sayokhat. uz; www.sayokhat.uz. Grubby & disorganised, the Sayokhat is partially redeemed only by its unexpectedly splendid rose garden & the incongruous, turquoise green Neoclassical portico. **$$$**

🏠 **Le Grande Plaza** [109 E3] (53 rooms) 2 Uzbekistan Ovozi; ✆ 120 6600; e reservation@ legrandeplaza.com; www.legrandeplaza.com. Reasonably priced hotel owned by Tata Group, situated in a convenient location. Some of the rooms have been renovated more recently than others, so ask to be shown several before you check in. The 2 restaurants on site serve up various interpretations of Indian & Chinese cuisine. B/fast inc. **$$$**

🏠 **Malika Tashkent** [92 A6] (27 rooms) 53A Chupon-ata; ✆ 150 3020; e info@malika-tashkent. com; www.malika-tashkent.com. Tricky to find but worth the effort. As you travel along Lufti, Chupon-ata is the last road on the left before you reach the ring road. The 2 carriageways on Chupon-ata are separated & so you will need to drive past the hotel to the junction with Katartal before you can double back to the Malika. Look for the large cream plaster & stone façade with green blinds in the ground-floor windows. The Malika has comfortable rooms with twin beds & reasonable bathrooms. Meals are fairly basic but the small garden at the rear is a pleasant place to drink tea & relax. We were accosted by an overly enthusiastic, German-speaking *babushka* trying to sell paintings in the lobby, but managed to escape unscathed. Free Wi-Fi. **$$$**

🏠 **Retro Palace Hotel** [108 D6] (55 rooms) 65 Vahidov; ✆ 256 3106; www.retropalace.uz. Large, clean rooms with plenty of light. The staff

are pleasant & the outdoor pool area has lots of sun loungers on which to relax. The gaudy pink bar is a good place to meet other travellers. Accepts payment by Visa & MasterCard. **$$$**

🏠 **Rovshan Hotel** [108 C7] (46 rooms) 118 Mirobod; ✆ 120 7747; e stay@rovshanhotel. com; www.rovshanhotel.com. Located in a quiet residential neighbourhood, the Rovshan has reasonable rooms that are generally clean. A few of the staff speak English & they're relatively helpful by Tashkent standards. **$$$**

🏠 **Sam-Buh Elite Hotel** [108 C7] (38 rooms) 10 Tsekhovaya; ✆ 120 8826; e sambus@albatros. uz. The décor at Sam-Buh is a rather nasty flashback to the 70s, but if brown & orange are your thing, rooms are a reasonable size & come with a b/fast buffet. **$$$**

☀ 🏠 **Sayram Hotel** [108 C5] (25 rooms) 73 Rakatboshi; ✆ 140 0858; e info@sayram.uz. Tashkent's best mid-range option. Rooms are clean with relatively new furnishings, the staff are unusually friendly & eager to please, & the b/fast buffet is a treat. Highly recommended. **$$$**

Budget

🏠 **Glen-Eden Hotel** [93 F7] (14 rooms) 16/18 Chavandoz; ✆ 120 6171; e rest@ gleneden.co.uz. Small, well-run hotel with old but clean bathrooms, AC & ping-pong table. B/fast inc. **$$**

🏠 **Grand Tashkent** [92 D6] (27 rooms) 57 A Kahhor Lane VI; ✆ 255 0599; e hotel@ grand-tashkent.com; www.grand-tashkent.com. Unremarkable option with rock-hard beds & the finest synthetic furnishings China produces. The Wi-Fi & in-house travel agency are useful. **$$**

☀ 🏠 **Gulnara Guesthouse** [102 A5] (8 rooms) 40 Ozod; ✆ 160 2816; e gulnarahotel@ gmail.com. Friendly, family-run guesthouse offering comfortable rooms, & b/fast in the courtyard garden. Recommended for those travelling with children or who have had their fill of 'Soviet service' & want a human touch. Guests can use the kitchen & Wi-Fi. Some twin rooms have en-suite bathrooms. Dorm rooms US$15. **$$**

🏠 **Hotel Ali-Tour** [108 B5] (12 rooms) 26/2 Vokhidov; ✆ 256 7162; e ali_tour@globalnet. uz; www.alitur.narod.ru. Pleasantly furnished rooms & apts. Guests can prepare own food in the kitchen & there is also a sauna. Can also arrange visas. **$$**

🏠 **Mirzo Guesthouse** [102 B3] (12 rooms) 95 Saghban; ☏ 224 3794; e turkturizm@mail.ru; www.turkturizm.uz. Small blue guesthouse built around a courtyard. Service is friendly but beware the squat toilets. **$$**

🏠 **Orzu Tashkent Hotel** [108 C6] (34 rooms) 14 Ivleva; ☏ 120 8822; e orzu@grandorzu.com; www.grandorzu.com. One of Tashkent's better budget options. Rooms are small but clean &

the attached bathrooms & AC are definitely welcome. **$$**

Shoestring

🏠 **Hotel Al Hosilot** [108 A2] (156 Rooms) 95 Sh Rustavelli; ☏ 253 3196; e lot@hosilot.uz. Close to the south railway station, Al Hosilot is one of Tashkent's cheapest options & currently seems free of the cockroaches that plague so many other bottom-end establishments. Some of the bathrooms are better than others so ask to see several options. **$**

✕ **WHERE TO EAT AND DRINK** Forced migrations within the Soviet Union had one remarkable benefit for central Asia's capitals: the diversity of food now available. Whereas in the provinces you'd better get familiar with mutton, Tashkent has a pleasantly surprising array of restaurants, with options ranging in price from the economic to the exorbitant. Vegetarians may still go hungry (though see Sunduk, page 98), but everyone else should be well fed.

Perhaps predictably, Tashkent's most expensive restaurants are predominantly in upmarket hotels and the streets around Amir Timur. This is also where you'll find the greatest range of international cuisine. Central Asian restaurants tend to be cheaper and scattered more widely across the city; they cater predominantly to local diners and are therefore found in more residential areas as well as commercial districts. Chorsu Bazaar is the best location for cheap eats, both in terms of fresh produce but also shashlik and other hot snacks cooked right under your nose. Unless otherwise stated, restaurants are open for both lunch and dinner.

Most of Tashkent's larger hotels are equipped with **cafés** open around the clock, but it's cheaper and more interesting to head out into the city. Traditional Uzbek **tea houses** can be found in many of Tashkent's parks and are open late into the evening, particularly in summer. They're great for people-watching as the locals come to gossip, read the paper and do business. In Chorsu Bazaar taking tea is a rather more frantic affair as shoppers and stallholders tend to be in a hurry, but a cup of tea will set you back a fraction of what it would elsewhere and it is fun to be part of the hustle and bustle.If you prefer more Western surroundings (and/or want to drink coffee and eat cake), the places on pages 97–8 are recommended. They typically open late morning for coffee and pastries, and are busy around lunchtime, and stay open until 21.00 or so, often serving light dinners and alcoholic drinks as well as snacks.

Finally, Tashkent has no shortage of **bars and clubs**, particularly if vodka is your thing. The 'in' places to be seen are constantly changing, but usually revolve around one of the larger hotels where the clientele are wealthy and the drinks expensive. The Russian-language website www.afisha.uz has the most up-to-date listings.

Although generally fairly safe, visitors should note that many of the attentive single women in bars and clubs are working girls. Men simply interested in a quiet drink (or a genuine date) need to be clear about what they are and are not paying for, and women should be prepared to fend off unwanted advances.

Central Asian cuisine

✕ **Caravan** [108 B7] 22 A Qahho; ☏ 150 3959; www.caravangroup.uz; ⏱ 11.00–midnight daily. Central Asia-themed restaurant overrun with tourists

& children. Food is delicious & the atmosphere lively, but prices are many times higher than for similar dishes elsewhere. **$$$$–$$$$$**

✗ **Sato** [108 B7] 18 Kakhkhara; ☎150 0660; www.caravangroup.uz; ⏲ 11.00–03.00 Sun–Thu, 11.00–06.00 Sat. An unusual menu fusing Uzbek & Middle Eastern cuisines, upstairs from Izumi (see below). $$$$

✗ **Manas** [108 C6] Cnr Shota Rustaveli & Bog Saroy; ☎152 3811; ⏲ 10.00–midnight daily. Large yurt restaurant popular with wedding parties: ask to be seated in a yurt away from the music & dancing! The menu is Kyrgyz & the decor is reasonably authentic. Staff are helpful, though don't speak English, & a beer with your meal will set you back just 8,500 som. $$$$

✗ **Bagizagan** [108 D6] 43 Mirobod; ⏲ 10.00–23.00 daily. Formerly known as Dervish, this relatively modern restaurant is inspired by a Silk Road caravanserai. You pass through the door into a large open courtyard with charpoys, & smaller dining rooms are arranged off the courtyard. It is possible to eat inside & out, & the place is popular with groups. $$$–$$$$

✗ **Mangyt** [92 C6] 12 Usmon Nosir; ☎252 3811. 2 yurts erected in a residential courtyard is a surprising place for a restaurant, but the crowded interiors give an authentic feel for nomadic life in Kyrgyzstan. Dishes include roasted horse meat, shashlik & *beshbarmak* (noodles & mutton). $$$

✗ **Sharshara** [108 A2] 10 Bobojonava; ☎144 5835. Lively restaurant with great location (including manmade waterfall) & freshly baked bread. Menu helpfully has pictures so just choose & point. $$$

✗ **Milliy Taom** [102 D5] Gafur Gulyam; ☎244 7703; ⏲ lunchtimes only. Traditional Uzbek food including *shorpa* (soup) served in clay pots, *hasip* (sausage), *halim* (porridge) & *chuchvara* (ravioli). The restaurant is unmarked so you'll need to stop & ask. Exceptionally popular with locals. $$

✗ **Restaurant Bek** [108 B6] 13 Abdullaeva; ☎241 1752; www.bek.uz; ⏲ 09.00–22.00 daily. Always busy with local families, Bek offers a range of fairly tasty dishes, most of which are Uzbek or Russian. Also part of the same chain are Sim Café (*15 Mukimi*), Nur Restaurant (*124 Ergasheva*) & Mr Steak (*18 Bobura*). $$

✗ **Central Asian Plov Centre** [93 F2] Ergashev & Abdurashidov; ☎234 2902; ⏲ lunchtimes only. The best plov in central Asia is served up here. A passionate team cooks vast *kozon* (woks) of the stuff in an open-sided kitchen for the customers to watch before tucking in to plov & tea at one of the plastic patio tables on the terrace. Highly recommended for both the experience & the food. It's busiest on Thu as the special plov is believed to have aphrodisiac properties! $–$$

International cuisine

✗ **Affresco** [108 A7] 145 Babur; ☎129 9090; www.caravangroup.uz; ⏲ 11.00–00.30 daily. Excellent pizza & homemade pasta, with a variety of more unusual authentic Italian dishes, too. A number of the staff are Italian & the menu is available in both English & Italian. $$$$$

✗ **Gruzinski Dvorik** [108 C7] 15 Kakhkhara; ☎129 0770. The best Georgian restaurant in Tashkent. Quality of both food & wine is high, but so are the prices. There's often live music in the evenings. $$$$$

✗ **Izumi** [108 B7] 18 Kakhkhara; ☎150 3959; www.caravangroup.uz. Eye-wateringly expensive sushi restaurant but a great location if you fancy a blowout meal. Seating is on traditional Japanese *tatami* mats, & the adjoining karaoke rooms are ready & waiting for when you finish your meal. Discounts often available on Tue. $$$$$

✗ **Montgomery** [109 E5] 38 Taras Shevchenko; ☎150 3399; 🄵 fb.me/Montgomeryclub; ⏲noon–02.00 daily. Upmarket bar & restaurant popular with expats doing business or trying to impress a date. The atmosphere is lively, the food good, & the standard of service unusually high. $$$$$

✗ **Nam Dae Mun** [108 D4] 24 Bukhoro; ☎232 0107. Long-running sushi bar with attentive waitresses in kimonos. You get 12 assorted salads free with every order, so factor this in when choosing your dishes. Main dishes are around 35,000 som, & the teriyaki chicken is particularly good. $$$$$

✗ **Tokyo Sushi House** [93 E2] 95A Amir Timur; m 90 961 8888. Tashkent's smartest sushi restaurant is situated a stone's throw from the national bank & attracts a smart, wealthy crowd. Popular with businessmen. $$$$$

✗ **City Grill** [108 C2] 1 Shayhontohur; m 90 910 0450; ⏲ noon/midnight/daily. Top-end restaurant with high-quality food & imported wines, but predictably a price tag to match. The business lunch costs 18,500 som & is available weekdays 12.30–16.00. $$$$–$$$$$

✗ **Amaretto** [108 C6] 28 Sh Rustaveli; ☎ 215 5557. Popular Italian restaurant with take-away option for pizzas. The best tables are on the terrace. $$$$

✗ **Beryozka** [109 F4] 34 Shakhrisabz; ☎ 236 3595. Russian restaurant with accompanying micro-brewery & regular live music. Take-away option available. $$$$

✗ **Bistro** [109 E5] 33 Amir Timur; ☎ 252 1112. Gorgeous Italian restaurant in a courtyard setting with its own wood-fired pizza oven. Ingredients are fresh & authentic. $$$–$$$$

✗ **Al Delfin** [109 F1] 3 Malyasova; ☎ 233 1985. Wide range of Middle Eastern hot & cold meze with indoor & outdoor tables. Sheesha pipes available. $$$

✗ **Raaj Kapur** [109 E3] 2 Uzbekistan Ovozi; ☎ 120 6600; ⏰ 11.00–midnight daily. Inside the Tata-owned Le Grande Plaza Hotel (page 95), this is the closest Tashkent gets to an authentic Indian restaurant. The paratha & naan breads are particularly good. $$$

✗ **Italian Vero Ristorante** [108 D5] 1/35 Afrosiab; m (90) 910 0450; f fb.me/italianoverotashkent; ⏰ noon–midnight daily. Popular Italian restaurant with clean, white linens & authentic dishes. Most of the clientele are on dates, but if you're travelling solo the pizza is a fine cure for loneliness. $$–$$$

✗ **Efendi** [109 F5] 79A Azimova; ☎ 233 1502; ⏰ 09.00–midnight daily. Atmospheric Turkish restaurant with a wide menu of kebabs, salads & surprisingly good desserts – a rarity in Tashkent. Popular dishes do sell out, so arrive early for max choice & the chance for a table on the terrace. $$

✗ **Sunduk** [109 F4] 63 Azimova; ☎ 232 1146. Charming French-style restaurant with just a few tables. Service is fast & polite, & there are even vegetarian dishes on the menu. Try the business lunch for 5,000 som. $$

✗ **Yolki-Palki** [109 F3] 5 Shakhrisabz; ☎ 233 2259. Part of a Russian chain serving Russian & Ukrainian dishes – expect everything to come with dill. Service is slow but the food is cheap. $$

Fast food

✗ **Toronto Restaurant/Golden Wing** [109 E3] 30A Shakhrisabz; ☎ 232 2035. Turkish kebabs, French fries & the best selection of ice creams in Tashkent. Free Wi-Fi. $$$–$$$$

✗ **Papa Pizza** [109 E1] 2 Niyozbekyuli; ☎ 120 5970; ⏰ 09.00–02.00 daily. Home delivery only. $$$

✗ **Zamin Pizza Burger** [102 A5] Cnr Ozod & Beruniy; ☎ 177 4404. Surprisingly good pizzas & fried chicken. Standard pizzas cost 11,000 som; giant ones with fancier toppings are 24,000. Wash it down with a bottle of Fanta. $$–$$$

✗ **Gamburger Uzbechka** [109 E3] 45A Musakhanov; ☎ 113 1077. Literally the 'Uzbek Hamburger'. Wi-Fi available. $$

✗ **Angels Food** [108 D5] Oybek metro station. Stand selling cheap burgers & deep-fried snacks. $

Cafés and tea houses

🍵 **Cafe Bon** [108 D5] 63 Sh Rustaveli. Great European-style patisserie serving mouth-watering desserts & pastries. The *sachertorte* & *tiramisu* are particularly good if you're in need of an indulgent afternoon (or simply a change from shashlik).

🍵 **Café Jum** [108 C6] 34 Usmon Nosir; ⏰ Mon–Sat. Café serving real Italian roasted coffees & patisserie. Coffee machines, beans & other assorted coffee paraphernalia are also on sale.

🍵 **Dolce Vita** [93 F2] 1 Amir Timur. Paradise for coffee lovers & dessert fiends. If you have both a sweet tooth & dental insurance, try the espresso with crème caramel, orange liqueur & whipped cream.

🍵 **Il Perfecto** [108 D6] 9A Mirobod. Comfortable seating & a laid-back feel. Extensive menu of coffees served with a smile. The free Wi-Fi is an added attraction.

🍵 **Japanese Garden Teahouse** [93 E1] 107 Amir Timur. Built with the collaboration of the Embassy of Japan to Uzbekistan, this classical Japanese tea house is at the heart of the garden behind the UzExpo Centre (page 118) & contains all the items for the traditional Japanese tea ceremony.

🍵 **Studio Café** [109 F4] 1 Toytepa. Garish, Hollywood-themed café blaring Russian pop. If you're feeling hungry, the steaks are the best in Tashkent.

Bars and clubs

🍷 **Brauhaus** [109 F3] 5 Shakhrisabz; f Brauhaus - Tashkent; ⏰ noon–midnight daily. Lively German beer hall with a large bar & individual booths orientated around the copper brewing vats. The atmosphere is relaxed & so is the clientele. The German sausages aren't bad either.

🍷 **Docker Pub** [108 C7] 26 Ivlieva; ☎ 281 4825; f Docker Bar; ⏰ noon–midnight daily. Pretty ghastly but hugely popular bar with thumping music & good deals on drinks.

☆ **Fabrique** [109 E2] 1 A Kodiriy; ⊕ 22.00–05.00 Thu–Sun. The self-proclaimed Best Global Dance Club has R&B sets from resident DJs & a stylish clientele. Face control can be strict, so dress up for the occasion.

♀ **Gasthaus** [109 G6] 7 Fargona Yuli. German beer garden where home-brewed lager is served up by waitresses in Oktoberfest outfits. Half a litre of beer costs 3,000–5,000 som. Opens daily at 11.00 & closes when the last patron leaves.

♀ **Irish Pub** [109 E5] 30 Shevchenko; ⊕ 11.00–23.00 daily. A taste of the Emerald Isle in Tashkent: naff, but entertainingly so. Major football matches are screened on the big-screen TV & it draws a large (& loud) expat crowd. Beer from 5,000 som.

☆ **Neo Music Club** [109 E3] 2 Uzbekistan Ovozi; ⊕ 21.00–05.00 daily. Relaxed dance club with in-house DJ, large dance floor & good food & cocktails. Located on the 14th floor of Le Grande Plaza Hotel. Entrance costs 5,000 som for men but

is free entry for women. Also in the same location is the Sheikh Sheesha Lounge (⊕ until 07.00).

♀ **Timur** [109 F3] 9 Kory Niyozov; ⊕ 11.00–midnight daily. An Uzbek-named English pub serving Georgian food may sound like a slightly strange mix, but it's a pleasant place to hang out for a few hours, particularly if you're with a large group. Unusually for Tashkent, it's possible to pay by Visa & MasterCard.

♀ **Traktir Sam Prishyol** [108 D2] 2 Navoi; ⊕ 11.00–23.00 daily. Swanky brew-pub & restaurant with occasional live music in the evenings. Beers from 3,500 som.

♀ **Ye Olde Chelsea Arms** [108 C7] 25 Kakhkhara; ✆ 150 9989; ⊕ 15.00–05.00 daily. Chelsea claims to be an English pub, though the interior will leave most Brits bemused. Major sporting events are shown on the big screen, but it lacks the atmosphere of the Irish Pub.

ENTERTAINMENT
Theatres and music venues The theatre season in Tashkent runs roughly from October until June.

🎭 **Bakhor Concert Hall** [108 C3] Independence Sq; ✆ 139 0136. Formerly Government House, the Bakhor Concert Hall is now home to an Uzbek dance troupe & hosts occasional musical recitals.

🎭 **Ilkhom Theatre** [108 C2] 5 Pakhtakor; ✆ 241 2241; www.ilkhom.com. Founded in 1976, Ilkhom was the 1st independent theatre in the USSR: see box, page 31 for its history. Productions are typically in Russian (occasionally with English subtitles) & are highly innovative. The company tours internationally & is well regarded both at home & overseas. Performances 18.30 Tue–Sat (check website for season).

🎭 **Mukimi Musical Theatre** [108 A4] 187 Olmazaar; ✆ 245 1633. Popular theatre with programme of musicals & comedy in Russian.

🎭 **National Academic Drama Theatre** [102 D5] 34 Navoi; ✆ 244 1751; www.teatr.uz. Running since 1914, this theatre offers both classical & contemporary works by Uzbek playwrights. Performances are in Uzbek.

🎭 **Navoi Opera & Ballet Theatre** [108 D4] 28 Otaturk; ✆ 233 9081; www.gabt.uz; ticket office ⊕ 13.00–19.00. A trip to the ballet or opera at the Navoi Theatre is a highlight of any trip to Tashkent. The building, designed by the same architect responsible for Lenin's

mausoleum in Red Square, is set in an attractive square with musical foundations and was completed by Japanese POWs in the 1940s. A plaque in Japanese on the outside of the building commemorates their contribution. Inside, the central courtyard is covered with scenes from Uzbek folk tales. The standard of performance is high, & a live orchestra comes as standard. You can see the national opera & ballet companies, & foreign troupes often visit on tour. Guided tours start from the box office. Performances 18.00 Mon–Fri, 17.00 Sat–Sun. Matinées sometimes available at w/ends. The theatre was closed for a 2-year renovation in 2014–15 but should reopen, resplendent inside & out, sometime in 2016.

🎭 **Republican Puppet Theatre** [108 C4] 1 Afrosiab; ✆ 2567 395. 2 theatre companies perform a repertoire of more than 20 fairy tales with everything from marionettes to sock puppets. The elaborate building is almost as much of an attraction as the plays. Highly recommended. Performances 11.00 & 13.00 Sat–Sun.

🎭 **Russian Drama Theatre** [108 D3] 24 Otaturk; ✆ 233 8165; www.ardt.uz. Professional theatre companies perform both Russian classics & modern pieces in this 1930s theatre.

Performances 18.30 Mon–Fri, 19.00 Sat–Sun. Tickets start at US$2.

🎭 **State Conservatory** [108 B3] Cnr of Abai & Batyra Zakirov; ☎ 241 2991. Chamber concerts in Western & Uzbek styles.

🎭 **Tashkent State Circus** [102 C6] Khadra Sq; ☎ 244 3223. Purpose-built circus building hosting regular sell-out performances. The acrobats on camels are a Tashkent speciality. Performances Sat–Sun.

Cinemas

🎬 **Grand Cinema** [92 C7] 1 Kushbegi. Popular if slightly dingy multiplex showing both Hollywood & Russian blockbusters.

🎬 **Museum of Cinematic Art** [108 B3] 49A Uzbekiston. See page 110. Daily film showings take place at 19.00, often in English.

🎬 **Premier Cinema** [108 D6] 25 Mirobod. Watch the latest blockbusters dubbed into Russian on the big screen, or hire the intimate 12-seat hall to watch a film of your choice (*100,000 som*).

SHOPPING Tashkent is yet to mark itself out as a shoppers' paradise, but new money is spurring the opening of Western chain stores and, if you're happy to haggle, almost anything can be purchased in the city's bazaars.

The souvenirs on sale in Tashkent don't really compete with those in Uzbekistan's tourist hubs, either in variety or quality, as there's little market for them: the appeal of shopping here instead comes from barging elbows with Tashkent locals and snatching a glimpse of everyday life. From the mounds of melons to the wafting smell of freshly cooked *non* bread, the street-side butchers, the chinking and sparking of metal workshops, and a gay array of rainbow-coloured plastic goods from China, an hour or two spent shopping here is a multi-sensory feast.

🛍 **Chorsu Bazaar** [102 B5] 48 Navoi; ⏰ 09.00–18.00 daily. Meaning 'the crossroads', Chorsu is the commercial heart of Tashkent & has been for hundreds of years. Originally open to the air (as parts of it still are today), the maze of covered stalls was largely cleared away in the mid 20th century. In their place Soviet architects designed & built vast mosaic-covered domes, blue & turquoise space bubbles that still protect merchants & their goods from the elements & give the bazaar's skyline its distinctive shape. Each dome or area of the market houses a different type of good: take a stroll around the dried fruit & nut stands if you want to try plenty of free samples but beware of the dried cheese balls: they're something of an acquired taste.

If you have the time to hunt, almost everything is for sale here: plastic Chinese household goods battle for attention with hand-painted ceramics & fox fur hats, almost-antique nick-nacks, dried fruits & imported car parts in varying states of decay. The market is liveliest first thing in the morning when the wholesale deliveries are made, & the cheap chai & kebab stalls provide ample sustenance while you watch the world go by. Come here to get a feel for 'real' Tashkent &

an echo of Silk Road trade in centuries past. The easiest way to reach the market is to take the metro to Chorsu station, which is just a minute's walk from the first stalls.

Books

🛍 **Knizhny Mir** [109 F3] 1 Azimova; ⏰ 09.00–19.00 Mon–Sat. Well-stocked bookshop including a small selection of maps & English-language titles.

🛍 **Sharq Ziyokori** [108 D4] 26 Bukhara; ☎ 233 3590; ⏰ 09.00–18.00 Mon–Fri, 09.00–14.00 Sat. Best option for buying maps, including the Uzbek-equivalent of Ordnance Survey (*Ozbekiston Viloyatlari*). Most of the titles are in Uzbek or Russian, but they do have some language learning materials & guidebooks.

Souvenirs

🛍 **Abdul Khasim Madrassa** [108 A4] Alisher Navoi Park; ⏰ 10.00–16.00 daily. Take the opportunity to watch Tashkent's artisans at work & buy directly from them. The stringed instruments make particularly tasteful mementoes, & you can also buy miniature paintings, wood- & metalwork & lacquer.

Human House [108 C6] 30/9 Usman Nosir; www.humanhuman.net; ⊕ 10.00–19.00 Mon–Sat. One of Tashkent's coolest boutiques, Human House sells Uzbek textiles, ceramics, homeware & toys. Prices are high but the quality is good & the choice is wide.

Sharq-Guli [108 C1] 78 A Kodiry; ☏ 412 056. Once a Soviet women's collective, this embroidery company continues to use traditional designs to decorate *suzanis*, bags, skull caps & other textiles. More than 3,000 women still work here, doing embroidery by machine & by hand. This is a great option for gift shopping, particularly if you won't have the opportunity to travel beyond Tashkent, & if you call in advance you can usually see the women at work.

OTHER PRACTICALITIES

Emergencies In an emergency, you can call the following free numbers for assistance. It is unlikely, however, that the operator will speak any English, and help is not guaranteed to arrive. In the case of medical emergencies, you are usually better off hailing a taxi and transporting yourself (or the casualty) to the hospital in a private vehicle.

Ambulance ☏ 03   Police ☏ 02
Fire ☏ 01

Medical Tashkent's medical facilities are a mixed bag, and the quality is usually dictated by whether or not you can pay. In an emergency you should contact your embassy for assistance and to arrange medical evacuation (Medevac), but the following options should be able to patch you up if the worst comes to the worst.

✚ **Emergency Hospital** [92 A5] #16 2 Farkhad; ☏ 367 9001. Large, state-run hospital with proficient staff.

✚ **Safo Tibbiyot** [108 C7] 21 Ivlieva; ☏ 255 3136. Large, private clinic offering a full range of services including emergency care.

✚ **Tashkent International Medical Clinic** [93 F7] 4 Taras Shevchenko; ☏ 291 0142; www.tashclinic.org. Privately run medical clinic catering to the expat community in Tashkent. 24hr emergency care. Dental clinic also available. Consultations cost US$120–150.

Money Changing money in Uzbekistan is typically done on the black market (page 56), and it is here you will get the best rate. It is easiest to find **money changers** at Chorsu Bazaar and around the Gofur Gulom metro station. Dollars, euros, roubles and sterling are all widely accepted and you can typically haggle on the rate. It is, however, also possible to change money, cash travellers' cheques and get a cash advance from RBS [93 E2] (*77 Nosirov; ⊕ 09.00–14.00 Mon–Fri*) and the National Bank of Uzbekistan (*95 Gulomov; ⊕ 09.00–18.00 Mon–Fri, 09.00–16.00 Sat*), albeit at the poor official exchange rate. If you need to change Swiss Francs (CHF) or other less-common currencies, the NBU is the only place which will change them. There is still a severe shortage of **cash machines** in Tashkent (and even fewer actually have cash in them), but those belonging to Asaka Bank [92 D7] (*73 Abdulla Kahhor; also at 40 Akilov, 12 Usman Nosir & 60A Amir Timur*) are generally reliable, as are the ones in the foyers of Hotel Uzbekistan [109 E3] (*45 Musakhanov*), Hotel Lotte [108 D4] (*56 Buyok Turon*) and the International [93 E2] (*107A Amir Timur*). Not all machines accept all cards: the Ipak Yuli ATM at Hotel Lotte can only be used by Visa cardholders, for example.

Communications Tashkent's main **post office** [109 E3] (*7 Shakhrisabz*) is centrally located but tends to be busy and the staff are unhelpful. If you want to increase the likelihood of your post actually arriving at its destination, **DHL** [108 A5] has

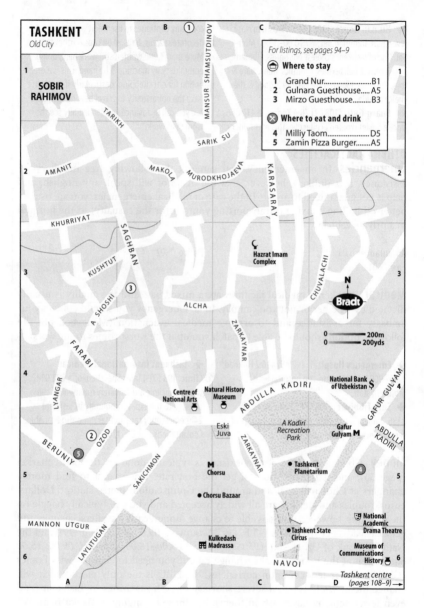

TASHKENT
Old City

SOBIR RAHIMOV

For listings, see pages 94–9

⬡ **Where to stay**
1 Grand Nur.....................B1
2 Gulnara Guesthouse.....A5
3 Mirzo Guesthouse..........B3

✖ **Where to eat and drink**
4 Milliy Taom.....................D5
5 Zamin Pizza Burger........A5

MANSUR SHAMSUTDINOV

TARIKH

SARIK SU

AMANIT

MAKOLA

MURODKHOJAEVA

KARASARAY

KHURRIYAT

SAGHBAN

KUSHTUT

A SHOSHI

ALCHA

Hazrat Imam Complex

CHUVALACHI

N

Bradt

ZARKAYNAR

FARABI

0 ——— 200m
0 ——— 200yds

LYANGAR

OZOD

BERUNIY

SAKICHMON

Centre of National Arts

Natural History Museum

ABDULLA KADIRI

National Bank of Uzbekistan $

GAFUR GULYAM

Eski Juva

A Kadiri Recreation Park

ZARKAYNAR

Gafur Gulyam **M**

ABDULLA KADIRI

M Chorsu

● Tashkent Planetarium

● Chorsu Bazaar

MANNON UTGUR

LAYLITUGAN

Kulkedash Madrassa

●Tashkent State Circus

NAVOI

National Academic Drama Theatre

Museum of Communications History

Tashkent centre
(pages 108–9)

several offices (*16B Said Barak; also at 2 Uzbekistan Ovozi & 4 Turkestan*) and there is a branch of **UPS** [92 A7] (*52A Khalklar Dustligi*). Uzbekistan's own Express Mail Service (*4 Turkiston;* ☎ *081; www.ems.uz*), which operates both domestic and international services, tends to be slightly cheaper than its foreign competitors, and will collect mail from you for dispatch.

Getting online in Tashkent is becoming easier, though connections are often rather slow. Wi-Fi in hotels and cafés is increasingly common, internet dongles are widely available (page 77) and new internet cafés seem to open and close every other day. The following were open at the time of going to print.

Business Communications Centre [108 D5]
16A Shakhrisabz. Also rents out office space &
provides secretarial services.

Internet Center [108 C6] 13 Usmon Nosir
Internet Markazi [109 E3] 7 Shakhrisabz.
Located inside the main post office.

WHAT TO SEE AND DO

In and around the Old Town Tashkent's historic heart is jam-packed with
museums, mausoleums and mosques, many of which are within walking distance
of one another. They are the sole survivors of the 1966 earthquake (page 111) and
so it is here that you will get a sense of Tashkent in times gone by – the pace of life
is a little slower, the people-watching richer, and the ghosts of the past are veritably
trampling over one another to be seen.

Alisher Navoi Literary Museum [108 B2] (*69 Navoi;* ✎ *241 0275;* ⏱ *10.00–17.00
Mon–Fri, 10.00–13.00 Sat*) Although he was born in Herat, Afghanistan, the Uzbeks
have taken Alisher Navoi very much to heart and declared him the father of Uzbek
literature (see box, page 114). Housed in an attractive neoclassical building constructed
to mark the 500th anniversary of Navoi's birth, the museum contains manuscripts,
photographs and archive documents as well as a small number of paintings, some of
them replicas. The interior of the museum building is itself decorated with large-scale
murals depicting garden and palace scenes inspired by Navoi's *Khamsa*.

Aibek House Museum [93 E1] (*26 Tazetdinov;* ✎ *248 0900;* ⏱ *10.00–17.00 Mon–
Sat*) Situated inside Aibek's former family home in an old district of Tashkent, this
museum reveals much of everyday life for Uzbekistan's literary elite in the 1940s.
The six rooms, which are in a building designed by the author's wife Z N Said-
Nasirova, are stuffed with photos, magazines, press cuttings and of course, Aibek's
books. Canvases by Aibek's artistic contemporaries line the walls, and the extensive
archives are actively used by modern academics.

Centre of National Arts [102 B4] (*Zarqaynar;* ✎ *150 4012;* ⏱ *10.00–18.00 Mon–
Sat*) One of the most vibrant collections of art in Tashkent, this modern gallery
showcases everything from textiles and sculpture to dance, graphic art and cinema.
Its purpose is to exhibit and promote the folk arts and culture of Uzbekistan, in
both their traditional and contemporary forms, and all your senses are catered for,
from sight, to sound, to taste. Continually changing exhibitions in the main hall
attract a young discerning crowd, as does the regular programme of fashion shows
and modern dance demonstrations. A number of artisans have their workshops on
site; it is possible to view and to buy their handmade carpets, miniature paintings,
wood carvings, gold thread embroidery, jewellery and pottery.

Chagatai Cemetery [92 B1] (*319 Farabi;* ⏱ *daylight hrs*) Little-visited by tourists
but offering a fascinating insight into both Muslim and Soviet funereal habits,
this large cemetery is stuffed with mausolea to the great and the good of Tashkent
society. Lack of space has historically necessitated the burying of bodies on top of
one another, but the numerous plaques commemorate those hidden below. Look
out for the surprisingly un-Islamic busts and engraved depictions of the deceased,
and particularly the leading figures of the Uzbek SSR. The poet Aibek (see box, page
104) is buried here, as is former president Rashidov, and you'll also find memorials
to lesser-known Uzbek heroes, such as Hero of Labour Turson Akhunova, the first
woman to drive a cotton-picking machine. Tragically, she died aged 46 from cancer
caused by the unregulated chemical fertilisers sprayed on the cotton fields.

Chorsu Bazaar See page 100.

Geology Museum [108 A2] (*1 Furkat;* ☉ *10.00–16.00 Mon–Fri; US$2*) Geology may not be the most fashionable of subjects, but we wouldn't be here without it. This unsophisticated museum explains the formation of the earth and our place in the solar system, and has a few tatty dinosaur displays. More importantly, however, it also has a large collection of precious stones and minerals from central Asia, and a set of the excellent Soviet geological survey maps produced to show the extent of the USSR's natural resources. It's popular with school groups during the week.

Hazrat Imam Complex [102 C3] (*Karasaray;* ☉ *09.00–13.00 & 14.00–16.00 Mon–Fri, 09.00–noon Sat*) North of Chorsu Bazaar is the historical spiritual heart of Tashkent, a glimpse of what much of the city must have been like before it was levelled by the 1966 earthquake or replaced with Soviet concrete. At its heart is **Hazrat Iman Square** (sometimes also written as Khast Imom Square), and, facing onto it, the **Hazrat Iman Mosque**, which was constructed in just four months in 2007 on the instruction of President Karimov. The largest mosque in the city, it was an expensive undertaking: the sandalwood columns came from India, the dark green marble is Turkish and the interior of the blue-tiled domes is decorated with genuine gold leaf.

Of the numerous sites surrounding the square, the most important is undoubtedly the **Muyi Muborak Library** (☉ *09.00–noon & 14.00–17.00 Mon–Fri, 10.00–15.00 Sat; US$1.50*). 'Muyi Muborak' means 'the sacred hair', a reference to a holy relic held here: a hair said to have belonged to the Prophet Muhammad. Amongst its rare manuscripts collection, the library also holds the world's oldest Qu'ran, produced just 19 years after the death of Muhammad. It is said to be stained with the blood of Caliph Uthman who was reading it at the time of his assassination in Medina in AD656, but in fact modern scientific analysis has shown

'AIBEK' MUSA TASHMUKHAMEDOV

'Aibek' was the pen name of Musa Tashmukhamedov (1905–68), a polymath born into a family of weavers in Tashkent. He took full advantage of the Soviet higher education system, graduating in turn from the Tashkent Teacher Training Course, Leningrad Economics Institute and then the Central Asian State University in Tashkent.

Aibek's literary career began in 1926 when he published *Emotions*, a collection of poetry about life in Soviet Uzbekistan. His subsequent poetic works included *Torch* (1932) and *Vendetta* (also 1932), both of which discuss the abandonment of the vestiges of traditional life. In the late 1930s, having completed his education, Aibek really began to establish himself as a writer. He published the remarkable *Sacred Blood* in 1943. It is recognised as one of the most outstanding works of social realism in Uzbek literature, and it describes the contribution of Uzbeks in WWI and their role in the 1916 uprisings. Also of note are Aibek's novels *Navoi* (1945) and *Khamsa* (1948) in which he gives fictionalised accounts of the inner feelings of the poets Alisher Navoi and Khamza Khakimzada Niyazi. Not only was Aibek a central figure in 20th-century Uzbek literature, but he was also a scientist, a translator and a publicist. He became a member of the Uzbek SSR's Academy of Scientists, and his translations of important Russian literary works, including writings by Pushkin, Gorky and Lermontov, are still widely read in Uzbekistan.

that the blood you see is of animal origin. This Qu'ran is one of four copies made shortly after the Caliph's death, and was brought to Uzbekistan by Amir Timur. It would have been displayed on special occasions on the vast stone Qu'ran stand in the centre of the Bibi Khanym Mosque in Samarkand (pages 159–60), which is still in situ. Today the Qu'ran is displayed in a glass-fronted display case, and although the text appears to be written on parchment, it is in fact on deerskin. Other highlights of the manuscript collection include Qu'rans from the 8th century onwards, illuminated pages, and modern Qu'rans in numerous foreign languages.

Next door to the library is the 16th-century **Barak-Khan Madrassa**, home to the Muslim Board of Uzbekistan until 2007. Unusually, this madrassa only ever had a single storey: it was built to educate local students from Tashkent and so there was no need to construct the accommodation cells that would have been situated on the first floor. Immediately opposite the madrassa is the **Tellya Sheikh Mosque**, formerly Tashkent's main place of worship. Built by Mirza Akhmed Kushbegi in 1856, the mosque is a peaceful place with some attractive carved pillars and painted ceilings, though notably less ornate than the Hazrat Iman Mosque (page 104) that has effectively replaced it.

On the western edge of the complex, no less visit-worthy, is the 19th-century **Al-Bukhari Institute** (once the Namozgoh Mosque), one of the few Islamic centres allowed to operate during the Soviet period. For much of the 20th century it was restricted in the scope of its work and limited to just 25 Imams; now there are more than 130 people studying here. Last but not least, the **Tomb of Kaffal Shashi** is a 16th-century shrine with a silver dome. It marks the final resting place of Abu Bakr Mohammed Kaffal Shashi, a local poet philosopher who died in the late 10th century. You can see his sarcophagus, and also the tombs of numerous later muftis. Pilgrims, in particular women hoping to conceive a child, still pray, donate alms and help with the cleaning and maintenance of the shrine in the hope that the saint will give them help.

Kulkedash Madrassa [102 B6] (*Chorsu Bazaar;* ⊕ *10.00–18.00 daily*) Tashkent's own Registan centres on the Kulkedash Madrassa, a 16th-century Islamic school built of mud bricks decorated with majolica and painted ceramic tiles. In the 18th century it was converted first into a caravanserai for merchants trading at the nearby bazaar, then into a fortress. Finally, it was used as the setting for public executions: women in particular were stoned to death with rocks hurled from the parapet of the central portal. Earthquakes in 1866 significantly damaged the structure, and it sadly lay in ruins until it was restored in the mid 20th century.

The towering archway that marks the entrance to the madrassa is decorated with stars; the lancet niche above the doors serves to emphasise its height. Once inside, follow the corridor through to the central courtyard, looking out for the *darskhona* (lecture hall) on the left as you pass by. The cells around the yard once housed the madrassa's students; their modern counterparts study in more comfortable, though less picturesque, surroundings.

Museum of Communications History [102 D6] (*28A Navoi;* ℡ *244 9909; www.aloqamuzeyi.uz;* ⊕ *10.00—17.00 daily*) A relatively new, free museum, this was built by the Uzbek Agency for Communication and Information to explain the history of communication from the Middle Ages to the present day. The postal service exhibition includes a historic mail wagon, models of the Timurid fortresses and their fire-signalling techniques, and you can make short-range phone calls on the antique telephones. Soviet era technology – computers, televisions, record players, etc, – is inevitably particularly well represented, and is a really fascinating way to look back at the past. Few of the exhibits are labelled but there are guides on hand who are keen to practise their English. For a taste of what is on offer, check out the virtual tour on the museum's website.

Natural History Museum [102 C4] (*1 A Niyazov;* `246 9531; *www.tabiatmuzey. skm.uz;* ☺ *10.00–17.00 Tue–Sun; US$2*) Tashkent's own dead zoo is home to more than 400,000 exhibits, amongst which are numerous stuffed birds and animals and their skeletons. The museum was founded in 1876 and includes what is probably the world's largest collection of central Asian flora and fauna, albeit in a sadly preserved state.

The museum is of interest to two types of people: serious naturalists who can look beyond the dust and fake blood-dripping plastic dinosaurs and appreciate the diversity of the region's wildlife, including many species now extinct; and those intrigued by the Soviet Union at large and its admirable attempts to educate the masses. The vast dioramas, including scenes of dinosaurs, mammoths and early man, provide an easy (if not always chronologically or anatomically accurate) introduction to pre-history for children.

Sheikhantaur Mausoleum Complex [108 C2] (*State Islamic University, Navoi*) Just three mausoleums remain here in what was once a necropolis of 16 tombs – the others fell prey to earthquakes and short-sighted Soviet planning.

The largest of the tombs is that of **Yunus Khan**, descendant of Genghis Khan, grandfather of Babur, and one-time ruler of Tashkent. Although you cannot go inside (it's almost always locked), it's still possible to appreciate the fine lancet arch of the portal, the turquoise dome and the Arabic calligraphy that decorates the façades. The tile work was restored in the 1970s.

Sheikhantaur's Mausoleum is the small, brick-built structure with dark blue majolica tiles and metal dome. Sheikhantaur (or, to use his real name, Sheikh Khovandi Tahur) was a local Sufi saint born in the late 13th century believed to be a descendant of the Rashidun Caliph Umar. As a child he was initiated into the Yasaviyya order of St Khodja Ahmed Yassaui and he was known in Tashkent as a spiritual guide. He died in Tashkent around 1360; his tomb is contemporary, though heavily restored.

The final site here is the **Kaldirach Bey Mausoleum**, a 15th-century ruler of Moghulistan. His tomb is particularly unusual because its turquoise roof is dodecahedral (12-sided) on the outside but domed on the inside. The *gurkhan* (burial room) has beautiful carved wooden doors and deep alcoves decorated with stalactite-like carving.

Tashkent Planetarium [102 C5] (*6 Zarqaynar;* `244 7720; ☺ *09.00–17.00 daily; US$2*) Close to Chorsu Bazaar, the planetarium combines exhibition halls with a 60-seat auditorium, with projectors showing the movement of the planets, meteors, comets, black holes and other fabulous things.

Founded relatively late, only in 2003, the planetarium has an admirable dual remit of entertainment and the promotion of astronomy, and so on weekdays you will most likely be surrounded by groups of school children. The building's design – a cube overlapped with a dome – is supposed to represent the earth beneath the heavens, and the exhibits are regularly updated to reflect the latest astronomic discoveries. The discovery of a new, minor planet named Samarkand in 2008, of course, caused particular excitement for Uzbekistan's astronomers.

Ural Tansykbaev Museum [93 H2] (*5 Cherdantsev;* ✆ *162 6230;* ◷ *10.00–18.00 Tue–Sun*) Central to this house museum is the easel of the USSR's People's Artist Ural Tansykbaev, with his final, unfinished work still stretched across it. The museum includes his studio, living quarters and small garden, as well as a purpose-built gallery displaying the work of contemporary Uzbek artists. Tansykbaev's own paintings, dating from the 1920s until his death in 1974, are also on view; his moody blue landscapes, including a depiction of men hauling in their nets on the shore of the then fish-filled Aral Sea, are also on show.

Around Amir Timur and Independence squares
Central to the modern city, Amir Timur Square is a lush, green space with plenty of flowers and fountains. Roads radiate from here to the north, east and south of Tashkent, and the city's most important buildings, both political and cultural, are concentrated on the square and in the immediate vicinity. A large statue of Timur himself (see box, page 14), sitting astride his horse and proclaiming 'strength is in justice', is the square's current centrepiece, but he is simply the latest in a long line of former residents: General Kaufmann, Josef Stalin and Karl Marx have all occupied this spot before him. This particular statue of Timur, a 7m high bronze weighing in at 30 tonnes, is the work of sculptor Jabarov and is one of three erected in Uzbekistan to commemorate the 660th anniversary of Timur's birth.

Independence Square (*Mustakillik Maydon*) covers 7ha and is the largest square in Tashkent. It is packed with monuments and fountains, including a particularly impressive one with 500 water jets. First the site of a fortress in the mid 19th century, it later became a parade ground for the military and for workers' processions on national holidays. The most important monument here is the golden globe on a pedestal, and beneath it a mother with a child in her arms. Erected in 1992, the monument marks Uzbek independence. Look out also for the World War II memorial fronted by an eternal flame and engraved with the names of the 400,000 Uzbek soldiers who died, and the giant, gold-coloured globe showing Uzbekistan's place in the world.

Earthquake Memorial [108 D1] (*Sharof Rashidov, near Museum of Olympic Glory*) This dramatic memorial, also known as the Monument to Courage, is dedicated to the men and women who rebuilt their flattened city following the earthquake of 1966 (see box, page 111). The monument was erected in 1976 to mark the tenth anniversary of the disaster, and it is in several parts: the broken labradorite cube bears the date on one side and clock-face showing the time of the earthquake (05.23) on the other. The zigzag crack through the cube directs the eye to the bronze sculpture alongside: a father protecting his wife and child from danger. The unusual shape of the statue's plinth is supposed to symbolise the earthquake's destruction, and the surrounding stelae remember those who rebuilt the city in the following months and years: the military, architects, builders and, of course, the ordinary people of Tashkent.

House of Photography [109 E4] (*4 Istikbol;* ✆ *233 5168;* ◷ *10.00–16.00 Mon–Sat; US$0.50*) This striking, unexpectedly light display space inside a 1930s building showcases exhibitions from internationally known photographers and is affiliated to the Academy of Arts. Though many of the photographers are Uzbek or have links with Uzbekistan, this is not always the case. The museum also arranges photography competitions, conferences and workshops. It is a good place to get in touch with Tashkent's artistic community.

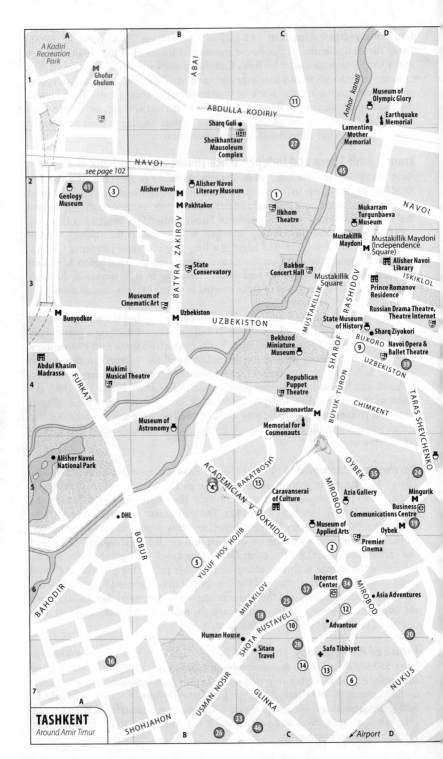

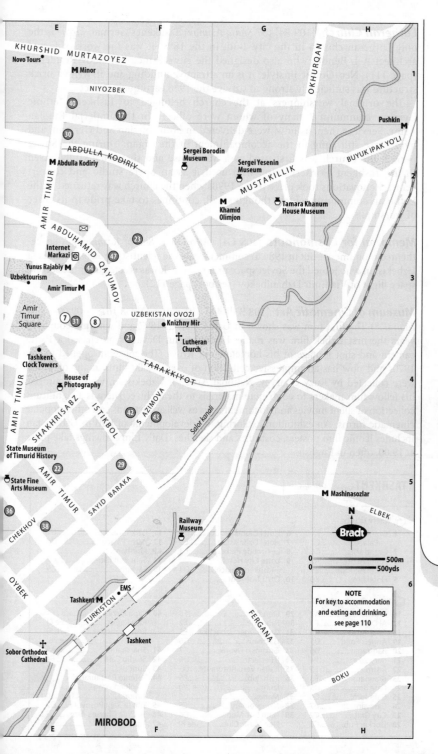

KHURSHID MURTAZOYEZ

Novo Tours

Ⓜ Minor

NIYOZBEK

40

17

30

Ⓜ Abdulla Kodiriy

ABDULLA KODIRIY

Sergei Borodin
Museum

Sergei Yesenin
Museum

OKHURQAN

Pushkin Ⓜ

BUYUK IPAK YO'LI

MUSTAKILLIK

Ⓜ
Khamid
Olimjon

Tamara Khanum
House Museum

AMIR TIMUR

Internet
Markazi ✉

ABDUHAMID QAYUMOV

23

47

Yunus Rajabiy Ⓜ

44

Uzbektourism

Amir Timur Ⓜ

Amir
Timur
Square

7 31

8

UZBEKISTAN OVOZI

Knizhny Mir

21

† Lutheran
Church

Tashkent
Clock Towers

House of
Photography

TARAKKIYOT

AMIR TIMUR

SHAKHRISABZ

ISTIKBOL

42

43

S. AZIMOVA

Solar kanali

State Museum
of Timurid History

22

29

AMIR TIMUR

SAYID BARAKA

State Fine
Arts Museum

36

38

CHEKHOV

Railway
Museum

Ⓜ Mashinasozlar

ELBEK

N

Bradt

0   500m
0   500yds

OYBEK

32

Tashkent Ⓜ EMS

TURKISTON

Tashkent

FERGANA

NOTE
For key to accommodation
and eating and drinking,
see page 110

† Sobor Orthodox
Cathedral

BOKU

MIROBOD

Tashkent and Environs   TASHKENT

3

Lutheran Church [109 F4] (37 *Sadiq Asimov*) Tashkent's German *kirche* is the only Lutheran church in the city. Built in the 1899, it was the work of famed architect A L Benoit, who also designed the city's Prince Romanov Residence (page 111). Neo-Gothic in style, it is an attractive building and its yellow-brick structure was sufficiently strong to survive the 1966 earthquake intact.

The original worshippers at the church belonged to Tashkent's ethnic German community, many of whom were officers in the Imperial Russian Army. Services then, as now, were delivered in both Russian and German, and hymns are still sung to the accompaniment of the organ. During the Soviet period, the church was first used as a warehouse and then, thankfully, given to the Tashkent Conservatoire, who used it as an opera studio and concert venue. Renovations took place in the 1990s when the church was returned to the Lutheran community which, though small, continues to take pride in its place of worship.

Memorial for Cosmonauts [108 C4] (*Afrosiab & Sharof Rashidov*) A space-themed monument built in 1984 to commemorate the scientists and cosmonauts of Uzbekistan who joined the Soviet space programme. It was erected after the second space flight of Vladimir Dzhanibekov (see box, page 112).

Museum of Cinematic Art [108 B3] (*49A Uzbekistan;* \458 161; ⏲ 09.00–18.00 *Mon–Fri*) The first film was shown in Uzbekistan in 1897 and within a couple of years the first Uzbek film was made: Hudoybergan Devanev purchased a Pathe camera and shot footage of his hometown of Khiva. The museum opened in the 1970s and now has an impressive collection of over 40,000 films, many of which were collected by Ruzy Charyev, National Artist of Uzbekistan, who encouraged his fellow film makers to contribute materials to the archive. There is a significant collection of silent movies and documentaries, as well as cartoons and other popular cinematic forms. An exhibition exploring the developments of film in Uzbekistan includes iconic film posters, costumes and sketches. Daily film showings take place at 19.00, often in English.

TASHKENT *around Amir Timur*
For listings, see pages 94–9

🛏 **Where to stay**

1 Domina Shodlik Palace.................. C2	6 Hotel Grand Raddus........D7	11 Park Turo...............................C1
2 Grand Mir.............. C6	7 Hotel Uzbekistan................E3	12 Retro Palace........................ D6
3 Hotel Al Hosilot.....A2	8 Le Grande Plaza.................E3	13 Rovshan................................C7
4 Hotel Ali-Tour......... B5	9 Lotte City Hotel Tashkent Palace.............. D4	14 Sam-Buh Elite.....................C7
5 Hotel Bek.................B6	10 Orzu Tashkent.....................C6	15 Sayram................................. C5

❌ **Where to eat and drink**

16 Affresco...................A7	29 Efendi............................... F5	40 Papa Pizza............................E1
17 Al Delfin....................F1	30 Fabrique............................. E2	Raaj Kapur.................. (see 8)
18 Amaretto................. C6	31 Gamburger Uzbechka......E3	Restaurant Bek........... (see 5)
19 Angels Food...........D5	32 Gasthaus..............................G6	Sato............................. (see 26)
20 Bagizagan...............D6	33 Gruzinski Dvorik...............C7	41 Sharshara.............................A2
21 Beryozka.................. F4	34 Il Perfecto..........................D6	42 Studio Café......................... F4
22 Bistro.........................E5	35 Italian Vero Ristorante.... D5	43 Sunduk................................ F4
23 Brauhaus.................F3	36 Irish Pub..............................E5	44 Torento Restaurant/
24 Cafe Bon..................D5	Izumi.............................(see 26)	Golden Wing....................E3
25 Café Jum..................C6	37 Manas.................................. C6	Timur...........................(see 23)
26 Caravan................... B7	38 Montgomery...................... E5	45 Traktir Sam Prishyol...........D2
27 City Grill................... C2	39 Nam Dae Mun.....................D4	46 Ye Olde Chelsea Arms......C7
28 Docker Pub.............C7	Neo Music Club..........(see 8)	47 Yolki-Palki...........................F3

At 05.23 on 26 April 1966, Tashkent's skyline changed forever. An earthquake measuring 7.5 on the Richter scale ripped through the city as residents slept. Remarkably, only ten people were killed, but the quake damaged an estimated 70% of all buildings in the city. More than 28,000 were flattened completely, and 100,000 people were left homeless. The old city was worst hit due to the number of traditional, adobe brick-built structures and their close proximity to one another.

In the aftermath of the earthquake, Tashkent became a blank canvas for the Soviet Union's leading urban planners: they envisaged a model Soviet city with wide, tree-lined boulevards, public squares for parades, and hundreds of apartment blocks with workshops, canteens and nurseries where the city's populace could live, work and play together. By 1970, an estimated 100,000 new homes had already been constructed, and further areas of the city continued to be cleared to implement the planners' grand new designs. This era of building contributed the heart of today's city.

Museum of Olympic Glory [108 D1] (*4A Sharof Rashidov;* \ *244 7602;* ⊕ *09.00–17.00 Mon–Sat*) Opened by President Karimov and the then president of the International Olympic Committee, Juan Antonio Samaranch, the museum holds a predictable collection of photographs, medals and trophies from international competitions.

Prince Romanov Residence [108 D3] (*Cnr Sharof Rashidov & Sayilgokh*) Built by Grand Duke Nikolai Konstantinovich Romanov (see box, page 113) in 1891, this private residence has gone through a number of different incarnations, being used in turn to accommodate the Museum of Art, National Palace of Young Pioneers (a Boy Scout-type organisation established by Lenin) and the Museum of Uzbek Jewellery. The palace is currently used by the Ministry of Foreign Affairs for official receptions. Though it is not currently possible for the public to go inside, the building, designed by architect William Solomonovich Geyntselman, is an attractive structure with rose windows, turrets and life-size sculptures of guard dogs. It is surprisingly small in size, but set among pleasant gardens just back from the street.

State Fine Arts Museum [109 E5] (*16 Amir Timur;* \ *136 7436;* ⊕ *10.00–17.00 Wed–Sun, 10.00–14.00 Mon; local/foreigner 3,000/10,000 som*) One of the largest museums in central Asia, the current buildings opened in 1974 to house an extensive collection of paintings, ceramics and other artefacts, the core of which were confiscated from Grand Duke Romanov (see box, page 113) in 1918 and once displayed in his former home (see above), functioning as the Museum of Art.

Some 50,000 paintings and artefacts are held now at the museum, originating not only from Uzbekistan and Russia but also from Europe. Uzbek art dominates the ground and first floors: the earliest pieces, which include sculptures, ceramics and murals, date back to the 1st century BC and are remarkably well preserved. Look here for 9th-century ceramics; tiles from Samarkand, Bukhara and Shakhrisabz; Bukharan court robes weighed down with decadent gold embroidery; and finely carved wooden shutters and doors.

European art works are displayed on the second floor, and the exhibition includes pieces from Prince Romanov's original collection as well as some remarkable

Unlike neighbouring Kazakhstan, Uzbekistan is less immediately associated with the space race. One man has, however, helped to put Uzbekistan on the map: Vladimir Dzhanibekov.

Born Vladimir Krysin in 1942, Dzhanibekov's family moved to Tashkent from Iskandar when he was a child. He briefly studied physics at Leningrad University before deciding his real passion was for flying and he enrolled at the V M Komarov Higher Military Flying School in Yeisk. On graduation, having also taken a course in radio engineering at Taganrog State University, Dzhanibekov became a flying instructor in the Soviet air force and joined the Communist Party. It was to do his career no harm.

Dzhanibekov was selected for cosmonaut training in 1970. Over the next 15 years he was to make five space flights, spending a total of 145 days in space. His missions were to the Salyut 6 and Salyut 7 space stations, and included two space walks.

Dzhanibekov became a Soviet celebrity: he was twice Hero of the Soviet Union, five times recipient of the Order of Lenin, and received both the Order of the Red Star and an additional Medal for Merit in Space Exploration. Foreign recognition included becoming a Commander of the Legion of Honour in France, and receiving honorary citizenship of Russia, Kazakhstan and Houston, Texas.

On retiring from space travel, Dzhanibekov entered politics in Uzbekistan and became interested in hot air ballooning. Sadly his ballooning exploits were about as successful as Richard Branson's, and his round-the-world attempt in 1993 lasted just 30 minutes. He survived the ordeal and now occupies himself making paintings about space, keeping his feet firmly on the ground.

medieval Russian icons from Novgorod. Though they are not to everyone's taste, admittedly, and neither are the 20th century Russian landscapes chosen for their lack of controversy, the standard of exhibits is generally high and whether you have a preference for Russian portraits in oils, Chinese scrolls or Uzbek art from the early Soviet period, there will undoubtedly be something that catches your eye.

If you have time at the end of your visit, step out behind the museum into the **Fidoliyar Garden**. Initially laid out in the 1880s, it became the burial place (and de facto memorial to) Bolshevik fighters who died in street fighting in Tashkent in 1917 and the 14 Turkestan Commissars betrayed by Ossipov in 1919. Yuldush Akhunbabaev (1885–1943), the first Chairman of the Uzbek SSR, and Sabir Rakhimov, the first general of the Uzbek SSR, are also buried here.

State Museum of History [108 D3] (*3 Sharof Rashidov;* \239 1083; *www.history-museum.uz;* ⏱ *10.00–17.00 Tue–Sun; US$3.50*). The State Museum of History has had two lives. The building, first opened in 1970, the centenary of Lenin's birth, was a memorial to the Soviet Union's first leader and a means of expounding the Lenin cult far beyond Russia's borders. Amongst the Communist propaganda, copies of the blood-stained clothing he wore when he survived an assassination attempt in 1920 were some of the more gory artefacts on display.

Independent Uzbekistan has done away with Lenin and, to some extent, his memory. The 250,000-plus exhibits now housed here have been relocated from the Aibek Museum (now closed). The collection, which began as Uzbekistan's first public museum in 1876, includes some 60,000 archaeological finds, 80,000 coins and 35,000 remarkable negatives, black-and-white photos and reports from early archaeological digs. It is the largest repository of historical artefacts in central Asia.

The museum's main floor displays ancient history, from skeletal human remains uncovered in the Selangor grotto thought to be 1.5 million years old, to a 4th-century BC bronze cauldron carved with writhing animals. Uzbekistan's only complete Buddha figure (1st to 2nd century AD), from Surkhandarya in eastern Uzbekistan where ancient Silk Road monasteries flourished, is here. The exhibits are arranged more or less in chronological order, with plenty of information boards, maps, models and graphics to help you understand what you are looking at.

Don't miss the Sarmishay rock carvings in the first room you enter: the ibex petroglyphs found in the Fergana Valley date from around 5,000BC. There are models of key items from the Oxus Treasure (the originals of which are in the British Museum), and there is an excellent display on Khorezm (6th–4th centuries BC), which includes statuary, fresco fragments, cooking vessels, ossuaries and architects' models of the fortresses.

A small gift shop on the ground floor sells the usual selection of souvenirs as well as a few books in English. Guided tours (*US$3*) are available in English and are the best way to understand the collection and ensure you don't miss the highlights. If you want to take photos in the museum, you will need to buy a photo permit (*US$7*) from the cashier at the same time as getting your entrance ticket.

State Museum of Timurid History [109 D4] (*1 Amir Timur;* ╲ *232 0212;* ⏰ *10.00–17.00 Tue–Sun; US$1.50*) One of Tashkent's more iconic buildings, the Amir Timur Museum with its turquoise dome and crenulated roofline is undoubtedly an attractive, if slightly out of place, addition to the city's skyline. Inside is a succession of beautifully painted displays about the history of central Asia, in particular the Timurid period (pages 14–15). Exhibits include copies of historical documents and illustrated manuscripts, weapons, jewellery and astronomical instruments, some of which are purportedly linked to Timur himself and to Babur, the central

THE EXILE OF GRAND DUKE ROMANOV

Cousin of Tsar Nicholas II and grandson of Nicholas I, Nikolai Konstantinovich Romanov was born in St Petersburg in February 1850, the first son of Grand Duke Konstantin and Grand Duchess Alexandra. He had a successful military career but was an infamous womaniser and allegedly stole three of his mother's diamonds to give to his American lover, Fanny Lear. When the theft was discovered, Nikolai was declared insane and banished in perpetuity to Turkestan.

Nikolai put his time in Tashkent to good use, building two large canals (the Bukhar-aryk and the Khiva-aryk) to irrigate lands between Tashkent and Dzhizak. He ordered the construction of his own palace in 1890 in part to showcase his vast art collection, which now forms the core of the collection at the State Fine Arts Museum (pages 111–12).

Nikolai died in 1917, though sources disagree as to whether pneumonia or Bolshevik bullets caused his demise. He was buried in St George's Cathedral (now demolished) and was survived by his wife, two sons, and at least six illegitimate children.

Mir 'Alī Shīr Navā'ī (Russified as Alisher Navoi) was born in Herat (now in Afghanistan) on 9 February 1441. He was a politician, mystic, linguist, painter and poet, and is considered by many to be the founder of Uzbek literature.

Herat was an important city in the Timurid Empire, and a cultural and intellectual centre. Navoi was born into the city's political elite, and so he had access both to education and to patronage. His father was one-time governor of Sabzawar, and when he died the ruler of Khorasan became the guardian of the young Navoi. Navoi studied in Herat, Mashhad (now in Iran) and Samarkand, returning to Herat to work at the court when his childhood friend Husayn Bayqarah seized power there in 1468.

Navoi was a fearsome administrator and keen builder, endowing and constructing 370 mosques, madrassas, libraries and caravanserais in Khorasan and managing the running of 40 caravanserais, 20 pools, 17 mosques, ten mansions, nine bathhouses and nine bridges in Herat. When time allowed, he was patron of scholarship and the arts, a composer, calligrapher, painter and sculptor, and wrote such impressive literature that the English historian Bernard Lewis declared him to be 'the Chaucer of the Turks'.

In the course of 30 years, Navoi produced 30 literary works. Most of these were in Chagatai Turkish, though he also wrote in Persian (under the pen name Fāni), Arabic and Hindi. Navoi produced four collections of poetry amounting to some 50,000 verses, each collection corresponding to a different phase in a man's life: *Ghara'ib al-Sighar* (Wonders of Childhood), *Navadir al-Shabab* (Rarities or Witticisms of Youth), *Bada'i' al-Wasat* (Marvels of Middle Age), and *Fawa'id al-Kibar* (Advantages of Old Age). His other important works include *Khamsa*, a collection of five epic poems that includes the famous love story of Layla and Majnun, a comparison of the Turkic and Persian languages, and an exploration of his views on religion and Sufism.

Navoi never married or had children, and he remained in the service of Husayn Bayqarah until his death in 1501. He was buried in Herat but is commemorated across Uzbekistan with statues and street names. The Alisher Navoi Opera and Ballet Theatre in Tashkent is also named in his honour.

Asia-born first emperor of Mughal India. The museum also features an exhibition on Uzbekistan's modern leader, President Karimov (see box, page 21), who appears to deftly align himself with the great rulers of Uzbekistan's past.

Tashkent Clock Towers [109 E4] (*Amir Timur Sq*; ⊕ *09.00–16.00 daily*) Built more than 50 years apart, these twin clock towers on Amir Timur Square have fast become Tashkent icons. The first tower was constructed in 1947 to house the clock mechanism from the City Hall in Allenstein in East Prussia, a war trophy brought back to Tashkent by watchmaker Ayzenshteyn.

The architectural design was chosen from competition entries and the 30m tower now displays an ethnographic collection of traditional Uzbek textiles (including embroidery), woodcarving and ceramics. The external decoration was done by Usto Shirin Muradov, a famous Uzbek ganch carver.

The second tower, completed in 2009, contains a showroom exhibiting antique and modern jewellery made by Uzbekistan's master craftsmen.

Lamenting Mother Memorial [108 D1] (*Independence Sq;* ⊕ *09.00–18.00 daily*) Inside a quiet garden, this memorial remembers soldiers who gave their lives for peace and the mothers they left behind. The names of the deceased are inscribed on granite walls of the Alley of Memory, at the centre of which is the Eternal Flame and the Lamenting Mother statue. The monument is accompanied by busts of two war heroes, Viktor Malyasov and Jurakhon Usmanov.

Alisher Navoi Library [108 D3] (*1 Independence Sq; www.natlib.uz;* ⊕ *08.00–20.00 Mon–Fri, 08.00–17.00 Sat–Sun*) The National Library of Uzbekistan, named in honour of the 15th-century polymath Alisher Navoi (see box, page 114), is a sprawling modern building that opened at the end of 2011. Dating back to 1870, the core of the collection includes books and manuscripts originally belonging to General Kaufman. The rare books department has a vast number of pre-revolutionary Turkic-language newspapers, and separate catalogues list Uzbek and Russian sources, materials in Kyrgyz Kazakh and Soviet-era journals relating to Uzbekistan. Though not of such great interest to general visitors due to the language barriers involved, it is nonetheless an invaluable resource for research, and many of the items are visually appealing whether you can read them or not.

Mukarram Turgunbaeva Museum [108 D2] (*5 Independence Sq;* ☎ *139 1296;* ⊕ *09.30–17.00 Mon–Sat*) One of the best-presented small museums in Uzbekistan, this collection showcases the life of Mukarram Turgunbaeva, one of the country's most famous dancers and the founder and director of the Bahor folk dance ensemble. Focused on dance in the late 1920s and 1930s, exhibits include elaborate and beautifully displayed dance costumes, performance posters and memorabilia. There is also an extensive archive of Uzbek folk song and music recordings. Fascinating and highly recommended.

In and around Alisher Navoi Park [108 A5] This celebrated and rather attractive park, located to the west of Tashkent's city centre, is a much-needed green space in the over-crowded capital city. Manmade lakes, canals and fountains, cafés and ornamental gardens seem to cool the air in the sweaty summer months, and they make it a pleasant place to relax or picnic if you have an hour or two to spare. With the **Navruz Wedding Palace**, the **Istiqlol Concert Hall** and the **Parliament of Uzbekistan** (pages 19–20) all within the confines of the park, there are plenty of opportunities for people-watching.

Abdul Khasim Madrassa [108 A4] (*Alisher Navoi Park;* ⊕ *10.00–16.00 daily*) Although medieval in style, this madrassa in fact dates from the early 19th century. It was famously the location of the signing of the peace treaty following the capture of Tashkent by the Russian general Chernyaev in 1865, and from 1919 to 1974 it was home to more than 70 Russian families who had fled from famine in Samara.

The madrassa was restored to its former glory in 1987 and today each of its cells houses workshops for Tashkent's artists and craftsmen. More than 30 artisans work here producing fine jewellery, paintings, ceramics and prints. It is possible (and recommended) to buy souvenirs straight from these producers.

Bekhzod Miniature Museum [108 C4] (*K Bekhzod Memorial Park;* ⊕ *10.00–18.00 Tue–Sat; US$2*) The Bekhzod Miniature Museum and accompanying Memorial Park were opened in 2002 to commemorate Kamoliddin Bekhzod's work and to popularise the art of miniature painting. More commonly known as Bihzad, this 16th-century, Herati-born artist is to Persian miniatures what Constable is to English landscapes or Da Vinci is to anatomical drawing. He is, quite simply, the master, and his original paintings (or at least those attributed to him, as it was rare for miniaturists to sign their work) are prized pieces in national collections from New York and London to Tehran.

The museum holds nearly 100,000 illustrated manuscripts, though sadly few are the work of the master himself. Around 500 items are on show at any one time, and they include printed books and lithographs as well as miniatures and manuscripts. Displays change frequently.

Museum of Astronomy [108 B4] (*33 Astronomicheskaya*; ⊕ *10.00–18.00 Tue–Sun; US$2*) The year 2009 was the UN's International Year of Astronomy and also the 615th anniversary of the astronomer and emperor Ulug Beg's birth (see box, page 164). Tashkent marked the event with the opening of this new museum, supported by UNESCO. Exhibitions chart the development of astronomy from ancient times through medieval discoveries to the present. The most interesting artefacts are the huge number of telescopes and quadrants, and, for those unable to make it to Samarkand, a scale model of the meridian quadrant once used in Ulug Beg's Observatory. Though not on the standard tourist itinerary, the museum is well worth a visit.

Sergei Yesenin Museum [93 H5] (*20 Tolstoy*; \ *237 1179*; e *esenin@mail.tps. uz*; ⊕ *09.00–17.00 Mon–Sat*) House museum of Russian lyrical poet Sergei Yesenin (1895–1925), who visited Tashkent and stayed here for a month in May 1921. The current exhibition, which opened in 1999, contains 3,000 manuscripts, photographs and autographs, along with furniture typical of a Tashkent home in the 1920s. It often hosts poetry recitals. Free guided tours are available in Russian.

Yesenin himself was an interesting character. Born to a peasant family in Konstaninovo, he began writing poetry at the age of nine. Having studied first in Moscow and then moved to St Petersburg, he became well-known in Russian literary circles. He published *Ritual for the Dead* in 1916 before being drafted to fight in World War I. Initially a supporter of the Bolshevik Revolution, he quickly became disillusioned, and some of his subsequent poems, including *The Stern October Has Deceived Me*, were openly critical of the new regime. Although initially celebrated, his works were later banned by the Kremlin. Only in 1966 were his poems re-published.

Yesenin was a hit with the ladies, and married four times during his short life. He was a tormented soul, however, and though he continued to write, he suffered from alcoholism and mental illness. Following a month's hospitalisation, he cut his wrist, wrote a farewell suicide poem in his own blood, and hanged himself from the heating pipes in his hotel room. He was just 30 years old.

Parliament of Uzbekistan [92 C4] (*Alisher Navoi Park*) Constructed with Bukharan granite and marble from Samarkand, capped with a turquoise dome, and decorated with a 10m-high, 4.5-tonne chandelier of crystal and gold in the central hall, Uzbekistan's parliament building is designed to impress. Uzbek nationals can gain access to the ground floors of the building; foreigners must be content viewing the ostentatious structure from outside.

North Tashkent
Hidden in suburbia to the north of the city centre are a few sites that may be of interest to those with a little more time to spend in Tashkent.

Aqua Park [93 E1] (*107 Amir Timur;* ✆ *238 5625; www.uzexpocentre.uz;* ⊕ *May–Sep 09.00–20.00; adult/child 20,000/10,000 som*) Inevitably popular with Tashkent's youth, this large water park has numerous flumes, wave pools and other watery attractions, ideal for cooling down during the heat of the summer. Tickets are valid for 3 hours and adults can either get wet with the kids or chill out in the cafés and jacuzzi.

Botanical Garden [93 G1] (*232 Bog'ishamol;* ✆ *289 1060; www.academy.uz;* ⊕ *10.00–17.00 daily; US$0.50*) Belonging to the Academy of Sciences, the botanical garden was founded in 1920 and now covers 66ha in the northeastern part of the city. The extensive arboretum has more than 4,500 species of plant, divided into five geographical zones within the park: central Asia, Europe, the Americas, south Asia and the Far East. Medicinal tropical plants are housed in a number of hot houses and specialist nurseries.

Though attractive year round, the garden really comes into its own in autumn when the heat of summer days has subsided and the trees are sliding from green into every shade of red, orange and gold. Inquisitive squirrels, some nearly tame, raid picnics and dart back and forth across the gravel paths while the garden's guides introduce visitors to the more important specimens in the botanical collection.

Tashkent Zoo (⊕ *08.00–17.00 Tue–Sun; US$1.50*), the oldest scientific zoo in central Asia, is situated in the south of the garden. It covers 22ha of the site. There are more than 300 species of animal, including bears, gorillas and giraffe, and an aquarium houses freshwater and marine creatures. Children will enjoy watching feeding time, which takes places in different enclosures throughout the day.

Museum of the Victims of Repression [93 F1] (*Martyrs Memorial Sq;* ⊕ *10.00–17.00 Tue–Sun*) This harrowing museum close to the TV Tower opened in 2002 and focuses on the violent Soviet repression of the Uzbek people, starting with the clamp-downs of the Tsar in the late 19th century and the elimination of the Basmachi uprising after the 1917 Revolution (page 16), through Stalin's purges to ethnic cleansing and the gulags. Even recent history – the cotton trials of the 1980s – is represented. Exhibits include moquettes of the gulags and prisons, a prison van, photos, documents and personal belongings of those who were imprisoned or killed. Though the curators are inevitably espousing a very specific message, the displays are informative and help to flesh out understanding of what was, until very recently, a particularly secretive aspect of life in Uzbekistan. The archives are widely used by academics, and the building in which the collection is housed is an attractive affair that incorporates various aspects of traditional Uzbek design.

Tamara Khanum House Museum [109 G2] (*1/41 Tamara Khanum;* ✆ *267 8690;* ⊕ *10.00–16.00 Mon–Sat*) Located just off Mustakillik is the house museum of actress and dancer Tamara Khanum (1906–91), an ethnic Armenian born in the Fergana Valley who was the first woman in Uzbekistan to perform publicly with her face uncovered. Awarded the title of 'People's Artist of the USSR', she toured internationally in the 1940s and 50s, winning fans as far away as Norway and China. Small but lovingly curated, the museum contains 70 or so ballet and folk dance costumes, around 30 of which are on display at any time, as well as photographs, letters and gifts received by Khanum herself.

TV Tower [93 F1] (*Amir Timur;* ⊕ *10.00–17.00 daily*) Rising 375m above the city, Tashkent's TV Tower is the tallest structure in central Asia. It took six years to complete, starting in 1979, and was, until 1991, the third-highest tower in the world. The architects responsible, D Semashko and N Terziev-Tzarukova, were tasked with coming up with a design capable of withstanding earthquakes up to 9.0 on the Richter scale, and their solution was the lattice-style trunk supported by three inclined slips.

Entering the TV Tower's lobby, you'll see the slightly incongruous Romanesque mosaic created by artist A Buharbaev. The three high-speed elevators will take you to the top of the tower at a rate of 4m per second; you can step off at one of the revolving restaurants or at the observation deck. Situated 97m up, it has predictably impressive views in all directions. On occasions it is also possible to visit the metereological station in the upper reaches of the tower; ask in the lobby if you're interested.

If heights aren't your thing and you prefer to keep your feet on the ground, the TV Tower is floodlit at night, making for memorable photographs.

UzExpo Centre [93 E1] (*107 Amir Timur; www.uzexpocentre.uz*) Uzbekistan's main exhibition centre hosts a revolving schedule of trade fairs, most of them linked to the energy and chemical sectors. Forthcoming fairs are listed on the centre's website. In the same complex you will also find the Aqua Park (page 117) and the Japanese Garden Teahouse (page 98).

The **Japanese Garden** (⊕ *09.00–21.00 daily; entrance fee 20,000 som*) is a small but tranquil space, popularly used as the backdrop for wedding photos. Though not authentically Japanese in its design, it is charming nevertheless, with a wooden bridge across the water, lotus flowers in the pond, and carved granite lanterns along the walkways. Storks, ducks and peacocks roam freely. Cultural events are occasionally hosted in the garden, and the events calendar is listed on the UzExpo website.

Sergei Borodin Museum [109 F2] (*18 Lashkarbegi*; ☏ *133 0932*; ⊕ *10.00–17.00 Wed–Mon*) Northeast of Tashkent's ring road is the house museum of Sergei Borodin (1902–74), a Tashkent-born writer of fiction. His most famous novels, *Dmitriy Donskoi* and *Stars over Samarkand*, brought him Soviet prizes and a degree of international fame. Museum displays chart his life and work through photographs, manuscripts and personal effects, the most important of which are the autographed books given to him by contemporaries including Maxim Gorky and Boris Pasternak. There is also an extensive numismatic collection in which every coin has been lovingly described.

South Tashkent
South of the city centre, a little removed from the political and commercial heartland, are a variety of attractions for culture vultures and, appropriately situated next to the train station, the Railway Museum.

Azia Gallery [108 D5] (*25 Kunaeva; www.aziagallery.com*; ⊕ *11.00–18.00 Mon–Fri, 12.00–17.00 Sat*) This private gallery in a barn-like structure has regular exhibitions of contemporary art and design, and looks to promote the work of Uzbek artists abroad.

Caravanserai of Culture [108 C5] (*37A Yusuf Hos Hojib; www.caravanserai. uz*; ⊕ *09.00–18.00 daily*) Dedicated to the cultures of the Silk Road, this modern caravanserai (decorated, somewhat incongruously, with a miniature pagoda) and the surrounding Garden of Friendship host a succession of exhibitions, a permanent collection of archaeological artefacts and a large library of books on the history, architecture and ethnography of the Silk Road.

Museum of Applied Arts [108 C5] (*15 Rakatboshi*; ☏ *256 4042; www.artmuseum. uz*; ⊕ *09.00–18.00 daily; US$3*) Possibly the best-looking museum in Tashkent, the Museum of Applied Arts is situated in the former home of Imperial Russian diplomat Alexander Polovtsev. Polovtsev was an avid collector of handicrafts and his personal possessions still form the heart of the museum's superb collection of decorative arts. The first public exhibition was held here in 1927, and it was classified as a national collection a decade later.

As photographs on display inside show, the façade of the building has changed surprisingly little since its construction in the early 20th century: the gardens have matured, but the delicate columns and the pale blue colour scheme are original. In the museum's central hall, it is the building itself that is the attraction: it is a stunning space with an ornately carved and vividly painted ceiling. The wooden doors and their frames are particularly elaborate, as are the decorative pillars supporting the roof. The walls are painted and tiled with so many contrasting designs that in any other context they'd make your eyes go funny. Here, however, they look exquisite.

Other galleries are arranged by the type of item on display, and their exhibits include fine ceramics, crystal and glass, clothes and embroidered textiles, musical instruments, jewellery and carpets. The costume and textile displays are particularly good. Though there are items of considerable note in each of the galleries, our particular favourites are the musical instrument and the textile rooms, where you can see not only the finished garments and accessories but also the different types of *ikat* fabric, each with their own distinctive designs. Although these aren't labelled, your guide will be able to explain them to you.

Two workshops at the museum restore antique pieces and give classes in various crafts, whilst three shops sell a refreshing selection of handmade items, prints and vintage clothing. There is a small café in the central courtyard where you can have a tea or coffee. Guided tours are available in various languages (*US$4pp*). If you want to take photos, you will need to buy a camera permit (*US$2*) from the ticket desk.

Railway Museum [109 F6] (*6 Turkiston;* ✆ *299 7040;* ⊕ *09.00–13.00 & 14.00–21.00 daily; US$2*) Appropriately located beside Tashkent station, the open-air Railway Museum may not be top on everyone's sightseeing list, but it offers a charming insight into the early development of the railway in central Asia. Here, you will find 13 well-preserved steam engines, as well as 20 diesel and electric locomotives, train carriages and communication systems. The collection of coaches reveals the different uses of the railways, both for passengers and cargo, and there are numerous accessories (semaphore and radio systems, etc), too. The exhibits are generally impressive in scale and in good condition, and you are welcome to climb inside. A small engine and carriages transport visitors the 1km across the park.

Sobor Orthodox Cathedral [109 E7] (*20 Avliyoota;* ⊕ *09.00–18.00 daily*) The Assumption Cathedral (Uspensky Sobor) is one of four Russian Orthodox churches in Tashkent. The cathedral began life as a chapel at Tashkent's military cemetery in the 1870s. Wanting something more impressive, General von Kaufman allotted 3,000 rubles for the construction of a larger church, and the city's mercantile guilds also contributed. The new building was consecrated in 1879 and dedicated to St Panteleimon the Healer. After the Bolshevik Revolution, the church was used as a sanitary depot for the military and it wasn't returned to religious use until after World War II. The church had to be almost completely rebuilt (which took until 1960), and it was at this time that it was given its current name and upgraded to the status of a cathedral. Best visited on a Sunday morning when a service is in full flow, this small but attractive building, replete with solemn icons, onion domes and lots of gilt, was heavily restored in 1996 for the visit of His Holiness Patriarch Alexy II. In 2009, 13 new bells were added to the bell tower, and an additional tower was completed the following year. The cathedral's ark is said to contain relics of the Holy Cross.

AROUND TASHKENT

Within an easy day trip of Tashkent, the following sites provide interest for both long-term expats and visitors keen to get away from the usual tourist sites. They're listed in order of distance from the city centre.

ZANGIOTA COMPLEX Some 15km out of the city along the M34 brings you to Zangiota village, which has grown up around the Timurid-era mausoleum of Zangiota, a 13th-century Sufi saint and shepherd who is still believed to have healing powers. People come here to pray and seek his blessings. Surrounded by a well-maintained garden, this is a tranquil spot and far less visited than Uzbekistan's other Timurid sites, despite its similarly beautiful portal, dome and tile work. Zangiota's inscribed marble tombstone is particularly fine. The neighbouring cemetery, still in use, contains the tomb of Zangiota's wife, Anbar Bibi, to whom women hoping to conceive pray for children.

LAKE CHARVAK Around 60km northeast of Tashkent, approximately 2 hours' drive from the capital, is the Lake Charvak resort. The lake here is in fact a manmade reservoir, created in 1970 behind a rock-filled dam at the confluence of the Chatkal, Kok-Su and Pskem rivers. The clear blue waters run down from the Tian Shan Mountains.

The beauty of the lake, which is ringed by green-sloped mountain peaks that are frequently topped with snow, combined with its easy access from Tashkent, have made it a popular holiday destination for Uzbek families and the few expats who know of its existence. In the summer months, there are plenty of opportunities for watersports (swimming, parasailing, banana boating, etc) and lazing around on the beach; but in the winter when everything is frozen, you had better wrap up warm.

Archaeologists have found evidence of prehistoric settlements, including petroglyphs and around 150 ancient monuments, in the area where the lake now lies, but after the 1966 earthquake (see box, page 111), rapid reconstruction and the provision of electricity to Tashkent took priority over archaeological conservation. The Charvak Hydropower Station was conceived and built, and so those archaeologists who still have an interest in the site must now content themselves with digging in the mud and sludge.

Nevertheless, the vast majority of visitors come solely for recreational purposes. The lake has a shoreline 100km in length, and so hotels and campsites have popped up in many of the villages. The most developed of these is Charvak Oromgokhi (*208 rooms;* ✆ *232 2282;* **$$$**), also known as the Pyramid Hotel, in Bokachul village. Situated a stone's throw from the sandy beach on the lakeside, it is split into three gigantic pyramid-shaped buildings. Standard rooms have queen-sized beds, central heating and air conditioning, and there is 24-hour room service. The hotel is popular with conference organisers, so rooms may well be booked up by groups in advance, but individual travellers can still make use of the restaurant and other facilities.

KANKA (*open access*) On the outskirts of Eltamgali village, 80km southwest of Tashkent, are the archaeological remains of Kanka, the earliest incarnation of Tashkent. You will need your own transport: take the M34 from Tashkent towards

Although there are plenty of short day or half-day hikes in the Ugam-Chatkal National Park, if you have a greater length of time to explore, especially in the late spring and early summer when the wildflowers are in bloom, it is well worth doing so on foot. If you purchase a detailed topographical map of the area from one of the book shops in Tashkent, you should be able to pick out and follow the basic route we have described below, but it is generally recommended to hire a local guide: not only are they better able to assess changes in the weather and landscape, but they will also be able to enlighten you about the local flora and fauna, and to introduce you to local people and their customs along the way. This trek is suitable for someone of moderate fitness, wearing proper walking boots or walking shoes. Campsites are unofficial but are used regularly for pitching tents.

Day 1: Starting at Beldersay village (1,600m), follow the Marble River, with its sparkling waterfalls and lush scenery, up and over the Urta Kumbel Pass (1,820m). It is then an easy descent to the Beldersay River, where you can pitch a tent for the night. The camp has superb views of Big Chimgan Mountain (3,309m), a magnet for skiers and snowboarders in winter but a photogenic peak at any time of the year.

Day 2: Start early on the second day as there is plenty of distance to cover. A short climb to the top of the Chet-Kumbel Pass (1,850m) grants you panoramic views of the **Beldersay River** and the western slopes of Big Chimgan Mountain. Having caught your breath, continue along the Beldersay Gorge, climbing steadily to its highest point (2,450m). Look out for the ancient rock paintings along the way, then cross over the Kumbel Pass (2,550m) and into another small gorge. Arrive sufficiently early to sit, beer in hand, and watch the sunset and then one of the most incredible night skies you'll ever see. You can pitch your tent by the river at the bottom of the gorge.

Day 3: There is a straight track up to the Tahta Pass (2,620m), which overlooks the distant Pulatkhan Plateau, where you'll often see patches of snow even in the height of summer. The route continues along the slopes of the plateau, which is a natural fortress surrounded by a ring of peaks, and then to the bank of the Kara-Archa River where you can camp for the night.

Day 4: This is the hardest day of trekking, with a descent of 1,000m in altitude. The day begins with a short climb up the southeastern slope of Chimgan Mountain, then a very long descent into the Gulkam Gorge, during which you will have a clear view of Okhotnichiy Peak (3,099m) and, in the distance, Lake Charvak (page 120). The lower you descend, the lusher the flora, and amid the grassy meadows and groves of juniper trees you are likely to meet shepherds with their flocks of sheep and goats. The final campsite is on the bank of the Gulkamsay Stream (1,650m).

Day 5: Start the morning with a short diversion into the Gulkam Canyon, a haven for climbers. If you want to climb here, you will need to bring your own helmet and ropes. Complete your trek with one last climb over the Pesochniy Pass (1,820m) which overlooks Chimgan village, an hour's walk further along the track. Arrange your onward transport from here.

Yangi-Chonoz, and just before you reach that town, turn left and head to Soldatskiy. Eltamgali and Kanka are reached along an unmade road heading southeast from the town. The vast Kanka site, which has been only partially excavated, is clearly demarcated with defensive walls, ditches and a large citadel which at one stage would have risen more than 35m above the surrounding land. Climbing to the top of the site it is possible to see the footprint of both towers and temples. Archaeologists working on the site are more than happy to show you ceramics, coins and even bones they have unearthed in the most recent phase of digs.

UGAM-CHATKAL NATIONAL PARK The Chatkal Mountains rise up from the steppe 80km northeast of Tashkent, creating one of the most picturesque landscapes in Uzbekistan. Whether walking and picnicking, windsurfing and climbing, or heli-skiing at rock-bottom rates is your thing, in little over an hour's drive from central Tashkent you can be making the best of the great outdoors.

From December to March, the **Chimgan Ski Resort** is packed each weekend with Tashkent's beautiful people and a host of foreign adrenalin junkies. Though not comparable to European resorts in scale (there are only half a dozen or so slopes, none more than 1,500m in length), it's a popular excursion nonetheless and a cheap place for beginners to develop a taste for the powder. The majority of skiers take the chairlift up Great Chimgan (3,309m), the highest peak, to race down the Kumbel track, but it is also possible to fly up to 3,000m and be deposited on virgin snow. Asia Adventures (page 90) has heli-skiing packages from US$500 per day but, if your budget won't stretch quite that far, a day's lift pass is a snip at US$10. Ski and snowboard gear is available to hire.

Once the snow has melted, the Chatkal Park becomes an ideal **trekking** ground. There are numerous routes suitable for all degrees of fitness: serious trekkers should take a guide and a border permit to reach the glaciers of the Pskem Mountains alongside the Kyrgyzstan border, but there are also ample opportunities for more casual trekkers with a day or two to spare. Routes around the **Chatkal Reservoir** at the confluence of the region's rivers are strikingly beautiful and easy underfoot, and a stroll through juniper forests of the **UNESCO Chatkal Biosphere** will reveal not only ancient petroglyphs but also 280 species of fauna and more than 2,000 species of plants.

 Where to stay and eat Camping is common and encouraged. Make sure you take your rubbish away with you in spite of the poor example set by the locals. However, if you prefer a proper bed there are a couple of options:

🏠 **Beldersoy Oromgohi** (30 rooms, 16 cottages) m (90) 176 3826; www.beldersoy.uz. This swish hotel has a stunning position, swimming pools & restaurants. **$$$$**

🏠 **Charvak Oromgohi** m (90) 188 0553. Comfortable option with great views across the mountains from its more expensive rooms. **$$**
🏠 **Hotel Chimgan** m (90) 105 5002. An authentic Soviet-era sanatorium with hard beds but low prices & all meals inc. **$**

RAFTING ON THE CHATKAL RIVER The Chatkal River is 3 hours' drive northeast from Tashkent, beyond the ski resort and further up into the Tian Shan Mountains. It offers some of the best white water in central Asia, and 183km of its 223km length is suitable for rafting. It is known colloquially as the Five Canyons River. Waterfalls, cascades of rapids, whirlpools and rocky gorges all offer physical challenges, but the landscape is diverse, and the route is filled with excitement.

Spring and autumn are the ideal times for rafting. The first canyon contains a perilous waterfall, with two steps, each of around 4m. It is followed by a 100m stretch of rapids, and the confluence of the Chatkal and Ters rivers. The rapids here are considered one of the most difficult parts of the route.

In the second canyon, the stone walls tower high above the river on either side.

The third canyon is narrow; the river winds through a corridor 200–300m high, the rocks pitted with grottoes and caves. Cornices overhang the water, in places blocking out the sky. The riverbed narrows to just 6m wide, but then opens out again to floodplains of forest and meadow. Chatkal Peak (4,503m) rises majestically in the distance.

Traversing the fourth canyon is relatively straightforward, but you quickly enter the most dangerous rapids of the trip, situated in the fifth canyon. The rocks narrow into a corridor known as 'the diaphragm', after which the river calms and widens. There are sandbanks and pebble beaches either side of the water. The final stretch of rapids is after the fifth canyon at Aurahmat. They occur only when dams upstream are opened for irrigation.

Rafting on the Chatkal is particularly delightful in the spring, when the waters are at a safe level and the spring flowers are a riot of colour in the surrounding meadows. You should satisfy yourself as to the condition of any equipment you use, particularly if it is hired locally, and should wear a life jacket and helmet at all times. Comprehensive medical insurance is essential. For guided rafting tours and equipment hire, the Tashkent-based ✷ **Asia Raft Tour Company** (*77 M Riezey*; ☏ *267 0918*; e *asiaraft@fromru.com; www.asiaraft.uz*) is highly recommended. Booking on to their ten-day rafting trip along the Chatkal gets you all meals, transfers and camping equipment as well as raft, medical kit, life jacket and safety helmet.

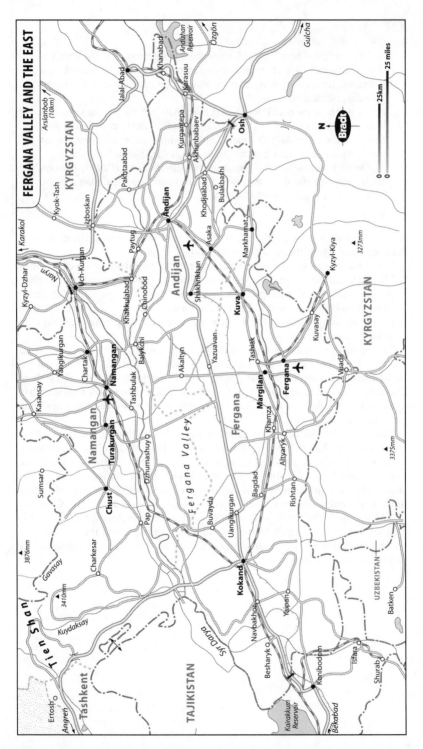

FERGANA VALLEY AND THE EAST

25km

25 miles

KYRGYZSTAN

KYRGYZSTAN

UZBEKISTAN

TAJIKISTAN

Tashkent

Tien Shan

F e r g a n a   V a l l e y

Namangan

Fergana

Andijan

Syr Darya

Narym

Andizhan Reservoir

Kairakkum Reservoir

Arslanbob (10km)

Karakol

Gulcha

Özgön

Jalal-Abad
Khanabad
Karasuu
Osh
Kurgantepa
Akhunbabaev
Khodjaabad
Bulakbashi
Markhamat
Kyzyl-Kiya
3273mm
Kyok-Tash
Pakhtaabad
Izboskan
Andijan
Asaka
Shakhrikhan
Kuva
Kuvasay
Viadil
Pajtug
Uch-Kurgan
Khakkulabad
Chinobod
Akaltyn
Yazuavan
Tashlak
Margilan
Fergana
Khamza
Altyaryk
Kyzyl-Dzhar
Yangikurgan
Chartak
Tashbulak
Balykchi
Namangan
Turakurgan
Dzhumashuy
Uangikurgan
Bagdad
Rishtan
3375mm
Kasansay
Sumsar
Chust
Pap
Buvayda
Kokand
Charkesar
3410mm
Kuydaksay
Gavasay
3876mm
Navbakhor
Yapan
Batken
Besharyk
Konibodom
Istara
Shurab
Bekabad
Ertosh
Angren

4

Fergana Valley and the East

The Fergana Valley is a depression between the Tian Shan Mountains in the north and the Gissar-Alai range in the south. Some 300km long, up to 70km wide and naturally irrigated by two tributaries of the Syr Darya, it is the most fertile part of Uzbekistan and hence the country's agricultural heartland. Agricultural wealth historically gave rise to Silk Road trading towns, fortresses and, most importantly, the 19th-century Khanate of Kokand.

For much of the past 100 years it has also been an area that is deeply troubled. Stalin's border policies divided the valley between Uzbekistan, Kyrgyzstan and Tajikistan; not only are there main international borders here, but also a bewildering number of enclaves and enclaves that are nigh on impossible to administer but are fiercely defended at great financial and human cost. Communal violence has regularly reared its ugly head, most recently between Kyrgyz and Uzbeks in the summer of 2010, often spurred on by governments and other regional players when it suits their political objectives to do so.

NAMANGAN _Telephone code: 69_

Some 300km east of Tashkent in the northern part of the Fergana Valley, not far from the border with Kyrgyzstan, is Namangan, the second-largest city in the country. The confluence of the Karya Darya and Naryn rivers, two tributaries of the Syr Darya (or Jaxartes), lies just outside the city's confines, and the local area has been populated at least since Sogdian times, as is attested to by the remarkable ruins of Aksikent, Namangan's biggest draw.

HISTORY Namangan city, which takes its name from a local salt mine (_namak_ meaning salt), grew up in the 17th century as the Fergana Valley's religious centre. At its height there were more than 600 mosques in the district, and a population of a third of a million people.

The religiosity of the local population, which was never fully suppressed during the Soviet period, has been a cause of concern since independence. Wahhabism, an extreme Islamic sect from Saudi Arabia, took root in the area, and in the mid 1990s it was the heartland for the now banned Islamic Movement of Uzbekistan (see box, page 27).

GETTING THERE AND AWAY Namangan is in the northern central part of the Fergana Valley, roughly equidistant between Kokand and Andijan.

By road Namangan has two bus stands: the **long-distance bus stand** is about 2km north of the city centre, and from here you can get buses to Andijan (*1hr*) and Fergana (*2hrs*). There are no direct minibuses to Tashkent, so you'll need to haggle with a shared taxi driver. The 290km (180 mile) journey to Tashkent along the A373 takes 5 hours and a seat should not cost more than US$14. The **local bus stand** is by the bazaar and the spaghetti junction at the eastern end of Navoi. The most useful minibus is No 4, which runs between the local and long-distance bus stands, and a succession of minibuses also run along the length of Navoi and from the bazaar to Dustlik.

If you are travelling to or from Kyrgyzstan, the **Uch-Kurgan border post** between Namangan and Karakol (not the famous Karakol on Lake Issyk-Kul) is now open to foreigners (⏱ *08.00–20.00 daily*). It's considerably closer to Tashkent than the crossing between Andijan and Osh (see boxes, pages 132 and 133), which is beneficial if you're simply passing through the valley to get to northern Kyrgyzstan and Bishkek. Many foreign nationals (including all EU passport holders) no longer need a visa to enter Kyrgyzstan. If you have your own vehicle, or to arrange a taxi on each side, you can cross in around an hour. If you are reliant on public transport, you should take a minibus from Uch-Kurgan town (1,500 som) to the border, and on entering Kyrgyzstan, walk to the main road to hail a minibus or taxi travelling along the Bishkek–Osh highway.

By train The train station (✆ *233 0338*) is on A Timur but in all honesty you're unlikely to use it: there is only a train once a week to Tashkent, and as it transits through Tajikistan you would need a Tajik transit visa and a double-entry Uzbek visa in order to complete the journey, making it an unviable way to travel for foreigners.

By air Namangan's airport (✆ *232 2890; e ap.nma@uzairways.com*) is 12km west of the city centre, and Uzbekistan Airways has a flight to Tashkent three times a week (*Tue, Thu & Sun*) for around US$75. The flight takes 55 minutes and tickets can be purchased either from the ticket desk at the airport, or from their ticket office in the city (*41 Mashrab*).

Travelling to or from Russia, there are also scheduled departures between Namangan and Moscow (VIM Airlines, Uzbekistan Airways, Ural Airlines), Yekaterinburg (Uzbekistan Airways, Ural Airlines) and Saint Petersburg (Uzbekistan Airways).

GETTING AROUND Minibus 1 links the town centre with the 3rd Microdistrict and, if you are travelling beyond the city limits, Namangan Travel (see below) can arrange a car and driver.

TRAVEL AGENTS The following travel agents can arrange onward transport (including general flight ticketing) and accommodation bookings.

Adelaida Travel 32 Mashrab; ✆ 226 5533; e adelaida_trevel@inbox.ru
Akram Trans Servis 16A Nodira; ✆ 226 5453; e umarov.79@mail.ru

Namangan Travel 1 Nodira; ✆ 226 1733. Guided tours, transport & trekking options.

 WHERE TO STAY *Map, page 127*
Namangan has a number of places to stay, though sadly none of them are particularly exciting.

🏠 **Hotel Dustlik** 23 Dustlik; ✆ 232 7610; e liliya7777@yandex.ru. Currently

the best place to stay, Hotel Dustlik is inside the tennis complex in the 3rd

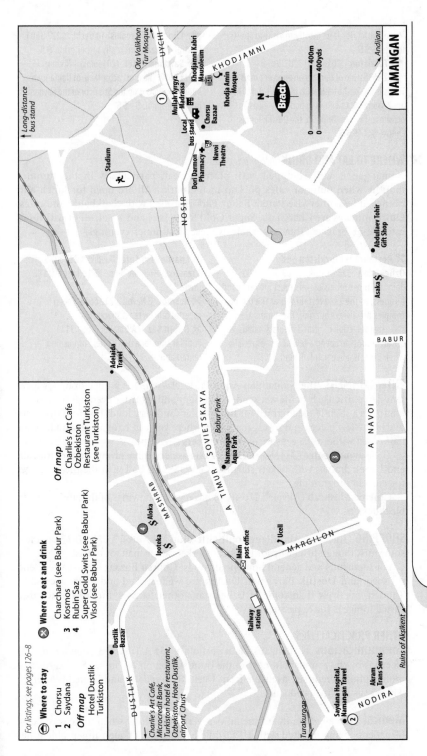

For listings, see pages 126–8

Where to stay
1 Chorsu
2 Saydana

Off map
Hotel Dustlik
Turkiston

Where to eat and drink
Charchara (see Babur Park)
3 Kosmos
Rubin Saz
Super Gold Swits (see Babur Park)
Visol (see Babur Park)

Off map
Charlie's Art Cafe
Ozbekiston
Restaurant Turkiston
(see Turkiston)

NAMANGAN

Microdistrict. It caters mostly to visiting sports teams. **$$$**

🏠 **Turkiston** (30 rooms) 32B Dustlik; ☎232 3535. One of Namangan's newer hotels, the Turkiston is comfortable with pleasant staff. There are 2 saunas & a swimming pool, as well as an on-site restaurant. Opposite the Dustlik Tennis Centre. **$$–$$$**

🏠 **Chorsu** (50 rooms) 10 Uychi; ☎227 3501. Central & cheap, but really rather grim. **$$**

🏠 **Saydana Hotel** (20 rooms) 1 Nodira; ☎223 0017. The most acceptable of Namangan's budget options is on the 5th floor of the Saydana private hospital. **$–$$**

✕ WHERE TO EAT AND DRINK *Map, page 127*

Namangan is well equipped with places to eat, particularly in the summer months when outdoor cafés pop up in the parks. All are open for lunch and dinner unless otherwise stated. Babur Park is stuffed with chaikhanas and cafés. Our favourites are Charchara, Super Gold Swits [*sic*] and Visol, all of which fall into the **$$** bracket. They're at their liveliest on summer evenings.

✕ **Restaurants Turkiston and Ozbekiston** 32B Dustlik; ⊕ 09.00–02.00 daily. All those tennis players must provide good business, as the 2 big restaurants at the tennis complex are always buzzing. The menus are the usual selection of grilled meats & salads, & are ideal spots to spend a few hours, especially when there is a live band playing. **$$$**

✕ **Charlie's Art Café** Dustlik; ☎232 3375. A reasonable option, home of the best pizza in town. **$$$**

✕ **Kosmos** 8 Navoi; ☎212 6606. Cheap & cheerful cafe for tea & snacks. **$$**

✕ **Rubin Saz** 7A Galaba; ☎681 3131. Popular spot for a quick bite, but nothing remarkable. **$$**

ENTERTAINMENT The **Namangan Aqua Park** (*A Timur*) is a huge draw for local families, particularly at the weekends. On Friday and Saturday evenings in summer it attracts a slightly older crowd for the popular (and very loud) open-air disco. It's one of the few places in the Fergana Valley where you can have a beer and let your hair down without the censure of more conservative types.

The **Navoi Theatre** (*2 U Nosir*; ☎*226 2432*) has occasional productions of Russian and Uzbek dramas with tickets starting from US$2–3. Call in at the theatre to get the current programme.

Cinema Mashrab (*Navoi*; ☎*226 4039*) has regular showings of the latest Russian blockbusters.

SHOPPING The small **Abdullaev Tohir Gift Shop** (*31 Navoi*; ☎*275 0101*) has a few souvenirs, though primarily for the local market rather than for tourists.

For foodstuffs and general household goods, **Chorsu Bazaar** at the eastern end of Navoi and **Dustlik Bazaar** on Dustlik are well stocked and easily accessible. Though less lively than some of Uzbekistan's other bazaars, they're still worth a casual forage if you're passing by.

OTHER PRACTICALITIES

Communications Namangan's main post office (*54 A Timur*; ⊕ *Mon–Fri 09.00–18.00*) is by the roundabout next to the train station on A Timur. SIM cards and mobile phone credit are available from Ucell (*8 Margilon*), and Unitell (*46 Ibrat*), which sells Beeline products.

Medical Namangan sadly hit the news several years back when there was a case of patients being infected with HIV while in hospital. Though this problem has hopefully been solved, you should still bring your own needles and sterile kit (purchased from a local pharmacy if there isn't already one in your first-aid kit) to ensure peace of mind.

In an emergency you need the Republican Centre of Science of Emergency Medicine (2 Go'zal; ☎ 226 2815). For more general health problems, it is better to go to Polyclinic #1 (Namangani; ☎ 226 3600) or the private Saydana Hospital (see Saydana Hotel, page 128). There is a branch of the Dori Darmon pharmacy chain at 12 U Nosir.

Money Namangan has no shortage of banks for currency exchange and money transfer, though ATMs are still largely absent.

$ **Aloka Bank** 5A Galaba; ☎ 232 2359; ⏱ 09.00–18.00 Mon–Fri

$ **Asaka Bank** 27 Navoi; ☎ 427 0853; ⏱ 09.00–17.00 Mon–Fri

$ **Ipoteka Bank** 2 Mashrab; ☎ 223 0300; ⏱ 09.00–17.00 Mon–Fri

$ **Microcredit Bank** 9 Dustlik; ☎ 224 4859; ⏱ 09.00–17.00 Mon–Fri

WHAT TO SEE AND DO Namangan is home to a number of attractive religious sites, one of which is closely linked with the controversial Wahhabi sect.

The **Mullah Kyrgyz Madrassa** (built 1910), just east of the bazaar on Uychi, is the work of a talented local architect, Usto Kyrgyz. It is said that one day the architect sat in the middle of the madrassa building site drinking tea and watched a particularly useless apprentice trying (and failing) to build a wall. Exasperated, Usto Kyrgyz hurled a brick at the young man from across the courtyard but, not unsurprisingly given the distance, missed him. The brick hit the top of the wall in exactly the right place, just as if Usto Kyrgyz had carefully placed it there by hand.

The madrassa, which is an irregular pentahedron in shape due to the local topography, is surrounded by evenly placed *hujras*. It was closed by the Soviets and spent much of the 20th century operating as a literary museum, but it was restored by local residents following independence and briefly served as a madrassa again before being closed by the Uzbek government. It is now a museum-monument, not in active use, and named in honour of the craftsman responsible for its construction.

There is some attractively carved woodwork, both ceilings and columns, and the main portal is decorated with a fine mosaic depicting flowers in blue, green, yellow and white. A scramble up the steep and uneven steps inside brings you up on to the rooftop, from where you'll catch a pleasant breath of fresh air, even in the sticky heat of summer, and also get good views across the bazaar.

A short walk south along a lane that rings and sparks with the striking of metal sheets and bars in tiny workshops brings you to the **Khodjamni Kabri Mausoleum** and neighbouring **Khodja Amin Mosque,** which has been recently renovated. Both of these buildings date from the 18th century and are the work of architect Usto Muhammad Ibrahim. The portal-domed mosque, open on all four sides, is typical of local mosque architecture of this period. The intricate terracotta tilework on the front of the mausoleum is particularly interesting as the tiles were produced using a method revived from the 12th century that had more or less disappeared in Fergana. You should note that only men are permitted inside these particular buildings.

Further east along Uychi is the **Ota Valikhon Tur Mosque** (built 1915) with its unusual stripes of blue mosaic, star-shaped carvings in the entrance way and cylindrical monumental drums illuminated with Arabic calligraphy. It has one of the largest domes in central Asia, a ribbed construction with a diameter of more than 13m, but is better known as a centre for the extreme Islamic Wahhabi sect during the

1990s. They spent large sums of money (mostly gifts from Saudi Arabia) developing the site as a modern madrassa, only for it to be closed by the government.

In the centre of town, **Babur Park** is a pleasant spot to spend an hour or two. It began life in the late 19th century as the garden of the Russian governor, but is now open to the public. If you arrive in the late afternoon you'll see Namangan's elders gathering in the dappled shade beneath the Chinor trees to drink steaming bowls of tea and play games of chess or *nards* (a Persian board game similar to backgammon); it's an unexpectedly civilised haven of calm.

AROUND NAMANGAN

Aksikent Namangan's most interesting site is outside the actual city. Some 22km to the southwest are the ruins of Aksikent, a fortified city at the confluence of the Kasansai and Syr Darya rivers.

Aksikent (also known as Akhsi) was already well established by the 3rd century BC. Along with 60,000 soldiers, the Chinese commander Li Guanli besieged Aksikent for 40 days in 103 BC in an attempt to gain control of the surrounding territory and, in particular, its famed blood-sweating horses.

Early in the 1st millennium AD, the city was conquered first by the Kushans and then by the Turks. It was a caravan stop *en route* from Kashgar to Byzantium, and locally made goods were traded all along the route: the strong but flexible steel produced in kaolin-lined smelting furnaces here was famous as far away as Baghdad and Damascus. By the early medieval period the town had grown to such an extent that the perimeter wall was 18km long, and the central citadel contained a palace, mosque and bathhouse. Soldiers kept an eye on the trading domes and hostels from watchtowers along the walls.

In the early 13th century Aksikent was sacked first by the Karakhitai and then by Jebe Noyan, one of Genghis Khan's commanders. The city fell into decay and though attempts were made to rebuild it on the riverbank, it never really recovered. What little remained collapsed during an earthquake in 1620.

Aksikent is not a popular site for tourists, despite its historical significance, so you're likely to have the ruins to yourself. Start by climbing to the top of the site where a modern pylon stands incongruously atop a sweeping, manmade mound of earth. This was once the centre of the fort and, as the Emperor Babur recorded in his memoirs, the *Baburnama*, the suburbs of Aksikent stretched out from here for 3km in each direction. Looking down the steep drop to the row of plain trees alongside the river, you can clearly see the strategic value of this site: it's a spot that is easy to defend, and you could see enemies advancing from any direction.

Although initially the earthen mounds around you look just like arid humps, if you look closely you'll be able to differentiate between the underlying earthworks and the stocky mud-brick walls. Millions of bricks, each one made by hand, comprised walls more than 2m thick: it's little surprise that it took Li Guanli's forces so long to break inside.

Chust The town of Chust, some 30km due west of Namangan, is famed for its production of knives and skull caps, and a visit here will enable you to see the workshops and purchase fine examples of Uzbek craftsmanship. In the National Knife Factory (*46 Chusti;* \ *36 942*), which is open to the public, metal workers smash and grind their knives from short lengths of steel or iron, honing each blade into the desired shape with a meticulous attention to detail. The tip of each knife should curl, a trademark of the Chust design. The neighbouring rooms owe more to artists' ateliers than the blacksmith's shop next door. Whilst some knife makers carve the haft, or handle, of the knife from animal horn, others painstakingly slice slivers of mother of pearl and arrange them in elaborate patterns of flowers and geometric designs.

The *tubeteika*, the black, tetrahedral skull cap worn throughout the Fergana Valley, is also made in Chust but unlike the knives, these are the handicraft of the town's womenfolk. Each black cap is lovingly embroidered in white: the four arches represent impenetrable gates that will keep all enemies at bay; the burning peppers protect against the evil eye; and the almonds, or *bodom*, are said to symbolise life and fertility.

ANDIJAN *Telephone code: 74*

Uzbekistan's fourth-largest city, Andijan has a rich past and vibrant Uzbek culture but a troubled recent history, and consequently few foreign tourists come here unless they're passing quickly through *en route* to Kyrgyzstan. Though at the time of going to print it was considered safe, you are advised to avoid large gatherings of people, and to check with the FCO (*www.fco.gov.uk*) and media reports as to the current security situation.

HISTORY Andijan was founded sometime in the 9th century and was just getting onto its feet when Genghis Khan rode through and razed it back to the ground. Fortunately for Andijan, his grandson Kaydu Khan saw potential in the ashes, rebuilt the town and made it his capital. This was a shrewd move, as the city became

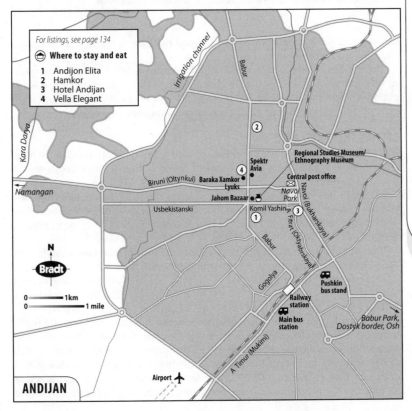

For listings, see page 134

🍽 **Where to stay and eat**

1 Andijon Elita
2 Hamkor
3 Hotel Andijan
4 Vella Elegant

ANDIJAN

131

The 13 May 2005 must surely rank amongst the blackest days in Uzbekistan's recent history. One of the few things about this event that is certain is that National Security forces opened fire into a crowd of protesters gathered in Andijan's central square; the identity of the protesters, the purpose of their protest and the number of fatalities are facts that are hotly contested.

According to Human Rights Watch (*www.hrw.org*) and the BBC, on the morning of 13 May gunmen broke into a prison in Andijan to release 23 local businessmen on trial for alleged religious extremism, a particularly sensitive issue in the country since the end of the civil war in Tajikistan in the late 1990s and the invasion of Afghanistan in 2001. There had been several days of peaceful protest in the city beforehand, and following the men's release the number of protesters swelled to several thousand, their grievances ranging from the heavy-handedness of the government to economic woes.

Around 18.00, security forces were given orders to break up the protesters and regain control of the government buildings that they were occupying. Using snipers and troops in armed personnel carriers, they shot repeatedly into the crowd. The government maintains only 187 were killed, 60 of those being protesters, and that all of them were shot by gunmen in the crowd. President Karimov has refused to allow an independent inquiry into the massacre and denies responsibility for the killings of unarmed protesters; the United Nations believes lethal force was used excessively.

the lucrative gateway between Samarkand and Bukhara in the west, and Kashgar and Chinese Turkestan in the east.

The Andijan you see today is mostly of 20th-century construction: an earthquake in 1902 more or less levelled the Old Town, taking with it 4,500 lives. In the Soviet period Andijan industrialised and grew wealthy on the profits of black and white gold: oil and cotton. They're still the mainstays of the local economy.

GETTING THERE AND AWAY

By road Most visitors arrive in Andijan by road as it is well connected to the other cities in the Fergana Valley, and it is usually faster to drive to/from Tashkent than it is to go by train.

The **main bus station** is on A Timur, close to the train station, and from here you can pick up both minibuses and shared taxis to destinations within the valley. The ride to Namangan takes 1 hour and the shared taxi costs US$3. The minibus to Fergana takes 1¼ hours and costs US$3, or US$4 by shared taxi.

If you're going to Tashkent by bus, you need the **Pushkin bus stand** near Pushkin Park. Shared taxis take around 5 hours and cost US$12 per seat.

There are two **border posts** close to Andijan, but as of 2013 only one of these is actually open for foreigners to cross into Kyrgyzstan. The border crossing at Khanabad, which is on the road between Andijan and Jalal-Abad, is shut.

The open border crossing is at Dostyk between Andijan and Osh, and public transport is plentiful on both sides. Note that the opening times of the two sides of the post differ: while the Uzbek side will let foreigners pass in and out at any time of day or night, the Kyrgyz side operates only between 07.00 Uzbek time, which due to the time difference is 08.00 Kyrgyz time, and sunset. The border also closes for half an hour at lunchtime. If you get stuck in no man's land (as we did), expect

A significant number of visitors to the Fergana Valley will be continuing their journey and crossing the border into Kyrgyzstan. Though politically troubled in recent years, it's nonetheless a remarkable country with some of the most beautiful and unspoilt mountain scenery on earth. Within easy striking distance of the border are several sites of interest.

OSH Just 5km from the border is Osh, the second city of Kyrgyzstan, which celebrated (accurately or otherwise) its 3,000th birthday in 2000. Though there is little to see of the original citadel, a bastion of Islam against the marauding, infidel nomads, but the Tacht-i Suleiman (Throne of Solomon), the looming hill that dominates the city's skyline, is one of the holiest sites in central Asia and an important pilgrimage site. Osh is also home to a sprawling bazaar, a vast statue of Lenin that was supposedly brought here from Bishkek, and the Silk Road Museum, which has a number of reasonable ethnographic displays. Osh's accommodation options were largely destroyed during the violence of 2010 but the Community Based Tourism (CBT) programme (e *cbtgulcho@mail.ru; www.cbtkyrgyzstan.kg*) is able to make homestay bookings, advise on recently opened or restored hotels, and arrange tours and transport.

ÖZGÖN An hour's drive northeast of Osh on the banks of the Kara Darya river is Özgön, the erstwhile capital of the Karakhanid dynasty. A stone's throw from the town's bus station are three mausoleums and a minaret, important by virtue of the fact they are amongst the few surviving examples of pre-Mongol architecture. Each of the sites is finely decorated, and it is an intriguing sight to watch women touching the walls of the tombs with reverence. You can reach Özgön by bus from Osh (60 Kyrgyz som).

ARSLANBOB Three hours' drive through the mountains from Andijan is Arslanbob, a Shangri-La scene with snow-capped peaks, waterfalls and alpine lakes. The area is famous for its ancient walnut forests, which support a diverse range of wildlife, and for the nomads who drive their flocks here to fatten them in the lush, green pastures. Arslanbob is cloaked in snow in the winter months, but an ideal place for horse trekking and hiking during the summer. Homestays, trekking and horse hire can be arranged through CBT (m *(77) 334 2476;* e *arslanbob_2003@rambler.ru; www.cbtkyrgyzstan.kg*).

to spend an uncomfortable night sleeping in your vehicle or bunking down with the lorry drivers in one of the long, low buildings to the side of the road.

By train Once a week there are trains between Andijan and Bukhara (*Fri; 12.45; 23hrs 30mins*), and Andijan and Tashkent (*Sun; 14.35; 16hrs 30mins*). Both of these train services route via Margilan. Tickets can be bought from the train station (*A Timur*) or, more easily if you don't speak Russian, through a travel agent.

By air Andijan's airport is southwest of the city centre, immediately outside the ring road. Uzbekistan Airways operates four flights a week between Andijan and Tashkent (*US$75; 1hr 5mins*); there are less regular services to Bukhara and Urgench, and also to Moscow, Krasnoyarsk and Novosibirsk.

Tickets can be bought from the ticketing desk at the airport or, more conveniently, from the Aviakassa at 1 Koltsevaya.

GETTING AROUND Set minibus routes cover most of Andijan city. Minibus 8 links the city centre and the airport and 33 goes from the Old Town along Bobur. To reach Babur Park, minibuses 16 and 21 run from the bazaar.

TRAVEL AGENTS The main ticket office of Uzbekistan Airways is at 1 Koltsevaya (\ 224 4864). For other airline tickets and hotel reservations, try Baraka Xamkor Lyuks (*38 Bobur;* \ *263 4311;* e *baraka_xamkor@mail.*ru) or Spektr Avia (*43 Bobur;* \ *224 5937;* e *spektr-avia@bk.ru*).

WHERE TO STAY *Map, page 131*

There are several options some of them quite reasonable and others rather grim. The same contrast sometimes applies to rooms within a single hotel, so if in doubt you might want to ask to see a couple of options before committing to checking in.

Andijon Elita (48 rooms) 13B Bobur; \ 224 6947; e andijon_elita@mail.ru. Relatively modern (2005), this mid-size hotel has large, comfortable rooms, good bathrooms & a restaurant. Sgl, dbl & quad rooms available. **$$$**

Hamkor Hotel (26 rooms) 53 Babur; \ (71) 150 3020. Modern business hotel in the centre of Andijan. Staff are professional & polite. Facilities include conference & business centre & large restaurant & bar. Free Wi-Fi. Book through Advantour. **$$$**

Vella Elegant (14 rooms) 40 Bobur; \ 200 6336; e vellaelegant@mail.ru. Split between 2 buildings, old & new, either side of the road, Vella Elegant has large rooms, clean bathrooms & a pleasant, grassy courtyard & outdoor pool. Choose a room in the new building. **$$**

Hotel Andijan 241 Fitrat; \ 226 2388. Andijan's best shoestring option is close to the bazaar. Some rooms have been renovated; opt for one with a private bathroom. **$**

WHERE TO EAT AND DRINK Andijan is famous for its plov, so even if you haven't eaten it anywhere else in Uzbekistan, you should probably try it here. It's served up to a hungry local crowd in the chaikhana (**$$**) in Babur Park. There are also restaurants at the Elita and Vella Elegant hotels, though they're fairly uninspiring and often booked out for weddings. The hotel restaurant at Hamkor (*53 Babur;* **$$$**) is slightly better, however.

Bosco 8 Istiqlol. This is the place for good Russian food, though it is a little more expensive than elsewhere. **$$$**

Dolma 43 Kusharik. This is popular with a younger crowd, & on summer evenings it's pleasant to sit outdoors by the fountains. **$$**

SHOPPING The Jahom Bazaar (⊕ *09.00–18.00 daily*) on Biruni is Andijan's commercial centre, and though it is open daily, it is significantly larger on Sunday and Thursday when the villagers flock into town. Head first to the fringes of the market where you'll find blacksmiths banging and clanging away in their forges, knife-makers shaping and polishing steel blades, and the occasional dusty carpentry workshop. Among the craftsmen, keep your eyes peeled for the wizened old pigeon fanciers; their dove-grey birds sit twitching and cooing and watching the world with alert, beady little eyes. The people-watching here is unrivalled, and the photographic opportunities somehow sum up life on the Silk Road.

Zahir-ud-din Muhammad (1483–1530), also known as Babur, was a direct descendant of Timur through his father's line, and a supposed descendant of Genghis Khan through his mother. He was born in Andijan, the eldest son of the ruler of Fergana, Omar Sheykh Mirza of the Barlas tribe. He was educated in both Chaghatai Turkish and Persian, and as a young man excelled not only on the battlefield but also as a poet.

In 1495 Babur succeeded his father as ruler of Fergana, but he lacked widespread support. Though he successfully besieged Samarkand in 1497, a rebellion of nobles back in Fergana forced him to abandon his prize, and his troops deserted on the way back. A second attempt to take Samarkand two years later was no more successful, and Babur was forced to retreat to Badakhshan (now in Afghanistan).

Perhaps realising that he was not destined to rule central Asia, he turned his attention south to Timur's other imperial domains: Afghanistan and India. Here he had more luck. He captured Kabul in 1504 and again in 1510, briefly occupied Herat, had one final go at taking Samarkand in 1511, then turned his attention to defeating the Lodi rulers of northern India and seizing their capital, Delhi. *En route* Babur successfully took Kandahar and the plains of the Punjab, finally winning Delhi at the Battle of Panipat in 1526.

Babur fell ill late in 1529 and was succeeded by his eldest son, Humayun. He wished to be buried in Kabul, in his mind a far more civilised city than the cultural wilderness that was India, so after a brief interment in Agra, he was reburied in his garden tomb in Kabul. His descendants, the Mughals (a corruption of Mongols, in reference to their central Asian heritage), would rule much of India and what is now Pakistan until being finally deposed by the British in 1857.

In addition to fresh produce (the melons are enormous!) you can pick up spices, embroidered hats, good silks, embroidered skull caps and the traditional Fergana knives, all (so long as you haggle) without the usual tourist mark-up.

OTHER PRACTICALITIES

Communications Andijan's central post office (⊕ *08.00–17.00 Mon–Fri*) is on the northeast corner of Navoi and Biruni, and you can also make long-distance calls in the same building.

There was a crackdown on internet cafés in Andijan in the late 2000s and they still seem to get closed down with little reason or notice. You will need to ask at your hotel for the closest option. You have to show your passport when using an internet café, and the owner will take a photocopy. You may find that some sensitive sites (including news sites) are blocked, as are their proxy servers.

Money Cash advances for Visa cardholders, as well as the usual currency exchange services, are available from the National Bank of Uzbekistan (*42 Navoi*). The following banks do money transfer and Forex:

$ **Asaka Bank** 2A Furkat; ☏ 226 2391;
⊕ 09.00–17.00 Mon–Fri

$ **Hamkor Bank** 17 Otabekov; ☏ 237 5537;
⊕ 09.00–16.00 Mon–Sat

$ **Savdogar Bank** 1 Anisi; ☏ 225 3281;
⊕ 09.00–16.30 Mon–Fri

WHAT TO SEE AND DO Andijan's main sites are clustered around Eski Bazaar in the Old Town. It has a bunch of small museums, the most important of which is the **Babur Literary Museum** (*21 Bazernaya*; \ *225 7302*; ⊕ *09.00–18.00 Tue–Sat; foreigners US$0.75*). Babur (see box, page 135) studied in a madrassa on this site, and the design of the heavily rebuilt structure harks back to its original use. When Babur fled Uzbekistan in the early 16th century the building was destroyed and it was 200 years before it was restored, first for use as Andijan's town hall, and then as the private residence of a prominent local family. It opened as a museum in 1990 and the carefully laid-out garden with formal planting also dates from this time.

The exhibits inside the museum celebrate Babur's poetry and prose: his autobiographical chronicle, the *Baburnama*, is one of the most important historical sources we have from the 1500s and he was a fine wordsmith as well as a warrior and statesman. Text displays (which can be a little monotonous) are interspersed with attractive reproductions of miniature paintings and larger-scale scenes from Babur's life, fleshing out the picture of a man who changed the fate of the Indian subcontinent.

The museum also displays the poems of Nadira Beg (1792–1842), wife of the Khan of Kokand and a celebrated literary figure in Uzbekistan. Babur is also remembered with a statue in Babur Square (formerly Lenin Square), the site of the 2005 massacre (see box, page 132).

The **Regional Studies Museum** and neighbouring **Ethnography Museum** (*Oltinkul*; ⊕ *09.00–16.00 Tue–Sun; foreigners US$1*) are not in themselves terribly exciting, but the latter is housed inside the 19th-century Juma Madrassa and Mosque (⊕ *09.00–17.00 Tue–Sun*), the only building in the city to have survived the 1902 earthquake. Built as Andijan's chief religious complex in the late 19th century, it's a stocky reddish building with a façade more than 120m long. There are some attractive vaulted halls, and the traditional portal at the centre of the mosque is crowned with ornamental minarets. If you climb up onto the rooftop (accessible until 16.00), you can appreciate both the layout of the inner courtyards and the scale of the summer *iwan*. The easy climb also provides for fine views across the city and, if you're lucky, a waft of much-needed breeze.

There are two large, public parks in Andijan. In **Navoi Park** (*Babur Sq*), an unexpectedly green haven with numerous trees and boating lakes, there is an elaborate 19th-century industrialist's house (now an office building). Built in 1897, this was once the home of factory-owner Ahmed Beg Khoja, but he was forced to abandon the building when he fled to China to escape the Bolsheviks. The house was, for a time, a folk museum but now houses the office for Andijan Muslims. During office hours visitors are permitted to explore living quarters and guest rooms on two of the floors. Inside the park there is also a gaudy new mosque sponsored by Saudi Arabia, situated on the foundations of an older mosque and madrassa from 1903.

Babur Park is 7km southeast of the city centre (a quick taxi ride or an hour's walk). Babur was supposedly fond of coming here (to the hill, not the park) and it is said that he stood atop the hill to get one last, panoramic view of the city before leaving his homeland forever. Earth from his grave in Kabul was scattered here when the park opened in 1993, and like a relic, the earth is now entombed in marble. The park is at its busiest on Sundays and holidays when there are craft stalls, music and dancing; you can also take the somewhat rickety chairlift up to a hilltop fairground.

Margilan is the centre of Uzbekistan's silk industry, and much of the silk you see for sale in Samarkand and Bukhara is in fact made in factories here. Like those better-known cities, the population of Margilan is also predominantly ethnic Tajik, which gives it a slightly different feel to other places in the Fergana Valley. It's only a small place, but well worth a few hours of your time.

HISTORY Margilan's history and its name are entwined, for local legend claims that Alexander the Great stopped here on his conquest of central Asia and was fed both *murgh* (chicken) and *naan* (flat bread). It was certainly a flourishing Silk Road town by the 9th century in large part due to its location on the road to Kashgar, and it became famous for both its fruits and its handwoven silks. Industrial silk production became the mainstay of the town's economy during the Soviet period, and Margilan was also noted as a centre for black market trade.

GETTING THERE AND AWAY Margilan lies 14km to the north of Fergana along a well-maintained road. It is just a 20 minute drive between the two towns, and all of the significant onward connections come into Fergana, so you should expect to transit through there.

Margilan's **bus stand** is close to the junction between Mustakillik and B Margilani, just behind the cinema. The ride to Fergana costs US$0.50 by minibus and US$1 by shared taxi.

Margilan has its own **railway station** (*1 Mashrab*; \ *237 5728*), which is on the southern side of the town. On Wednesdays, the #659 starts in Andijan at 17.55, stops in Margilan at 19.24 and then reaches Tashkent at 09.45 the following morning. In the opposite direction, the #660 departs from Tashkent at 17.20 on Thursdays, stops in Margilan at 07.58 on Friday morning, then reaches Andijan at 09.25.

GETTING AROUND Once in Margilan, the best way to get around is on foot. Almost all of the city's sites are situated along a 300m stretch of B Margilani and on Mustakillik, which crosses its western end.

TOURIST INFORMATION The best way to see the silk factories and workshops is with a guide, but if you want one who speaks English, you'll need to summon one from Uzbektourism in Fergana (page 140). The staff are generally helpful and knowledgeable about the silk industry, as well as having the inside track on what to buy and where (albeit, no doubt, with a hefty commission).

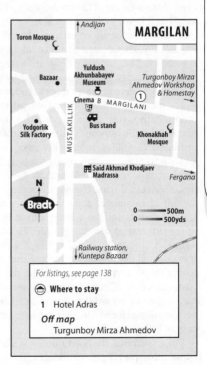

MARGILAN

Toron Mosque

↑ Andijan

Yuldush Akhunbabayev Museum

Bazaar

Turgonboy Mirza Ahmedov Workshop & Homestay

(1)

Cinema B MARGILANI

Yodgorlik Silk Factory

MUSTAKILLIK

Bus stand

Khonakhah Mosque

Said Akhmad Khodjaev Madrassa

N

Fergana

0 ▬▬ 500m
0 ▬▬ 500yds

Bradt

↓ Railway station, ↓ Kuntepa Bazaar

For listings, see page 138

⊖ **Where to stay**
1   Hotel Adras
Off map
    Turgunboy Mirza Ahmedov

WHERE TO STAY AND EAT   *Map, page 137*

Most people choose to visit Margilan on a day trip from Fergana, but if you do decide to stay, the hotel listed is the best available option. A homestay is also available with the silk painter Turgunboy Mirza Ahmedov (page 139). Call into his workshop to book. It costs US$25 per person, and US$5 for dinner. For food, head for the bazaar where there are basic cafés and shashlik stalls, as well as plenty of fresh bread, tomatoes, cucumbers and fruit.

Hotel Adras (21 rooms) 32 B Margilani; 279 0075; e hoteladras@gmail.com. The reasonably new Hotel Adras is not quite as cheap as you would hope, but the location is good & the sheets & bathrooms are clean. There is a medium-sized restaurant serving European & Uzbek dishes & large conference hall on site. **$$$**

SHOPPING   Buy your silk in Margilan; it would be foolish to do it anywhere else. The Yodgorlik Silk Factory (see below) has reasonable, though unimaginative, products, and silk designer Turgunboy Mirza Ahmedov also has a workshop at 129 Orol Buyi if you're looking for something a little more unusual.

WHAT TO SEE AND DO   Put simply, silk, silk and more silk. The **Yodgorlik Silk Factory** (*Imam Zakhriddin*; 223 8824; ◷ *Mar–Nov 08.00–17.00 Mon–Fri; admission 10,000 som*) was established in 1983 in a bid to preserve traditional silk weaving techniques in the face of industrialisation. The focus on high-quality, handmade goods has clearly paid off as the buoyant factory has now expanded to employ more than 2,000 workers. All parts of the production process are undertaken here, from the feeding of the big, fat silk worms with mulberry leaves, through dyeing with natural vegetable and mineral dyes, to the weaving of the final cloth, and it is fascinating to follow it through step by step: you'll never look at a silk scarf or tie in quite the same way again. Informative tours (*US$5, but can be off-set against purchases in the shop*) are fortunately available in English, French, German and Russian, so you can understand the intricacies of what is going on. The guides are delighted to answer questions and, if you show particular interest in part of the process, they really get into their stride, pull colleagues out of their work to demonstrate things to you, and may even let you have a go yourself.

For its sheer scale, and the contrast in production methods (machines feature prominently), you can also visit the state-run **Margilan Silk Factory** on a tour organised by Advantour (page 90). At its peak it employed 15,000 workers, who produced 22 million square metres of silk each year, but the economic downturn and electricity shortages mean the output now is just a fraction of this. If you're curious how centralised planning and mass-production were implemented in Uzbekistan during the Soviet period, this is a prime place to come as little if anything has changed since independence.

On Sundays and, to a lesser extent, Thursdays, the **Kuntepa Bazaar** (*5km west of the city centre*) springs into life: it's one of the most vibrant markets in central Asia and, unusually, is still selling the product that gave the Silk Road its name. It is open all day, but busiest in the mornings. The bazaar is a feast for the senses, with glorious textiles for sale on the stalls but also being worn by the traders and customers alike. Chatter, drink tea, wander around, haggle, drink more tea, buy a hat, engage in yet another complicated conversation of charades, eat shashlik, try on something else in silk, then collapse in a heap with yet more tea. This experience cannot be beaten.

Once you're all shopped out (or if silk just isn't your thing), Margilan also has some attractive **religious buildings**. The Khonakhah Mosque (*off B Margilani*), the

Silk weaving in Margilan is a family business, the secrets and skills passed down from father to son. Turgunboy Mirza Ahmedov is head of the seventh generation of silk weavers in his family. He was born in Margilan in 1944 and was one of the founder members of the Yodgorlik Silk Factory, for which he has created more than 100 designs.

Turgunboy is both a designer and a maker of silk fabrics, and his particular interest is in researching and reviving traditional styles of handweaving. His work has come to the notice of UNESCO, who has recognised its significance, and he will proudly show you samples of *adras*, *banoras*, *beak slab* and *shoi* cloths, all of which ceased production during the Soviet period but that he is now making once again.

Keeping the weaving tradition alive, Turgunboy has trained his son Rasul to carry on his work. The two men work closely to develop authentic patterns, and Rasul has begun his own project to reproduce Ala Bakhmal silk, which was last made in Bukhara in 1910 and was even then produced only in tiny quantities for the most elaborate of royal costumes.

city's religious centrepiece, has an impressive pair of minarets each 26m high, and the main buildings are a showcase for the mastery of Margilan's woodcarvers. The mosque was first built in the 16th century and much of the decoration is original. Non-Muslims are welcome inside providing that they are appropriately attired and behave in a respectful manner.

The elegant Toron Mosque (1840), situated just north of the bazaar, has a superb and sensitively restored painted ceiling, as does the Said Akhmad Khodjaev Madrassa just off Mustakillik. Said Akmad Khojaev, the madrassa's patron and namesake, was a wealthy philanthropist and advisor to the tsarist administration. He fled Margilan during the revolution, first to Afghanistan and then to Saudi Arabia. In the 20th century the building was used first as a jail and then as an office, returning to its original function in 1992. Some 300 students study here; boys and girls are taught in separate shifts and they are keen to practise their English on any foreigner who steps inside. Visitors are welcomed by the administration as well as the children.

Last but not least, you can also visit the small **Yuldash Akhunbabayev Museum** (*1 Ozodlik Sq;* ⟍ *233 5117;* ⊕ *Tue–Fri 10.00–17.00*), which covers the life of this former leader of the Uzbek Communist Party and also has a few more general displays on the city's history. The exhibits are a little dry, and very typical of house museums in Uzbekistan, but it's worth an hour of your time if you're politically inclined or want a break from silk and mosques.

FERGANA   *Telephone code: 73*

Founded in 1876 as a Russian garrison town, Fergana has gone though a succession of name changes. From its origin as the less than imaginative New Margilan, it became Skobelov in 1907, then finally Fergana in 1924. It is now the capital of Fergana Province and is also a regional centre for oil refining and chemical fertiliser production. The majority of foreigners visiting the town are either here for work reasons, or passing through *en route* to somewhere with more cultural capital.

Fergana Valley and the East   FERGANA

4

139

GETTING THERE, AWAY AND AROUND

By road Some 350km from Tashkent and 75km from Andijan, Fergana is easily accessible from either direction should you feel the need to go there: it lies just south of the A373, the main road through the valley. Shared taxis to Tashkent leave from the Yermazar Bazaar bus stand (*4hrs; US$12*), and the minibus/shared taxis to Andijan leave from the old bus station on Rahimov (*1¼hrs; US$3/4*). The minibus/shared taxis to Margilan also leave from this point (*20mins; US$0.30/0.70*). For Kokand, minibuses departs from the new local bus stand on Kurbunjon Dodhoh (*2hrs; US$1*).

Though Fergana is a fair-sized city, most of the sites you are likely to want to visit fall within a few streets of each other and so are conveniently reached on foot. If you are travelling further afield within the city, buses 3 and 4 run from the airport, along M Kasimov and eventually to the bazaar. Minibus 22 takes a more direct route from the city centre to the airport.

By air Fergana's airport is 5km south of the city. Uzbekistan Airways has scheduled departures three to four times a week, depending on the season, to Tashkent (*1hr*) and also a weekly flight (*Wed; 3hrs*) to Nukus via Tashkent.

TOUR OPERATORS The state-run Uzbektourism have an office in Fergana (*2A Dodkhokh;* ✎ *224 7740*) and are able to provide English-speaking guides to Margilan and other local sites of interest. **Vodiy Sayyox** (*3 Al Fargoni;* ✎ *224 2502*) offer flight and accommodation bookings, although there is no English spoken.

WHERE TO STAY *Map, page 141*

Fergana is a much larger city than Margilan, and has a correspondingly greater number of accommodation options. You might, therefore, want to base yourself in Fergana, and to visit Margilan on a daytrip.

Asia Hotel (95 rooms) 26 Navoi; ✎ 580 3994; www.asiahotels.uz/en. Upmarket chain hotel aimed at foreign tour groups. The hotel is large, comfortable & well located but utterly characterless. There is a restaurant on site. B/fast & Wi-Fi inc. **$$$**

Club Hotel 777 (32 rooms) 7A Pushkin; ✎ 224 3777. A slightly brash resort hotel for package tourists on coach trips, where you'd expect to fight for a sun lounger by the pool. Facilities are fine; the atmosphere & clientele can be ghastly. **$$$**

Ziyorat Hotel (72 rooms) 2A Dekhon; ✎ 224 7742. Recently reopened after much-needed renovations, Ziyorat has gone from being a bit of a dump to a perfectly acceptable (if uninspiring) mid-range option. **$$$**

Golden Valley (3 apts) 10 Shakirov; ✎ 215 0733. Large, comfortable apts a short walk from the town centre. Each one is equipped with AC & ample kitchen equipment to self cater should you wish. **$$**

Sonia B&B 49 Ahunbabaev; ✎ 979 9099. The friendliest homestay in town is with Sonia & her warm & welcoming family. Join them for excellent dinners & comfortable beds in a central location. Highly recommended. **$$**

WHERE TO EAT AND DRINK *Map, page 141*

For cheap and tasty eats, there are numerous chaikhanas and shashlik stands in Al Fargoni Park and around the bazaar. Otherwise, we recommend the following.

Bavaria 89 Kuvasoy. For something a little different, head to Bavaria & cry sweet tears at the sight of actual German sausages (or at least a very good approximation of them) in Uzbekistan. **$$$**

✗ Bravo Cafe 12 Khojand. This scruffy outfit close to Asia Hotel is a reasonable option, where Fergana's arty types hang out. The espresso is suitably strong; the baristas certainly know their stuff! $$

OTHER PRACTICALITIES

Communications Fergana is better stocked with internet cafés than the cities in the valley. Infinity Internet (*18 Navoi;* ⏲ *09.00–22.00 daily*) is the most popular spot: it's round the corner from the telephone and telegraph office on Al Fargoni. The main post office is at 35 Mustakillik (⏲ *07.00–19.00 Mon–Sat*).

Money Fergana has plenty of places to change money and receive Western Union transfers. The most centrally located banks are listed here, though there are plenty more. None of them have ATMs. Cash advance is available for Visa cardholders at the National Bank of Uzbekistan (*35 Al Fargoni*). The best place to find unofficial money changers is in the bazaar or around the bus stands, where someone is in any case likely to approach you to offer to exchange som for dollars.

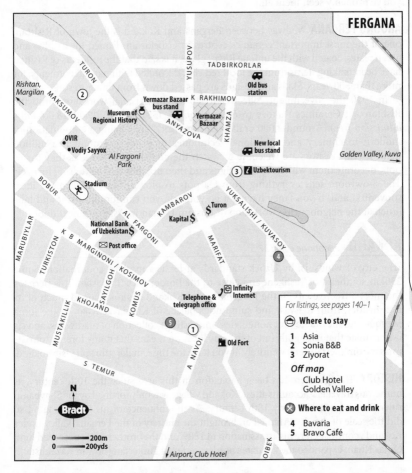

FERGANA

4

For listings, see pages 140–1

⬒ **Where to stay**
1 Asia
2 Sonia B&B
3 Ziyorat

Off map
   Club Hotel
   Golden Valley

⊗ **Where to eat and drink**
4 Bavaria
5 Bravo Café

0 ▬▬▬ 200m
0 ▬▬▬ 200yds

141

$ Hamkor Bank 74 Naqshbandi; m 95 401 7175; ☉ 09.00–16.00 Mon–Fri
$ Kapitalbank 43 Marifat; ☎ 224 3322; ☉ 09.00–17.00 Mon–Sat

$ Turon Bank 44 Marifat; ☎ 224 0617; ☉ 08.30–17.00 Mon–Fri

Registration Fergana's Office of Visa and Registration (OVIR) is at 36 Ahunbabaev (☉ *08.00–17.00 Mon–Fri, 08.00–12.00 Sat*).

WHAT TO SEE AND DO To be honest, you don't come to Fergana to see Fergana: you sleep here and make use of the good transport connections to explore other parts of the valley.

Fergana's sole piece of remaining history, a section of the mud-brick walls of its Russian fort, is now sadly hidden from view (and usually inaccessible) inside the army compound on Kasimov.

The **Museum of Regional History** (*26 Murrabiylar;* ☉ *09.00–17.00 Wed–Sun; foreigners US$1*) is a Soviet relic, and some of the dioramas probably haven't been dusted since then either. It gives some insight into what the USSR felt was important for its citizens to learn about, but once you've seen one museum of this type then you've probably seen them all.

AROUND FERGANA Midway between Fergana and Kokand is the town of **Rishtan**, one of the most important ceramics centres in Uzbekistan. Famed for its blue and green plates, coated with the unique *ishkor* glaze, it is said that the residents of Rishtan have been making items from the local red clay, decorated with natural pigments, for more than 800 years. Skills and designs are passed down from father to son.

In 1920 the government collectivised 30 small, artisanal workshops into the Rishtan Art Ceramics Factory (*6 B Roshidoni;* ☎ *452 1549;* ☉ *09.00–18.00 daily; admission free*). Around 2,000 craftsmen now work here, using a combination of modern machinery and traditional techniques to produce around five million items a year. Visitors are welcome to watch the craftsmen at work as they throw pots, decorate them with delicate designs and then fire them in the roaring furnace. The showroom sells everything from tea pots to plov dishes (which make ideal souvenirs) and, if you fancy having a go yourself, you can mould, paint and take lunch at the neighbouring workshop of Rustam Usmanov. Ask for it next door.

KOKAND *Telephone code: 37*

'The city of winds' is, by Uzbek standards at least, a modern conurbation. Some 230km southeast of Tashkent and close to the border with Tajikistan, it is perhaps the most attractive city in the Fergana Valley. Kokand has maintained much of its rich history, from the vast and sumptuous palace of Khudayar Khan to the Juma Mosque and inevitable (but nonetheless interesting) collection of madrassas, and it's unfortunate that its slightly out of the way location means that many foreign tourists miss it from their itinerary entirely. If you have the time, make sure you visit Kokand.

HISTORY Though there has been habitation in this area since the 10th century, as numerous travellers' accounts attest, Kokand village was only fortified by the Shaybanid ruler Shahrukh in the early 18th century. As the influence of his khanate grew, so did the scale of the city. Alim Khan brought the entirety of the Fergana Valley under Kokand's control before his assassination in 1809, and the brother who succeeded him, Omar Khan, expanded the khanate's borders as far as Turkestan (now in Kazakhstan).

Kokand's power peaked under the rule of Madali Khan, Omar's debauched son, to whose court came both Russian and British agents, including the ill-fated Captain Conolly (see box, page 218). The Bukharan emir Nasrullah murdered Madali in 1842 and seized Kokand, but the people revolted against him, starting two decades of bloody warfare and several short-lived rulers. Political instability fatally weakened the Kokand state, leaving it at the mercy of the Russians.

Khudayar Khan was forced to accept a Russian commercial treaty in 1868, leaving him as little more than a puppet ruler. He continued to live in luxury despite the suffering of Kokand's citizens; insurrections followed and the khan died in exile in Russia. Kokand was annexed by General Kaufman in 1875 and became a province of Russian Turkestan.

Russian rule never sat easily with Kokand's population, however, and in 1917 the revolutionary Mustafa Chokayev seized the opportunity to establish the Provisional Autonomous Government of Turkestan, an Islamic alternative to the Tashkent Soviet. It took just three days for the Red Army to sack and burn the city. Some 14,000 people died and Chokayev fled to Paris, taking with him the Basmachis' greatest hope for an Islamic state in central Asia.

GETTING THERE AND AWAY Kokand's airport has frustratingly been mothballed and train routes to Tashkent go through Tajikistan, so for foreign visitors the best way to reach or depart from Kokand is by road.

The **main bus station** is at 102 Furkat by the Dekhon Bazaar. In the daytime, buses leave every 15 minutes to Fergana (*2hrs; US$1*) and every 45 minutes to Andijan (*2hrs; US$1*). Minibuses and shared taxis ply the same routes but are slightly faster. Expect to pay twice the bus fare if you go by shared taxi.

The best way to Tashkent is by **shared taxi** (*4hrs; US$10–12*). These can be picked up from the Krug stop (circle roundabout) 5km north of the city centre, though it is sometimes possible to get a ride from the main bus station, too.

Kokand has a **railway station** (*40 A Timur*) on the A376 in the south of the town, at the end of Turon. There is a slow local service to Andijan, though it is usually preferable to drive.

GETTING AROUND Getting around Kokand is straightforward. The most useful buses are No 8 between Hotel Kokand, the railway and bus stations, also passing the Khudayar Khan Palace and the Juma Mosque; and No 14 between the airport, railway station and Hotel Kokand. Minibuses 2 and 4 link the Dekhon Bazaar with Hotel Kokand; minibuses 15 and 40 go north from the bazaar to the Juma Mosque.

Most taxis are hail and ride. However, if you do want to pre-book a car, try Grand Taxi (☏ *200 2121*).

TOUR OPERATORS Uzbektourism (*83 Khamza;* ☏ *552 5892*) offer transport and accommodation bookings, as well as guided tours; the walking tour of Kokand is particularly interesting. For airline tickets and other transport services, try Khavo Sayyokh Air Company (*9I I Bukhari;* ☏ *552 3102*).

WHERE TO STAY AND EAT *Map, page 144*
Kokand has a reasonable selection of accommodation options and places to eat, all of which are within easy reach of the city centre.

Hotel Khudyar Khan (21 rooms) 31 Istiqlol; ☏ 542 2244; www.khan.uz. Kokand's

best option is this modern hotel with AC & Wi-Fi. Staff are helpful & will usually change money as well as offering tips on what to see. **$$$**

🏠 **Hotel Kokand** 1 I Bukhari; ✆ 552 6403. Recently reopened after a much-needed refurbishment, rooms & public areas are now significantly improved, as are the bathrooms. Situated in the west of the city opposite the telegraph office. **$$**

🏠 **Khadirov Homestay** [not mapped] (2 rooms) 1A N Urinbaeva. Feel like one of the family in this attractive traditional building. B/fast inc; other meals on request. **$$**

✕ **Jahan Chaikhana** 1 I I Bukhari; ⏱ 08.00–18.00. For a quick bite to eat or an early supper,

this has the usual range of soups & kebabs & tends to be quite lively at weekends. **$$$**

✕ **Capri** 1 I I Bukhari. For something a little more substantial, this has some fairly solid Russian dishes sprinkled amply with dill, to be washed down with plentiful vodka. **$$$**

✕ **Café Markhabor** (cnr Khamza & Turkiston) This is another good option & overlooks the canal. **$$**

✕ **Jassurbek** Independence Sq. This is well placed for a light, quick snack if you've spent the afternoon at Khudayar Khan Palace. **$$**

SHOPPING As you would expect, Kokand's Dekhon Bazaar, the main bazaar, is well stocked with fresh produce and basic household goods. There are some underwhelming souvenir stands chancing it outside the Khudayar Khan Palace but, for something a bit more unusual, try the Khaidarov Wood Workshop (*67 K Khaidarov*) where enthusiastic young apprentices will show you their latest woodcarving projects.

OTHER PRACTICALITIES

Communications There is an internet café at 1 Navoi, and you can also use the Wi-Fi at Hotel Khudayar Khan. The main post office is at 38 Urda-Dogi.

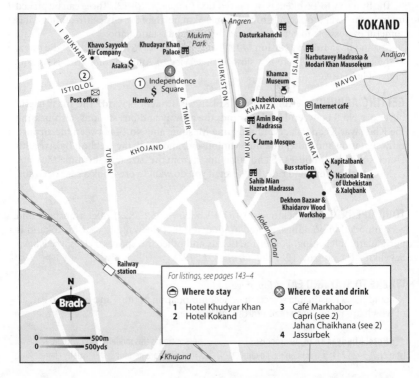

Medical Kokand has several hospitals, but in an emergency you would need the Central Kokand Hospital of Urgent Medical Care (*132 Kokandi;* ☎ *552 9493;* ⊕ *24hrs*). There are a number of Apteka around the hospital and also another at 66 Istiqlol.

Money Visa cardholders can get cash advanced at NBU. The other banks listed can send and receive Western Union transfers and exchange money at the official rate. You will find unofficial money changers in Dekhon Bazaar and around the main bus station.

$ **Asaka Bank** 25 Istiklok; ☎ 552 6110; ⊕ 09.00–15.00 Mon–Fri
$ **Hamkor Bank** 51 U Nosira; ☎ 554 1135; ⊕ 09.00–16.00 Mon–Sat
$ **Kapitalbank** 82 Furkat; ☎ 553 0698; ⊕ 09.00–17.00 Mon–Sat
$ **National Bank of Uzbekistan** 100 Furkat; ☎ 552 5926; ⊕ 09.00–17.00 Mon–Fri
$ **Xalqbank** 100 Furkat; ☎ 255 1868; ⊕ 09.00–17.00 Mon–Fri. Mini branch only.

Registration Although Kokand has an OVIR (*cnr Turkiston & Istiqlol*), it is not currently possible for foreigners to register here. You have to go to Fergana instead (page 142).

WHAT TO SEE AND DO Without a shadow of doubt, Kokand's most impressive sight is the **Khudayar Khan Palace** (*2 Istiqlol;* ☎ *553 6046;* ⊕ *09.00–18.00 Mon–Sat; foreigners US$1*), one of the most glittering royal residences in central Asia and a structure that would make fairytale princesses jump up and down for joy. At the tail end of the 19th century, just before the Russians put paid to his architectural (and political) ambition, Khudayar Khan indulgently commissioned a sumptuous palace with 113 rooms set around seven courtyards. His mother lived in one of these courtyards, housed in her very own yurt.

Of the original rooms, only 19 remain, but walking here in Khudayar Khan's footsteps you gain a fascinating glimpse into the life of an oriental despot just before everything around him fell apart: it is a palace built on the cusp of history, and you can almost sense the unfulfilled dreams tied up in its walls and furnishings. The collection of objects on show is somewhat eclectic (everything from jewellery and weaponry to a beautifully carved hall), probably due to the fact that most of the original contents were dispersed or destroyed in the early years of Soviet rule. Some of the interiors have fortunately survived (some partially restored), however, and these are the palace's real attraction. The craftsmanship is exquisite, and you can clearly see the influence of Russian and European tastes on more traditional Uzbek designs. The museum's English-speaking director gives guided tours (*US$3.50*) of the site, and these are the best way to understand not only the physical building but also the lives and times of Khudayar Khan and his family.

A few general exhibits about life in Kokand have been relocated from the palace to the **Khamza Museum** (*2 A Islam;* ☎ *552 2329;* ⊕ *09.00–17.00 Tue–Sun; foreigners US$1*), which commemorates the life of Khakim Khakimzade Niyazi, the Soviet poet, dramatist and propagandist. It's a fairly dingy spot, however, so don't bother coming unless you've plenty of time on your hands.

Rather more worthy of your time are Kokand's religious sites. The **Juma Mosque** (*5 Khamza;* ⊕ *09.00–17.00 daily; foreigners US$1*) swings back and forth between being a mosque and a museum, so goodness knows which it will be by the time you visit. If it's a mosque, non-Muslims may not be allowed to enter: you will, however, be permitted to stand in the gateway and look across the football pitch-sized courtyard to the mighty *iwan*, supported on 98 glorious redwood columns, carved and imported from India.

In any case, the building itself was built by Umar Khan between 1809 and 1812 and it was the khan's primary place of worship. The mosque remained shut for most of the 20th century but reopened following a much-needed period of restoration in 1989.

THE SHOHIMARDON RESORT

An hour's drive from Fergana, lost among the mountain peaks of the Alai range, is the picturesque city resort of Shohimardon. The physical landscape is nigh on perfect: to the south is Lake Kulikubbon (the Blue Lake), reached by a cable car that creaks alarmingly but has breathtaking views, and the Oak-Su and Kok-Su rivers run by. Trekking routes are numerous, as are the picnic spots, and the lake and river waters are clean and fresh for swimming, albeit a little on the chilly side.

Local legend has it that Hazrat Ali, son-in-law of the Prophet Muhammad and the fourth caliph, visited Shohimardon. The name Shohimardon, which is Persian for 'Lord of the People', is in fact a reference to Ali. Ali was assassinated in Iraq, but shortly before his death he is said to have instructed his followers to dig him seven graves in seven places, and to bury parts of his body there. Of these seven graves, three are said to be in Uzbekistan: in Nurata, in Khiva and in Shohimardon. The city is therefore considered to be a sacred place. The Hazrat Ali Mosque and Mausoleum, which lies in the city centre, was destroyed by the Soviets in the 1920s but has been rebuilt since independence and it still attracts a constant stream of pilgrims, in particular barren women.

A second, rather more recent historical figure is also buried in Shohimardon: the Uzbek poet Khamza Khakimzade Niyazi. Born in Kokand in 1889, and a key figure in the early development of modern literature, Khamza was stoned to death by Islamic fundamentalists in Shohimardon in 1929. Khamza was an ardent supporter of the communist revolution, and his tomb here is said to be cut from the same pink Pamiri marble as Lenin's tomb in Red Square.

The city lies 80km south of Fergana along a well-maintained road. If you don't have your own vehicle, there are plenty of shared taxis running the route, especially at weekends and other holidays. Taking a private taxi will cost around US$20. Be sure to stop at the village of Vuadil *en route*, where there's a maple tree with a circumference of nearly 28m that is said to be 800 years old.

For its history and its beauty, Shohimardon should rightly be a key tourist destination in the Fergana Valley. However, thanks to Stalin's meddling with central Asia's borders, it is unfortunately situated in an Uzbek enclave within Kyrgyzstan. Foreigners wishing to visit require a multiple-entry Uzbek visa, a multiple-entry Kyrgyz visa, and also a permit from the Internal Affairs Bureau in Fergana. The permit can be gained from a local travel agent (page 143).

There are several pleasant places to stay in Shohimardon, including sleeping in wooden chalets at Turbaza Shakhimardan (contact Uzbektourism in Fergana; page 140), a Soviet-style holiday camp on the hill overlooking Ali's tomb.

A short walk north brings you to the **Amin Beg Madrassa,** which was built in the 1830s for a son of Madali Khan. The madrassa has a particularly attractive tiled façade: indeed, the tilework is so fine that the madrassa is also known as Khomol Khozi Madrassa in honour of the craftsman who restored its ornamental mosaics in 1913. It was closed when we visited but is due to reopen as a museum, hopefully within the lifespan of this edition.

There are three other madrassas of note in the town: the 18th-century Narbutabey Madrassa (*Nabiev*) has an attached graveyard that includes the Modari Khan Mausoleum where Omar Khan and his wife, the poet Nadira Beg, are entombed; the Dasturkahanchi, a madrassa for teenage girls first built in 1833 (originally for male students) where they now study embroidery and other sewing skills; and the 19th-century Sahib Mian Hazrat Madrassa (*Muqimi*), which houses a small museum to the Uzbek poet Mohammad Amin Muqimi (1850–1903).

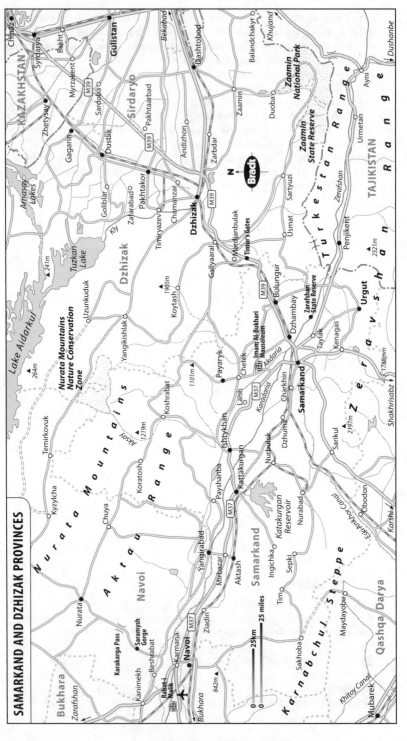

SAMARKAND AND DZHIZAK PROVINCES

5

Samarkand and Dzhizak Provinces

Samarkand and Dzhizak benefit both from their proximity to Tashkent and from the wealth and variety of tourist sites they contain. The Zaamin National Park and Zarafshan mountain passes of Dzhizak show Uzbekistan's natural landscapes and wildlife at their best; this small province bordering Tajikistan is one of the country's most picturesque and a prime location for climbing and trekking.

A stone's throw away, the manmade wonders of Samarkand never cease to amaze even the most sated of culture vultures. A dynamic city of well over half a million people, Samarkand is quite rightly a must-see stop on every tourist's itinerary. Masterpieces of Timurid architecture soar above the otherwise low-rise Old Town, and surely there's as much archaeological history underfoot as above ground.

SAMARKAND *Telephone code: 66*

> For lust of knowing what should not be known,
> We take the Golden Road to Samarkand.
>
> *James Elroy Flecker (1884–1915)*

Buildings of breathtaking beauty in the heart of regal Samarkand caught imaginations long before Flecker's and have continued to do so ever since. Medieval merchants must have marvelled at every sight, from the exotic goods on sale to the spectacular manmade backdrops of madrassas, mosques and mausoleums. Centuries on, visitors are still struck by the beauty, the number and the scale of Samarkand's architectural sites, and are often moved by thoughts of the ambition, dedication and, no doubt, personal sacrifices required to turn dreams into concrete reality.

The Registan, with its central square and three exquisite madrassas, is Samarkand's biggest draw and makes a picture-postcard scene. It's far from the only attraction, however, as the ruins of Afrosiab, the observatory of Ulug Beg and the Shah-i Zinda, the necropolis of the Living King, are sights that you'll never forget. The time of year you visit Samarkand will have a significant impact on your experience: coming out of season, especially in the autumn months, will enable you to get close to the building's physical details and to linger as long as you like. The city always was a bustling, cosmopolitan place, however, so even if you are sucked into the summertime crowds, your experience will be no less authentic: the residents of Samarkand have for centuries made money from the foreigners passing through.

HISTORY Samarkand's past is built up in myth and legend, its beauty extolled by chroniclers and travellers for two millennia or more. There was certainly a city here from the 6th century BC, around the Afrosiab hill fort (pages 163–5), and two centuries later, when Alexander the Great seized the Sogdian city, he is alleged to have said, 'Everything I have heard about Marakanda is true, except that it is more beautiful than I ever imagined.' The city's beauty was not enough to spare its buildings or its inhabitants, however, and Alexander's forces torched the citadel to punish the Sogdian general Spitamenes for his resistance.

Samarkand entered a dark age and it was not until the 7th century AD that Silk Road trade returned and the city flourished again. It became one of the most populous cities in central Asia (far larger than it is today), a cultural and mercantile centre whose reputation spread even to Tang China. The Zoroastrian rulers of Samarkand sent luxurious gifts to neighbouring states, which included wild animals, dancing girls, musicians and all manner of natural and manmade curiosities.

As in so many of Uzbekistan's cities, life came to an abrupt halt with the arrival of the murderous Qutaiba ibn Muslim in AD 712. Much of the population was killed or exiled, though Qutaiba did thoughtfully compensate the city by building its first mosque in which they could pray for the slain.

In the centuries that followed, Samarkand passed successively through the hands of the Samanids, Karakhanids, Seljuks, Karakhitai and Khorezmshah before being struck down yet again by Genghis Khan. It is said that the city's irrigation canals ran red with the blood of the people. The population was decimated, either killed or driven out so that scarcely a man remained.

Remarkably, Samarkand bounced back. Marco Polo and Ibn Battuta both commented on the city's size and splendour, and in 1370 Timur decided to make it his capital. Samarkand became the epicentre of one of the largest empires the world had ever seen, and to make it great Timur drew on resources both human and financial from as far afield as Damascus and Delhi. He built madrassas and mosques, palaces and caravanserai, mausoleums and trading domes. The whole known world brought their goods to sell in Samarkand, and they marvelled at the scale and beauty of the city, and of the speed of its construction.

Timur had put Samarkand on the map, but it made the city a target for any ambitious competitor. Timur's grandson, Ulug Beg, maintained control long enough to build his observatory (page 165), but the power of the Uzbek clans was rising, and they would ultimately chase the last Timurid emperor, Babur, out of central Asia altogether. After two failed attempts to regain control of Samarkand, he fled south to India and there founded the Mughal Empire instead.

Silk Road trade declined, Samarkand began to fall into disrepair, and an earthquake caused significant damage to the taller buildings in particular. The Russian general Kaufman seized the city with a force of just 3,500 men in 1868; the Russians then set about demolishing the walls, constructing a modern fortress in the citadel and building wide, tree-lined avenues in the European style. The Trans-Caspian railway arrived in 1888, and Samarkand was dragged into the modern age.

In 1917 Samarkand fell to the Bolsheviks with none of the violence seen in Bukhara. Samarkand was declared the capital of the Uzbek SSR in 1925, in spite of the fact that the majority of its population were ethnic Tajiks, the population swelled to around 400,000 people, and Lenin Square and the Opera House were built atop what was once Timur's Blue Palace.

GETTING THERE AND AWAY

By road Samarkand is an easy 4- to 5-hour drive from either Tashkent or Bukhara. The surface has been fairly recently tarmacked, and vehicles of all shapes and sizes speed along. Samarkand's **Ulug Beg bus stand** [154 D1] is 200m east of the Observatory, and it is from here you will pick up most long-distance minibuses and shared taxis. A seat in a minibus costs US$5 to Tashkent and US$5 to Bukhara, and just over twice as much if you travel by shared taxi. In either direction, the minibus ride takes around 5 hours. Buses are the same price but take significantly longer.

To travel south to Termez you need the **Grebnoy Kanal bus stand** on the eastern outskirts of the city. Shared taxis cost around US$17 and take 5 hours. Arrive early and be prepared to wait, as there are frequently more would-be passengers than seats. The bus is cheaper (*US$8*) but allow twice as long for the journey.

If you are driving your **own vehicle** into Samarkand, expect to get terribly lost. The signposts are almost non-existent, and there are so many one-way sections and dead ends it would make the Pope swear. We've found the easiest

TRANS-CASPIAN RAILWAY   *Bijan Omrani*

The Trans-Caspian railway was developed as a necessary part of Imperial Russia's conquest of central Asia. At the end of the 1870s, Russia was fighting to overcome the fearsome Tekke Turcomans, but was experiencing serious problems of military transportation across the central Asian deserts. In 1879, their army lost 8,000 out of 12,000 baggage camels in the Karakum Desert, as a result of which they suffered a dangerous setback at the hands of the Turcomans. Two years later in 1881, although the formidable General Skobelev was able to break the Turcomans by capturing their stronghold of Geok-Tepe, the Russian Army and camels faced even worse difficulties. At the end of this campaign, only 350 of the latter were left out of an original 12,500. A railway was clearly needed to secure the army's supply routes.

The railway was the brainchild of General Mikhail Annenkov, who was then in charge of the Army Transport Department. He decided that the railway should have a spacious five-foot gauge, and be powered not by burning wood as was common elsewhere on Russian railways, but by naphtha, a by-product of crude-oil refining which was easily available from Baku across the Caspian.

Annenkov had to overcome a range of engineering challenges. Timber, iron and steel had to be imported all the way from central Russia, and stone quarried from the Persian mountains. Although the land was flat, the newly laid tracks could easily be covered by shifting sands, or washed away by flash floods. Nevertheless, when the conditions were favourable the skilled workforce of 1,500 men could lay up to 6km of track a day.

The line was started in 1881, and by 1895 it reached over 1,000km from the Caspian Sea to Bukhara, Samarkand and Tashkent. The old Silk Road cities were at first hostile to the line, calling it Shaitan's Arba, or the 'Devil's Wagon'. The strong feelings of Bukhara's citizens caused the Russians to put the station 16km away from the city. However, once the trains started opinions reversed. Locals and merchants flocked to use the new service, and business rapidly drained from the heart of the old cities to cluster around the new railway stations. The initial unwillingness of the people to embrace the new means of transport sapped the dynamism of their old cities, and led to them being treated for much of the 20th century as nothing more than museum pieces.

way is to drive in the general direction of the city centre, then flag down a taxi and pay him to drive in front of you to the Gur-i Amir where there is plenty of free, fairly well-lit parking.

By train Samarkand's **railway station** is 6km northwest of the city centre at the junction between Rudaki and Beruni. It is on the main railway line between Tashkent and either Bukhara or Urgench (they're on different lines), so it's fast and relatively straightforward to reach the city by train.

The new, high-speed **Afrosiab service** between Tashkent and Samarkand runs daily and takes just 2½ hours. Tickets start from 50,000 som. The older **Sharq service** (train 9 or 10 depending on the direction) runs every morning and compartments have air conditioning. Trains 49/50 and 661/662 also run daily and have sleeper carriages. These services take between 3 and 4 hours, but the ticket prices are correspondingly lower: basic tickets on these slower services start from 20,075 som one way.

Travelling west from Samarkand, there are twice-daily departures to Bukhara (trains 9/10 and 661/662) and the journey takes between 3 and 5 hours depending on the service. Trains to Urgench (No 56 and 58) run daily apart from Wednesday. Two- and four-berth sleepers are available and they are highly recommended as it is about 12 hours travel in each direction.

For the latest departure times and ticket prices see www.uzrailpass.uz. Tickets can be bought online by card, or paid for in cash at the station. If you are buying your tickets in advance and want them delivered, hassle-free to your hotel, Caravanistan (*www.caravanistan.com*) offers a hugely helpful reservations service.

By air Given the ease of road and rail travel between Samarkand and Tashkent and the relatively short distance involved, it seems unnecessary to fly. However, if you do feel the need, **Uzbekistan Airways** flies at least four times a week in each direction. The flight takes 55 minutes and costs US$60 one way. Departures are in the early morning. Payments for tickets can only be made in cash, and the **airport** is northeast of the city centre on V Abdullo.

GETTING AROUND Most of Samarkand's important sites are within easy walking distance of one another, and hotels tend to be fairly central, too. Tashkent has been pedestrianised (and lined with souvenir shops), so walking between the Registan and the Bibi Khanym Mosque and bazaar is particularly straightforward.

It is possible to get around Samarkand in your own car, but not really advisable due to the nonsensical road system. Concrete bollards now blockade the north side of the junction of Dahbet and Registan, which is a particular nuisance.

There is a good network of **minibuses** in Samarkand. Minibuses 17 and 45 are particularly helpful as they link the bazaar with Afrosiab and Ulug Beg's Observatory. Minibus tickets cost 1,000 som.

The most useful **bus route** is the 73 linking Registan with the train station. Bus 60 links the airport to the town centre, as does 31 and 19. Bus tickets cost 500 som.

If you're travelling further afield within the city (for example to the railway station), you may want to take a **taxi**. There are the usual number of hail and ride options, or you can pre-book a cab with **Taxi Co** (\ *727 9064*) or **Dinamo Taxi** (\ *261 020*).

To reach Khoja Ismail village (for the Imam Al-Bukhari Mausoleum), which lies 20km north of Samarkand, you need to take a minibus headed to Chelek

The striped Islam Khoja
Minaret adds height to Khiva's
otherwise low-rise skyline
(j/S) page 245

above left It's possible to see Alpine ibex in Ugam-Chatkal National Park (M/D) page 122

above right Tulips are a common sight in Uzbekistan (SI) pages 167–8

left Ship skeletons on the bed of the Aral Sea are a poignant memorial to the environmental disaster (DP/D) page 257

below Nomadic herders still live in traditional yurts in the Kyzylkum Desert and around Aiderkul (AL/D).

above **Lake Charvak glimmers like a turquoise jewel in the Tian Shan mountains** (EK/D) page 120

below **Uzbekistan's foothills are prime areas for trekking and make a cool retreat in the summer months** (SS) page 37

above left Gold thread embroidery is a traditional craft that makes popular souvenirs (R/D) page 33

above right Spices have been traded along the Silk Road since time immemorial (EM/D)

left You can see decorative metalwork being worked at the Bukhara Artisan Development Centre (AB) page 214

below The chaikhana at Lyabi Hauz in Bukhara is central to the community (MEP) page 217

above Round, flat breads are served at every meal and are treated almost reverentially (EF/D) page 67

right Uzbekistan's artisans produce all manner of curious souvenirs, including hand-carved gourds (MEP)

below Though in modern buildings, the merchants of Chorsu Bazaar continue an ancient trade (JS/AWL) page 100

above left & above right   **The Timurid Emperor Ulug Beg** was a notable astronomer as well as ruler (SS); his observatory survived destruction and can still be used to survey the stars (E/D) page 164

left   **The Ark Fortress at Bukhara** is Uzbekistan's architectural icon (DP/D) pages 215–17

below   There would be little reason to come to Nukus at all if it weren't for the **Igor Savitsky Museum**, an unexpected treasure trove of Soviet avant-garde art from the 1920s and 30s (C/WC) page 255

above The archaeological site of Kampir Tepe is superbly preserved, and empty of tourists (MEP) pages 192–3

below Amir Timur is commemorated in front of the Ak Serai, his palace in Shakhrisabz (P/S) page 176

above Politician and poet Alisher Navoi is commemorated across Uzbekistan, such as this statue in Tashkent (MM/S) page 114

from the bus stop by the Shah-i Zinda and jump off at Khoja Ismail, which is 4km before the end of the route.

TOURIST INFORMATION AND TRAVEL AGENTS Most hotels in Samarkand are able and willing to provide tourist information and make ongoing travel arrangements (including train reservations) on your behalf. Some general information about the city and its sites is online at www.samarkand.info.

For tours around the city, or indeed further afield, there are plenty of options to choose from. **Sogda Tour** [154 B5] (*38 Registan;* \ *235 3609;* e *info@sogda-tour.com; www.sogda-tour.com*) and **Asia Travel International Group** [154 A5] (*Afrosiab Palace, 2 Registan;* \ *233 7521;* e *tours@ati-uzbekistan.com*) both seem well organised and reasonably priced, though you can still haggle.

To buy airline tickets, you need **VIP Aviakassa** [154 B5] (*38 Registan;* \ *235 0061*).

WHERE TO STAY Samarkand has plenty of places to stay whatever your budget, though the most popular tend to get booked up in high season. The larger hotels typically cater to coach parties, but this means independent travellers can often negotiate a hefty discount on the advertised rate if there are rooms going spare.

Top end

🏠 **Afrosiab Palace** [154 A5] (278 rooms) 2 Registan; \ 231 1195; e afrosiab@online.ru. Occupying what was once the site of Timur's Blue Palace, this architectural eyesore has a prime spot between the Registan & the Rukhobod Mausoleum. It's stuffed with coach parties watching the nightly belly dancing shows & lounging by the pool. Generally disappointing. **$$$$**

🏠 **Grand Samarkand** [154 A4] (30 rooms) 38 B Yalangtush; \ 233 2880; e grand-samarkand@mail.ru; www.grand-samarkand. com. West of the city centre, but still within walking distance of the Registan, is this modern property with spacious, well-maintained rooms & immaculate white linens. The décor is neutral, the furnishings comfortable, & the outside restaurant set in the courtyard garden is pleasant in summer. Guests can make use of the swimming pool, sauna, souvenir shop & exchange office at Grand Samarkand's sister property on the opposite side of the street. Wi-Fi is free. **$$$$**

🏠 **Hotel President** [154 C3] (165 rooms) 53 Sh Mirzo; \ 233 2475; e info@uzhotelpresident. com. The smartest hotel in town is the 4-star Hotel President. It's not exactly what you'd call cosy, but it has good facilities (inc a bar, business centre & sauna) & the staff are generally attentive. The hotel also has designated parking, a rarity in the city. Visa card payments are possible. **$$$$**

Mid range

🏠 **Hotel Asia Samarkand** [154 B4] (85 rooms) 50 Kosh Khauz; \ 235 8230; www. asiahotels.uz/en. Part of an Uzbek chain, this large hotel is uninspiring but rooms are comfortable enough & a sit down in the sauna or dip in the pool is welcome after a hard day's sightseeing. **$$$**

🏠 **Hotel Diyor** [154 C5] 43 Tashkent; \ 235 9076. Modern guesthouse with basic facilities situated on the pedestrian street between the Registan & the Bibi Khanym Mosque. The location is its best feature. **$$$**

🏠 **Hotel Malika Classic** [154 A5] (26 rooms) 37 Khamraeva; \ 237 0154; www.malika-samarkand.com. The Malika chain's 2nd property in Samarkand is a little away from the centre but has comfortable rooms with tasteful furnishings. B/fast inc. **$$$**

🏠 **Hotel Tumaris** [154 A5] (12 rooms) 149 Gagarin; \ 233 5851; e tumaristour@yahoo. com. Boutique hotel with AC rooms run by a local women's association. Hotel profits support Tumaris (page 157). Pool, sauna & on-site parking. B/fast inc. **$$$**

🏠 **Malika Prime** [154 A6] (22 rooms) 1/4 University; \ 233 4349; e malika-hotel@ mail.ru; www.malikahotel.com. Tastefully decorated hotel in a superb location alongside the Gur-i Amir, catering mostly to upmarket tour groups. All rooms have AC & Wi-Fi; those

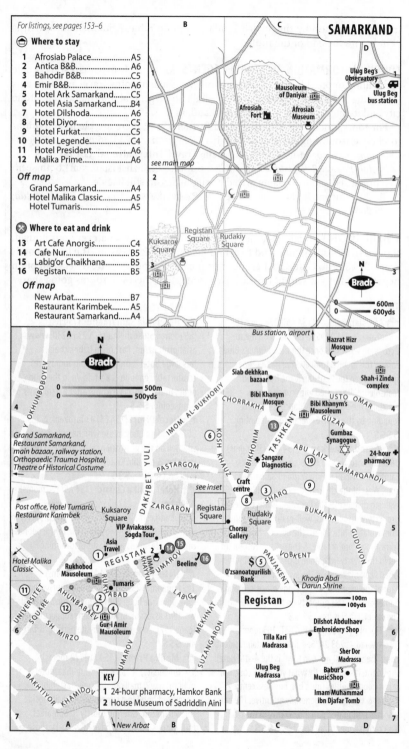

For listings, see pages 153–6

SAMARKAND

🛏 Where to stay

1 Afrosiab Palace..................A5
2 Antica B&B..........................A6
3 Bahodir B&B.......................C5
4 Emir B&B.............................A6
5 Hotel Ark Samarkand......C5
6 Hotel Asia Samarkand.....B4
7 Hotel Dilshoda..................A6
8 Hotel Diyor.........................C5
9 Hotel Furkat......................C5
10 Hotel Legende...................C4
11 Hotel President..................A6
12 Malika Prime......................A6

Off map
   Grand Samarkand...............A4
   Hotel Malika Classic...........A5
   Hotel Tumaris.....................A5

✖ Where to eat and drink

13 Art Cafe Anorgis................C4
14 Cafe Nur..............................B5
15 Labig'or Chaikhana............B5
16 Registan...............................B5

Off map
   New Arbat.............................B7
   Restaurant Karimbek.........A5
   Restaurant Samarkand......A4

Ulug Beg's Observatory
Ulug Beg bus station
Mausoleum of Daniyar
Afrosiab Fort
Afrosiab Museum

see main map

Registan Square
Rudakiy Square
Kuksaroy Square

Bradt

0 ——— 600m
0 ——— 600yds

Bus station, airport

Hazrat Hizr Mosque
Siab dekhkan bazaar
Shah-i Zinda complex
Bibi Khanym Mosque
Bibi Khanym's Mausoleum
Gumbaz Synagogue
24-hour pharmacy
Sangzor Diagnostics
Craft centre
Rudakiy Square
Chorsu Gallery
O'zsanoatqurilish Bank
Khodja Abdi Darun Shrine

Bradt

0 ——— 500m
0 ——— 500yds

Grand Samarkand, Restaurant Samarkand, main bazaar, railway station, Orthopaedic Trauma Hospital, Theatre of Historical Costume

Post office, Hotel Tumaris, Restaurant Karimbek

Kuksaroy Square
VIP Aviakassa, Sogda Tour
Asia Travel
Hotel Malika Classic
Rukhobod Mausoleum
Tumaris
Gur-i Amir Mausoleum

see inset
Registan Square
Beeline

Register

0 ——— 100m
0 ——— 100yds

Dilshot Abdulhaev Embroidery Shop
Tilla Kari Madrassa
Sher Dor Madrassa
Ulug Beg Madrassa
Babur's Music Shop
Imam Muhammad ibn Djafar Tomb

KEY
1 24-hour pharmacy, Hamkor Bank
2 House Museum of Sadriddin Aini

New Arbat

on the upper floors have balconies overlooking the mausoleum. B/fast inc. Discounts available for 2+ nights. Pay in som to guarantee the best rate. **$$$**

🏠 **Hotel Ark Samarkand** [154 C5] (14 rooms) 9 Panjakent; 📞 235 6941; e arksamarkand@mail. ru. Though the Ark's location by the Registan is unbeatable, & many of the rooms are large, a smattering of good taste would not go amiss. The building is ugly inside & out, & smoking anywhere in the vicinity risks sending the whole lot up in polyester-fuelled smoke. **$$–$$$**

🏠 **Hotel Furkat** [154 C5] (27 rooms) 105 Mullakandov; 📞 235 6299; e hotelfurkat@ mail.ru. A stone's throw from the Registan, this comfortable, if rather higgledy-piggledy, guesthouse is built around a courtyard where you can relax on the wooden *topchan* beds. Some rooms have balconies with impressive views, & it's definitely worth paying a bit extra for one of these if they're available, though you can also see the panorama from the rooftop café. If your budget won't stretch to a dbl room, dorm beds in the basement cost US$7, & dinner is US$5 (book by 10.00 if you plan to eat in). Payment is by cash or Visa. **$$–$$$**

Budget

✳ 🏠 **Antica B&B** [154 A6] (9 rooms) 58 Iskandarov; 📞 235 2092; e anticasamarkand@ hotmail.com. If we have the choice of where to stay in Samarkand, we always opt for this family-run B&B built around a lovingly tended courtyard garden with mulberry trees & numerous flowers. Many of the rooms have traditionally painted ceilings (as does the b/fast room), & all

are decorated with gorgeous antique textiles. The b/fasts are the best in Uzbekistan – this book isn't long enough to finish extolling the virtues of the homemade jams – & evening meals are also available if you request them in advance. Can also organise dinner in a 19th-century house (see below). **$$**

🏠 **Emir B&B** [154 A6] (8 rooms) 142 Ok Saroy; 📞 235 7461. Well-located Old Town guesthouse with pleasant rooftop terrace. **$$**

🏠 **Hotel Dilshoda** [154 A6] (13 rooms) 150 Ok Saroy; 📞 235 0387. Located on an alley behind the Gur-i Amir, this is really a B&B rather than a hotel. It's basic, clean, comfortable enough & is equipped with Wi-Fi, but lacks the warmth of Antica. **$$**

🏠 **Hotel Legende** [154 C4] (18 rooms) 48/62 M Ulug Beg; 📞 233 7481; e info@legendm7.com; www.legendm7.com. Hidden 10 mins' walk from the centre in Samarkand's little-visited Jewish quarter is this 170-year-old property with an airy, double-storey veranda, a lush green courtyard with its own vines, & hundreds of antique fabrics, carpets & intriguing knick-knacks. It's a hotel with a great deal of character. French & English are both spoken. **$$**

🏠 **Bahodir B&B** [154 C5] (16 rooms) 132 Mullokandov; 📞 235 4749. The cheapest beds in Samarkand are to be had at this B&B. Dorm beds cost US$6-8 inc b/fast, & the best of these is the 4-bed as it has an en suite. Sgls & dbls are available with & without bathrooms. AC is available & you can request an electric heater for your room in winter. Ask for one of the newer rooms. Those away from the courtyard are quietest. **$**

✕ **WHERE TO EAT AND DRINK** For a city with quite so many visitors, it's a shame Samarkand hasn't yet upped its game in the culinary stakes. Hotel restaurants are bland, and the larger restaurants tend to cater mostly to coach parties. You might be privy to an unauthentic belly dance or two, but most of us would happily swap that for a decent meal. Restaurants are open for both lunch and dinner unless otherwise stated.

For a more authentic dining experience, the staff at **Antica B&B** (see above) can arrange dinner in a traditional 19th-century house with a beautiful painted interior. The menu is set but inevitably tasty, and you will also have the opportunity to try locally produced wine. If you're in luck, the house's owner, a local history expert and curator of one of the local museums, will be present to tell you about her family, the building and its history. What is more, at around US$7 per person it is no more expensive than eating at a restaurant in town. Book one day in advance at Antica.

✗ Labig'or Chaikhana [154 B5] 6 Registan. With its wooden veranda & columns, low tables & kitchen open to the street, Labig'or has significantly more character than most. The salads are a bargain (*2,500 som*) & the shashlik tasty & fresh. Plov is available at lunchtime only. **$$$**

✗ New Arbat [154 B7] 124A Ulugbek; m 895 509 2200. Ostentatious Neoclassical pillars & a sweeping staircase greet guests at this well-run restaurant favoured by tour groups. Romantic murals of Moscow street scenes grace the walls, it is clean & the Russian menu is tasty, **$$$$**

✗ Registan Restaurant [154 B5] 5 Registan; 742 1548; ⏰ 08.00–23.00 daily. Decorated with *suzanis* & paintings copied from tilework on the Registan, the Registan Restaurant has the best location in town, staring across the road at its namesake. It's possible to enjoy a sheesha here after your meal. **$$$**

✗ Restaurant Karimbek [154 A5] 194 Gagarin; 237 7739; ⏰ 10.00–23.00 daily. Large restaurant at the cnr of Gagarin & A Timur serving menu of Uzbek & European dishes. Uzbek wines, cocktails & draft beers are served at the bar. Live music each evening during summer months. **$$$**

✗ Restaurant Samarkand [154 A5] 54 M Kashgari; m 95 500 5599. Hugely popular with local groups, this restaurant is large & elaborately decorated, albeit with questionable taste. Spread over 2 floors, groups tend to be put upstairs, leaving individual guests with the run of the garden & ground floor. The music can be too loud in the evenings. Opt for the salads & shashlik as the chips are disappointing. **$$$**

⊡ Art Café Anorgis [154 C4] 12 Tashkent; 235 0402; ⏰ 08.00–19.00daily. Next to Bibi Khanym, this Western-style café serves various salads, soups & cakes (3,600 som). The menu is available in English. **$$**

⊡ Cafe Nur [154 B5] 9 Registan. Fast-food joint with a menus of pizzas, grilled meats & other quick snacks. **$$**

ENTERTAINMENT There is no nightlife in Samarkand per se, but most nights it is possible to watch a cultural performance somewhere in the city. The best of these is **Instant of Eternity** at the Theatre of Historical Costume [154 A4] (*27 Alisher Navoi Sq;* 233 8125; US$20). Produced with the assistance of the Hermitage in St Petersburg, this historical fashion show takes you through millennia of Uzbek costume, starting with the Scythians and Achaemenids, moving on to the Timurids, and ultimately to clothing of the 19th century. The live performance is accompanied by music and video. It is well produced and the costumes are historically accurate. Performances take place at 18.00 most nights during the high tourist season. Call the theatre to confirm.

SHOPPING Samarkand's commercial centre is the **main bazaar** [154 A4] (⏰ *05.00–19.00 daily*), right next to the Bibi Khanym Mosque. It's primarily aimed at the local market, so although you may not find many souvenirs here, it is a good place to pick up a picnic. Having tasted multiple samples, haggle hard for the fruits and nuts, and follow your nose to the stands of flat, fresh bread. Enjoy the people watching.

The **Ozik Ovqatlar** and **Siyobnon** supermarkets, both of which are close to the Registan, have the usual selection of dried and processed goods.

All over Samarkand are numerous **souvenir shops** selling low-quality and usually fairly samey products. The greatest concentration of these are on Tashkent, inside the Tilla Kari Madrassa, and in the cells surrounding the Rukhobod Mausoleum.

If you want something a little different, however, you need to look a little harder. Ethnographer **Dilshot Abdulhaev** sells both antique and modern embroideries from his former teacher's room (identified by its numerous bookshelves) inside the Tilla Kari Madrassa. Abdulhaev speaks good English and is exceptionally knowledgeable about Uzbekistan's textile heritage. His shop is only open April to November as he travels in the winter to textile exhibitions overseas.

In the **craft centre** [154 C5] alongside Hotel Diyor on Tashkent you can watch a number of artisans at work and buy directly from them. The long, striped *chapan* (coats) are dramatic but, for those less keen on drawing attention to themselves in public, also make good dressing gowns.

Tumaris [154 A6] on Rukhobod is a bespoke hat maker, though if you are short on time they also have samples ready to wear. Assuming you have no moral objection to wearing wild animal fur, you choose your style, select a pelt and *voila!* You have something unique to keep your ears warm in winter.

Visiting the **Chorsu Gallery** [154 C5] on Tashkent is a fascinating experience. Though the contemporary artworks on sale may leave you cold, the building itself dates from the 15th century and director and artist Bakhrom Uldashev has his studio just inside. He produces fine pen and ink drawings, and is happy to chatter away at length about Samarkand's artists and their work.

The best carpets, both in terms of quality and ethical production, are available from the **Samarkand Bukhara Carpet Workshop** (page 166). The workshop prides itself on having exemplary conditions for its workers and that every carpet here is made by hand.

If you're having a panic that you've come to Samarkand and your memory card is already full, **Foto Magazin** (*8 Registan*) will sort you out. They also have batteries, tripods and a selection of old Russian cameras for sale. **Babur's Music Shop** can be found in the former students' cells in the Sher Dor Madrassa in the Registan (page 159).

OTHER PRACTICALITIES
Communications Samarkand is well connected with the outside world. To send your postcards, albeit with no guarantee they'll arrive, you need the **main post office** [154 A5] (*5 Pochta;* ⊕ *08.00–17.00 Mon–Sat*). You can also buy stamps from the craft shop (*127 Aksaray;* ⊕ *09.00–17.00 daily*) by the Gur-i Amir: look out for the post office sign. International stamps cost 1,000 som, and they will post things for you, too.

There are Paynet points to top up your mobile phone all over the city, including at the Ozik Ovqatlar supermarket. If you need to buy a SIM card, there is a **Beeline** [154 B5] shop opposite the Registan.

Many of Samarkand's hotels and restaurants now have Wi-Fi, and this is the most convenient way to get online – **Art Café Anorgis** (page 156) is probably the easiest to get to. The **Foreign Language Institute** (*23 Ahunbabaev*) and **International Telephone Office** (*9 Pochta*) both have internet terminals for 1,000 som an hour.

Medical Samarkand has several private clinics and hospitals that you could go to in an emergency. **Sangzor Diagnostics** [154 C4] (*Tashkent;* ⊕ *09.00–17.00 Mon–Sat*) is right in the city centre and is akin to a GP practice. For more severe incidents, you will need the **Doctor Plus Medical Centre** [154 A4] (*26 Lufti;* ✆ *233 5638*) or the **Orthopaedic Trauma Hospital** [154 A4] (*73 Haliduna;* ✆ *2229 3274*).

For minor incidents and medication, there is a **24-hour pharmacy** [154 E2] at 7 Registan.

Money Samarkand suffers from the same ATM shortage as everywhere else in Uzbekistan, so you will need to bring sufficient cash (local or foreign) or get cash advanced on your Visa card. The two most conveniently located banks for this are **O'zsanoatqurilish Bank** [154 C5] (*cnr Panjakent & Registan;* ⊕ *08.30–16.00 Mon–Sat, closed 13.00–14.00*) and **Hamkor Bank** [154 B5] (*7 Registan;* ⊕ *09.00–16.00 Mon–Sat, closed noon–13.00*).

It is straightforward to change money with the unofficial money changers in the bazaar, and the smaller hotels and souvenir shops will all be able to help you exchange dollars at favourable rates.

Registration Samarkand's **OVIR** is located on the corner of Ulug Beg and M Kashgari.

WHAT TO SEE AND DO For most visitors to Samarkand the challenge is not what to see but what to leave out: the city is packed with fascinating sites from all eras of its history, and unless you have a full week to spend here, you're unlikely to see them all. Below are the city's highlights.

The Registan [154 C5] (*Registan; ⊕ Apr–Oct 09.00–20.00 daily, Nov–Mar 09.00– 17.00 daily; local/foreigner 1,000 som/US$7*) Samarkand's central square will make even the most architecture-weary visitor stand up and take note. Pausing for a minute (and a photo) on the raised viewing platform, the square unfolds below you. An almost infinite number of contrasting patterns swirl and dance on every surface but somehow never clash; the equally garishly patterned textiles worn by Uzbek women walking by appear almost as a continuation of the buildings themselves. The effect is completely mesmerising.

The Registan grew up around the tomb to the 9th-century saint Imam Muhammad ibn Djafar, but by the 14th century this was also the commercial heart of the town. Six roads ran through the square, and it was connected directly with Timur's citadel. Imperial decrees were shouted from the rooftops, and people would also have gathered here to watch military pageants and other forms of spectacle. The three magnificent buildings you see today are the successors to this medieval centrepiece.

The **Ulug Beg Madrassa** on the left of the square is the oldest of the three madrassas. It was built between 1417–20 by Timur's grandson Ulug Beg, an intellectual who, sadly for his faltering empire, spent more of his time concentrating on maths and science than he did on affairs of state. His love of astronomy is shown in the mosaic tilework above the 15m arch on the main portico: it's a depiction of the sky and the stars.

The madrassa itself measure 56m by 81m and is built around a large, open courtyard. At its peak some 100 students lived in the 50 cells, many of them making use of the astronomical instruments housed here before the construction of Ulug Beg's Observatory (page 165). Unusually, this was not a religious madrassa: the students here were studying mathematics and the sciences. If you tip the security guard you can climb over the dust and builders' rubble and up the steep and narrow staircase to the top of the right-hand minaret, finally pulling yourself up through the metal hatch and onto the rooftop. There's scarcely any room to move and you sit in a precarious position with an awfully long drop below, but if you can overcome any fear of heights, this is an exhilarating place from which to view the tiger mosaic on the Sher Dor Madrassa opposite and you feel like you're on top of the world.

The madrassa in the centre is the **Tilla Kari Madrassa**. When the Bibi Khanym Mosque started to fall into disrepair in the mid 17th century, Yalangtush Biy decided a replacement was needed, so he commissioned this combined mosque and madrassa complex. Construction was completed in 1660 after 20 years of hard work; the dome was reconstructed in the 20th century as the original was destroyed by Nadir Shah's forces in the early 18th century. Though it is easy to get caught up looking at the exterior, this is the one madrassa you must go inside: the golden ceiling is utterly enthralling, and it is this gilt that gives the madrassa its name. Tour groups inevitably spend a while lingering here and blocking the view, but be patient and wait for space. Position yourself immediately beneath the centre of the golden dome and then look straight up to appreciate the full effect.

Sher Dor Madrassa, the Tiger or Lion Madrassa, is a 17th-century construction and must be one of the most photographed buildings in existence. There are two ribbed domes (best seen from inside rather than from the Registan Square) and two minarets flank the façade. The elaborate mosaic work on the portico shows two sun gods, two strange big cats with each with tiger's stripes but a lion's mane, and two deer, and must therefore contravene so many Islamic prohibitions on art, but still this was a religious building. The mosaic was ravaged over time, but was heavily restored in the 20th century to the condition you see today. Restoration work is ongoing, so parts of interior courtyard may well be under scaffolding.

The former students' cells now house small souvenir shops and workshops. Among these, the most interesting is **Babur's Music Shop**, where master Babur gives demonstrations of traditional Uzbek instruments including various stringed instruments, tambourines, flutes and trumpets. He explains about each instrument in English, then gives a short performance. This is free to attend, and you can then buy his CDs if you wish. There is no pressure.

The madrassa stands on the site of a previous *khanagha* (hospice or resting place for holy men) belonging to Ulug Beg that didn't survive as long as the contemporaneous Ulug Beg Madrassa. In the southeastern corner of the madrassa is the tomb of the saint **Imam Muhammad ibn Djafar**, no longer the *raison d'être* of the Registan, but a side show encompassed by architectural splendour.

During the summer months, there is a nightly **sound and light show** in the courtyard at 19.30 which gives a light (excuse the pun) introduction to each of the buildings and their history. It is usually in English or French, and you can ask at the Registan's normal ticket office for details.

Bibi Khanym

Two of the three buildings once associated with Bibi Khanym, Timur's Chingizid wife, are still standing. The third, a madrassa with a portico so large that it rivalled that of the neighbouring mosque, was destroyed by Nadir Shah's Persian troops when they invaded in 1740.

The **Bibi Khanym Mosque** [154 C4] (*Tashkent;* ⊕ *08.00–19.00 daily; foreigners US$0.50*) is one of Samarkand's most impressive sites, but also one of its most controversial due to the heavy reconstruction that has taken place. What you see before you is an almost total rebuild dating from the 1970s as much of it collapsed after an earthquake in the 15th century, not that long after it was built. It seems that the speed of the mosque's construction led to shoddy workmanship, and hence it could not survive the tremor.

It is said that Bibi Khanym built the mosque as a gift to Timur while he was away on campaign in India. The mosque's architect fell deeply in love with her, and demanded he be allowed to give her a kiss in part payment for his work. The kiss left a permanent stain on her cheek; Timur saw it on his return and had the architect executed for his insolence. Legend has it that Bibi Khanym was beheaded too, but in fact she outlived Timur by four years and was then poisoned by one of her daughters. When her body was excavated from its grave in the 1950s, it was remarkably well preserved. She had been buried wearing expensive jewellery (now in the Hermitage in St Petersburg), a nod to her royal Mongol heritage as this was not an Islamic practice.

Building the mosque, one of the largest in the Islamic world, pushed Timurid engineering to its limits. Skilled workmen were brought to Samarkand from across the empire to design and build the 41m-high cupola, and Indian elephants were purportedly used for the transportation and heavy lifting. The original bronze gates, stolen by Nadir Shah, rung out when struck; the 129m by 99m courtyard was floored with marble on which worshippers knelt and prayed. There were 400 marble pillars and the interior was decorated with painted papier mâché. Sadly, during the 20th century the mosque was used as a storage area for the neighbouring market, and almost all of the papier mâché decoration was lost when some goods caught fire.

In the centre of this courtyard survives a vast stone Qu'ran stand, under which childless women still occasionally crawl in the hope of conceiving a child. This is where the world's oldest Qu'ran (now on display in Tashkent, page 104) would have been shown on holy days.

The mosque is typically a quiet spot (far more so than the Registan), and at prayer times you may well see both men and women prostrating themselves in the courtyard or immediately outside the mosque's main entrance. If you want to take photos inside, you will need to buy a photo permit (*US$2*).

Opposite the mosque is **Bibi Khanym's Mausoleum** [154 C4] (*foreigners 7,000 som*). It's a simple, brick-built structure with a turquoise dome on top. This building is entirely new, the upper parts having been constructed only in 2007, though the graves beneath it date from the 14th century. They include the sarcophagi of Bibi Khanym, her mother and two other female family members, which are just about visible down a shaft in the floor. The interior has some fine decorative mosaics, including a depiction of paradise.

Shah-i Zinda (*U U Dzhurakulov;* ⊕ *summer 08.00–19.00 daily, winter 08.00–17.00 daily; US$2*).

The Registan may be Samarkand's poster child, but for us the real star of the show is the line of blue-and-turquoise tiled tombs known as the Shah-i Zinda. The best time to visit is in the early evening. We have always entered through the graveyard and come into the complex at the top of the hill, which gives a strange sense that you are walking back through time, a thousand ghosts your guides through the long grass and headstones. The main entrance and ticket booth are actually at the bottom of the hill by the street.

The name Shah-i Zinda translates as 'Living King' and it is a reference to Samarkand's patron saint, Kusam ibn Abbas, a cousin of the Prophet Muhammad who came to Uzbekistan to preach Islam but, legend has it, was wounded, crept beneath the city walls and, so they say, lives there to this day. Regardless of whether he died or not, one of the mausoleums within the complex is dedicated to him: the 11th-century (and predictably named) **Mausoleum of Kusam ibn Abbas**. Excavations have revealed there is a body inside (that of a middle-aged man), but his exact identity is unknown. A mufti is employed to sit inside the tomb and pray each day, and because of this it is not always possible to enter the inner sanctum.

The tombs at the Shah-i Zinda are loosely grouped. The earliest tombs are those at the north of the site, which date from the second quarter of the 14th century when the site was revived following the city's sacking by the Mongols. The tiles used here are made from a terracotta base that has been painted blue–green or blue–grey prior to being glazed and fired. The same blue–grey tiles were used 70 years later to decorate the neighbouring **tomb of Tumanaga**, a wife of Amir Timur.

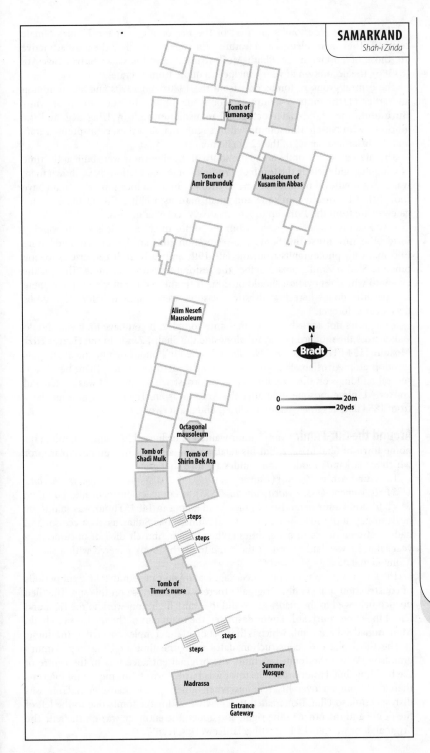

Tomb of
Tumanaga

Tomb of
Amir Burunduk

Mausoleum of
Kusam ibn Abbas

Alim Nesefi
Mausoleum

N

Bradt

0 ————————— 20m
0 ————————— 20yds

Octagonal
mausoleum

Tomb of
Shadi Mulk

Tomb of
Shirin Bek Ata

steps

steps

Tomb of
Timur's nurse

steps

steps

Summer
Mosque

Madrassa

Entrance
Gateway

The sapphire blue tombs are part of the necropolis built for Timur's female relatives. These mausoleums also feature painted majolica tiles. The most attractive are those of Timur's niece, **Shadi Mulk** (d1372), and his sister, **Shirin Bek Ata** (d1386), the decoration of which includes a quote from Socrates.

The central group of tombs date from the 1380s and 1390s and are built atop an earlier (11th century) madrassa. Look out for the 16-sided **tomb of Amir Burunduk**, the slightly later **octagonal mausoleum** built by Ulug Beg, and the glorious **Alim Nesefi Mausoleum** with its relief majolica tiles, eight-pointed stars and the inscribed names of the 12 Shi'ite imams.

The latest group of tombs are to the south of the site. These were built at the time of Ulug Beg and include the **tomb of Timur's nurse**. Excavations have shown there was also a **medieval bathhouse** here (a strange choice of location, one would have thought). The **summer mosque** and small **madrassa** either side of the entrance gateway are from the 19th century, so relatively recent additions.

If you can tear your eyes away from the tombs themselves, it is worth popping inside the tiny **museum**. Some pre-restoration tiles are on display and, more informatively, photographs from the late 19th and early 20th centuries showing how the Shah-i Zinda looked before the restoration work was done. Though the extent to which renovation should be done is frequently a contentious issue, there can be little doubt here that drastic measures were required before the tombs disappeared forever.

Though it's not actually part of the same complex, if you have time you should walk across the modern graveyard alongside the Shah-i Zinda to the **Hazrat Hizr Mosque** [154 F1] (*admission 7,000 som*). Named in honour of a mythical saint, its position atop Afrosiabs Hill gives superb views across the city. There have been several buildings on this site. It was first a Zoroastrian temple, but was sacked and converted into a mosque soon after the Arab invasion. The present mosque dates from 1854 and has finely painted ceilings and plasterwork.

Around the Gur-i Amir
Amir Timur wanted to be buried in a simple tomb in his home town of Shakhrisabz, but his relatives and advisers had grander plans, for which Samarkand's modern tour guides are no doubt grateful

The **Gur-i Amir** [154 A6] (*University;* ◷ *08.00–19.00; locals/foreigners 600 som/ US$4.50; camera US$3, video camera US$5*), a compact but gem-like building, was built for Timur's grandson Muhammad Sultan in 1404. Timur was said to be heartbroken at this loss: he had appointed Muhammad Sultan as his successor and had great confidence in his abilities. When Timur himself died of pneumonia a year later, he was laid to rest in the same tomb, his body covered with a slab of Mongolian jade.

The Gur-i Amir was built in three stages, and you can spot the different periods of construction quite easily. Originally there was a madrassa on this site. The tiled portico belonged to the madrassa, as did the waist-high stonework to the right and left of the main courtyard. Timur destroyed the main part of the madrassa to build Muhammad Sultan's tomb, which is the portion of the complex covered by the dome.

The third phase of construction dates from the time of Ulug Beg, Timur's grandson. When the tomb was built, the original entrance was in the centre of the building, but Timur's religious tutor was buried near to his pupil, and pilgrims therefore tromped over his remains when entering the mausoleum. This was disrespectful, so Ulug Beg created two new wings for the tomb, one to the left of the dome and the other to the right, and added the entrance way on the left. The original door was blocked up with a latticework screen.

Inside the Gur-i Amir, Timur's final resting place is marked with a single slab of jade, said to be the largest in the world. Brought back by Ulug Beg from Mongolia in 1425, it is inscribed in Arabic calligraphy with the following words: 'When I rise, the World will Tremble.'

The first supposed victim of the curse was the Persian invader Nadir Shah, who carried it off to Persia in 1740 and sadly broke it in two. Nadir Shah's son fell gravely ill, and things started to go wrong to such an extent that his advisers demanded the jade be returned to the tomb. It was brought back, and the son recovered, though Nadir Shah himself met a sticky end just a few years later, assassinated with a sword.

On the night of 22 June 1941, a team of Russian scientists began to exhume Timur's remains. Within hours the Nazis had begun rolling into the Soviet Union. Many wondered if this was Timur's curse. The scientists found him to be a tall man, and as his name suggested, lame in the right leg. He had also suffered a wound to the right arm. Analysis complete, Timur's remains were reinterred with full Muslim burial rites, and the Nazis eventually left.

The Gur-i Amir effectively serves as the Timurid dynasty's necropolis, for in addition to Timur and Muhammad Sultan, the bodies of two of Timur's sons, Miranshah and Shahruh, and his grandson, Ulug Beg, are also here. The stone tombs you see are in fact purely decorative, as was traditional: the bodies are in fact interred in crypts beneath the floor.

If you're fortunate enough to step inside the mausoleum after dark, the central chamber sparkles as light flickers from the colossal crystal chandelier hanging beneath the dome. The gilt on the ceiling seems to glow, and it feels like you're in a very holy place indeed. Regardless of the time of day, be sure to also look at the onyx panelling on the walls. The original onyx (the duller green tiles) came from Persia; those that are a brighter green date from the modern restoration.

Before you leave the complex, stop in the main courtyard and have a look at the stonework beneath the plastic lean-to in the corner. These pieces were all excavated from the ruins of Timur's Ak Serai palace, now lost beneath modern Samarkand. The large stone block with exquisite carving on its side is thought to have been Timur's coronation stone. At its side, what looks like a huge stone font would once have been filled with fresh pomegranate juice to be drunk by Timurid soldiers.

Diagonally across the car park from the Gur-i Amir is the **Rukhobod Mausoleum** [154 A5] (⊕ 09.00–18.00 daily; admission free), Samarkand's oldest surviving monument. Built in the late 14th century, this simple, cream stone structure marks the burial place of Sheikh Byrhan ad Din Sagarji, a Sufi preacher who spread the message of Islam from central Asia to India and was mentioned by the Arabic traveller Ibn Battuta after they met in the 1340s. Sagarji's son, Abu Said, was Timur's religious tutor. Though often locked, it is occasionally possible to go inside the mausoleum, climb to the upper floors and look back towards the Gur-i Amir.

Afrosiab and northern Samarkand

Samarkand's earliest history is tied up with the rise and decline of the **Afrosiab Fort** [154 C1], northeast of the modern city. The ruins cover a vast site of 120ha and include a **citadel** with foundations two storeys deep.

Religion disperses like a fog, kingdoms perish, but the works of scholars remain for an eternity.

Ulug Beg

Not content with their earthly domains, kings have often looked to the stars for confirmation of their divine right to rule, and indications of what the future might bring. Their patronage and personal interest in astronomy have driven forward our understanding of not only our own solar system but also the planets beyond.

Astronomy had been a royal pursuit for thousands of years: the ancient Egyptians aligned their pyramids to the stars and were able to accurately predict the flooding of the Nile by sightings of Sirius and the summer solstice, whilst the Babylonians were producing star catalogues as long ago as 1200 BC. It would be the medieval Emperor Ulug Beg (1394–1449) who would take astronomy into the modern age, however, building a vast observatory and producing the most detailed star catalogue before that of Tycho Brahe. Ulug Beg was born in Samarkand in 1394 and was the grandson of Amir Timur. He lacked the political skills of his predecessors but instead focused on turning his capital into an intellectual centre for scholars from across the Islamic world. Having travelled to both India and the Middle East as a child, he was well aware of scientific developments in both those regions, and was determined to build upon them in Samarkand. The young Ulug Beg constructed a huge madrassa on the Registan square and invited numerous astronomers and mathematicians to study there.

Although Ulug Beg was himself a fine mathematician, his real interest lay in astronomy. The observatory he built, the Gurkhani Zij, contained a sextant 11m long and with a radius of 40.4m. It was the largest such instrument in the world and had to be kept underground to protect it from earthquakes. Long before the invention of the telescope, this instrument enabled Ulug Beg to accurately position over 1,000 stars, determine the year with such accuracy that it would even surpass Copernicus' calculations, and to work out the exact tilt of the earth's axis.

Given that Ulug Beg and his astronomers were working without optics, the accuracy of their calculations is unnerving. Even today we do not have a more accurate calculation of the earth's axial tilt than Ulug Beg's 23.52°, and his assertion that the year is 365 days, six hours, ten minutes and eight seconds in length is only one minute longer than modern electronic calculations.

Had Ulug Beg and his astronomers had more time to study the stars, they may yet have been more impressive, but fate was to intervene: the observatory was destroyed by religious fanatics in 1449 and would lie forgotten underground until it was rediscovered by an archaeologist in 1908. Ulug Beg himself hardly met a more glamorous fate: he was beheaded by his own son *en route* to Mecca and his remains were interred in Timur's tomb.

Unlike Samarkand's other sites, the fort has been excavated but not restored, so unless you already have an in-depth historical knowledge and a very active imagination, you should first go inside the informative **Afrosiab Museum** [154 D1] (⏲ *09.00–17.00 daily; foreigners US$2*). Along with well laid out excavation plans, photos and, of course, the archaeological finds themselves (which include pre-Islamic ritual goods, ceramics, weapons and coins) are a remarkable set of murals found in 1965. Dating from the 7th century AD, each panel is more than 2m high and shows scenes of the Sogdian elite at play: there are hunting scenes, a Chinese princess in a boat, and men on horseback and camel. The figures' physical appearance and dress show the cosmopolitanism of Samarkand in this period: all the known world is shown coming to trade and play. The murals were painted with vegetable and mineral pigments, including large amounts of lapis lazuli, the precious stone from neighbouring Afghanistan which makes the vivid aquamarine blue.

The best way to understand the murals is to watch the short video in the room alongside their exhibition space, which costs US$1. The voice-over is in English and computer graphics draw attention to one section of the mural at a time, showing you details that aren't necessarily visible to the naked eye. You also get a good idea of what was in the damaged sections.

If you want to take photos inside the museum, you need a photo permit (*US$2*). In reality, the only things you are likely to want photographs of are the murals, and you might be better off buying a postcard of these.

Medieval Samarkand was a centre for both religious and secular learning, and its rulers patronised the sciences as well as the arts. **Ulug Beg's Observatory** [154 D1] (*Tashkent; ⊕ 09.00–18.00 daily; foreigners US$2*), the largest astronomical observatory in the world at the time it was built, lies a brisk, 10-minute walk past Afrosiab and into the foothills. The observatory lay forgotten and in ruins for some 500 years prior to its partial restoration, the important work undertaken there remembered only in Ulug Beg's astronomical works, which had been published posthumously in Europe.

The centrepiece of the observatory, rediscovered and excavated by the Russian archaeologist Vladimir Viyatkin in 1908, is part of a quadrant arc 63m in length that was used to chart the progress of celestial bodies across the sky. Using this arc, Samarkand's medieval astronomers produced a star catalogue charting the movements of 1,018 stars, which was still known and studied in Oxford in the 17th century.

When you first arrive at the site you'd be forgiven for thinking that there's nothing to see: only a modern portal is visible. The arc itself is sunk below ground, which is the reason it survived when the rest of the observatory was destroyed by fanatics in 1449. Descend into the gloom, and you will be struck by the scale of the arc but also the precision with which it was made: tiny niches are cut into the surface for calibrating the once-accompanying astrolabe, enabling exact calculations to be made. In fact, their accuracy would not be beaten until the invention of the computer.

Alongside the arc and its portal is the **grave of Viyatkin** and a small **museum** (⊕ *09.00–17.00 Mon–Sat; admission free*) about Ulug Beg's life and works. It is well worth going inside the museum as the displays are excellent and really help to explain not only the historical context of Ulug Beg's work, but also how he made his calculations. Architectural models, maps and information boards, which include descriptions in English, are well done, and there are a number of replica astronomical instruments, including Ulug Beg's double quadrant and armillary sphere.

The tiled portico that is the entrance to the museum, and the similar structure around the entrance to the arc, are both new, as is the large statue of Ulug Beg enthroned that you see on the way up the hill. It was erected only in 2010, on the site of an older statue of Ulug Beg standing. Apparently he now looks more regal.

Everyone has heard of Daniel and the lion's den, but few people could tell you that his final resting place, the **Mausoleum of Daniyar** [154 D1] (*Tashkent;* ⏰ *09.00–18.00 daily; US$0.50*), is in Samarkand, on the northern edge of Afrosiab. Daniel (Daniyar in Uzbek) is considered a patron saint and protector of Samarkand, and brings wealth and prosperity to the city, and his tomb is amid landscaped gardens.

Timur supposedly brought Daniel's remains here from Susa in Iran, and it is still a pilgrimage place for the followers of all three Abrahamic religions. On the site is an ancient spring, and the water is said to have healing properties.

The mausoleum is unadorned, and this is even more noticeable given the contrast with the elaborate decoration of Samarkand's other sites. The long, thin stone building, the latest of many on this site, dates from the 19th century and supports five simple domes. Inside is Daniel's tomb; it's considered a holy site and so visitors are not allowed to actually go inside, but you have to look in through the doorway. A photo permit (*US$2*) is available, but it is not worth buying one.

Local legend has it that despite being dead, Daniel's severed leg continues to grow within his sarcophagus. This unusual miracle has necessitated the lengthening of his white marble sarcophagus several times during its history. If the leg reaches 18m, the length of the latest sarcophagus, it it is said that the world will surely end.

The sarcophagus is covered in green and gold prayer rugs. Green is the colour of Islam; the gold denotes the importance of the saint. It is not only Islam that reveres Daniel, however. If you stand at the entrance way to the mausoleum and look left, you will see a flag pole with a small bundle of horse hair hanging from its top. This is a traditional symbol used by local nomads to denote the burial place of a respected leader.

Other sites Of potential interest to fans of Uzbekistan's literary heritage is the **House Museum of Sadriddin Aini** [154 B5] (*7B Registan;* ☎ *2355 153;* ⏰ *09.00–17.00 daily*). Built around a peaceful, whitewashed courtyard just metres from the Registan, the house museum has none of the crowds of its more famous neighbour. It was in these rooms that Aini (1878–1954) wrote his most famous texts, including the novels *Slaves* and *Dokunda*, and the collection includes early editions, photographs and personal papers, as well as pre-revolution interiors and furniture. The elderly curator is passionate about his subject and shows you around the museum with surprising vigour. Sadly he only speaks Russian, so you'll need a translator to fully benefit from his knowledge.

To see traditional carpet weaving, go to the **Samarkand Bukhara Carpet Workshop** (*12A Hujom;* ☎ *231 0726;* e *badghisia@hotmail.com*). Established in 1992 in a bid to revive traditional techniques, the workshop is run by the affable and exceptionally knowledgeable Haji Baba (Muhammad Ewaz Badghisi). The workshop produces around 400 handmade carpets a year and prides itself on having exemplary working conditions and benefits for its weavers and dyers. Workers undertake a four-month training programme and work no more than 40 hours a week. All of them are over 18. The plants required to make many of the natural dyes are grown in the workshop garden, which you are welcome to wander around, and the women take painstaking care to show you each stage of the carpet making process. There is no hard sell, just a fascinating insight into the industry, and if you do decide to buy a carpet, you can either choose from one of those already made, or design one yourself and be confident of having it delivered.

Southeast of Samarkand, on the outskirts of the city, lies the **Khodja Abdi Darun shrine** [154 C6]. Slightly dilapidated, but still beautifully adorned with fine carved pillars, attractively painted ceilings, and decorative tigers on the doors (likely a model for those later depicted on the Sher Dor Madrassa, see page 159), the shrine is in a far more authentic condition than the less sensitively rebuilt structures in the city centre.

The buildings you see today date from the 12th to the 19th centuries, and a new madrassa is also under construction on the site. The oldest part was built by the Seljuk Sultan Sanjar to be his mausoleum, and it was then reconstructed by Ulug Beg (see box, page 164) three centuries later, who added a khanagha. The water reservoir, mosque and madrassa date from the most recent phase of construction in the 1800s.

Last but not least, you may be interested to visit the **Gumbaz Synogogue** [154 D4] (*2 Ilyazarov*; \ *223 6516*), which is tucked down an alleyway beside a hammam: you might have to ask to find it. Situated within the old city wall, this synagogue was used by the Bukharan Jewish community in Samarkand,, which today numbers only about 250 people, but has lived in the area for several centuries. It is an interesting place to visit, architecturally, and has a pleasant courtyard. The rabbi is keen to display the old books as well as the Torah scroll, which was written in the city.

AROUND SAMARKAND

Imam Al-Bukhari Mausoleum (⊕ *09.00–18.00 daily; admission free*) This lies 25km (15 miles) north of Samarkand in Khoja Ismail village. Al-Bukhari was born in Bukhara in ad810, and at the age of 16 he embarked upon his life's work: scouring the Islamic world for Hadith, the sayings of the Prophet Muhammad. Over the next 16 years, Al-Bukhari collected some 600,000 sayings. The resulting book ran to 97 volumes.

The mausoleum complex comprises an impressive gateway, a large courtyard with manicured lawns and flowerbeds, prayers rooms and a water tank, and a minaret. This is in addition, of course, to the tomb itself, which is covered by a blue dome raised upon marble pillars. The symbolic tomb (the real tomb is in fact buried beneath the floor, as is the case in the Gur-i Amir in Samarkand) is made of highly polished marble. The inscription on the accompanying gravestone, engraved in Arabic, describes Al-Bukhari's life.

The mausoleum complex is an active religious centre, though non-Muslims are welcome to visit providing they are appropriately dressed (women must cover their heads) and ask permission at the entrance. There is no entrance fee, though you may be asked to make a small donation towards the upkeep of the shrine.

Amankutan Gorge Natural Preserve
The 2,158ha Amankutan Gorge Natural Preserve is some 50km from Samarkand, not far from Urgut. It has been an important and successful conservation site since the late 19th century: the governor of Turkestan saw the devastating impact that mud slides had on local communities, and consequently orchestrated an ambitious reforestation programme in whichseveral thousand trees were planted, including apricot, almond, and walnut – some of these trees still stand today. Their roots help knit the soil together, making it less vulnerable to subsidence during the rains, and the trees also offer pleasant shade.

The gorge is famed for having some of the most impressive views in central Asia, as well as being a pristine natural environment (which is sadly a rarity in this part of the world). Emperor tulips (*Tulipa fosteriana*), the ancestor of modern, domesticated varieties of tulips, grow wild here, as do many medicinal herbs. There are a number of short trekking routes, ideal for day hikes, through the woodlands, where you can see many flowers, birds and butterflies. You can also visit the archaeological remains of a Neanderthal site (discovered in 1947), and small villages, still inhabited, which were originally established when this was the migration path from ancient Bactria to Sogdiana.

DZHIZAK *Telephone code: 72*

Though many people do pass through Dzhizak, and it is a fair-sized town with a long history, for today's tourists it really is just a convenient transit point. You won't want to schedule any time here.

HISTORY Dzhizak grew up as a trading post at the crossroads between Samarkand and the Fergana Valley, a gateway to Western riches. Anxious to control the valuable trade passing through, it was fortified in turn by the Sogdians, the Arabs and the Bukharan Khanate; it was so well defended that it slowed the advance of General Chernayev in 1866, though the Russians ultimately won out, slaughtering more than 6,000 men.

GETTING THERE, AWAY AND AROUND Dzhizak is just 203km and 95km from Tashkent and Samarkand respectively along the M39 or M34 (pages 88–9 for details on this route), but if you don't have your own vehicle then getting there can be a bit of a drag on account of the fact that the **intercity bus stand** is 10km out of the city on the M39 highway.

The **minibus** ride to Tashkent takes 2½ hours and costs US$3; the journey to Samarkand is 2 hours and costs US$2. Shared taxis cost twice as much but reduce the travel time by about a third.

The No 1 minibus plies the route between the intercity bus stand and the town centre. Local minibuses can be picked up from the bazaar or from Rashidov Square and are the most convenient means of getting around.

Dzhizak does have a **railway station** off A Navoi, but relatively few of the long-distance trains stop here. If you do want to take the train to Samarkand, it takes just over an hour. Trains run several times a day, and tickets cost around US$2.

TOUR OPERATORS The regional branch of Uzbektourism (*1 Dustlik*; \ 226 3940) provides basic tour services, including airline tickets and reservations for accommodation in the Zaamin National Park.

🏠 **WHERE TO STAY AND EAT** Dzhizak is sadly not blessed with many accommodation options as few people visit and even fewer spend the night.

🏠 **Comfort Continent** (9 rooms, 1 apt) 1A S Nasimov; \ 771 7100. Opened in 2012, this mid-range business hotel has large, light rooms with modern bathrooms. There is a bar on site & the best room has a jacuzzi. Also has a convenient bar & restaurant serving Uzbek & European cuisine. **$$$**

🏠 **Khalk Markazi B&B** 3 K Marx; \ 237 222. Dzhizak's most unusual accommodation option is this somewhat quirky B&B run by the People's Centre, a Sufi group that offers healing & pilgrimages aimed at locals rather than tourists. Facilities are basic but the company is fascinating. **$$**

Dzhizak is the birthplace of Sharaf Rashidovich Rashidov, and from Rashidov Square to S Rashidov Street, the town is clearly proud of its most famous son.

Born to a peasant family in 1917, Rashidov was a writer and teacher. Having been called up to fight in World War II he was severely injured, but the war inspired him to write a collection of poems entitled *My Wrath*, and their publication brought his work to national attention and a promotion to head of the Uzbek Writers' Union in 1949.

Within a year, Rashidov had slid across from literature and into politics, and for the next 24 years he was First Secretary of the Uzbek Communist Party. His regime became synonymous with corruption, so much so that Brezhnev spoke out against his excesses. His death in 1983 spared Rashidov an inevitable fall from grace; satellite images showed that his much lauded cotton fields were in fact barren. Those responsible for the deceit were arrested and executed, an embarrassment to the nation.

🏠 **Sangzor Camp** Karasai Village. Soviet-style holiday camp close to Timur Darvaza (see below). **$**

✕ **Amir Timur** Karasai Village ⊕ 08.00–23.00 daily. This small restaurant next to the Sangzor Camp serves salads & other snacks. **$$**

WHAT TO SEE AND DO Almost nothing is left of Dzhizak's past: what you see is a 20th-century industrial town. **Rashidov Square** and the **Rashidov Memorial Museum** (⊕ *Mon–Sat 09.00–18.00; admission 1,000 som*) are both named in honour of Sharaf Rashidovich Rashidov despite his subsequent fall from favour. The latter houses a fairly underwhelming collection of political memorabilia, including the understandably forlorn stuffed crocodile that was an official gift to Rashidov from Fidel Castro.

AROUND DZHIZAK The two reasons you might come to (or through) Dzhizak are both located out of the city.

Timur Darvaza (Timur's Gates) These mark the narrow opening to the Zarafshan Mountains, the bottleneck that numerous soldiers have sought to defend (or at least died trying). Ulug Beg left an inscription here to mark his triumphant return home in 1425; other historic inscriptions are sadly hidden amongst the modern graffiti. Although the site itself is in some ways unimpressive (there are no structures to see), it's a place charged with history and you can easily appreciate its strategic importance in keeping invading hordes at bay.

The Dzhizak–Samarkand minibuses pass right by, so it's easy to jump off, take a look, and hop back on the next one passing through.

Zaamin National Park (*www.zaamin.uz*) This national park lies 75km southeast of Dzhizak, along an uninspiring road that traverses a dusty steppe and former collective farms before taking a last-minute turn up into the rolling hills and snow-capped mountains that ring Tajikistan. The oldest national park in Uzbekistan (founded in 1926), it covers around 156km² of apricot orchards, juniper forest and alpine meadow and is criss-crossed by four rivers, the Aldashmansoy, Baikungur, Guralsh and Kulsoy.

The park entrance lies just above a large, manmade reservoir where you can swim and camp in the summer months (mosquito repellent is advised if you do the latter). The visitor centre (situated inside the sanatorium, see opposite) lies a short way further on in the Uryuklisai Gorge, though you're unlikely to have much use for it. At the head of the gorge is one of the park's most striking sites, the 100m Sharilak Waterfall, the course of which was diverted artificially to entertain the demanding clientele of the Sharshara Dacha (see below), including President Karimov.

The park's true wilderness lies beyond the road and hotel infrastructure, in the alpine meadows over the Suffa Pass where Kyrgyz nomads make their camp. The ring of peaks, several of which climb to more than 4,000m, make a spectacular setting, especially in the early evening when the sky turns burnt orange and there's not a sound in the air save for the breeze and the twittering of birds. A new observatory is still under construction, and around 150km of designated trails give walkers and wildlife spotters ample opportunity to explore. If you leave the trail, keep your eye out for animal tracks and, if you're really lucky and the area is quiet, the animals themselves, including Turkestan lynx, bearded vultures and Asian black bears, can all potentially be spotted. A pair of binoculars will come in useful.

In 2012, a 350m **ski slope** for beginners was constructed close to the sanatorium. Active visitors with a passion for mountaineering may also use the park to attempt an ascent on Shaukartau and Tokalichuk, though both climbers and skiers will need to bring their own equipment.

You can reach Zaamin village by minibus (*1½hrs from Dzhizak*) and then sleep either at the **Sharshara Dacha** (✆ *21 550;* **$$**), a popular spot with attractive gardens, or the vast and rather ugly **Zaamin Sanatorium** (*Nomalum;* ✆ *221 0010;* **$$**). Meals are included with the room rates in both cases. Unusually for Uzbekistan you are also allowed to **camp** in the park, though you will need to bring everything with you and confirm permitted locations at the park office when you arrive. Regardless of whether you will be staying in the confines of the park or not, you need to register with the park office (which doubles as the visitors centre) on arrival.

6

Qashqa Darya and Surkhan Darya Provinces

Uzbekistan's two southernmost provinces are rarely visited by foreigners, especially now that few tourists travel back and forth across the border with Afghanistan. This is a real pity, however, as the area has some of the country's most attractive natural landscapes, with the Gissar-Alai range providing a dramatic backdrop to any road trip or stay. The cities of Shakhrisabz and Termez, in Surkhan Darya and Qashqa Darya respectively, are both equally rich in history and provide an insight into Uzbekistan's past that is largely devoid of the gloss applied to Samarkand and Bukhara. It is for this reason that you can justify spending several days travelling south to visit them.

SHAKHRISABZ *Telephone code: 75*

There has been a settlement here, in the upper reaches of the Qashqa Darya River, for at least 2,700 years. The modern highway to Samarkand overlies a much older route through the mountains to Samarkand, but though it was a well-situated trading post, it would never have come to our notice if it were not for the city's most famous son: the 14th-century emperor, Amir Timur.

Amir Timur dominates Shakhrisabz, and quite rightly so. Join the throngs of wedding goers in Amir Timur Park to have your photo taken with the modern bronze statue of the great man himself and, more importantly, to see what's left of the Ak Serai, his once mighty palace with its unrestored medieval tilework. Head then along the main street to the Dor at-Tilyavat and Dor as-Siadat for the Timurid mosque and family necropolis.

In 2014–15, large parts of central Shakhrisabz were demolished as part of a beautification programme. Though the monuments remain standing, many of the 20th-century buildings, in particular those near the city walls, have been cleared and at the time of going to print, nothing yet had replaced them. When you visit you are likely to find yourself in the midst of a building site, and it will be some time before the new generation of hotels, restaurants, shops and other amenities are up and running.

HISTORY Shakhrisabz originated as the Sogdian town of Kesh sometime before the 6th century AD. It survived the Arab invasion but was a place of relatively little importance until the birth of Timur-i Leng (Timur the Lame; see box, page 14) in Khoja Ilgar, a village 12km to the south, in 1336. Though he made his capital at Samarkand, Shakhrisabz was not forgotten: he fortified the town, enlarged his family burial ground, gave the city its present name (which means 'Green City')

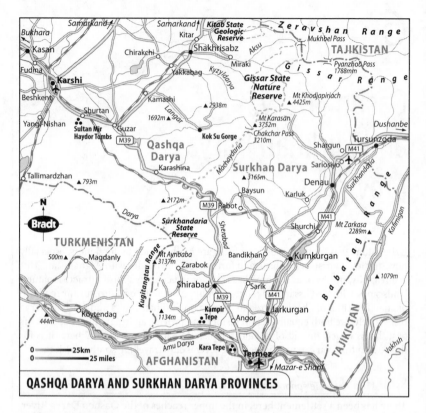

QASHQA DARYA AND SURKHAN DARYA PROVINCES

and began to construct the fabulous Ak Serai (White Palace), whose magnificent gateway remains unrestored but virtually intact to this day. Timur hoped to be buried in Shakhrisabz in a simple crypt but his relatives had other ideas and he was eventually interred in the sumptuous Gur-i Amir in Samarkand.

Shakhrisabz was sacked in the late 1700s by Abdulla Khan of Bukhara, but remained nominally independent until it surrendered to the infamous Nasrullah Khan in 1856. In addition to the city, the emir also seized the ruler's sister, only to have her executed on his deathbed. Shakhrisabz fell to the Russians 16 years later, and it dwindled into insignificance with neither wealthy patrons nor Soviet governors to steer its development in the 20th century.

GETTING THERE, AWAY AND AROUND Shakhrisabz is 90km from Samarkand and the **drive** across the mountains takes around 2 hours and considerably more if there is snow on the pass. Coaches are not allowed to cross the pass for safety reasons, and so must take a slightly longer route around the mountains instead. **Minibuses** between Samarkand and Shakhrisabz (*2hrs; US$4*) leave from Samarkand's Suzangaran stop, near to the Registan, and require you to change at Kitab. There are two **buses** a day on the same route (*4hrs; US$3*). Minibuses run directly between Tashkent and Shakhrisabz (*8hrs; US$6*). **Shared taxis** also operate this route; they're faster but about twice the price. To reach Bukhara, go first to Karshi and then change there. The total journey takes 5 hours (excluding waiting around for your connection) and costs US$12–14.

Once you've reached the city, Shakhrisabz is best explored **on foot**; all the sites listed here are within 10 to 15 minutes' walk of one another along Ipak

Yuli. Amir Timur Park and the Ak Serai are at the northern end of the road, the bazaar is in the middle, and the Dor at-Tilyavat and Dor as-Siadat are slightly further south. As you traipse between them you'll have the chance to take in the sights and smells of a place that wears its heritage lightly, entwining the past and present effortlessly.

TOUR OPERATORS AND TRAVEL AGENTS There are several Aviakassa along Ipak Yoli, the most organised of which seems to be **Mobil Servis Aviakassa** (*Ipak Yoli*), immediately opposite the bazaar.

WHERE TO STAY *Map, page 174*
Shakhrisabz is just a few hours' drive from Samarkand, so it's easily done as a day trip. If you want to have a little longer to look around, however, or are travelling the long way to Bukhara, there is only one option at the present time: other choices were demolished as part of the beautification programme and are yet to be rebuilt.

Hotel Shakhrisabz Yulduzi (50 rooms) 2 Ipak Yoli; 521 0554; e shakhrisabzstar@inbox. ru. Opened in 2009, Shakhrisabz's only hotel is also its best, though don't expect 5-star standards. Situated overlooking the city walls, it is clean, comfortable & all rooms have AC. The swimming pool is welcome in summer. Unusually for Uzbekistan, some rooms have access for travellers with disabilities. There is a restaurant on the roof, & a souvenir shop & small art gallery in the foyer. Service is slow & lacklustre. Wi-Fi costs 6,000 som for 300 MB. **$$$**

WHERE TO EAT AND DRINK *Map, page 174*
Providing you like shashlik or 'hot dog' (sheesh kebab in half a naan bread), Shakhrisabz has a number of places to eat, though as demolition of the Old Town continues, who knows which will actually be open by the time you visit. If you're a vegetarian or have a hankering for more variety, you're unfortunately out of luck.

Most of the chaikhanas are along Ipak Yoli, all of which are open during daylight hours and spread out onto the street. The smell of the shashlik grilling will catch your nose long before you can see the premises and will start your tummy rumbling. The pick of the chaikhanas are **Xush Kelibsiz** ($$) midway between the mosque and the bazaar on the eastern side of Ipak Yoli, and **Mantixona** ($$) next door to the caravanserai.

SHOPPING Though it lacks the variety of souvenirs you'll find in Samarkand, the quality in Shakhrisabz is reasonable and prices are relatively low. Inside the Dor at-Tilyavat and Dor as-Siadat complexes (pages 175–6) you'll find various stands selling embroidered bags, hats and other gift items. The same is true at the Ak Serai, where there are a number of stalls and also usually artists displaying their paintings. One of these artists also has a gallery inside Hotel Shakhrisabz Yulduzi.

For foodstuffs, in particular fresh and dried fruits and the morning's bread, the **Main Bazaar** (*Ipak Yoli;* ⊕ *06.00–18.00 daily*) is well stocked and also a fine spot for people-watching. Men with handcarts gather in the central courtyard to smoke, talk and watch the world go by, occasionally breaking to deliver a sack of potatoes or two. For dry goods, chocolate, etc, **Sargon Market** (*32 Main Bazaar;* ⊕ *07.00– 17.00 daily*) has basic supplies at fixed prices.

OTHER PRACTICALITIES
Communications There is a **Paynet** station and mobile phone stand on the left as soon as you come through the main gate of the bazaar. There are **Beeline, Ucell**

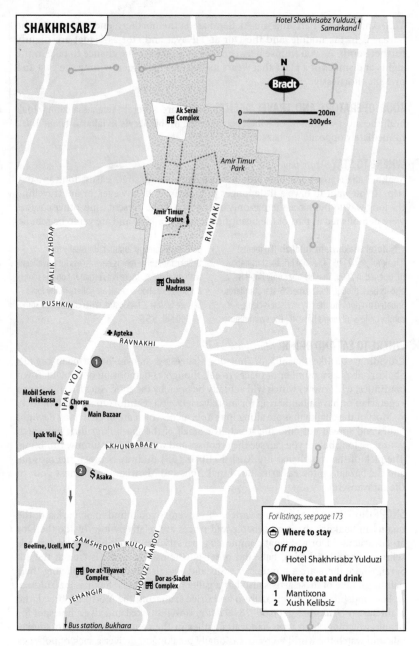

For listings, see page 173

SHAKHRISABZ

Hotel Shakhrisabz Yulduzi,
Samarkand

Ak Serai
Complex

Amir Timur
Park

Amir Timur
Statue

RAVNAKI

Chubin
Madrassa

MALIK AZHDAR

PUSHKIN

Apteka
RAVNAKHI

Mobil Servis
Aviakassa

IPAK YOLI

Chorsu

Main Bazaar

Ipak Yoli

AKHUNBABAEV

Asaka

Beeline, Ucell, MTC

SAMSHEDDIN KULOL

Dor at-Tilyavat
Complex

KHOVUZI MARDOI

Dor as-Siadat
Complex

JEHANGIR

Bus station, Bukhara

For listings, see page 173

Where to stay

Off map
 Hotel Shakhrisabz Yulduzi

Where to eat and drink
1 Mantixona
2 Xush Kelibsiz

and **MTC** offices on Ipak Yoli immediately to the north of the mosque. It is possible to get Wi-Fi at Hotel Shakhrisabz Yulduzi (page 173). Internet cards are for sale, which allow you to logon to the hotspot.

Medical There are several Apteka on Ipak Yoli, the best stocked of which is on the corner with Ravnaki (*08.00–18.00 daily*).

Money There are no ATMs in Shakhrisabz, so if you need more cash you will need to get cash advanced on your card in a bank branch, or receive a money transfer. **Ipak Yoli Bank** (*Ipak Yoli;* ⊕ *09.00–16.00 Mon–Fri*) is most convenient for this. If you only need to exchange dollars for som, **Asaka Bank** has a booth in the covered section of the bazaar by the vegetable stalls.

WHAT TO SEE AND DO Shakhrisabz has a wealth of historical sites, and they are far less visited than the big name draws of Samarkand and Bukhara. All of the below-mentioned sites are open 09.00–18.00 unless otherwise stated. There are currently no entrance charges, though you will be charged if you take a guided tour: half-day tours cost around US$15 per person and can be booked through Hotel Shakhrisabz Yulduzi. All of Shakhrisabz's tourist sites are on Ipak Yoli, the main street.

Dor at-Tilyavat Complex The **Kok-Gumbaz** (Blue Dome) is an aptly named mosque, south of the bazaar, which was built by Timur's grandson in 1434–35, not long after his father had moved the centre of Timurid power from Samarkand to Herat. On the site of an older, Karakhanid-era mosque, it once had a dome larger than that of the Bibi Khanym Mosque in Samarkand, as well as 40 domed galleries to house additional worshippers. The original dome collapsed sometime in the late 18th century but was rebuilt 200 years later.

Stepping across the threshold, you'll find the interior mosque of the complex cool and calm, particularly when compared with the heat of the courtyard outside. The interior decoration, gently peeling in places due to damp, may come across as a little garish, but it should not be forgotten that even in its original state it would still have been brightly painted and tiled; the only change is in the quality of the workmanship and its maintenance.

Surrounding the Kok-Gumbaz is a pleasant courtyard lined with craft stalls (mostly selling embroidery and gaudy knitted socks) and an area of whitewashed pillars with a vaulted ceiling. Protected from the elements, a few traditional **stonemasons** work here, mostly producing elaborately carved headstones, some of which include realistic depictions of the deceased. Watching them work is mesmerising and the chink-chink of their chisels against the marble echoes back from the curved roof.

On the opposite side of the courtyard are two heavily restored mausoleums: the **Gumbazi Seidon** (dome of the Sayyids) and the **Mausoleum of Sheikh Shamsuddin Kulyol**. The former marks the graves of various Timurid-era holy men; the latter is for the 14th-century missionary who is credited with converting the Chagtai tribes to Islam. Remove your shoes at the door and remain quiet inside; these are considered holy places.

Dor as-Siadat Complex Following the brick path through the park immediately behind the Dor at-Tilyavat brings you to the clearly visible Dor as-Siadat (Abode of Might), the family necropolis built by Timur himself when his eldest son, Jahangir, died in 1376. It's a pleasant spot with plenty of mature trees, a haven set back from the street. Construction of the necropolis took 25 years, and a second son, Omar, is also buried there. It is thought that Timur also wished to be entombed here, and a **crypt** discovered by archaeologists beneath the floors of the memorial mosque supports this idea, though he was ultimately interred at the Gur-i Amir in Samarkand (pages 162–3).

On the mausoleums' northern side is the **Hazrati Imam Mosque,** a 19th-century building with an attractive wooden *avian* (veranda). Though it is not explicitly named in honour of one particular man, the inscription across the doors perhaps links it to Abu Abdulla Muhammad ibn Nasr al Keshi, a local holy man in the 9th century.

Ak Serai Complex At the northern end of Ipak Yoli is Timur's Ak Serai (White Palace), which was quite possibly the largest and most impressive building he commissioned. The portal alone would have reached 50m in height and been flanked by a pair of tapered minarets each 65m tall. Construction of the palace began in 1380 and it took the labourers and artisans, drawn from across the Timurid Empire, 20 years to complete. According to the Castillian ambassador Claviho, the rear courtyard was 300 paces wide (in all an estimated 1.6ha) and the reception halls were painted azure blue and richly gilded. It must have been quite a sight.

Envisaging the scale and might of this structure today requires a little imagination. In their attempt to wipe out memory of the Timurids, the Shaybanids destroyed many of the original structures, leaving just 38m of the central gateway intact. This may not sound a great deal, but it still rises dramatically above the surrounding parkland and is visible from quite a distance. Unlike many of Uzbekistan's other historic sites, to date very little restoration work has been done here, and UNESCO's current project seems to focus, quite rightly, more on shoring up the building than touching up its magnificent (albeit time-ravaged) tile work. This approach enables you to appreciate what is original and what is a modern interpretation of the site, far more so than is possible in Samarkand.

Immediately in front of the gates is Shakhrisabz's modern **statue of Amir Timur**. It's big, it's brash and it probably looks nothing like the man himself, but every bride and groom in the vicinity, plus their inebriated entourages, are clamouring to have their photos taken alongside. If you stray too close, expect to be enveloped into the fold and to have a glass thrust into your hand: foreigners are popular additions to wedding photographs, it seems, even if you've previously never met.

A small section of Shakhrisabz's mud-brick **city walls** has been preserved just behind the gateway. Originally at least 8m thick and 11m high, and broken up with a tower or archway every 50m, they must have been an imposing prospect for any would-be invader. More sections of the walls are being rebuilt as part of the town's beautification programme, and the buildings abutting them have largely been demolished.

Other sites Three other sites in the city are worthy of mention. Outside the main entrance to the bazaar (page 173) is **Chorsu,** a medieval trading dome that still serves its original purpose. The external dome covers an octagonal hall, which is surrounded by four smaller domes, each with its own portal. The bustling stalls inside spill out onto the square outside and there are some curious objects on sale: the handmade wooden cribs, for example, are constructed with a hole in the base to facilitate the easy cleaning of baby in the absence of a nappy!

Closer to Ak Serai, the **Chubin Madrassa** dates from the late 17th century. It was restored in the 1990s, the theological students and their teachers long gone; in their place is a small museum with local archaeological finds including rather fine relics from a Zoroastrian ossuary, and a scale model of Shakhrisabz as it would have looked in its Timurid heyday.

Shakhrisabz also has a small, mud-brick **caravanserai** next to the junction between Ipak Yoli and Ravnakhi. It was, however, closed indefinitely, supposedly for renovation, at the time of research and so we were unable to look inside.

AROUND SHAKHRISABZ In the Kok Su Gorge, 60km south of Shakhrisabz, is the **Lyangar Ata Mausoleum**, the final resting place of 15th- and 16th-century sheikhs from the Iskiya order, rivals to the dominant Naqshbandi order, who had them driven out of Samarkand during the Timurid period. The hilltop mausoleum is clearly visible from all around, and the mosque by its side once held both an early Qu'ran and a cloak said to belong to the Prophet Muhammad. These artefacts have sadly long-since been removed, but it's still worth stopping off here for half an hour, if only to break the journey south.

KARSHI *Telephone code: 75*

The capital of Qashqa Darya Province, this small city of 200,000 people is a regional hub due to the proximity of natural gas plants and the numerous cotton fields that surround it, all of which are irrigated with water diverted from the Amu Darya.

THE GISSAR STATE NATURE RESERVE

The Gissar State Nature Reserve (*(0375) 522 7669; www.hisor.uz/en*) is an 80,000ha site at the western end of the Pamir–Alay mountain range, which begins around 40km to the east of Shakhrisabz. Since 2008 it has been on UNESCO's Tentative List for inclusion as a World Heritage Site on account of its combination of unique geological outcroppings, biodiversity and ancient historical sites.

The territory of the reserve, which was formed in 1985 when the Kyzyksui and Mirakin reserves were merged, is comprised of gorges, caverns, small glaciers, streams and waterfalls, so it is exceptionally photogenic. There is very little human habitation in this part of Uzbekistan, so the indigenous wildlife thrives: there are snow leopards (which have been successfully photographed with the use of camera traps), marmots, Tolai hares and porcupines. The mixed habitats – forest, shrub, grassland, rocky areas and wetland – attract diverse birdlife, including large birds of prey. You can expect to see of Himalayan snowcock, Hume's lark and yellow-billed chough, and may be lucky enough to spot the endangered saker falcon and near-threatened cinereous vulture and himalayan griffon.

To date, more than 800 species of flora have been recorded in the reserve, and experts estimate that there may be as many as 300 more to find. Scientists working in the reserve are collaborating with the National University of Uzbekistan, as well as local universities in Samarkand and Karshi, to create a gene pool of the reserve's flora and fauna. They are also monitoring changes in the reserve's ecosystem, and trying to identify unique and fast-disappearing species.

Of historic interest (and hence of interest to UNESCO) are a dinosaur's footprint; a pilgrimage site dedicated to the Muslim saint Khodji Daud; and a vast subterranean lake in a natural cavern, which was settled in the Stone Age and occupied until about the 3rd century BC. All of these sites are accessible if you have a knowledgeable guide and are prepared to hike.

There is currently nowhere to stay within the reserve, and no public transport to reach it. You will need to travel to Shakhrisabz by minibus or shared taxi (page 172), and then hire a taxi to take you onto the reserve. The journey to the edge of the park will take about an hour.

6

The city has Sogdian roots, but it is the surviving medieval madrassas, mausoleums and mosques, not to mention a reputation for producing finely worked flat-weave carpets, that attract an occasional tourist.

HISTORY There have been three cities on this site: Sogdian Nakhshab, the Arab Nasaf, and lastly Karshi, which took its name from the two 14th-century palaces built by the Mongol khans. Timur erected the city's citadel and protective moat in 1364; successive rulers extended the city walls and constructed caravanserais, gardens and religious buildings.

Karshi was annexed by the Russians in 1868, and the documents reducing Bukhara to merely a Russian protectorate were also signed in the city five years later.

After a long hiatus, Karshi emerged briefly to international attention following the US invasion of Afghanistan as the site of the Khanabad airbase. Though this was initially used to supply US troops, it was forced to close in 2005 following US criticism of the Andijan massacre (see box, page 132) and replaced with the Manas airbase outside Bishkek in Kyrgyzstan.

GETTING THERE, AWAY AND AROUND Karshi is 455km from Tashkent and it's an 8-hour drive, so if time is of the essence many people choose to fly. **Uzbekistan Airways** has four flights a week (*1hr 25mins; US$75*) thanks to the need to move workers swiftly down to the natural gas plants, and there are occasional flights to Russia with **Rossiya**. The **airport** is in the southwest of the town past the railway tracks.

The **main bus station** is southwest of the city centre, and there are regular buses, minibuses and shared taxis to Bukhara (*3hrs*), Shakhrisabz (*2hrs*) and Termez (*5hrs*). By shared taxi, expect to haggle hard and end up paying US$8–10 to Bukhara, US$6 to Shakhrisabz and US$15 to Termez. Once in the city, minibus 12 runs past the war memorial and the Kok Gumbaz Mosque to the bazaar. It's the cheapest and easiest way to get around.

The **train station** (*7 Uzbekistan*) is next to the airport. There are daily departures to Samarkand (*2hrs*) and Tashkent (*3½hrs*).

TOUR OPERATORS

Avia Marka 2 Mustakillik; ☎ (93) 722 0900. Airline tickets & other transport bookings.
City Tour 11A Uzbekistan; ☎ (75) 221 3003. Basic travel agency. No English is spoken.

Nasaf Travel Company 2A Bogzar; ☎ 225 0665. The owners of Hotel Nasaf Travel (page 179) also run this small, professional outfit & can arrange guided tours, onward transport & make hotel bookings.

 WHERE TO STAY AND EAT Don't expect to be impressed by Karshi's hotels and restaurants: they're functional, but certainly nothing special.

The easiest places to eat are the **hotel restaurants** at Hotel Nasaf Travel and Hotel Afsona where food is inevitably bland but at least predictable. The restaurant at the Afsona does a reasonable selection of salads, which goes down well if you've had your fill of shashlik. There are a number of unnamed **chaikhanas** in the bazaar and also to its east on Nasaf. Follow your nose and expect to eat either standing or squashed on a bench with a stranger at busy times.

🏠 **Hotel Afsona** (40 rooms) 5A Sherkulov; ☎ 771 0091. Modern hotel with a candyfloss pink exterior that would make Barbie proud. Bedrooms are a little on the small side, as are the bathrooms, but it's clean enough. Note that it is in the business district rather than the city centre. **$$$**

🏠 **Hotel Nasaf Travel** (20 rooms) 2A Bogzar; 📞 225 0665. Medium-sized, renovated hotel in the city centre. All rooms have AC & satellite TV. The hotel has internet & a large restaurant. **$$$**

🏠 **Hotel Sarbon** (18 rooms) 10A, Microrayon 4; 📞 223 0808. Well-located, comfortable hotel with clean rooms, a restaurant & bar, & a swimming pool. B/fast inc. Probably the best accommodation option in Karshi. **$$**

OTHER PRACTICALITIES

Communications To send and receive mail you need the **central post office** (*19 Mustakillik;* ⊕ *09.00–18.00 Mon–Fri*). In addition to the regular postal service, you can also courier letters and parcels with **EMS Falcon** (*also 19 Mustakillik*).

The main office for **Ucell** is at 49 Uzbekistan (⊕ *09.00–17.00 Mon–Sat*).

Medical For general medical issues, the **Multidisciplinary Medical Centre of Qashqa Darya Region** (*413 Uzbekistan;* 📞 *226 1760*) is your best bet. In an emergency, however, you should go to the **Republican Centre of Science of Emergency Medicine** (*5 X Bashir;* 📞 *227 6616*).

There are **Apteka** around both of these hospitals, and you can also get medications, dressings and other basic items from **Asklepiy** (*85A Uzbekistan*) and **Dori Darmon** (*25 Uzbekistan Ovozi*).

Money You will find unofficial **money changers** in the bazaar, and hotel staff are also able to assist. The following banks offer Western Union and currency exchange at the official rate.

$ **Agrobank** 2 Navoi; 📞 221 1876; ⊕ 09.00–16.00 Mon–Fri

$ **Microcredit Bank** 4 Sohibkor; 📞 227 6757; ⊕ 09.00–17.00 Mon–Fri

$ **Uzpromstroibank** 2A Khonobod; 📞 223 0683; ⊕ 09.00–16.00 Mon–Fri

WHAT TO SEE AND DO Karshi's medieval heart is centred on the bazaar, though you have to look past the 20th-century's less tasteful architectural creations if you're to get a sense of what historic Karshi would actually have been like.

The 16th-century **Odina Mosque**, now restored, is built on the site of a Mongol palace. It houses Karshi's **Regional Museum** (⊕ *09.00–17.00 Tue–Sat; foreigners US$1*), though this is rather underwhelming: it is the building's domed exterior that is the main attraction, though you may also want to take a look at the covered pool by the wall as this would have been the mosque's main source of water, essential for the faithful to perform their pre-prayer ablutions.

Elsewhere on the same square are the **Bekmir, Kalizbek** and **Khodjaev Abdul Aziz madrassas** (all 19th century). These somewhat forlorn structures are caught in limbo due to the government's policies on religion: they can no longer function as religious buildings, but are surplus to other requirements and hence generally lie empty, collecting dust and pigeons where once their students trod. If you ask their guardians, they will be happy to let you inside to look around, and they may even give you a tour.

Karshi's **bazaar** is well stocked and a good spot for people-watching. On Fridays you'll see numerous men flitting through in long black *chapan* coats and embroidered skull caps on their way to the **Kurgancha** and **Charka mosques**. It's also worth stopping to take a look at the 16th-century **bathhouse,** once the social centre for men in the city, which legend has it was magically heated by the warmth of a single candle. On our next visit we'll have to bring one and see; it seemed rather drafty without.

A 5-minute walk along Nasaf brings you to the attractive **Kok Gumbaz Mosque.** This late 16th-century mosque is richly tiled and not dissimilar to those built by the Timurids in Shakhrisabz, though it is less heavily restored than similar mosques elsewhere.

At the opposite end of Karshi (take the No 12 minibus to get there) is a sprawling **war monument** that remembers the Soviet casualties of the Great Patriotic War (World War II). One of the largest such monuments in central Asia, it's an eclectic mix of plaques, walkways, an eternal flame and a red star-topped tower with a series of stained-glass windows. Karshi's students tend to hang out in the square, and you'll need to co-opt one of them to locate the elderly guardian with the key to the upper levels of the tower and show you the stained-glass scenes, contrasting images of children harvesting wheat and soldiers departing for the battlefield.

AROUND KARSHI On the road north to Bukhara, about 15km outside Karshi, is the **Khasim Ata Mosque Complex** in Fudina. Entrance is free, but donations for the site's upkeep are welcome. Centred on the mausoleum of Hazrati Khasim Ata, an 11th-century Islamic missionary and teacher, it is unusual in Uzbekistan by virtue of the fact that it is still an active religious site: the mosque is functional, and pilgrims still come to the tomb to pray. The building, which includes additional tombs from the 13th and 14th centuries, is run-down and definitely in need of repair, but the fact that it still has life makes it a welcome contrast to so many madrassas left empty and purposeless by the government's continuing crackdown on religious establishments.

Half an hour southeast of Karshi towards Termez is a second, better-preserved architectural site: the **Sultan Mir Haydor tombs.** In close proximity here is a medieval **covered reservoir**, the 17th-century **Namazgokh Mosque**, and a series of decorative brick-built tombs, the earliest of which dates from the 1200s. The tombs can appear as a land that time forgot: white-bearded men who seem almost as old as the architecture linger in the courtyard, waiting for goodness know's what.

DENAU *Telephone code: 76*

Surkhan Darya's second town is Denau, also known as Denov. It is the border town with Tajikistan when entering into the west of the country for Dushanbe and the Pamir Highway, and transiting between the two countries is the most likely reason you'll find yourself here.

The valley around Denau has a subtropical climate, which has enabled it to become a relatively successful wine-producing area and also to support a wide range of non-native plants in the R Shreder Dendrarium. The archaeological remains of two important Kushan-era cities, Kalchayan and Dalverzin Teppe, are also within easy reach of Denau.

GETTING THERE AND AWAY

By road Denau is well connected with other cities in Uzbekistan. Most arrivals from Tajikistan will be heading by shared taxi or minibus along the picturesque road through the hills to Samarkand (*5hrs; US$18*), Bukhara (*6hrs; US$22*) or Termez (*2hrs; US$5*). These prices are for journeys by shared taxis; minibuses are about 30% cheaper. There is also a **daily bus** to Tashkent but it will easily take you 12–14 hours. All of the public transport options leave from Denau's bus station on Makhtumkuli, close to the bazaar. For the shared taxis you will need to haggle to get a fair price.

By train There are two helpful train routes out of Denau. The **local train** to the border town of Sariosiyo (*4hrs; US$1*) is irritatingly slow, but cheaper than taking a taxi. There are three departures a day. There is also a less-frequent **sleeper train** to Tashkent (*15hrs; US$24*), which departs at 15.40 every other day and travels via Karshi, Navoi and Samarkand. You don't have to change, just be very patient. The **railway station** is to the east of the town centre, within walking distance of S Rashidov.

WHERE TO STAY AND EAT Visitors have distinctly limited options of places to stay in Denau; indeed, if you have the choice, it is best to continue on to your next destination rather than try to find a bed here. The only hotel in town, **Hotel Denau** (*cnr Mustakillik & Rashidov; $*), is a miserable hole of a place with unimaginably horrific bathrooms and belligerent staff. Avoid it if at all possible.

Denau's **bazaar** is a lively place and well stocked with foodstuffs and crafts from both Uzbekistan and Tajikistan. In addition to fresh produce there is the usual array of shashlik stands and chaikhanas, all of which serve hot, tasty food for a dollar or two.

The valleys around Denau are known for their **winemaking**, in particular the production of Novbakhor and Morastel, two local varieties of grape. Local rum is also produced using sugar cane. Your best chance of tasting Denau wines or rum is in someone's home, though it is also worth asking for it in the bazaar.

OTHER PRACTICALITIES

Communications Ucell has agents in the bazaar on Mustakillik and also at 101 and 241 S Rashidov. **Beeline** and **MTC** SIM cards can also be topped up from stands in the bazaar.

Medical Denau's **district hospital** is on S Otaboev. It is a small hospital with only basic equipment and cannot be relied upon to give emergency care. There are two **Apteka** immediately next to the hospital, and a third by the bazaar.

Money **Money changers** are to be found in the bazaar and also around the bus station. Denau has several banks that exchange money at the official rate and provide Western Union services. Most conveniently located among these are the **National Bank For Foreign Economic Activity** (*20 Mustakillik;* ✆ *412 4839;* ⏱ *09.00–18.00 Mon–Fri*) and Microcredit Bank (*204 Registan;* ✆ *412 1687;* ⏱ *09.00–17.00 Mon–Fri*).

CROSSING INTO TAJIKISTAN

The **Tajik–Uzbek border crossing** is northeast of Denau on the road to Tursunzoda. It is open year-round, but the opening and closing times seem to vary depending on how the officials feel: sometimes it is open 24 hours, and at other times it closes around 20.00. It is best to cross in daylight in any case, as then it will definitely be open. It is significantly faster crossing from Uzbekistan into Tajikistan than the other way round as the customs checks are far less arduous. Both minibuses and taxis wait on both sides of the border for onward journeys, and there is sufficient foot traffic that you can always find someone with whom you can split the taxi fare. Expect to pay US$15 per seat in the shared taxis from Tursunzoda on to Dushanbe.

WHAT TO SEE AND DO In the centre of Denau, close to the bazaar, the **Sayyid Atalik Madrassa** dates from the 16th century and is one of the largest madrassas in central Asia. Its scale and elegant symmetry are more than ample compensation for the lack of ornamentation, and if you enter the building with the director, Murat, who you can ask for at the gate, he'll show you every last fascinating corner. The madrassa has officially been closed for renovation since 1997 but there is no sign of restoration work being under way. You are likely have the site to yourself; the atmosphere is somewhat eerie, as if echoing that a generation of students is missing and mourned.

A surprising discovery on S Rashidov is the **R Shreder Dendrarium**, an arboretum with more than 1,000 species of plants brought here by scientists and official visitors from around the world. Among the more common trees, flowers and herbs, many of which are native to Uzbekistan, are also imported varieties including kauchuk, bamboo and sequoia. The arboretum also has a notable collection of persimmon: more than 200 species are represented in the garden. Stop here for an hour or two if you've overdosed on madrassas and ruins: the plants will refresh your mind.

AROUND DENAU The hinterland around Denau contains a number of intriguing sites which, though probably not worth a visit on their own, can be combined into a worthwhile day trip, particularly if you are already in the area.

The **City of Kalchayan**, 10km northeast of Denau, is a Graeco-Bactrian city first settled in the fourth century BC. The Soviet archaeologist Professor Galina Pugachenkova led extensive excavations here in the mid 20th century, and found a large number of Kushan-era sculptures, many of them particularly lifelike. The variety of dress, hairstyles and ethnic features displayed in the figures reveals both the diversity of people living and trading in ancient Kalchayan, and the skill of the city's artisans. The most important finds have been taken from the site and are now displayed in the State Fine Art Museum in Tashkent (pages 111–12).

The ruined **Fortress of Yurchi**, south of the city on the road to Termez, dates from the 10th century, and the author Colin Thubron visited the village while researching *The Lost Heart of Asia* in the hope of finding the burial place of the Basmachi leader and World War I Turkish war minister, Ismail Enver Pasha (see box, page 183). Thubron failed to find a trace of Pasha (who likely died and was buried across the border in Tajikistan), but instead found in the village the grave of Licharov, the regional Bolshevik commander who was killed here in 1924.

Around 30km south of Denau, on the road to Termez, is the small town of Shurchi and neighbouring archaeological site of **Dalverzin Teppe**, a Kushan-era (1st–4th century AD) settlement that was once an important defensive site on the Surkhan Valley branch of the Silk Route. The settlement, which was protected by walls 10m thick, housed an important and wealthy Buddhist complex; archaeologists have unearthed the remains of a *stupa*, prayer hall and also the so-called King's Room, a hall richly decorated with sculptures that show both Buddhist and Hellenistic influences. The neighbouring complex contained a Bactrian temple, numerous statues of the Buddha and bodhisattvas and, remarkably, a treasure hoard of gold and silver items, many of them set with precious stones. The total hoard weighed in at 36kg, and the most important items are now exhibited at museums in Tashkent and in Russia.

The Dalverzin Teppe site is rather better preserved than Kalchayan; significant portions of the city wall are still clearly visible, as is the Buddhist temple and part of a Bactrian shrine. There's no charge to enter and no set opening times, though you'll need to go during daylight hours to stand a chance of seeing anything.

In the dying days of the Ottoman Empire, a young revolutionary called Ismail Enver Pasha cut his military teeth fighting guerrillas in the Balkans, then rose to prominence as Turkey's minister of war. His rallying cry to his troops was 'war until final victory'.

When the Russian Revolution took place in 1917, Turkey's Committee of Union and Progress (CUP), of which Enver was a founding member, befriended the Bolsheviks and sent their own troops into the Caucasus, where a power vacuum had been created by the withdrawal of tsarist forces. Enver named his new army the Army of Islam.

Enver's fortunes changed with the end of World War I. He was court-martialled in absentia for acting beyond his official remit, and condemned to death. Enver fled first to Germany, then offered his services to the Bolsheviks. He thought he could incite the Muslim world to join the revolution.

Lenin dispatched Enver first to Bukhara in 1921, and then to Tajikistan. Caught between his religious brethren and his paymasters, Enver switched sides and joined the Basmachi. He led a successful attack on Dushanbe in February 1922 but failed to unite his forces and lost the city to the Red Army just five months later.

Enver was killed by the Bolsheviks in the summer of 1922. A truce had been called for Eid, but an informant betrayed Enver's location. He attempted to defend himself with a single machine gun but was shot by a sniper's bullet. The Basmachi hid his body to prevent its capture, and it is likely that it was buried more than once. A body thought to belong to Enver Pasha remained in Tajikistan until the Turkish government carted it back to Istanbul for a state funeral in 1995.

TERMEZ *Telephone code: 76*

The city of Termez is the final frontier. Few foreigners venture this far south, save those heading across the border into Afghanistan, and so making the journey seems like quite an adventure regardless of whether you are continuing across the border or not. The city is home to a population of 15,000 people, including large numbers of Tajiks and Afghans, and its history stretches back some 2,500 years. From ancient Buddhist monasteries to medieval mausoleums, there is plenty to see, all nestled in the sweeping curve of the mighty Amu Darya.

HISTORY Termez marks the border between Uzbekistan and Afghanistan, and its history is therefore inevitably caught up with developments in both those territories. In the wake of Alexander the Great's invasion, Greek troops built a line of fortifications along the banks of the Oxus, and Termez grew up at a crossing point on the river. A Graeco–Bactrian city, it thrived financially, culturally and spiritually at the meeting point of Mediterranean, Indian, Persian, Chinese and central Asian civilisations. Termez became a centre for Buddhism and for Gandharan art, a fusion of Indian and Hellenistic styles.

The Bactrian state eventually fractured and slid into decline, torn apart by warring factions. The Arab general Musa ibn Qasim seized Termez in AD689 and proclaimed himself king, only to be overthrown by Caliph Uthman in AD704. From then on, Termez began to look north to central Asia rather than south to Afghanistan.

Alexander the Great spent around two years in Uzbekistan during his conquest of the Achaemenid Persian Empire. He experienced there not just some of the most difficult fighting of the entire campaign, but also some of the most remarkable events of his expedition into Asia.

Through 330BC, Alexander had chased the Persian nobleman Bessus around Afghanistan. Bessus was leading the Persian resistance to Alexander, and Alexander had to capture him to ensure the complete submission of the Persian Empire. In 329BC, Alexander crossed the Oxus after leaving the Afghan city of Balkh, and was shortly able to get hold of Bessus, who was sent off for execution.

However, Alexander remained in the region to consolidate his power. Perhaps foolishly, he did not make use of his natural allies in the region. Shortly after crossing the Oxus he discovered a town that was inhabited by Greeks, who welcomed him wholeheartedly. However, on discovering that they had collaborated with the Persians when they had invaded Greece in 480BC, he executed the entire settlement and levelled it to the ground. Proceeding northward, he captured Samarkand and then reached the Syr Darya (River Jaxartes) where he founded Alexandria Eschate, 'Alexandria-the-Farthest', modern-day Khojend in Tajikistan.

Despite this immediate success, there was considerable disquiet in the area. Alexander faced a number of uprisings from the indigenous Sogdians and Scythian tribesmen. They were able to employ guerrilla hit-and-run tactics again relying on their mastery of horsemanship and archery to strike at his columns from a distance. Alexander had not faced this sort of warfare before, and he had to develop new tactics to defeat the nomadic warriors, including the combined use of catapults and archers, as well as hunting his opponents down to their fortresses and carrying out a conventional campaign of sieges. Despite being badly injured and suffering from dysentery, Alexander was able to lead his men to a notable success against the Scythians on the Syr Darya River.

As Alexander gained the upper hand, his opponents rallied at a fortress called the Sogdian Rock on top of a large escarpment. Its site is not known for certain, but it is thought to be near Samarkand. They thought it impregnable, and taunted Alexander that he would need soldiers with wings to capture it. Alexander was so irked by their jibes that he called for volunteers to scale the sheer cliffs up to the fortress. Three hundred men came forward and, using ropes and tent pegs, they made the ascent in the dead of night. Although 30 were lost in the climb, by morning they were inside the fortress. Alexander's herald shouted that they had found the soldiers with wings, and the defenders, amazed, surrendered immediately.

According to Greek historians, Alexander met on the rock a princess named Roxane, the daughter of one of the local rulers, Oxyartes. They record that he fell in love with her on sight and arranged a marriage with her. Having made such an alliance, he was ready to proceed out of Uzbek lands on his attempt to conquer India. The legend of Roxane still lives today, and many distinguished families in the region claim descent from the union of Alexander and Roxane.

In the 12th century Termez slipped swiftly through the hands of the Karakhanids, Seljuks, Ghaznavids, Gurids and Khorezmshah and thence into the clutches of Genghis Khan. A census was taken of the population, and every man, woman and child listed on it was killed. The bulk of the city walls was demolished and flung into the Oxus. Old Termez would never recover.

New Termez rose up in the 14th century; Ibn Battuta visited here on his travels. Timur built a line of pontoons across the Oxus so as to tax traffic entering the city; the city's perfume and soaps were particularly valuable commodities.

The third and final city of Termez is a 19th-century creation, a Russian garrison town on the southernmost border of the Russian Empire. A naval base was built on the river at nearby Chardzhou, and military boats monitored the border closely. The military would remain Termez's *raison d'être*, first as the entry point for the Soviet invasion of Afghanistan in 1979 and then for fuel, supplies and aid crossing the railway bridge after the US-led invasion in 2001.

GETTING THERE AND AWAY Termez is an intriguing destination, but a long way from anywhere, and this will inevitably influence your itinerary and preferred mode(s) of transport. For reference purposes, it is 375km from Samarkand, 380km from Bukhara, 660km from Tashkent, 855km from Khiva, and a whopping 1,100km from Namangan.

By road Termez's **main bus station** is in the city centre at the western end of Navoi. The city is pretty well connected with other destinations in Uzbekistan though the journeys are inevitably long.

Buses leave early in the morning to Samarkand (*10hrs; US$8*) and Tashkent (*16hrs; US$17*) and **shared taxis** run the same route throughout the day in half the time but at twice the price. To reach Bukhara you'll need to take a shared taxi to Karshi (*4hrs; US$8*) and pick up westward transport there. The road is slow, and in parts rough. Even in your own vehicle, you will need to allow at least 8 hours for the drive. If you are heading northeast to Denau (for Tajikistan), you have the choice between a minibus (*US$2*) and a shared taxi (*US$5*), both of which take around 2 hours.

By rail Termez's **railway station** is at the northern end of Termezi, an easy walk from the town centre. Train 379/380 goes daily to Tashkent (*16hrs; platskartny tickets from 57,306 som*) and stops *en route* at Karshi and Samarkand.

CROSSING INTO AFGHANISTAN

If you are travelling to or from Afghanistan, you'll cross the border at the **Termez–Hairatan border post**, which lies on the main road to Mazar-i Sharif. These days getting through customs and immigration on either side is likely to be completely uneventful (disappointingly so), though do allow plenty of time if you're entering Uzbekistan, as the anti-narcotics teams are thorough but not especially efficient. Public transport is plentiful (minibuses from Termez leave from the stand opposite the post office on Termezi), and it's around an hour's drive from the border to Mazar.

You should not attempt to cross the border anywhere other than the official border crossing: there is a high (and often jumpy) military presence and a large number of mines.

There are also regular services to Denau (*3hrs; US$1*), from where you can easily get road connections across the border to Tajikistan.

By air There are ten direct flights a week to Tashkent with **Uzbekistan Airways** (*1hr 35mins; US$90*), and these have reasonable connections across the rest of Uzbekistan and to Russia. The **airport** is a 20-minute drive north of the city, and can be reached either by taxi or by taking minibus No 11 from the stand by the bazaar on Termezi.

Tickets are available from the ticketing desk at the airport, and also from Uzbektourism (page 187).

GETTING AROUND Termez's **public transport** system is actually quite well organised, with buses, minibuses and minivans linking most parts of the city where you're likely to venture. The following minibus routes are most helpful for visitors:

Minibus 4	Along Termezi to the train station
Minibus 6	Along Navoi to the main bus station
Minibus 11	Yubileyny Bazaar to the airport

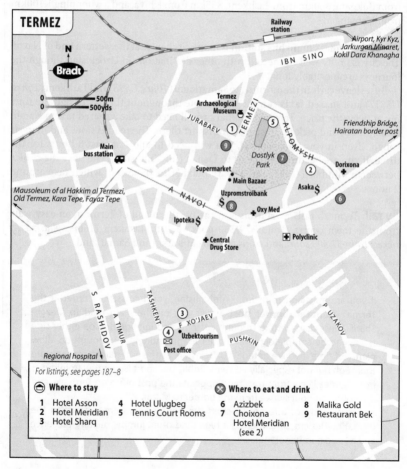

TERMEZ

N

0 — 500m
0 — 500yds

Railway station

Airport, Kyr Kyz, Jarkurgan Minaret, Kokil Dara Khanagha

IBN SINO

Termez Archaeological Museum

JURABAEV

TERMEZI

ALPOMYSH

Friendship Bridge, Hairatan border post

Main bus station

Dostlyk Park

Supermarket

Main Bazaar

Dorixona

Asaka $

Uzpromstroibank $

A NAVOI

Oxy Med

Ipoteka $

Mausoleum of al Hakkim al Termezi, Old Termez, Kara Tepe, Fayaz Tepe

Central Drug Store

Polyclinic

S RASHIDOV

A TIMUR

TASHKENT

F XO'JAEV

Uzbektourism

Post office

PUSHKIN

P UZAKOV

Regional hospital

For listings, see pages 187–8

⊖ **Where to stay**
1 Hotel Asson
2 Hotel Meridian
3 Hotel Sharq
4 Hotel Ulugbeg
5 Tennis Court Rooms

✗ **Where to eat and drink**
6 Azizbek
7 Choixona
  Hotel Meridian
  (see 2)
8 Malika Gold
9 Restaurant Bek

| Minibus 14 | Yubileyny Bazaar to Namuna (for the Sultan Saodat Mausoleums) |
| Minibus 15 | Yubileyny Bazaar to the Hakkim al-Termezi Mausoleum |

So long as the weather is not too hot (temperatures here sear in the summer months), it is also quite feasible to explore the central areas of Termez on foot. Hotel Asson, the bazaar and the Termez Archaeological Museum are just a couple of blocks away from one another, and if you walk through the park rather than around it, it is only another 5–10 minutes on to Hotel Meridian.

Travel agents in the town can arrange a **car and driver** if you want private transport to get between the outlying historical sites, but it doesn't come particularly cheap: budget US$50–60 depending on your itinerary.

TOUR OPERATOR Uzbektourism (*17 F Xo'jaev;* 223 1668; e *info@uzbektourism. uz; www.uzbektourism.uz*) can provide guided tours in a variety of languages, as well as making transport and accommodation bookings. There is also a travel desk at Hotel Ulugbeg (see below).

WHERE TO STAY *Map, page 186*

Termez is surprisingly well equipped with hotels, and some of them are even quite pleasant places to stay: no mean feat for a provincial town without a significant footfall of tourists!

Hotel Meridian (50 rooms) 23 Alpomysh; 227 4851. The best hotel in Termez is this modern, mid-sized hotel with large, clean, if somewhat uninspiring, rooms. All rooms have AC, which is essential in the summer months, & there is a shower over the bath in the bathrooms. German Technical Cooperation Agency (GTZ) have their office in the building, so there are usually a number of expat guests, some of them staying long term. The staff speak a few words of most European languages. There is a mediocre restaurant in the lobby (see below) & the bar sells beers for 8,000 som. Take your drink up onto the rooftop terrace for views across Termez. Free Wi-Fi. **$$$–$$$$**

Hotel Asson (74 rooms) 27 Termezi; 227 4366; www.asson-hotel.com. Situated next to the archaeological museum, the Hotel Asson has perhaps a little more character than the Meridian, & is easier on the pocket. It is, however, rather dark & gloomy & no English is spoken. The outdoor swimming pool is a real bonus in summer, even if it looks rather rundown. Non-residents can use the pool for 5,000 som, & exclusive hire of the sauna will set you back 30,000 som. **$$$**

Hotel Ulugbek (37 rooms) 13A Xo'jaev; 223 3099. Comfortable, family run hotel with large, clean rooms & helpful staff. Rooms have AC & the water supply seems to be fairly good, though we were warned it is sometimes switched off during the day. **$$$**

Hotel Sharq 28 Xo'jaev; 223 4613. Soviet-era hotel that has fortunately undergone a thorough renovation. All rooms have AC & the dbl rooms are large: you might think about taking one even if you're on your own. **$$**

Tennis Court Rooms 29B Termezi. Very basic dorm beds at the sports centre opposite the archaeological museum. It is targeted at athletes & students rather than tourists, so there's no service to speak of, but it's the cheapest option in town. **$**

WHERE TO EAT AND DRINK *Map, page 186*

The restaurant at **Hotel Meridian** is open 24/7, so if you're craving something bland covered in mayonnaise at 03.00 then this is the place for you. At more sociable hours it's a better bet to wander out into the city, as prices tend to be lower & flavours a little more distinct. We particularly recommend the following:

✗ **Malika Gold** A Navoi; ⊕ 11.00–23.00 daily. Large, clean restaurant popular with tour groups. The private dining room seats 14. The menu includes good, fresh salads, manti, noodle soups & tasty kebabs, all of which can be washed down with beer (5,000 som) or vodka (2,000 som). $$$

✴✗ **Azizbek Restaurant** 48 A Navoi; ✆ 225 2034; ⊕ 11.00–23.00 daily. Our favourite place in town is this sprawling restaurant with indoor & outdoor space & even its own (slightly seedy) disco. Grab a patio chair & table, order a Baltica beer & choose from a wide menu of salads, different shashliks, cutlets & other mixed grills. English isn't spoken but it is easy to make yourself understood: if you're really struggling, just point to the neighbouring table's dinner & tuck in to the same. Whatever it is, it'll surely be tasty. $$–$$$

✗ **Restaurant Bek** Cnr Termezi & Jurabaev; ⊕ noon–22.00 daily. Tucked back from the junction, Bek is rather more rough & ready than Azizbek, but unless you're staying at Hotel Meridian, it's undoubtedly in a better location. The shashlik is good & the atmosphere lively, particularly in the evenings at w/ends. $$

⌨ **Choixona** Dostlyk Park. If you just want a tea, coffee or small snack, try this friendly café on the edge of Dostlyk Park. It's shady & a very pleasant spot to relax for an hour or 2. $

SHOPPING The **Main Bazaar** in Termez is on Termezi, very close to Hotel Asson but on the opposite side of the street. It's primarily for the local population rather than tourists, so most of the shops are selling foodstuffs and household goods. On the left-hand side of the bazaar there is also a large, western-style **supermarket**, which is a good place to go if you want to buy bottled water and soft drinks, packeted goods, fresh bread, etc. Unlike in the bazaar, prices in the supermarket are fixed.

OTHER PRACTICALITIES

Communications Termez's **central post office** is at 13 F Xo'jaev (⊕ *09.00–18.00 Mon–Fri*).

Medical The main hospital is **Regional Hospital #1** (*2 Chanishev*; ✆ *223 6203*) but there is also a more centrally located **Polyclinic** (*A Navoi*), which has its own ambulance. Some of the doctors speak a few words of English, and though conditions are very basic, the standard of care provided is admirable. If you need an Apteka, try **Central Drug Store** #14 (*11 Kashgariy*) or **Oxy Med** (*21 Navoi*). A third pharmacy, marked only as **Dorixona**, is on the corner of Alpomysh and A Navoi.

Temperatures in Termez can soar as high as 50°C in summer, so it is imperative that you keep drinking water and keep out of the sun around midday.

Money Unofficial money changers are to be found, as usual, in the bazaar, and also hanging around the bus and train stations. Banks include:

$ **Asaka Bank** 45 A Navoi; ✆ 770 8220; ⊕ 09.00–16.00 Mon–Fri
$ **Ipoteka Bank** 20 Kashgariy; ✆ 770 8300; ⊕ 09.00–17.00 Mon–Fri

$ **Uzpromstroibank** 66 Navoi ✆ 226 2336; ⊕ 09.00–16.00 Mon–Fri

WHAT TO SEE AND DO It's rare to say that a museum in Uzbekistan is a highlight of the city in which it operates, but in the case of Termez, it is actually true. Start your city visit with the **Termez Archaeological Museum** (*29 Termezi*; ✆ *227 3017*; ⊕ *09.00–18.00 daily; foreigners US$2*), built in 2002, as it will put into context everything you go on to see. It is an impressive modern building with a very attractive mosaic on the façade.

The history of Termez is quite complex (pages 183–5), so the museum's collection – which focuses mostly on the Buddhist period and the early centuries AD – helps to bring the lists of names, places and dates to life. The scale models of archaeological sites as they would have looked in their heyday are particularly helpful in this respect. There are information boards in English and a 3D map in the main hall shows you the location of each of the archaeological sites.

The museum is laid out over two floors, and the most impressive pieces of statuary are in the main hall on the ground floor. Key items to look at here are the beautiful head of a prince in a pointed hat, dating from the 1st to 3rd century AD and excavated from Dalverzin Teppe (the original of which is in the Hermitage); what is labelled as a 'sacred pond' but appears to be a font, found at Fayaz Tepe, where the water flows out through the mouth of a lion; and a magnificent and anatomically accurate carving of an elephant among lotus flowers, this time from the 2nd century AD, unearthed at Old Termez (see below).

The bulk of the collection is displayed in a series of galleries on the first floor, which are arranged chronologically. The immaculate display cases are labelled in English. Look specifically for the well-preserved Bronze Age ceramics from Buston and Jarkutan; head, hand and foot fragments of Buddhas from Fayaz Tepe; and the stone statuette of a Bactrian virgin (2nd century AD). There are also small pieces of the gloriously vivid wall paintings recovered from Balalyk Tepe and Tavka Kurgan: they're remarkable for their clarity and state of preservation, as well as for the insight they give into life on the Silk Road in the 5th and 6th centuries.

If you want to take photographs inside the museum, you will need to buy a camera permit as you enter (*10,000 som*).

Fired up and inspired (and hopefully a little better informed), it is time to get out of the modern city centre. **Old Termez** is 6km to the northwest, just off the main road to Karshi. Only small sections of the walls of the early medieval citadel remain – the Mongols certainly knew how to raze a town – but you can still get an idea of the scale and strength of this settlement, which once hosted not only houses, shops and bazaars, but also a mint, caravanserais, orchards and a sophisticated network or irrigation canals.

Also in Old Termez is the 15th-century, mud brick-built **Mausoleum of al Hakkim al Termezi** (⊕ *daily; admission free*), a 9th-century Sufi saint, jurist and writer who died in Termez in AD859. Much of what you see on the river bank was built at the instigation of Timur's son, Shah Rukh, though there have been a series of structures on the site since at least the 10th century. The three most important buildings are the mausoleum itself, replete with a large, marble tombstone but also a large chunk of the tomb missing, purportedly taken by British archaeologists for display in the British Museum; a 12th-century mosque; and a khanagha built by Shah Rukh which served both for accommodation and also as a debating hall.

If you come on Wednesday, expect to find the site packed as the faithful (and also the peckish) come to pray to al Hakkim (meaning 'the wise') and to eat the free mutton and tea doled out for them at lunchtime. The food is sponsored by local businessmen and you are welcome (and indeed encouraged) to join them in this feast. Expect to be fed until you're ready to burst, to be grilled mercilessly on your home, your family and what you earn, and to have your picture taken with absolutely everyone. There is, as they say, really no such thing as a free lunch.

The **old port**, for Termez took advantage of water trade on the Amu Darya as well as caravans travelling by road, lies between the mausoleum and the river. Unfortunately, the newly built security wall prevents you from accessing the site, though in places you can see across the wall. The archaeological remains here include an expansive wharf, customs house and rest house. Due to the proximity of the border and consequent sensitivity of the site, assess the situation carefully before taking a picture and keep your camera out of sight.

A further 2–3km along the main road brings you to Buddhist Termez, which also spreads out a little to the east. The oldest of the three sites (and possibly the oldest building in Uzbekistan still standing) is the **Zurmala Tower**, a brick-built structure 16m high that dates from the 1st to 2nd century AD. It is the only remaining part of a vast Buddhist *stupa* (mound containing relics) that would originally have been clad in stone and richly decorated, an expensive and labour-intensive design that demonstrates the significance of Termez as a Buddhist centre. There is no road access to the tower, and the closest stopping place on the road is about 200m away, with a waterlogged cotton field in between. If you want to get up close, therefore, be prepared for wet feet and muddy trousers.

Caught in the no man's land between Afghanistan and Uzbekistan is **Kara Tepe**, a rock-cut Buddhist temple complex that is unique in this region. Due to its sensitive location (emphasised by the presence of an intimidating electric fence) it is not always possible to gain access: ask at the Termez Archaeological Museum (pages 188–9) for an update on the current situation. If you are prevented from going, a short video of the site is online at http://tours-tv.com/en/kara-tepe_monastery.

Rather more accessible, and fortunately no less interesting, is **Fayaz Tepe** (*open access*), another Buddhist monastery and temple complex. Though the majority of the site dates from the 3rd century AD, the oldest part – the stupa protected beneath a modern dome and visible only through the window – is probably 400 years older than that. The stupa, which is a fraction of its original size (only the inner part survives) stood on the northern side of the temple courtyard, which was flanked to the east by the main refectory, and to the west by the monks' living quarters.

Amongst the usual artefacts excavated here (many of which are on show in the Termez Archaeological Museum), archaeologists discovered the remains of a 2km-long aqueduct that would once have carried water to the monastery straight from the Amu Darya river. Fragments of pottery containing Brahmi, Punjabi, Kharoshti and Bactrian scripts confirm that this was a truly international site, with visitors to the monastery coming from across the known world.

A visitor centre explaining the significance of both Kara Tepe and Fayaz Tepe is planned and is likely to be funded and executed by UNESCO and the Japanese government. There is, however, as yet no scheduled date for this to happen.

AROUND TERMEZ

Kyr Kyz Just past the airport to the northeast of Termez is the intriguingly named Kyr Kyz: the 40 Girls Fortress. The story behind the name has sadly been lost in the mists of time, but the options include 40 daughters, 40 virgins or 40 girls in a harem variously abstaining, avenging or procreating depending on the fantasy of the particular storyteller. Let your imagination run wild.

Regardless of quite what they were up to, the Kyr Kyz dates from the 9th century, and it is not actually a fortress at all: archaeologists believe it was either a substantial caravanserai, or a Samanid-era summer palace. The architecture is typical of structures built in this region just prior to the Arab invasion. Thick, mud-brick walls ran 54m on each side of a square and encompassed some 50 rooms over two floors. Enough remains that you can wander from one obvious room to the next and get a sense of the impressive scale of the place. One section of the façade has

been restored, so you can compare easily the old and the new. Kyr Kyz attracts few visitors, so it is likely that you will have the site to yourself.

Sultan Saodat Complex Slightly further out on the same road is the Sultan Saodat Complex, the family necropolis of the Termez Sayyids, supposed descendants of Ali. They were politically powerful, exceptionally influential in religious matters, and wealthy to boot, enabling them to leave this lasting legacy. There are 120 graves on the site, most of which date from the 9th to 16th centuries, and they are arranged along a street not dissimilar to the Shah-i Zinda in Samarkand (pages 160–2).

Unlike the Shah-i Zinda, this was the burial place for holy men, not royal family members, and so the decoration is much simpler. There is some decorative brickwork, especially in the main mausoleum, where the symbolism of the star-like motif on the columns pre-dates the arrival of Islam: it is a Zoroastrian symbol of infinity and fertility. The mud bricks from which the complex is made are not held together with conventional mortar but rather with a durable mixture of clay, egg yolk, camels' blood and milk.

Timur visited Sultan Saodat to pay his respects to the saints buried here, and also because he had a practical use for the Sayyids: when he planned to attack a town he would send one ahead to convince the local people to surrender, and said that doing so was the Islamic thing to do. Timur used similarly persuasive tactics to encourage newly conquered peoples to pay taxes without rebelling. His grandson, Khalid Sultan, thanked the Sayyids for their contributions by erecting the elegant portico, the only tiled part of the complex, between the mosque and the main mausoleum. It dates from the 15th century and was restored at the same time as the rest of the site in 2002. It's a striking focal point among the otherwise mud-brown façades.

Almost next door is the Timurid **Kokil Dara Khanagha**. Originally a resting place for itinerant Sufi dervishes and other holy men, the building's design owes much to cultural links with Afghanistan, especially in the styling of its vaulted

THE FRIENDSHIP BRIDGE

The Friendship Bridge is something of a misnomer. Built by the Soviets in 1982, the bridge was required to supply the invasion of Afghanistan, an act that was far from friendly. It links Termez with the town of Hairatan in Balkh, spanning the Amu Darya.

The bridge closed in 1997 when the Taliban seized Mazar-i Sharif, and as it was (and remains) the only road and rail link between Uzbekistan and Afghanistan, the border remained shut until after the US invasion in 2001. It is the main transport route for imports into Afghanistan, and the railway is currently being expanded south as far as Mazar, which will ease congestion on the road.

ceilings. The tall, symmetrical portico appears imposing even now: it must have made quite an impression on early visitors.

The khanagha was built by Abdullah Khan II of Bukhara in the 16th century. The main portal and two wings survive. It's a simple structure – it was never decorated – and the domed interior is unique within Uzbekistan as normally the portal opens onto a courtyard. Here there isn't one. This khanagha was a space for meditation and debate. The different orders of sufis have their own ways of meditating: the dervishes here didn't whirl, unlike their counterparts in Turkey – they preferred to meditate quietly and alone. Today, there are no dervishes at all in Uzbekistan; they are banned by the government.

Jarkurgan Minaret Continuing out on the road to Denau, at a point 38km from Termez, is the Jarkurgan Minaret in Minor village (also known as Kommunizm Kolkhoz). Though a truncated version of its former self (only the first 22m of an estimated 50m remain intact), this 12th-century structure is remarkable by the wave-like shape in its brickwork: it appears to be made from a rounded concertina of herringbone-patterned bricks, broken up with occasional Kufic inscriptions. The minaret narrows towards the top, cheating the perspective to make it appear taller than it is.

Kampir Tepe Northwest of Termez, about 30km (40 minutes' drive) out of the city, is the Buddhist site of Kampir Tepe. You need your own transport to get here, but it is well worth taking a taxi to see it. This was once a Buddhist city thriving on the banks of the Amu Darya from the 3rd century BC for about 400 years, until the river changed its course and the city's inhabitants had to move on. Built on the riches of both river and overland trade, there were stupas, temples and monasteries, as well as civic buildings and common homes.

The site was first discovered in 1972 during a survey of the Amu Darya river bank, and the fortress (also known as the Kafir Qala) was excavated in the 1980s. The excavations lasted seven years and unearthed one of the most complete Kushan era settlements ever found.

You should park some distance from the core of the site and walk across the plateau to appreciate the scale of the city. Looking carefully at the hillocks you'll see they are in fact mud-brick ruins, melted over the past two millennia back into the earth from which they came. Under foot you'll see plenty of terracotta pottery shards, and occasional pieces of glass.

One section of wall has been rebuilt around the main excavation site, so it is easy to spot where you are heading for: it stands out considerably taller than anywhere else on the site. Behind this, the original walls are still at least waist-high, and sometimes reach well above your head. Rooms and alleyways are clearly visible, and you can also pick out the wells and pantries. Larger pieces of pottery, possibly from heavy terracotta storage jars, lie here, too.

Standing atop the reconstructed wall gives you a superb view of the labyrinthine site, and thence across the irrigated fields to the Amu Darya and, on the horizon, the hills of Afghanistan. Devoid of visitors, it can feel slightly eerie, but the sense of history and its lingering ghosts makes this one of our very favourite places to go in Uzbekistan.

Mausoleum of Khoja Abu Isa Muhammad Imam Termez

Continuing along this road, close to the town of Shirabad, is the Mausoleum of Khoja Abu Isa Muhammad Imam Termezi. A significant figure in Islam, he travelled across the Islamic world for 30 years collecting sayings of the Prophet to contribute to the Hadith, the holiest book after the Qu'ran. The tomb is less impressive than one might expect, but it is still an important pilgrimage site.

Friendship Bridge

Travelling south of Termez brings you to the Afghan border and this ironically named bridge (see box, page 191) over which Soviet tanks and troops poured into Afghanistan in 1979. Somewhere along this stretch of riverbank must also have been discovered the Oxus Treasure (page 192), though quite where nobody is sure. If you find the spot then let us know: we wouldn't mind having a hunt for some more!

Qashqa Darya and Surkhan Darya Provinces TERMEZ

6

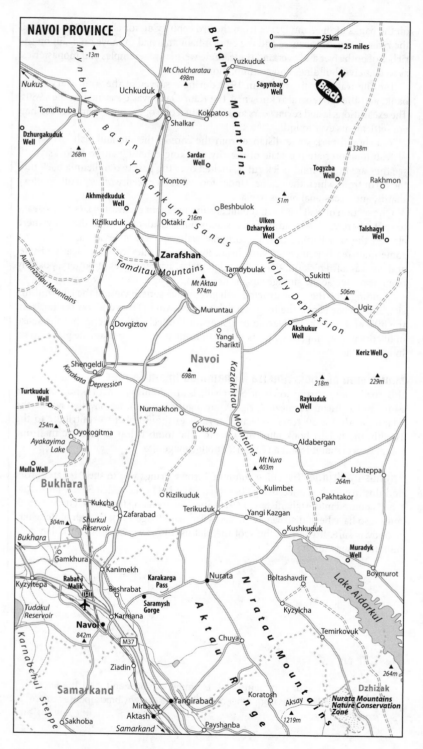

NAVOI PROVINCE

0   25km
0   25 miles

Mynbulak Basin

Bukantau Mountains

Nukus

▲ -13m

Mt Chalcharatau 498m

Yuzkuduk

Sagynbay Well

Uchkuduk

Tomditruba

Kokpatos

Shalkar

Dzhurgakuduk Well

▲ 268m

Sardar Well

▲ 338m

Togyzba Well

Rakhmon

Kontoy

Akhmedkuduk Well

Beshbulok

▲ 51m

Ulken Dzharykos Well

Talshagyl Well

Kizilkuduk

Oktakir

▲ 216m

Yamankum Sands

Zarafshan

Tamditau Mountains

Tamdybulak

Sukitti

▲ 506m

Ugiz

Molaly Depression

Aurminzaktau Mountains

▲ *Mt Aktau 974m*

Muruntau

Dovgiztov

Yangi Sharikti

Akshukur Well

Navoi

▲ 698m

▲ 218m

▲ 229m

Keriz Well

Karakata Depression

Shengeldi

Turtkuduk Well

Nurmakhon

Raykuduk Well

254m ▲

Oyokogitma

Oksoy

Aldabergan

Ushteppa

Ayakayima Lake

▲ 264m

Mulla Well

Bukhara

Mt Nura ▲ 403m

Kulimbet

Pakhtakor

Kizilkuduk

Kukcha

Zafarabad

Terikuduk

Yangi Kazgan

Kazakhtau Mountains

304m ▲

Shurkul Reservoir

Kushkuduk

Muradyk Well

Bukhara

Gamkhura

Kanimekh

Nurata

Boltashavdir

Boymurot

Lake Aidarkul

Kyzyltepa

Rabat-i Malik

Beshrabat

Karakarga Pass

Saramysh Gorge

Kyzylcha

Tudakul Reservoir

Karmana

Temirkovuk

Navoi

▲ 842m

M37

Chuya

▲ 264m

Nuratau Mountains

Aktau Range

Ziadin

Karnabchul Steppe

Samarkand

Mirbazar

Yangirabad

Koratosh

Aksay

▲ 1219m

Dzhizak

Nurata Mountains Nature Conservation Zone

Sakhoba

Aktash

Payshanba

Samarkand

7

Navoi Province

The vast province of Navoi covers almost a quarter of Uzbekistan's territory but includes just a fraction of the country's population, as much of the region is covered by the inhospitable Kyzylkum Desert. Despite the arid climate, cotton is still grown here, though Navoi's real income comes from what lies beneath the ground: natural gas, oil and precious metals.

For short-term visitors (and those without a few billion dollars handy to start building a gold mine), Navoi Province offers camel trekking and desert safaris, Bronze Age petroglyphs and medieval caravanserais. The Nuratau-Kyzylkum Biosphere Reserve is one of the most important conservation sites in Uzbekistan, there are hikes of all difficulty levels among the mountains, and Lake Aidarkul is a fine spot for birdwatching, especially in the spring. If you've had enough of hotels and towns, plan a few days in the biosphere, staying in a family homestay and learning to appreciate rural Uzbekistan.

NAVOI *Telephone code: 436*

Both the province and the provincial capital take their name from the Timurid poet and politician Alisher Navoi (page 114). Navoi is a small, modern city, refounded and renamed only in 1958. It makes its money from mining and processing minerals (including gold), natural gas, and producing chemical fertilisers. The majority of foreigners coming here are on business, though you may also pass through *en route* to Karmana and Nurata.

GETTING THERE AND AWAY Navoi is situated quite centrally within Uzbekistan, 435km from Tashkent, 155km from Samarkand and 125km from Bukhara.

By road If you're travelling with your **own vehicle**, Navoi is just south of the main road (M37) between Samarkand and Bukhara and it is clearly signposted.

Travelling by **minibus** or **shared taxi**, you will need the bus station in Karmana, which is just to the north of Navoi. Local minibuses link the two. From Karmana you can easily find onward transport to Bukhara (*every 1½hrs; 1hr; 5,000 som*), and Samarkand (*2hrs; 8,000 som*) and Tashkent (*5hrs*). Buses are marginally cheaper, but take longer. Taxis also run around the clock to Bukhara and cost 25,000 som per vehicle (one-way), or 40,000 to Samarkand. They are the fastest way to travel.

By train Trains pass through Navoi from Tashkent and Samarkand *en route* to Bukhara and Urgench, though it is faster to travel by road as not many trains actually stop here. The railway station is at the southern end of Galaba.

By air Navoi airport (*www.navoi-airport.com*) is 25km west of the city on the road to Bukhara. It is becoming somewhat of a regional hub, especially for cargo, and passenger flights operate to Tashkent (*1hr 30mins; daily*), Moscow (*4hr 30 mins; 1 per week with Ural Airlines*) and St Petersburg (*8hr 45mins; 1 per week with Ural Airlines via Moscow*). There is a ticket office at the airport (☏ 539 3523), though you might find it more convenient to book online or go to the Uzbekistan Airways office in the city centre (*52 Kh Dustligi;* ☏ 223 3471).

GETTING AROUND It is a 25-minute drive from Navoi Airport into the centre of the city, and taxis wait by the terminal. Minibuses run from 06.00 until 19.00 and cost 1,000 som; taxis run around the clock and cost around 10,000 som each way. Within the city centre, expect to pay between 500 and 1,000 som for a minibus ride, depending on distance. The most useful routes run from the railway station north along Galaba, passing the bazaar and continuing on to Karmana and the intercity bus station, or west from the bazaar along A Timur.

TOUR OPERATORS The ever-present Uzbektourism have an office here (*8 Navoi;* ☏ 223 9546) and are able to make transport and accommodation bookings and provide guides for city tours, desert trips and camel trekking. Sputnik Navoi (*16/14 Matvienko;* ☏ 225 5417) can also help with ticket and accommodation bookings.

WHERE TO STAY Due to its position as a business centre, Navoi has a number of upmarket hotels with price tags to match. Fortunately, however, there are also a few reasonable budget options for those of us not travelling on a company expense account.

⌂ **Grand M Hotel** (33 rooms & 3 apts) 77A Kh Dustligi; ☏ 770 3737; e info@grandm-hotel.uz; www.grandm-hotel.uz/en. Navoi's newest business hotel opened in 2011, & it is a step above the other options in town. The architecture may not be to everyone's taste, but service is of a high standard, the outdoor pool is huge, & the 2 restaurants' menus include both continental & Uzbek dishes. Apts are available for long-term rent. **$$$$**

⌂ **Silk Road Palace** (66 rooms) Malik Rabot; ☏ 780 2000; e info@silkroadpalace.uz; www. silkroadpalace.uz. Technically, the Silk Road Palace is in Karmana, but it is so close to the airport that we've included it here. It's a well-run, mid-size business hotel with its own bar & restaurant, conference facilities & fitness centre. The hotel also has Wi-Fi & designated parking. **$$$$**

⌂ **Hotel Kamilla** (27 rooms) 2/2 Ahunbabaev; ☏ 223 1473. One of the more surreal designs for a hotel interior that we've come across: there's a tree growing through the staircase, & some of the public

spaces look like a set from *Day of the Triffids*. Plants aside, the rooms are large & clean with new linens. Restaurant & small conference hall on site. Free Wi-Fi. **$$$**

☀ ⌂ **Hotel Yoshlik** (43 rooms) 138B Kh Dustligi; ☏ 224 4021; e info@hotel-yoshlik.uz; www.hotel-yoshlik.uz. Centrally located, mid-range option with friendly, helpful staff & a relaxed atmosphere. There is a fitness centre & banya on site. Recommended. **$$$**

⌂ **Hotel Zarafshan** (58 rooms) Free Industrial Economic Zone; ☏ 224 3302; e info@hotel-zarafshan.com; www.hotel-zarafshan.com. Situated outside the city, close to the airport & cargo zone. Modern business hotel with immaculate bathrooms, conference centre, swimming pool & gym. B/fast buffet served until 11.00. **$$$**

⌂ **Hotel Navoi** 73A Kh Dustligi; ☏ 223 1164. Central, budget hotel with hard beds & well-worn sheets. Haggle hard to get the price down. Payment in som only. **$$**

WHERE TO EAT AND DRINK Navoi has a large number of restaurants serving a selection of European and Uzbek dishes. Their primary clientele are a mixture of businessmen and wedding parties, but there are usually a few extra tables even if a party is in full swing. The hotel restaurants at Grand M and Silk Road (both $$$–$$$$) are also pretty good, and the staff don't fuss around you while you're eating. You can also get a drink at their bars and take it outside, which is ideal on a summer's evening.

✗ Richard Microdistrict 6; ✆ 223 3581. Probably the best restaurant in Navoi, if a little removed from the centre. Indoor & outdoor tables, & a mixed menu of European & Uzbek dishes. $$$

✗ Vstrecha 57A Kh Dustligi; ✆ 225 0327. A particular favourite with the Korean Air staff from the cargo centre, Vstrecha prides itself on its chicken dishes. $$$

✗ Yoshlik Cafe 4B Zarapetyan; ✆ 223 1886. Although Yoshlik does have indoor seating, the café's main attraction is its garden. Sit back & enjoy a cold beer & salads in the shade of the trees. $$–$$$

✗ Shams Fast Food 52 Kh Dustigli; ✆ 770 3030. High-calorie snacks delivered to your table at speed. The pizzas are the pick of the dishes, though the doner kebabs aren't bad either. $–$$

✗ Khoja Nasriddin 2 Abduramoanova. Shashlik, *manti* (steamed dumplings) & plov are the mainstays on the menu at this bustling Uzbek café. The plov is the best in the city. Ignore the monstrous mock-stone interior – the food is better than the décor. $

ENTERTAINMENT For a provincial city with no major tourist traffic, the cultural scene in Navoi is surprisingly vibrant.

The Alisher Navoi Cinema (*Cnr Ibn Sino & Janubiy*) has regular showings of Russian and Uzbek blockbusters. The Farkhad Cultural Centre (*cnr Kh Dustigli & Tolstoy;* ✆ *223 4261*) and the Jewish Cultural Centre (*5A Kurilish;* ✆ *225 2627*) have occasional recitals, film showings, plays and exhibitions. Call in for programme details.

SHOPPING Navoi's Central Mall is on Kh Dustligi, just south of the main post office. The Central Bazaar is by the roundabout at the eastern end of A Timur, and this is the best place to pick up fresh produce, bread and snacks.

OTHER PRACTICALITIES

Communications Navoi's main post office is at 3A Kh Dustigli. More reliable for international shipments, however, is DHL (*44A Kh Dustigli;* ✆ *770 2117*).

Mobile phone users can buy SIM cards and top up at Ucell (*Galaba Shokh*) and UzMobile (*3A Kh Dustigli;* ✆ *221 1044*).

For internet access, try UzNet (*also 3A Kh Dustigli;* ✆ *223 3519*) or, for Wi-Fi, Cafe Sensorika, which is close to the junction of Kh Dustigli and A Timur.

Medical General ailments can be diagnosed and treated at Polyclinic #1 (*3A Yujnaya;* ✆ *223 1588*) and the private General Urban Polyclinic (*5A Yujnaya;* ✆ *223 7182*). In a medical emergency, however, you should go instead to the Republican Centre of Science of Emergency Medicine (*27 Ibn Sino;* ✆ *223 1341*).

Money Unofficial money changers are to be found around Navoi's Central Bazaar. The following banks are centrally located:

$ Aloka Bank 3A Druzhba Narodov; ✆ 223 4140; ⏰ 09.00–18.00 Mon–Sat

$ Asaka Bank 2A A Timur; ✆ 770 2129; ⏰ 09.00–16.00 Mon–Fri

$ National Bank of Uzbekistan 14 Ibn Sino; ✆ 227 8384; ⏰ 09.00–18.00 Mon–Fri

$ Turon Bank 48/1 Kh Dustigli; ✆ 225 0449; ⏰ 09.00–17.00 Mon–Fri

Registration Navoi's OVIR is at 4 Matvienko (✆ *223 6081*).

This biosphere was established to protect the fragile ecosystems of the Nuratau Mountains, preserving both the diverse natural landscapes and the numerous varieties of wildlife the land and waters support. The United Nations Development Programme (UNDP) has for several years funded the development of the Nuratau Ecotourism Project (*www.nuratau.com*), a community-based tourism initiative, and consequently the biosphere now has the best-developed tourism infrastructure of any nature reserve in Uzbekistan. If you've had your fill (quite understandably) of mosques and madrassas, a few days in Nuratau is the perfect antidote.

There are plenty of activities available to fill your time. Treks and horseriding are perennially popular and enable you to get deep into the heart of the reserve, exploring the walnut and pistachio forests, sandy desert and Aidarkul and Tuzkan lakes. The best **short hikes** within the biosphere start from the village of Sentob. Trails are as yet unmarked, so you are advised to take a local guide: staff at the Nuratau Ecotourism Project (page 201) can effect an introduction, as well as arrange homestays in the village. In addition to the dramatic mountain peaks, you can also expect to see waterfalls, petroglyphs and archaeological ruins. If you have particular interests in spotting flora and fauna, guides will do their best to accommodate this, though sightings are inevitably seasonal and do require an element of luck.

If you have the time and stamina for a **full-day hike**, one of the most rewarding options that you can take is from Sentob to Lake Fazilman (*22km; 10hrs*); it's long but not difficult. Highlights of the route include the Chavaksoy Valley, where you'll meet local families transporting firewood and fodder by donkey; crossing

WHAT TO SEE AND DO Navoi grew out of the desert in the 20th century, so there's unfortunately little to see within the city itself. You can take a walk in Victory Park (*block north of Tolstoy & Galaba*) or around the manmade Lake Navoi in Alisher Navoi Park, where there is also a statue of the great man himself. For more options, you'll need to head to Karmana instead.

KARMANA *Telephone code: 436*

These days Karmana and Navoi virtually run into one another not far from the airport. But you'll notice the difference between the two: while Navoi is modern and includes far too much concrete, large parts of Karmana are still made from traditional mud brick, and the pace of life seems slower.

HISTORY Karmana is old Navoi, and it is likely a settlement that was founded here around the time of the Arab invasion. The town lay within an independent kingdom, Karmana and Paikend, one of several such kingdoms within the Bukhara Oasis, and the local rulers had the right to mint their own bronze and copper coins. The town was a stopping point on the Silk Road – as testified to by the caravanserais and *rabats* that remain – and it was the significant trade wealth that made it a target for Arab invaders seeking plunder. Karmana-Paikend fell to the Arab forces in 706, before experiencing a prolonged period of decline.

Karmana's fortunes slowly revived from the 11th century onwards when the area became a popular hunting ground for the Karakhanid rulers, and, for some, also the Gaukum Pass; and picnicking on the lake shore. You will get the most out of the trek if you go with a local guide.

The official horse trekking route is from Asraf to Sentob and goes from village to village, but guides are again able to tailor itineraries according to your level of fitness and the amount of time available.

Travelling without a vehicle increases your chances of spotting rare wildlife, from the protected Severtsov's wild sheep to lammergeier vultures, golden eagles and Eurasian griffons. It is a birdwatcher's paradise, especially in the spring when the migratory birds arrive, so make sure you bring your binoculars and a camera.

On spring and autumn weekends the Nurata Ecotourism Project lays on games of **kupkari** (the Uzbek variant of *buz kashi* or 'dead goat polo'), much to the delight of spectators. The horses sprint and sweat, the men shriek and fight, and both ride high on adrenalin. You'll need to keep your wits about you, even if you're only standing on the sidelines, as in all the excitement it's not uncommon for men and beasts to come thundering off the pitch, scattering the crowd in their wake. If you're particularly brave (and/or foolhardy), they'll even let you join in.

One of the highlights of visiting the reserve is the option to stay with a family in their home, which could be a house or a yurt. The most picturesque yurt stays are on the shores of Lake Aidarkul, and there are also atmospheric, comfortable guesthouses in the villages of Asraf, Eski Forish, Hayat, Sentyab, Uhum and Upper Uhum. All of these can be booked through the Nurata Ecotourism office in Yangikishlak (page 201). Expect to pay US$24 per person for bed and breakfast at the guesthouses, and US$40 per person (full board) in the yurt camps.

their final resting place. The Mir Said Bakhrom Mausoleum (page 200) and the Rabat-i Malik (page 200) both attest to the wealth and status of Karmana during the medieval period. Wandering dervishes and itinerant holy men walked along the same routes as the merchants, and this is why the Kasim Sheikh Khanagha (page 200) was erected here in the 16th century.

Karmana sank into commercial and political obscurity following the establishment of Navoi in 1958, but it retains a certain charm and there are several historic sites of note.

GETTING THERE AND AWAY The main bus station for both Karmana and Navoi is outside both towns, and close to the junction between the M37 and the M379, the road through the desert to Nurata. For destinations and journey times, as well as air, rail and local minibus options, see page 195.

WHERE TO STAY AND EAT The best accommodation options and restaurants are in Navoi (page 196), though it is possible to get a shashlik (or three) and a cup of tea in one of Karmana's chaikhanas if you need a break from exploring the sites. The best-located one is the Chahalpak Cafe ($$) next door to the Kasim Sheikh Khanagha (page 200).

WHAT TO SEE AND DO Life in Karmana still centres on the main bazaar. When we visited in November, the watermelons were the size of beach balls, and the pomegranates incredibly sweet and pink. Eating a pomegranate requires patience and a certain amount of skill, especially if you want to do it without getting covered in the sticky red juice, but it's definitely worth the effort. You can buy them one at a time or, more commonly, by weight.

Near to the bazaar is the **Mir Said Bakhrom Mausoleum**, an 11th-century brick-built tomb that, with its dome and monumental portal, served as an architectural model for many later structures, probably including the Ismail Samani Mausoleum in Bukhara. The portico is decorated with a Kufic inscription but, unusually, this is not made from mosaic or painted onto larger tiles but rather depicted with certain bricks raised out from their surroundings. The mausoleum was added to the tentative list of UNESCO World Heritage sites in 2008 in recognition of its importance as an architectural prototype.

Close to the point where the river crosses Navoi is the **Kasim Sheikh Khanagha**, a 16th-century hostel built by the Bukharan emir Abdulla Khan for itinerant holy men. The turquoise dome atop a lapis lazuli-coloured drum still stands, and the latter is strikingly decorated with calligraphy, stars and floral motifs. The khanagha is still in daily use, though now as the town's main mosque the chambers echo in a spine-chilling fashion with the sound of the muezzin's voice if you are fortunate enough to be present as he calls the faithful to prayer.

AROUND KARMANA AND NAVOI West of Karmana, 26km along the road to Bukhara, is the **Rabat-i Malik**, an ambitious and heavily fortified caravanserai built by the Karakhanid ruler Abu'l Hasan Shams al Mulk Nasr in the late 11th century. Though this was once a large complex of cells, stables, guardhouses and storerooms around a courtyard, only the portico remains fully intact: it is 12m tall, domed and with an impressive façade of embedded columns, connected at the top with arches. The only other example of this particular style is the Jarkurgan Minaret in Surkhan Darya (page 192).

Further north on the road to Nurata, about 40km from Navoi, the **Saramysh Gorge** sits hidden amongst the Bukantau Mountains, just before you reach the Karakarga Pass. Cones of volcanic rock rise up around an oasis, and on their surface is a gallery of more than 4,000 petroglyphs that give a panoramic view of life from the 9th millennium BC right through to the 18th century AD when wandering Sufis are thought to have taken refuge here. The number of petroglyphs, their variety, and their state of preservation, are truly remarkable. They have both been painted onto the cave surfaces and hewn out of the rock with chisels and other basic tools. In addition to the usual figures of hunters, horses and deer, there are also dancers, strange camels with three humps, and even stranger men with two heads. Engaging a guide from Uzbektourism in Navoi (page 196) is the best way to get the most out of the site, as the finest petroglyphs are not always that easy to find.

NURATA *Telephone code: 436*

Nurata city is surrounded by the Nuratau Mountains and is home to not only a fortress supposedly built by Alexander the Great but also a medieval pilgrimage site supposedly linked to Hazrat Ali. The city also serves as the transport hub (and occasional overnight stopover) for those camel trekking in the Kyzylkum Desert or trekking and birdwatching in the stunning and remarkably unspoilt Nuratau-Kyzylkum Biosphere Reserve.

HISTORY Local people believe that Nurata was founded as Nur by Alexander the Great in 327BC. They credit Alexander with building the hilltop fort (page 202) and also the *kariz*, a complex water system that brought drinking water several kilometres from a spring right into the centre of the citadel.

Nurata became important again at the start of the Islamic era as Hazrat Ali, son-in-law of the Prophet Muhammad, is said to have struck the ground here with his staff, and the Chashma Spring spurted forth. The 10th-century Bukharan chronicler Muhammad Narshakhi recorded people having visions of the Prophet in Nurata, and hence it became an important regional pilgrimage centre, with all the mosques, resthouses and other supporting structures you would expect.

GETTING THERE AND AROUND Shared taxis to Nurata from Navoi leave from the main bus station in Karmana (*1hr; US$2pp, or US$1.50 by minibus*). If you are travelling on to Lake Aidarkul and the yurt camps, you will need a private car or taxi. Expect to pay around US$20 each way.

Nurata itself is a small town and easily traversed on foot. There is also a minibus service running between the old and new parts of the town.

TOUR OPERATORS There are no travel agents actually in Nurata itself. However, there are a number of small companies in the surrounding towns and villages that specialise in camel trekking, home and yurt stay, and wildlife watching in the biosphere. All of them can provide suitable transport and guides.

Kyzylkum Safari Dungalak village, Kanimekh district; m (90) 732 4393. Guided tours on foot & by 4x4. Homestay bookings possible.
Nuratau Ecotourism Project 1 Bogdon, Yangikishlak; ☎ (72) 452 1200; e nuratau.ecotourism@gmail.com; www.nuratau.com.

UNDP-backed community tourism project offering guides, trekking & home & yurt stays in the Nuratau Mountains.
Nuratau-Kyzylkum Tour Nomalum village, Farish district; ☎ (72) 709 9966. 4x4 transport & guides.

WHERE TO STAY AND EAT The accommodation options in Nurata town are best avoided. If you have the choice, stay in one of the safari camps in the surrounding desert (page 199) or in a local homestay within the biosphere reserve, which can be booked online at www.nuratau.com. Prices are fixed at US$24 per person, which includes all meals.

Komil Homestay (3 rooms) Sentob ; m 090 265 0680; www.nuratau.com. Sentob's newest homestay was built in 2012 & sleeps 9. There's an outdoor shower in summer & a hot hammam in winter. Meals are prepared with vegetables grown in the garden, & there's a waterfall a short hike away. **$$**
Yahshigul Homestay (4 rooms) Asraf; m 090 265 0680; www.nuratau.com. Large homestay sleeping 16 guests, with 2 showers & flushing toilets. Drinking water comes from the spring, there's a wonderful orchard, & musical entertainment can be arranged on request. **$$**

Zamira Homestay (2 rooms) Eski Forish; m 090 265 0680; www.nuratau.com. Built in 2009, Zamira's Homestay sleeps up to 6 guests. A solar panel provides hot water for the shower, & there's a flushing toilet. Zamira's son is a qualified mountain guide. **$$**
Hotel Nur Situated on the main road between the Chashma Spring and Nurata's town centre is Hotel Nur, a very basic set-up with shared bathrooms & occasional electricity. There is a simple restaurant on the ground floor serving bread & shashlik. **$**

OTHER PRACTICALITIES
Medical Nurata has a small and overstretched district hospital, but in a serious situation you would still need to get to Navoi and seek treatment at the emergency hospital there (page 197).

Money There is, as usual, no ATM in Nurata, but the NBU can theoretically advance money to Visa cardholders.

$ Agro Bank 10 Timur; 770 3573; ⊕ 09.00– 17.00 Mon–Fri

$ National Bank of Uzbekistan 49 Rashidov; 523 1651; ⊕ 09.00–18.00 Mon–Fri

$ Xalqbank 3 Yusupova; m (795) 523 1153: ⊕ 09.00–17.00 Mon–Fri

WHAT TO SEE AND DO First and foremost, if you are sightseeing in Nurata you will want to visit **Alexander's Fort**. It is strategically located on the top of a hill to the south of the town, and Uzbek sources suggest that Alexander instructed one of his generals to build an impenetrable fortress here while he continued his conquest of Bactria and Sogdiana. When Alexander returned, his troops could neither break down the gates nor scale the walls, such was the strength of the construction.

We first came to the fort one Sunday afternoon in September, expecting it to be a visit of an hour or so. We stayed until nightfall, necessitating a scramble back down in the dark. It is a steep climb to the top of the site. What appears to be clay underfoot is, in fact, adobe bricks, compacted by thousands of sandalled feet and the elements over two millennia. In places you can still make out their individual shapes, and it's slightly eerie if you're on your own to think of the men who built it, lived and worked here. It's timeless. The central citadel, once measuring half a kilometre in each direction, has long gone, but one glance at the view, across the mountains and across Nurata itself, reveals exactly why Alexander (if indeed it was he) chose this spot, and why it was such a good decision.

Down below the fort, close to the modern town, is the **Chashma Spring** (*open access*), which is linked with Hazrat Ali (page 146). The centre of the complex is a pool where the faithful come to bathe, have their children blessed or collect water to take to sick relatives and friends. Regardless of the time of year, the mineral-laden spring water is said to remain at a consistent 19.1°C. The fish population in the pool is thriving as it is considered a holy spot, and hence no-one is allowed to catch them.

By the spring is the **Juma Mosque**, first built in the 10th century to accommodate visiting pilgrims when they came to pray. The mosque has been rebuilt several times; the current structure (mostly 16th century) has 25 cupolas, one of which has a diameter of 16m and hence is amongst the largest in central Asia.

There is also a small **museum** (⊕ *08.00–17.00 Tue–Sun; US$0.25*) on the site and a mausoleum, which dates from the 9th century and is said to cover the grave of one of Alexander's generals who died here whilst on campaign.

AROUND NURATA Nurata is a stone's throw from the Kyzylkum Desert. Named after its red sand, it is the 15th-largest desert in the world and spreads across northern Uzbekistan and up into neighbouring Kazakhstan. Between March and May, and September and October, you can trek a circuit on foot or by camel from the village of Yangi Kazgan, just north of Lake Aidarkul, and camel treks of two days or more include accommodation in the camel-hair yurts belonging to local Kazakh nomads. Expect to enjoy the best of local hospitality, from homemade bread dipped in still-steaming camel milk, to hunks of camel meat. Beds are made up on the floor from piles of rainbow-coloured blankets and rugs, and you'll often sleep cheek-by-jowl with other guests. You'll never forget the experience, and certainly won't get cold at night.

You can arrange camel trekking through the Nuratau Ecotourism Project (page 201) or, alternatively, approach the camel camps directly. The two companies that

The camel may be the pin-up of the Silk Road, but the two-humped Bactrian camel, with its scrawny legs, ungainly walk and hairy humps, is far from a sexy beast.

A fully grown adult camel can stand well over 2m tall, but chooses to mate sitting down. The male has a large, inflatable sack in its neck, an organ called a dulla. When in rut it extrudes from his mouth like a long, swollen, pink tongue in a bid to assert dominance and attract the glances of a passing female. When he finally catches her eye (possibly having pursued her at speed across the steppe: be warned if you're riding on top), they mate sitting side by side; in a single mating session, the male ejaculates three or four times in succession.

It's not only their sexual habits that make camels intriguing; they also have a number of physiological adaptations to help them live in dry climates. Camels' humps don't actually contain water, as was once commonly believed, but concentrated body fat. When this fat is metabolised, it releases more than 1g of water for every gram of fat. Unlike other mammals, a camel's red blood cells are oval rather than circular, which helps them flow when the body is dehydrated and also makes them less likely to rupture when large quantities of water are finally consumed. Consequently a camel can drink as much as 70 litres of water per minute, taking on 200 litres in total. Camels rarely sweat, even when temperatures reach 50°C, and when they do sweat they can lose up to 25% of their body weight before circulatory disturbance results in cardiac arrest. When a camel breathes out, water vapour is trapped in its nostrils and is then reabsorbed. They can, in fact, ingest sufficient moisture from eating green foliage to remain hydrated without drinking water at all.

dominate the market, both of which provide a high level of service, are Sputnik Camel Camp (✆ *223 8081;* e *sputnik-navoi@yandex.ru*) and the nearby Yangi Kazgan Yurt Camp (✆ *225 1419*). There's not really anything to choose between them, so just call up and see which has availability for your given dates. In each of these cases you'll pay US$40–50 per person per day for accommodation, meals and a camel trek. Don't expect to get too fond of your mount; camels are surprisingly hard creatures to love when you get up close and personal. Wet wipes will undoubtedly come in handy.

Navoi Province   NURATA

7

For additional online content, articles, photos and more on Uzbekistan, why not visit www.bradtguides.com/uzbek.

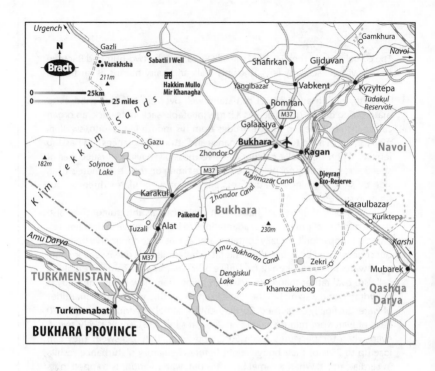

BUKHARA PROVINCE

8

Bukhara Province

You come to Bukhara Province for Bukhara itself. Whether you are drawn to the Ark, the city's medieval mud-brick citadel, and the grisly history of its Registan and zindan, or to the majestic beauty of the Kalyon Mosque and the buildings of Lyabi Hauz reflected in the gently shifting waters of the tank, everything you see is a treat for the eyes. Many people will quite understandably spend their entire stay wandering the labyrinthine streets of the Old Town, savouring each sight and sound and smell.

Those who do venture a little further afield will not be disappointed, however. The Bakhauddin Naqshbandi Complex outside the modern city's confines is considered among the holiest sites in central Asia, and huge numbers of visitors come both on pilgrimage and to admire the *mazar*. Close by is the Sitorai Makhi Khosa, the summer palace of Alim Khan, which gives a poignant insight into the last days of the Bukharan emirate before the Bolsheviks took control, and also the town of Gijduvan, famous for its handmade and finely painted ceramics.

BUKHARA *Telephone code: 65*

In our minds, Bukhara is the undisputed pearl (or perhaps that should be sapphire, given that its dominant colour is blue) of Uzbekistan. Samarkand and Khiva both have their charms, but they seem but pale mirages when you are standing alone on a late autumnal afternoon staring up at the Kalyon Minar, the most prominent sight on Bukhara's skyline, and with the vast and unbelievably sumptuous 16th-century Kalyon Mosque at your side.

HISTORY The founding of Bukhara is cloaked in mystery, the creation myths as rich and elaborate as the façade of Lyabi Hauz. The famed Persian epic, the *Shahnama*, tells us the city was founded by Siyavush, a Persian prince from the Pishdadian Dynasty. Accused by his wicked stepmother of seducing her, he was forced to undergo a trial by fire but emerged from the flames unscathed and crossed the Amu Darya in search of new lands and fortune. In Samarkand he wed the princess Farangis, daughter of King Afrosiab, and her dowry included the vassal state of Bukhara.

The story did not end there, however, as Siyavush was later accused of plotting to overthrow Afrosiab. Afrosiab had him executed in front of Farangis and his head was buried beneath the Ark's Kalyon Gate, a permanent reminder to the citadel's residents to remember their place and not to threaten the sovereignty of Samarkand.

Situated at the crossroads between Merv (now in eastern Turkmenistan and one of the largest cities in the ancient world), Herat and Samarkand, Bukhara was in a prime location to benefit from Silk Road trade. It was already flourishing by the 6th century BC when it was sacked by the Achaemenids, becoming a satrapy of the Persian Empire. The evident wealth of Bukhara would in many ways prove a curse, attracting the unwanted attentions of Alexander the Great in 329BC, then the subsequent invasions of the Seleucids, Graeco-Bactrians and the Kushans.

Bukhara became a centre of worship for the Iranian goddess Anahita, and devotees flocked to the city each year to exchange the idols they believed would ensure the fertility of their fields. The city also attracted Nestorian Christians and Manicheans, followers of a gnostic religion originating in Sassanid-era Babylonia, who were persecuted elsewhere in the Sassanian Empire but able to flourish in Bukhara.

When Arab invaders came to Bukhara in the 7th century, the residents were initially able to spare themselves by paying an annual tribute. Relations deteriorated, however, when 80 Bukharans were kidnapped and committed mass suicide *en route* to Medina, depriving their captors of slave profits they felt to be rightfully theirs. The crusading Qutaiba ibn Muslim arrived in AD709 and violently asserted direct control. The religious diversity for which the city was famed was quashed almost overnight and by the time Bukhara became the capital of the Samanid state in the 9th century, the city was known as Bukhoro-i Sharif (Noble Bukhara) and 'The Pillar of Islam'.

The 9th and 10th centuries were a golden age for Bukhara. The Samanid ruler Ismail ibn Ahmed maintained the political stability required for trade to flourish, and with his wealth he patronised some of the greatest intellectuals and artisans in the Islamic world. The scientist, philosopher and physician Ibn Sina (known in the West as Avicenna), the Persian poets Ferdowsi and Rudaki, and the chronicler al Beruni all thrived in the city and completed their most important works here.

The fall of the Samanids resulted in 200 years of attacks on Bukhara. The Karakhanids invaded in AD999, the Karakhitai attacked in 1141, the Khorezmshah in 1206 and, most catastrophically of all, Genghis Khan and the Mongol horde rode into town in 1220. Every one of Bukhara's 30,000 troops was slaughtered, the city was torched, the civilian population (including women and children) killed or enslaved, and the Great Khan himself stood in the Namazgokh Mosque and proclaimed himself the 'Scourge of God'. The city was utterly decimated and when the Arab traveller Ibn Battuta visited nearly 150 years later, he described it as still lying more or less in ruins.

Bukhara's revival came in the 16th century when it became the Shaybanid capital. Abdulla Khan united the Uzbek clans to resist the Shi'ite Safavids (Bukhara's rulers were Sunni), and artisans captured from the Safavid city of Herat (now in western Afghanistan) were instructed to rebuild Bukhara.

Bukhara once again became a regional religious centre, but this time to espouse Islam. Within the confines of the city were some 150 madrassas and nearly 300 mosques, each more ornate and better endowed than the last. By the late 18th century, Bukhara was struggling economically as trade took a back seat to religion and goods formerly traded along the Silk Road were now being transported along maritime routes, skipping central Asia entirely. Bukhara's rulers became known for their barbarism and for their religious extremism; the most notorious of them was 'the Butcher' Nasrullah Khan, who murdered 31 relatives (including three brothers) to ascend to the throne in 1826, and later cut his chief advisor in half with an axe. A succession of British and Russian officers, diplomats and spies trooped through Bukhara in this period, including Alexander 'Bukhara' Burnes, and it is Nasrullah Khan who was responsible for the imprisonment and execution of the British officers Conolly and Stoddart (see box, page 218).

Russia gained trading concessions in the Bukharan emirate in 1868 and though the khan remained nominally independent, Bukhara was essentially a Russian protectorate. The Trans-Caspian railway arrived in 1888, physically linking the city to Russia.

The emirate of Bukhara finally ended with the Bolshevik Revolution. The Bolshevik governor of Tashkent, Kolesov, came to Bukhara to request a peaceful surrender from Alim Khan, but the emir arranged a violent mob to slaughter both this emissary and the Russian detachment that followed. Ethnic Russians living in the city were also killed. Some 15 unfortunate Bolshevik spies were caught and dispatched, one by one, but this was to be the emir's swan song: in 1920 General Mikhail Frunze marched his troops into the city. Large parts of Bukhara were destroyed during four days of fighting, the emir fled to Afghanistan, and by the end of it the Bolshevik flag flew from the Kalyon Minar.

The Bukhara People's Republic was born, and within a matter of weeks the local Communist Party had 14,000 members. The republic joined the Uzbek SSR in 1924 and the transformation of Bukhara from a religious centre to a museum city began: mosques were converted into offices and workers' associations; *mullahs* were purged and exiled; madrassas became stables and storage yards. Rather than actively rebuild the city in the Soviet style, much of Bukhara was just left to decay, and it is for this reason that the old city is so well preserved: it was saved from 20th-century demolition crews, leaving later restorers much more original material to work with.

GETTING THERE AND AWAY
By road The M37 east of Bukhara to Samarkand and Tashkent is well maintained and a fairly fast drive on smooth tarmac. Travelling west to Khiva, the road was being upgraded (with resulting delays) at the time of going to print but the much-improved highway should be up and running during the lifespan of this edition, noticeably reducing the journey time.

ALEXANDER 'BUKHARA' BURNES

The dashing captain, Sir Alexander Burnes, FRS (1805–41), cousin of the Scottish poet Robert Burns, joined the East India Company's army at the tender age of 16 and set off to make his fortune. He learned Hindustani and Persian fluently while in service in India, and in 1831 he travelled up the Indus River to Lahore to deliver a gift of horses from King William IV to Maharaja Ranjit Singh, the Lion of the Punjab.

Burnes got a taste for adventure and decided to continue north into virtually unchartered territories, arriving in Bukhara in 1832 disguised as an Afghan trader. His command of Persian must have served him well. Burnes hoped to meet with Emir Nasrullah Khan in person but, probably fortunately for Burnes, he never got further than the Grand Vizier. Burnes collected as much information as he could about the city (particularly things of strategic importance) and left, his neck intact, a month later.

Returning to London, Burnes wrote *Travels into Bokhara*, which overnight became a publishing sensation. The first edition earned him £800 (a significant sum at the time) and a gold medal from the Royal Geographical Society.

With his new-found fame, Burnes was appointed to the court of Sindh and then as political agent to Kabul. He was assassinated in Kabul in 1841, quite possibly by the irate husbands of Afghan women he'd slept with, but not before he'd killed six of his assailants and earned, at least as far as the British were concerned, a heroic reputation.

Bukhara has three bus stations, and the one you need is dictated by your destination. The **Centralnee Avtovokzal** [209 B1] (central bus station) is on Gijduvania, 3km north of the city centre, and serves Samarkand (*8hrs; US$5*) and Tashkent (*14hrs; US$10*) – minibuses to the same destinations are roughly the same price but take approximately half the length of time. The **Avtostansiya Karvon Bazaar**, 1.5km further along the same street, has transport to Urgench (*bus 9hrs, US$9; minibus 6hrs, US$10*), and only shared taxis go from **Avtostansiya Sharq** [209 D2] to Karshi (*2hrs; US$10*) and Shakhrisabz (*5hrs; US$14*).

If you are arriving with your own vehicle, bear in mind that there is limited parking in the city centre, particularly in the Old Town. Unless your hotel tells you otherwise, you will need to park in the dozen or so parking spaces on the edge of Lyabi Hauz and then walk to your final destination from there. There is no parking charge.

By train The **train station** (✆ *524 6593*) is not actually in Bukhara at all but in Kagan, 10km to the east. You can get there by taking minibus No 68 from Lyabi Hauz (*25mins; US$0.50*).

The fastest train service to Samarkand and Tashkent is the Sharq train (No 9/10 depending on direction), which leaves Tashkent in the morning, stops in Samarkand around noon and reaches Bukhara by mid afternoon (page 88 for details). There is also a much slower sleeper service (train No 661/662 – page 88).

THE GRAND DERVISH OF ENGLAND

Few characters in Uzbekistan's history are more colourful than Joseph Wolff (1795–1862), a Cambridge oriental scholar and Jewish-Christian missionary born in Weilersbach, Germany, who wound his way to central Asia in the mid 19th century.

Wolff began his wanderings in Egypt and the Holy Land in the 1820s, working as a Christian missionary. He returned to England in 1826 and became obsessed with the idea of finding the Lost Tribes of Israel, a journey which took him through Turkey and the Caucasus, to Afghanistan and then on to India. Subsequent travels took him Africa and the Americas (where he was ordained as a deacon), and back again to the Middle East.

Wolff set out for Uzbekistan in the 1840s wondering if the Jews of Bukhara were one of the Lost Tribes. He arrived at the court of Nasrullah Khan dressed in full canonical garb, much to the surprise of everyone around him: they had never seen anything quite like it. Having heard of the incarceration of Conolly and Stoddart (who by this time, unbeknown to Wolff, had already been executed) – see box, page 218 – he attempted to negotiate their release; he escaped with his life only because the emir was so entertained (and, no doubt, bemused) by Wolff's appearance.

Wolff wrote and published two volumes of *Narrative of a mission to Bokhara, in the years 1843–1845, to ascertain the fate of Colonel Stoddart and Captain Conolly* in 1845 and despite its lengthy title, the book was huge success, running to no fewer than seven editions in as many years. When nearly 100 years later diplomat and writer Fitzroy Maclean visited central Asia, he retraced Wolff's journey and wrote about him in his own memoir, *Eastern Approaches*.

If you want to go west to Khiva and Urgench, you will need to travel first to Navoi and get the train from there as the main line splits near Navoi, and Bukhara and Urgench are on different tines of the fork. See pages 230–1 for details.

Current departure times and fares are listed at www.uzrailpass.uz. If you haven't bought your ticket online, you can get it from the train station or from the ticketing office on Nyzami.

By air Bukhara's **airpor**t is 5km east of the city centre. Getting there takes 10 minutes by taxi, and only slightly longer by public transport (*bus No 1 or minibus No 100; 500 som*). There are up to four flights a day to Tashkent (*1hr30mins; US$70*) and weekly services to Moscow, St Petersburg and Krasnodar.

Tickets are available from the **Uzbekistan Airways** desk at the airport, and also from their ticketing office in the city centre (*15 Navoi;* \ *223 5060*). For other departure points, including for international flights, you can also use **Lochin Avia** (*5 Mustakillik;* \ *223 3149*) and **Transaero** (*4 Khamza;* \ *227 0078*).

GETTING AROUND The best way to explore the centre of Bukhara is **on foot:** indeed, some sections of the Old Town are pedestrianised and others have a confusing one-way system, so at times walking may be the only possible mode of transport.

If you are travelling a little further afield, for example to the train or bus station, you can hail one of the city's **yellow taxis** (US$2 for short trips) or, for a cheaper ride, take a **minibus** or **bus.** The following routes are the most useful for tourists:

Minibus 100	City centre (various stops) to airport
Minibus 70 & 77	Nyzami to Centralnee Avtovokzal
Minibus 68	Lyabi Hauz to the train station
Bus 10	City centre (various stops) to airport

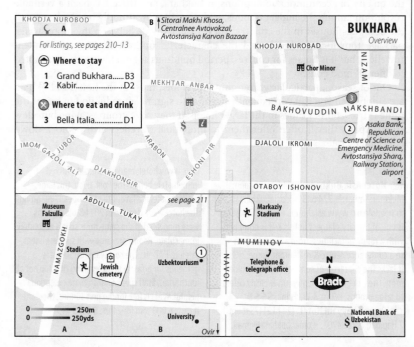

| Bus 17 | Vokzal to Sitorai Makhi Khosa |
| Bus 60 | Ark to Bakhauddin Naqshbandi Mausoleum |

It is also possible to hire **bicycles** from East Line Tours (see below) for US$10 per day.

TOURIST INFORMATION AND TOUR OPERATORS The following outlets can also assist with tickets, transport, accommodation and guided tours

ⓘ Bukhara Information and Culture Centre (BICC) [211 F3] 2 Eshoni Pir; ☏ 224 2246; ⏰ 09.00–18.00 daily. Established in 1995, this NGO-backed centre functions as the city's tourist information office. Director Zaynab Salieva & her team have an encyclopaedic knowledge of Bukhara & its sites & can arrange high-quality guided tours in most languages. They also make accommodation & transport bookings.

East Line Tours [211 F3] 98 B Naqshbandi; ☏ 224 2269. Professionally run outfit founded in 2004. They offer private, tailor-made tours of the city with bilingual guides & can also arrange excursions further afield.

Komil Travel [211 F4] 40 Barakiyon; ☏ 221 0800; e info@komiltravel.com; www.travelbukhara.com. Charming Komil Kadirov

arranges cultural tours of Uzbekistan & also more unusual trips such as camel safaris in the Kyzylkum Desert. He speaks good English & is particularly keen to show off the highlights of his home town, Bukhara.

Sarrafon Travel [211 E4] 4 Sarrafon; ☏ 221 0502; e info@sarrafon-travel.uz; www.sarrafon-travel.uz. Abdurakhmon Abdullaev is an attentive host (pages 212–13) & guide. He has a detailed knowledge of Bukhara, can make bookings for onward travel & makes reliable accommodation recommendations for other cities in Uzbekistan.

Uzbektourism [209 B3] 8 Muminov; ☏ 223 1236; e info@uzbektourism.uz; www.uzbektourism.uz. State-run tour company with an office situated inside the Grand Bukhara Hotel. Provides multi-lingual guides & tours to sites around Bukhara.

 WHERE TO STAY The competition for tourists' business has significantly improved the quality of accommodation options in Bukhara, and there has been a veritable revolution among the budget options, with the city now proudly boasting some of the best guesthouses in the country. There's still a divide between the more sterile, package tour-focused hotels and the characterful options serving independent travellers, but it is horses for courses: period buildings are not always easily adapted to offer all mod cons.

Out of season, particularly from mid-November, most of the hotels in Bukhara are empty, and you can consequently negotiate a significant reduction in price. The same is true at other times in the larger hotels: if they have groups staying but a few rooms spare, they'll often offer them to individual travellers at the knock-down commercial rate.

Upmarket

🏠 **Hotel Asia Bukhara** [211 E3] (95 rooms) Mekhtar Ambar; ☏ 224 6431; e asiabukhara@marcopolo.uz; www.asiahotels.uz. Asia Bukhara is one of the city's largest hotels & it is equipped with a range of facilities, from a sauna & gym to a conference centre & restaurant (page 213). It lacks the character of some of Bukhara's older properties, but it is efficiently run & easily caters to large groups. B/fast & Wi-Fi inc. **$$$$**

🏠 **Omar Khayyam Hotel** [211 E2] (75 rooms) 7 Haqiqat; ☏ 221 4707; e omar.bukhara@gmail.

com; www.hotelomarkhayam.com. Tucked immediately behind the Poi Kalyon, this large, modern hotel is a favourite of European tour groups. The hotel was extended in 2014 & older rooms were renovated at the same time, so it is absolutely immaculate. Rooms are large with spotless linens, satellite TV & AC. The courtyard restaurant is gorgeous for b/fast & in the evening (it is too hot at lunchtime). Staff speak English & are exceptionally helpful. Wi-Fi is free for the first 30mins, thereafter it costs 6,000 som for 24hrs. **$$$$**

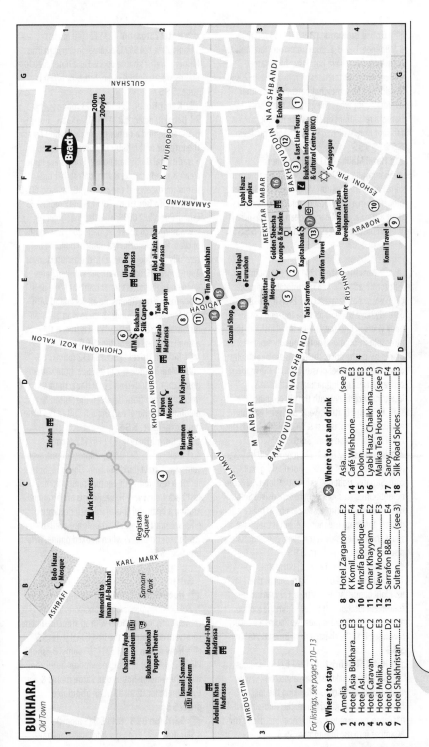

BUKHARA
Old Town

N

Bradt

0   200m
0   200yds

GULSHAN

KH NUROBOD

SAMARKAND

BAKHOVUDDIN NAQSHBANDI

Eshon Koja   1

East Line Tours   3

Bukhara Information & Cultural Centre (BIC)   12

Synagogue

Lyabi Hauz Complex   16

Bukhara Artisan Development Centre

ESHONI PIR

MEKHTAR AMBAR

Golden Sheesha Lounge & Karaoke

Kapitalbank   13

Komil Travel   10   9

ARABON

Magokiattari Mosque   5   2

Sarrafon Travel

Taki Sarrafon

K RUSHNOI

Ulug Beg Madrassa

Abd al-Aziz Khan Madrassa

Taki Telpal Furushon

Tim Abdullakhan   7

18

Suzani Shop

HAQIQAT   8   11   14   15

Mir-i-Arab Madrassa

Taki Zargaron

Bukhara Silk Carpets

ATM   6

CHOHONAI KOZI KALON

KHODJA NUROBOD

Kalyon Mosque

Poi Kalyon

M ANBAR

BAKHOVUDDIN NAQSHBANDI

Zindan

Ark Fortress

Hammon Kunjak

ISLAMOV

Registan Square

KARL MARX

ASHRAFI

Bolo Hauz Mosque

Memorial to Imam Al-Bukhari

Chashma Ayub Mausoleum

Bukhara National Puppet Theatre

Ismail Samani Mausoleum

Samani Park

Modar-i-Khan Madrassa

Abdullah Khan Madrassa

MIRDUSTIM

Bukhara Province   BUKHARA

8

For listings, see pages 210–13

Where to stay
1   Amelia...........................G3
2   Hotel Asia Bukhara......E3
3   Hotel Asl.......................F3
4   Hotel Caravan..............C2
5   Hotel Malika.................E3
6   Hotel Orom..................D2
7   Hotel Shakhristan.......E2
8   Hotel Zargaron...........E2
9   K Komil........................F4
10   Minzifa Boutique........F4
11   Omar Khayyam..........E2
12   New Moon...................F3
13   Sarrafon B&B..............E4
    Sultan...................(see 3)

Where to eat and drink
    Asia..........................(see 2)
14   Café Wishbone...........F4
15   Dolon.........................E3
    Lyabi Hauz Chaikhana..F3
16   Malika Tea House....(see 5)
17   Saroy.........................E4
18   Silk Road Spices.........E3

211

🏠 **Grand Bukhara** [209 B3] (153 rooms)
8 Muminov; ☎224 1236; e info@bukharatourist.
com. Vast, Soviet-era hotel that fortunately
underwent a comprehensive renovation in 2009.
Service can be somewhat patchy & it is rather
overpriced for what you get, but there are 2
bars & a restaurant on site & the rooftop bar is a
fab spot from which to watch the sun go down.
$$$–$$$$

🏠 **Hotel Malika** [211 E3] (34 rooms)
25 Shaumyana; ☎224 6256; www.malika-bukhara.
com. Part of the well-run Malik chain, the Bukhara
property is in a great location midway between Lyabi
Hauz & the Kalyon Minar. It's clean, quiet & there is
Wi-Fi in the public areas. B/fast inc. **$$$–$$$$**

Mid range

✴ 🏠 **Amelia Hotel** [211 G3] (10 rooms)
1 Bozor Hoja; ☎224 1263; e info@hotelamelia.
com; www.hotelamelia.com. Even if you do
actually have the budget for a top-end hotel,
book yourself into the Amelia Hotel instead: this
atmospheric boutique hotel soundly trounces
places twice the price. The rooms are beautifully
decorated with relief plasterwork, & the modern
conveniences (inc immaculate bathrooms)
integrate sensitively with the old building. The
staff are warm & attentive, & the hotel is in an
excellent location. B/fast & Wi-Fi inc. In short, this
hotel is a Bukharan gem. **$$$**

🏠 **Hotel Asl** [211 F3] (12 rooms) 100 B
Naqshbandi; ☎224 5839; e hotel.asl@gmail.
com. Situated right on Lyabi Hauz, Hotel Asl & the
neighbouring (& slightly more expensive) Sultan
Hotel have one of the best locations in the city. Tour
groups dominate the clientele, but if they have
space then independent travellers can negotiate a
discounted rate. B/fast inc. **$$$**

🏠 **Hotel Caravan** [211 C2] (28 rooms)
18 Muminov; ☎224 6144; e karavan1@intal.
uz. Right beside the Ark Fortress, Caravan has a
convenient location & the views from the rooftop
across the old city are impressive. Rooms are clean
& unfussy, if a little characterless. B/fast & Wi-Fi inc.
$$$

🏠 **Hotel Shakhristan** [211 E2] 53 Haqiqat;
☎224 2108; e shakhriston@yahoo.com; www.
shakhristan.narod.ru. Overlooking the Toki
Telpakfurushon trading dome, this mid-size hotel
has large, clean rooms with innocuous décor. The
AC comes into use in summer. **$$$**

🏠 **Hotel Zargaron** [211 E2] (40 rooms)
3 Haqiqat; ☎224 5821; e zargaron@mail.ru. This
former jeweller's house opened as a hotel in 2010.
Rooms are spacious & clean, & the inc b/fast is
large. **$$$**

🏠 **Kabir Hotel** [209 D2] (13 rooms)
2 L Babakhanova; ☎224 1641; e kabir_hotel@
mail.ru. Behind a rather unprepossessing façade,
the interior of the Kabir is loosely modelled on
a traditional Bukharan house. Rooms are large,
clean & comfortable, & the rooftop bar has
panoramic views of the old city. B/fast inc. **$$$**

🏠 **Minzifa Boutique** [211 F4] (12 rooms) 63
Eshoni Pir; ☎221 0628; minzifa_inn@mail.ru;
www.minzifa.com; see ad, page 204. Just south
of Lyabi Hauz, Minzifa is a modern building but
carefully designed to recreate the architecture of
19th-century Bukhara. Antique wooden gates
open on to the hotel's inner courtyard, the perfect
place to take tea. Rooms are all decorated with
local textiles & paintings, & there is an open-air
restaurant on the terrace. Wi-Fi is free, & there is
a small business centre, too. **$$$**

🏠 **Sultan Hotel** [211 F3] (12 rooms)
100 B Naqshbandi; ☎224 2435; e hotelsultan@
gmail.com. Situated on Lyabi Hauz, there's
little to choose from between the Sultan &
neighbouring Hotel Asl, though Sultan is a little
more expensive. **$$$**

🏠 **K Komil Hotel** [211 F4] (12 rooms)
40 Barakiyon; ☎221 0800; e info@komiltravel.
com; www.travelbukhara.com. Boutique hotel
inside a restored 19th-century family home,
just back from Lyabi Hauz. Rooms are arranged
around a beautiful courtyard with decorative
pillars & plasterwork. Discounts are available in
winter, for groups, & when booked online. B/fast
inc. **$$–$$$**

Budget

🏠 **Hotel Orom** [211 D2] (11 rooms) 9 Haqiqat;
☎224 6498; e hotel-orom@yandex.ru. Small,
conveniently located hotel with an attractive interior
courtyard decorated in the traditional style. **$$**

🏠 **New Moon** [211 F3] (10 rooms) 8 Eshoni
Pir; ☎224 4442; e xilol@newmoon-hotel.com;
www.newmoon-hotel.com. Large rooms & a
convenient location, all at an affordable
price. **$$**

🏠 **Sarrafon B&B** [211 E4] (5 rooms)
4 Sarrafon; ☎223 6463; e info@sarrafon-travel.

uz; www.sarrafon-travel.uz. The best of Bukhara's budget options, Sarrafon is comfortable & well located with friendly, accommodating staff, AC & private b/rooms. Dorm beds also available. B/fast inc. **$$**

✗ WHERE TO EAT AND DRINK
With a significant footfall of tourists, Bukhara is bound to have plenty of places to eat and drink. That's not to say that they all offer quality food, or value for money, as often their reason for staying in business is that they can house an entire coach party at once. These were the best options on our last visit. They are all open from mid morning until around 22.00, unless specified otherwise.

Restaurants

✗ Asia [211 E3] Mekhtar Ambar; \ 224 6431. The restaurant inside Hotel Asia Bukhara (page 210) has a bland menu of European dishes targeted at coach parties, but is redeemed by the nightly dance shows & 10 varieties of tea. **$$$$**

✗ Bella Italia [209 D1] Cnr B Naqshbandi & Presidential Hwy; \ 224 3346; ⊕ 11.00–23.00 daily. With a menu that offers such culinary delights as 'horse flesh & bear battered fish', you might be forgiven for wondering what you've let yourself in for. Fortunately it's a laid-back place with a good selection of salads, & freshly prepared pizzas & pasta dishes. The garlic bread is pretty tasty. 15% service charge. **$$$$**

✗ Dolon [211 E3] Haqiqat Sq. Take lunch on the roof of this centrally located restaurant for a fabulous new perspective on Bukhara. The Uzbek food is passable, but your attention will be on the views. **$$$**

✗ Saroy Restaurant [211 F4] Lyabi Hauz. On the corner of Sarrafon, this small but atmospheric restaurant has tasty dishes & efficient service. **$$$**

Cafés and teahouses

🖳 Café Wishbone [211 E2] Haqiqat Sq; m (94) 629 2132. For those craving a decent coffee & a small selection of homemade cakes (both sadly rarities in Uzbekistan), this German café is an absolute godsend. The interior is simple & there is an outside terrace for the warmer months. English & German are spoken. An espresso will cost you 5,000 som, & a slice of apple strudel to go with it 6,000 som. The cafe is within a stone's throw of the Kalyon Minar. **$$$**

🖳 Malika Tea House [211 E3] 25 Shaumyana; \ 224 6256. Traditional-style tea house on the 2nd floor of the Malika Hotel (page 212). The wooden beams supporting the roof were hand carved by local craftsmen in 2007. Enjoy your tea with a view of Bukhara's Old Town. **$$$**

🖳 Silk Road Spices [211 E3] 5 H Ibodov; \ 224 2268; ⊕ 09.00–19.00 daily. The proprietors of Silk Road Spices claim to have been in business since 1400, & the numerous teas & tisanes on their menu certainly suggest a long history in the spice trade. Coffee & cardamom, saffron tea & ginger tea all feature on the menu & can be enjoyed with the accompaniment of sticky national sweets such as *halva* & *nabat*. **$$$**

🖳 Lyabi Hauz Chaikhana [211 F3] Lyabi Hauz. On the edge of the reservoir, this must have the best location of any chaikhana in Uzbekistan. Though it is crowded with tourists in summer, out of season things are rather more relaxed & you'll be sitting alongside local chess players drinking endless bowls of tea. **$$**

ENTERTAINMENT Bukhara isn't exactly renowned for its nightlife, but during the high season there are various evening entertainment options that draw in the tourist crowds.

The annual **Silk & Spice Festival** takes place in May or June and includes a programme of music and dance performances and craft exhibitions. The BICC (page 210) can advise on exact dates.

Other options for an evening's fun include taking in a performance by the **Bukhara National Puppet Theatre** [211 B2] (*Nadir Divan Beghi Khanagha;*

⊕ *summer 18.00 & 19.00 daily; US$5*) or the **Bukhorcha Song and Dance Group** (*Nadir Divan Beghi Madrassa;* ⊕ *summer 19.00 daily; US$5*). Neither of these shows are particularly highbrow (or authentic), but they tend to be good fun and well-attended nonetheless.

For a drink and a sing along in the evening, head over to **Golden Sheesha Lounge and Karaoke Bar** [211 E3] (*Mekhtar Ambar;* ⊕ *noon–midnight*). Next door to Hotel Asia Bukhara, it is hardly classy, but has a reasonable selection of beers and spirits.

SHOPPING

Souvenirs Souvenirs are, quite predictably, everywhere in Bukhara, and quality is hit and miss. Expect to haggle hard, and don't be afraid to walk away if you think you're being fleeced as you probably are. There are numerous souvenir stalls in Bukhara's three restored medieval trading domes: **Taki Sarrafon** [211 E4] (the money changers' dome); **Taki Telpal Furushon** [211 E3] (the hat makers' dome); and **Taki Zargaron** [211 E2] (the jewellers' dome). Much of what they sell is uninspiring and probably made in China, but they are well worth a visit for the impressive (and historically significant) buildings that house them. *Taki*, incidentally, means dome or arch.

The following alternative options are friendly, knowledgeable about their products and will always haggle good-naturedly.

🏵 **Bukhara Artisan Development Centre** [211 F3] Lyabi Hauz. Inside this restored caravanserai are the numerous workshops of miniaturists, embroiderers, decorative metalworkers & weavers, each housed in a converted cell. You can watch them work (the embroidery with golden thread looks particularly striking, if not to everyone's taste), hear them explain about their crafts &, of course, buy directly from the producers. Handwoven *ikat* scarves, fresh from the loom, so to speak, are US$15.

🏵 **Bukhara Silk Carpets** [211 D2] Kh Nurobod; ☎ 722 0220; e Muhammad.mk@mail. ru. The lovely Sabina runs what is one of Bukhara's largest carpet shops. There is a wide range of styles, sizes & prices as carpets cover every surface, including the walls, & the staff are up front about which carpets are handmade & which are not. It's possible to watch carpets being woven in the shop by a gaggle of young women sat cross-legged & simultaneously knotting & gossiping at the looms in the corner.

🏵 **Suzani Shop** [211 E3] Haqiqat Sq. A mother & her teenage daughter run this Aladdin's cave of textile treasures. In addition to the usual *suzanis* & scarves (some old, some new) is a small but beautiful selection of traditional costume pieces that include *chapans* & short, embroidered jackets: it is a rail of these that will most likely catch your eye outside. The daughter is learning English in school & is keen to practise while you haggle for the inevitable discount. We left with a free gift, too.

🏵 **Tim Abdullakhan** [211 E2] Haqiqat Sq; ☎ 190 3720; e samira_fayz@mail.ru. Once the Tim-i Kalan (the Great Market), silks & other textiles have been traded in this covered marketplace since 1577. Large number of quality carpets & *suzanis* for sale inside the beautiful historic building with its cupolas, galleries & niches. Visit as much for the surroundings as for the stock, & be prepared to drink endless bowls of tea whilst making your final selection.

Food To buy picnic items, bottled water and snacks, go to **Eshon Xo'ja** [211 G3] (*cnr B Naqshbandi & Eshoni Pir*), a well-stocked convenience store. If you are coming from Lyabi Hauz you will inevitably pass **Food Market,** but keep going, as it is extremely overpriced and the staff are rude. It is just 2 minutes further on to Eshon Xo'ja.

OTHER PRACTICALITIES

Communications Many of Bukhara's hotels and cafés now have Wi-Fi and it's usually free if you're staying there or buy a coffee. If you're without your own laptop or smartphone, however, you can also get online at the **BICC** (page 210) and the two **internet cafés** [211 F3] on Lyabi Hauz. These are usually open 09.00–23.00 daily and charge 3,000 som per hour. The one on the left has a significantly faster connection speed.

The **telephone and telegraph office** [209 C3] is on Muminov opposite the stadium. There is a **post office** [209 B3] counter at Hotel Grand Bukhara, and another at the airport. These are only open on weekdays, usually between 09.00 and 17.00.

Medical For general aches, pains, stomach upsets and mild injuries **Polyclinic #2** (*61 B Naqshbandi;* ☏ *223 0503*) and **Polyclinic #4** (*80 Gijduvani;* ☏ *224 8374*) are the most centrally located. Medical emergencies will require a trip to the **Republican Centre of Science of Emergency Medicine** [209 D2] (*159 B Naqshbandi;* ☏ *225 1026*), which is well equipped by Uzbek standards but still not really comparable to a Western hospital.

Money If you have a Visa card, then you can get money out in Bukhara: it seems like a miracle! The city's solitary **ATM**, a yellow one belonging to Kapitalbank, is on Kh Nurobod on the wall outside Bukhara Silk Carpets (page 214). The machine only accepts Visa cards though, and works intermittently. Otherwise, you can withdraw money from the following:

$ National Bank of Uzbekistan [209 D3] 3 M Iqbol; ☏ 223 4588; ⏱ 09.00–18.00 Mon–Fri, 09.00–16.00 Sat

$ Kapitalbank [211 E3] cnr Sarrofon & B Naqshbandi; ☏ 224 1092; ⏱ 08.00–16.00 Mon–Fri

$ Asaka Bank [209 D2] 14 Khamza; ☏ 223 4030; ⏱ 09.00–17.00 Mon–Fri

Most hotel staff and shop owners will be happy to arrange currency exchange at the unofficial rate, but agree the rate with them before handing over your dollars as some tourists have reported being given a rate that falls somewhere between the official rate and the true unofficial rate.

Registration All of Bukhara's hotels should register you automatically. However, if you do need to go to the **OVIR** [209 C3] yourself, it's at 10/3 Murtazaev.

WHAT TO SEE AND DO

The Ark [211 C1] (*Registan Sq;* ⏱ *09.00–19.00 daily; adults US$2, includes entry to the Archaeology Museum & local history museum*) The mud-brick walls of the Ark Fortress grace almost every postcard of Bukhara: it is to this city as the Eiffel Tower is to Paris, or Tower Bridge is to London. It's both an architectural icon and, if we're truly honest, a slightly overrated tourist spot.

The exact origins of the Ark are lost in the mists of time, but archaeologists believe it to have first been built sometime between the 5th and 6th centuries AD. The original structure covered a roughly rectangular site of some 3ha and included a palace, Zoroastrian fire temple, administrative areas and guardrooms; the main functions of the town all took place within these city walls so that they could more easily be defended in the case of attack. The earliest structure recorded in local histories, built by Bukhar Khudat Bidun in the 7th century AD, collapsed and so did its successors. It was only when the fortress was reconstructed to reflect the shape and orientation of the constellation Ursa Major (the Great Bear) at the suggestion of a local seer that the gods were satisfied and the structure stood firm (at least for the time being).

The Arabs built Bukhara's first mosque in the confines of the Ark in AD713; it was built atop the smouldering ruins of the earlier Zoroastrian temple to assert physically and metaphorically the power of Islam over other faiths and their adherents. The site was heavily fortified by the Samanids and Karakhanids between the 9th and 13th centuries, during which time the vast, sloped ramparts were added, only to then be razed by the Karakhitai, the Khorezmshah and, last but certainly not least, the Mongols.

Most of what you see still standing at the Ark today dates from the 16th-century Shaybanid dynasty, with later additions from the Mangits (1753–1920). Under Shaybanid rule the Ark was expanded to accommodate not only the royal family but a population of some 3,000 people, their homes, workplaces and mosques. Everything from the royal mint and treasury to the dungeons and slave quarters were within the citadel's walls.

A similar-sized population was still living in the Ark in 1920 when a fire ripped through the site, destroying as many as 80% of the buildings. The fire was no accident, though no-one is really sure whether it was the Bolsheviks or the ousted, and therefore understandably irate, emir who was responsible for striking the match. Derelict and blackened, the corpse of the Ark was an easy target for Soviet propaganda and it continued to disintegrate throughout the 20th century, the only pitiful use of its remaining, decaying buildings being to house Bukhara's history museum and archives. Thankfully, the front part of the Ark has now been restored and reopened to the public, and an ongoing renovation project will bring back to life other parts of the site one section at a time.

Your visit to the Ark will inevitably begin with the **Registan** [211 B2], the vast square outside what is now the Ark's main gate. Historically it served as both a slave market and public execution ground, though now it lies empty save for tourists wielding cameras.

To picture the square at its height requires you to use your imagination: Soviet demolition crews made sure of that. Stand in the square facing the citadel walls and envisage the luxurious home of the *tupchi bashi*, the city's chief of artillery, surrounded by cannons seized in battle from the Kokand khanate. To your left would have stood a line of mosques and madrassas equal in beauty to those surrounding the Registan in Samarkand. The square itself would have been heaving: you'd have been jostled from every angle by courtiers and street hawkers, slave traders showing off their wares, and an occasional dervish spinning through on his way to the khanagha. When the drumbeat was heard from atop the city walls, the crowd would have surged forward for a grisly hour's entertainment: the ground would run red with the blood of publicly executed prisoners.

Entrance to the Ark is through the **Western Gate**, an imposing entranceway built by Nadir Shah in 1742. The second, southern or Kalyon Gate has long-since been destroyed. Two important items once hung from this gateway: a *khamcha* (six-stranded whip) to remind the people of the emir's power; and a mechanical clock made by an Italian clockmaker, Giovanni Orlandi, who was captured by Turkmen slave traders in Orenburg, Russia in the mid 19th century. Orlandi earned himself a temporary reprieve by offering to make the clock (at the time the only mechanical clock in Bukhara) for Nasrullah Khan but once it was completed, Orlandi was caught drunk and this gave Nasrullah the excuse he wanted to sentence the Italian to death. The skin on his neck was sliced off, and he was then beheaded.

Climbing the steep stone ramp and passing through the gateway brings you inside the Ark. There is a definite sense of shades of former glory, though as the renovation programme continues and as more areas are restored and opened to the public, you should get a picture of what life inside the citadel was like. You will come across a number of restored structures: the **mosque**, which now houses a small **exhibition of calligraphy,** including early Qu'rans and illuminated works of poetry; the **elchi khana,** an administrative building that contains the underwhelming **Regional Archaeology Museum** and a **plaque** to the 20 Bolshevik emissaries murdered here in 1918; the **salam khana** (public audience hall) where Conolly made his infamous (and ultimately fatal) error of judgement; and the **kurinesh khana** (throne room) where the emirs were crowned and lifted onto their new throne while sitting on a silk carpet. You will also find the **local history museum**, which has some fine royal costumes (including the emir's coronation robes and an accompanying 20m-long turban) and illuminating photographs of the Ark when it was still inhabited. The neighbouring courtyard overlooks the two-storey orchestra pit, the **nagora khana,** from which the court's musicians serenaded (or at least so he claimed) Joseph Wolff with a rousing rendition of *God Save the Queen* (see box, page 208).

For those with an interest in the Great Game, the most important, and also most harrowing, sight at the Ark is the **zindan**, the jail in which the unfortunate Conolly and Stoddart (see box, page 218) were kept prior to their execution. This is accessed around the back of the Ark and requires a separate admission ticket (*US$1*). Water and excrement washed from the floors of the royal stables rained down on the heads of already tortured bodies; wretched men, starving and chained by the neck, were packed into the overcrowded hole in the ground. The exhibits inside include a few items relating to torture, photographs of victims, and some rather feeble mannequins, forever imprisoned in the gloomy cells.

Lyabi Hauz Complex [211 F3] The photogenic Lyabi Hauz Square on B

Naqshbandi is centred on an **artificial reservoir** (a *hauz* in Persian) constructed on the orders of the Grand Vizier, Nadir Divan Beghi, around 1620. The surrounding mulberry trees pre-date the construction of the hauz by 150 years, suggesting the square has long been a shaded focal point in the city. Early visitors recall the presence of jugglers, storytellers and dancing boys, musicians and magicians, and even the occasional Indian snake charmer. It's a far cry from the serene, almost sleepy spot we see today.

The reservoir, which measures 42m by 36m and is 5m deep, is fed by an ancient sunken canal system known as the Shah Rud (the Royal Canal). It was built with stone steps to allow the city's water carriers to easily fill their leather buckets, regardless of the reservoir's current water level, though it's unlikely you'd actually have wanted to drink the water: until the Soviets drained, restored and re-filled the pool in the 1960s, it was stagnant and infested with all manner of worms and fleas, a perfect breeding ground for waterborne diseases.

Around the reservoir are the **Khanakha** (*Lyabi Hauz;* \ *224 4548;* ⊕ *09.00–18.00 daily*) and **Madrassa of Nadir Divan Beghi** (*Lyabi Hauz;* ⊕ *09.00–18.00 daily; US$1*), which are roughly contemporaneous with the reservoir. The elegant portal of the khanagha is the building reflected in the surface of the water, and it was constructed as a place where Sufi dervishes could stay and meditate. At the centre of the building is a mosque with a mihrab decorated with coloured stalactites in crimson red, ultramarine blue, a vivid green and gold. Around the mosque are two storeys of *hujras* (cells) in which the holy men would have slept. They've been replaced by souvenir sellers.

STODDART AND CONOLLY
Bijan Omrani

In 1838, as Britain was embarking on its first ill-fated invasion of Afghanistan, Lieutenant Colonel Charles Stoddart was sent as an envoy to Nasrullah Khan, the Emir of Bukhara. The British authorities wished to assure Bukhara's ruler that they had no intentions of marching beyond Afghan territory, and also to suggest measures, such as the abolition of slavery, which would make the Russians less likely to attack Bukhara.

Stoddart was admired as an army officer, but possessed no diplomatic training. Unaware of the niceties of central Asian royal protocol, he caused offence as soon as he arrived by failing to dismount before the emir outside the *arg*, or palace. On entering an official audience shortly afterwards, he compounded his offence by failing to make a symbolic gesture of respect. When a courtier tried to correct the mistake, Stoddart thought the official was attacking him and knocked him down. The emir, who had a volatile temper, was outraged and ordered Stoddart be thrown into a dungeon beneath the palace.

The dungeon was notorious as one of the worst punishments in Bukhara. It was dark, 6m deep and crawling with rats. Stoddart's first fellow inmates there were two thieves and a murderer. He was on occasion allowed out and kept under house arrest, but thrown back into the dungeon without any reason or notice.

The British government sent notes of protest to Nasrullah, but he failed to respond. Even the Russians attempted to free Stoddart, but Nasrullah ignored them too. The Russians had just failed in an attempt to capture the city of Khiva, and were not in a strong bargaining position. The British were reluctant to mount an expedition to save their countryman as they were bogged down in Afghanistan and could not extend themselves any further. When Stoddart's imprisonment had continued to the autumn of 1841, a fellow army officer, Captain Arthur Conolly, decided to stage a desperate attempt to rescue him. He was outraged not only by the British government's failure to act, but, as a devout Christian, by a report that Stoddart had been forced to convert to Islam. A failure in love, it seems, also drove him to this act of reckless courage. Conolly arrived at Bukhara in November 1841. He possessed rather greater diplomatic talents than his brother officer, and he negotiated for Stoddart, who was by then badly malnourished and ill from fever, to stay with him in better lodgings above ground. Yet, this happier situation did not last for long. At the beginning of 1842, when news came that the British garrison in Kabul had been annihilated, Nasrullah felt emboldened to defy Britain. Stoddart and Conolly were relegated to the dungeon, and then executed around the middle of June. They were forced to dig their own graves, and murdered by having their heads cut off.

The murders marked a lull in the Great Game, both Britain and Russia suffered serious setbacks in their central Asian engagements, and drew back from serious endeavours in the region until the 1860s.

The madrassa is on the opposite side of the square, as constructed in the 1630s. It was originally intended as a caravanserai, but Khan Imam Kuli mistook its elaborate façade for a madrassa, and the Nadir Divan Beghi felt compelled to change its function. This unplanned change of use accounts for the absence of typical madrassa features: the symmetrical layout, a mosque and teaching hall.

The mosaic of two *simurgh* (flying creatures from Persian mythology) and two deer on the madrassa's façade is one of the finest examples of figurative tile work in Uzbekistan. It makes for a truly dramatic scene, especially when you consider that it flies in the face of the widely accepted Islamic prohibition on figurative art. The Mongol sun, replete with human face, must have horrified orthodox visitors.

The **Kulkedash Madrassa** is on the north side of Lyabi Hauz, and it pre-dates all three of Nadir Divan Beghi's constructions, having been built in the late 1560s by the Kulbaba Kulkedash (foster brother) of Abdulla Khan II. Its footprint measures 86m by 69m, which makes it one of the largest madrassas in Bukhara, and the building includes 160 *hujras*. The madrassa's most famous student was the 20th-century writer Sadiriddin Aini (page 166).

During the Soviet period the madrassa was used for a variety of purposes, including as a hotel and a Soviet-era women's centre, a deliberate slight, one would assume, to those who believed the madrassa to be the realm of men. The Kulkedash Madrassa has now been restored to its original condition, if not its original function, and you can step inside the cool interior to admire the vaulted ceilings, colourful tile work and, of course, the numerous *hujras*.

Poi Kalyon [211 D2]

The Poi Kalyon square is the star in the Bukharan sapphire, the beating heart of the Old Town, and the visual high point (both literal and metaphorical) of the city's skyline. The name, which means 'at the foot of the Great', is derived from its place at the foot of the **Kalyon Minar** (the Great Minaret), the tapering, mud-brick tower which rises gracefully some 45m above the city.

The minaret was built in 1127 and it was, so an inscription tells us, the work of an architect named Bako. He ordered that the foundations be dug some 13m deep, and demanded the labourers use a special mortar that was mixed with bulls' blood, camel milk and eggs. It took two years to set. The exact original height of the minaret is unknown but it is thought to have been the tallest free-standing tower in the world. The uppermost section appears to have been lost (possibly due to an earthquake) and the part below reworked.

Bako died not long after the minaret was completed, purportedly broken hearted that it had failed to live up to his dreams. Genghis Khan looked upon it a little more favourably in the following century, however, and, having seen it for miles as he rode across the steppe and been suitably impressed, he spared the tower when all around it was razed. If you're feeling fit, you can climb to the top of the Kalyon Minar (*US$3 for access*). The 104 steps of the staircase spiral upwards, becoming ever narrower as the tower slowly tapers from a diameter of 9m to 6m. Leaning out through one of the 16 arches at the top grants you an unforgettable view of a peerless city. Don't lean too far, however, as the Mangits were fond of tying their prisoners up in sacks and chucking them off the top, a grisly but no doubt effective punishment that endured well into the 1800s, much to the disgust of Lord Curzon (see box, page 220).

In the sun dial-like shadow of the Kalyon Minar, the **Kalyon Mosque** [211 D2] (the Great Mosque) stands on the foundations of the earlier, 8th-century mosque in which Genghis Khan ordered that the pages of the Qu'ran be trampled beneath the feet of his horses and the entirety of Bukhara (with the exception of the Kalyon Minar) be destroyed. The mosque was burnt to a cinder.

This replacement, a worthy successor, is also known as the Juma or Friday Mosque and was built by the Shaybanids in 1514. An inscription on the mosque's façade attests to this completion date. Since then it has served as the city's main mosque: there is space for more than 10,000 worshippers to pray, the entire male population of the city at the time of its construction.

You enter through the eastern gate on Poi Kalyon and descend into a truly breathtakingly beautiful courtyard surrounded by 208 columns and 288 domes; the numerous pillars evoke the legendary court of Solomon and are an evocative statement in mosques and palaces from the Alhambra in Moorish Spain, to the forts and palaces of emperors in Mughal India. On the western side of the plaza is the turquoise-tiled **Kok Gumbaz** (blue dome), an architectural bubble, the shape of which belies its weight and width. Beneath it lies the mosque's wonderfully gilded mihrab and an unusual octagonal structure designed to improve the building's acoustics, amplifying the voice of the Imam as he speaks his Friday sermon. The inscription on the dome itself, a spider-spun web of Kufic calligraphy, reads 'Immortality belongs to God.'

Having been used as a warehouse during the Soviet period, the Kalyon Mosque reopened to worshippers in 1991. It continues to be a place of prayer, albeit on a fraction of the scale for which it was originally intended, but visitors and their cameras are welcome to come inside providing they are appropriately dressed and behave in a respectful manner.

Mir-i Arab Madrassa [211 D2] Opposite the mosque is the Mir-i Arab Madrassa, constructed, so they say, with the profits from the sale of 3,000

LORD CURZON IN UZBEKISTAN   *Bijan Omrani*

In the summer of 1888, the Honourable George Nathaniel Curzon – Old Etonian, classical scholar, precocious modern linguist, Fellow of All Souls Oxford and 29-year-old Conservative MP – set out on a journey via St Petersburg for central Asia. At that time the Great Game was in full swing, and debate in England about the intentions of Russia was at its height. Many believed that having taken over central Asia up to the northern borders of Afghanistan, Russia was now preparing to launch an attack on India. Few Europeans or non-Russians had been to central Asia, so Curzon wanted to visit the region and judge the situation for himself.

Curzon travelled along the newly built Trans-Caspian railway to Tashkent, where it then terminated, and from there by horse-drawn *tarantass* to Bukhara. The following year, he published his observations in a consistently entertaining 478-page work entitled *Russia in Central Asia and the Anglo–Russian Question*.

Curzon asserted in his introduction that his purpose was to write a work primarily dedicated to the problems of politics and foreign relations. However, he also admitted travelling at a 'unique' moment, when the railway had made travel suddenly easy, but had not yet changed the ancient way of life in the region, which he could see it would soon do. When he travelled, criminals were still hurled to their death from the great minaret of Bukhara, the city centres still bustled with their ancient trades and craftsmen, and the old rulers were still maintained (albeit as Russian puppets) in the medieval magnificence of their courts. Hence, Curzon's work is not only a well-informed assessment of Russia's objectives in the region, but also a compelling snapshot of the old Silk Road cities before the railways changed them forever.

Persian slaves. Its benefactor, the Shaybanid Khan Ubaidullah, clearly felt a need to salve his conscience, and hence in 1535 he endowed what is considered one of the most important educational establishments in the Islamic world. With the exception of a 21-year period when it was closed from 1925–46, it has remained fully functional, including throughout the Soviet period, and today around 180 students are studying here. They take a demanding four-year programme of Arabic and Qu'ranic studies, the first step on the path to becoming Imams. There is limited access for tourists to the madrassa: you can enter the foyer and look into the inner courtyard but, theoretically at least, can go no further. However, if you ask nicely and there is an appropriate guide present, you may also be permitted to view the tombs of Sheikh Abdullah of Yemen (known as Mir-i Arab, the prince of the Arabs), a close friend of Khan Ubaidullah who took responsibility for the madrassa's actual construction, and of Khan Ubaidullah himself. The tombs are marked with a white flag and a goat's tail, the traditional signs of saints.

Other madrassas The **Kosh Madrassa** (*Tinchlik & Mirdustim*) close to the Registan is in fact two madrassas: the small **Modar-i Khan Madrassa** [211 A3] built by Abdullah Shaybani Khan for his mother in 1566, and the rather more impressive **Abdullah Khan Madrassa** [211 A3] (1590) that Abdullah built for himself. You can see where his priorities lay. The architecture of this building was controversial (one might go as far as to say heretical) as rather than being orientated towards Mecca, its position is determined by the cardinal points, the façade mirroring that of the Modar-i Khan Madrassa opposite. Abdullah Khan is buried inside, his tomb lying on the north–south axis as is traditional for an Islamic burial; the building, one might argue, was laid out not for the glory of God, but for the convenience of Abdullah Khan.

East of the Poi Kalyon, the **Ulug Beg Madrassa** [211 E2] (*Kh Nurobod*) was built by Timur's grandson. Built in 1417, it is the earliest of three such madrassas, the other two being situated in Samarkand and Gijduvan.

Ulug Beg (see box, page 164) was an intellectual as much as a king, and it should therefore come as no surprise that the inscription over the madrassa's main door reads 'Aspiration to knowledge is the duty of each Muslim man and woman'. The architect's name, Ismael, is also inscribed among the tile work, the star patterns of which are surely a reflection of Ulug Beg's love of studying the heavens. Inside the madrassa is a small mosque, library and the **Museum on the History of Renovation** (⊕ *09.00–17.00 daily; US$1*), which includes photographs and tile samples taken from various buildings.

Immediately opposite is the unrestored **Abd al-Aziz Khan Madrassa** [211 E2] (*also Kh Nurobod*), built in 1652. Modelled on the Mir-i Arab Madrassa (pages 220–1), it was constructed for Abd al-Aziz after his defeat of the Mughal army in Balkh. The madrassa's footprint measures 60m by 48m, and the entire site is sumptuously decorated with mosaics in riotous colours and equally bright *ghanch* stalactites. A single side of the courtyard is unfinished and unadorned, the rest seemingly more spectacular for the contrast. The madrassa includes both summer and winter mosques, the latter of which now houses the fairly dusty and unremarkable **Museum of Woodcarving** (⊕ *09.00–17.00 daily; US$0.50*).

East of the Old Town, one block north of M Ambar, is the **Chor Minor** [209 C1], a stubby, brick-built structure with four turquoise domes. The uncharitable have described it as looking like an up-turned chair. The name Chor Minor, meaning 'four minarets', is a misnomer, however, as though the towers look like minarets,

8

they were never designed (or used) as a location from which the muezzin could call the faithful to prayer.

Built in 1807, the Chor Minor is the only known building in Uzbekistan in this style, though it was possibly inspired by the Char Minar Mosque in Hyderabad, India, where its patron, the Turkmen merchant Khalif Niyazkul, is thought to have travelled. It is said that the four towers, each subtly different from the next, represents one of his four daughters. The front-left minaret collapsed completely during an earthquake and so has been rebuilt; the other three have also been heavily restored. If you look closely at the tiles on the domes, you'll see each dome has a date: this is the date it was restored.

When it was built, the Chor Minor housed a library, accessed via the staircase in the front right tower. Students would take their books to read in the cells either side of the building, several of which still survive. You can climb the same staircase onto the roof (*4,000 som*), though in all honesty you can't see very far.

Before you leave, take a look at the stone barleycorn columns either side of the Chor Minor's front and back doors. No-one knows exactly where these came from, but they appear much older than the rest of the structure and were likely incorporated from an earlier building.

Other mausoleums In and around **Samani Park** [211 B2] (*cnr S Murodov & M Ashrafi*), west of the Ark, are three exceptionally important structures often overlooked by tourists in their bid to take in the big-name sites emblazoned on postcards and souvenir tea towels. The first is the **Chashma Ayub Mausoleum** [211 B2] (*09.00–18.00 daily; admission 2,000 som*), which purportedly marks the spot where the Prophet Job struck the arid ground and a spring of pure drinking water miraculously burst forth, saving his followers when those around them were dying of thirst. The city grew up around this holy site, and this may be a reason why the city's early Jewish community (page 225) chose to settle here.

First erected in the 11th century, the plain and slightly austere mausoleum you see today was raised by Timur in 1380 to protect the sacred tomb below. It is not known who is buried here, but it certainly isn't Job. On the roof are three domes, each one unique and dating from a different period of the building's construction. The shape of one of the domes, atypical in the region, is thought to have been derived from the roof of a Khorezmian nomads' tent.

Inside the mausoleum you will find a small **museum** (*09.00–18.00 daily; admission 2,000 som*) dedicated to Bukhara's water supply. There are displays on irrigation and water carrying, including a few photographs.

Immediately opposite the mausoleum is the modern **Memorial to Imam Al-Bukhari** [211 B1]. Born in Bukhara in 810AD, Al-Bukhari (page 167) collected 97 volumes of Hadiths, the sayings of the Prophet Muhammad.

More elaborate, and of great historical importance, is the early 10th-century **Ismail Samani Mausoleum** [211 A2], which gives the park its name. It is the oldest Islamic monument in Bukhara, a perfect cube of seemingly woven brickwork that marks the grave of the founder of the Samanid dynasty as well as his father, nephew and other family members. Pilgrims have been drawn to Ismail Samani's tomb for more than a millennium: it was one of the holiest sites in Bukhara, the final resting place of ancient kings.

Striking in its simplicity, the design incorporates aspects of Sogdian architecture, recent mathematical developments and even Sassanid fire temples. The cubic shape harks back to the *Kaaba* in the Masjid al-Haram in Mecca, and the dome above it

Medieval Bukhara was a hotbed for intellectuals from across the Islamic world, and one of its most remarkable sons was Abu ibn Sina (AD 980–1037), known in the west as Avicenna.

Born in the village of Afshona, the son of an Ismaili scholar from Balkh, ibn Sina gained a rigorous education in Bukhara, which was then the capital of the Samanid Empire. According to his biographers, he had memorised the entire Qu'ran by the age of ten, and he read Aristotle's *Metaphysics* more than 40 times during his teenage years. Ibn Sina then turned his attention to medicine, studying medical theory but also experimenting with his own treatments and remedies.

His appointment as court physician at the age of 18 gave ibn Sina access to the Samanid royal library, a treasure trove of scholarship. Ibn Sina was able to immerse himself in books, further educating himself in logic and astronomy. He remained in Bukhara until the fall of the Samanids in 1004, whence he travelled to Urgench, Merv, Tehran and Isfahan. In every place he sought more knowledge, and lectured on what he knew.

Throughout his life, ibn Sina wrote extensively. His most important works are in the fields of philosophy and medicine. His treaties on metaphysics and logic were written in Arabic and attempted to reconcile Aristotelianism and Neoplatonism; Avincennan philosophy became the leading school of medieval Islamic thought, and was also influential in Europe.

Ibn Sina's 14-volume *Canon of Medicine* was a standard medical textbook in European universities as late as the 18th century. He adopted ideas from the ancient Greeks about contagious diseases, but also made original observations on conditions from diabetes to facial paralysis, classified diseases and their causes, and laid down methodology for testing the efficacy of new medications. Ibn Sina was the first person to use a cannula to open the windpipe of a choking patient, and he recognised the importance of diet, exercise and psychology in good health.

The **Avicenna Museum**, opened to mark the 1,000th anniversary of his birth, is situated in Afshona village, but it is not of interest to general visitors and few of the exhibits are marked.

represents the heavens. The complex patterns in the brickwork add texture to the four equal façades, enticing visitors to run their hands across the grainy surface. There are two reasons for its unusually good state of preservation: it is made from fired bricks instead of sun-dried mud bricks; and it was partially buried beneath the sands until the 1930s. This protected it from both the wrath of Genghis Khan and the erosion of time and weather. When it was discovered in 1934 by Soviet archaeologists, it was fully excavated and the graves relocated. Only the dome has had to be rebuilt.

If you want to take photos inside, which in this case is actually recommended, the camera permit costs 2,000 som.

Other mosques Central Asia's oldest surviving mosque, the **Magokiattari Mosque** [211 E3], is situated between the Taki Sarrafon and Taki Telpal Furushon trading domes (page 214). Prior to the Arab invasion there was a Buddhist monastery and then a Zoroastrian temple on the site; archaeologists in the 1930s excavated the site down to a depth of 6m in order to get to the bottom (literal and metaphorical) of its 2,000 years of history.

The mosque you see today was founded sometime in the 9th century and gained its name from the herbalists (*attars*) trading in the bazaar next door. It was burned down and rebuilt in the 10th century, and again 200 years later, though the portal from the first structure remains. There is some suggestion that the columns at the sides of this portal may in fact be pre-Islamic, a tantalising suggestion of the appearance of the destroyed Zoroastrian temple. The domed portal on the eastern side is a relatively recent addition: it dates from 1547.

One of the most elegant-looking mosques in Bukhara is the **Bolo Hauz Mosque** [211 B1] close to the Registan. The 12m-high pillars, 20 in all, that support the *iwan* are so slim that they look like super-sized chopsticks. They are made from elm, poplar and walnut wood. Built in 1712, the Bolo Hauz Mosque is the only historic building on this side of the square to survive: all the others were destroyed in the early 20th century by the Soviets, and the mosque itself was turned into a working-men's club. This did, at least, save it from a far worse fate, and both the pool that gives the mosque its name (*hauz* meaning reservoir or pool) and the brightly coloured paintwork have been sensitively restored.

The interior of the mosque is less interesting than the outside, though as it is free to go inside, you might as well. Take your shoes off and put them on the rack by the door. The original painted mihrab is quite attractive; the modern chandelier hanging from the dome is hideous and out of keeping. If you want to take photos inside, put something in the donation box. – donations are used for the conservation of the building.

Other sites As in cities across the Roman Empire, bathing in historic Bukhara was a communal affair; you could drink tea, do business and gossip while having a rub in the communal tub. Several of the medieval bathhouses remain operational, though these days visiting is more of a novelty than an essential component of public hygiene. Our favourites are the 16th-century **Bozori Kord Bathhouse** [211 E3] (*Taki Telpal Furushon;* \ *301 1133;* ⊕ *06.00–15.00 men only, 15.00–19.00 mixed; US$7*) and the **Hammon Kunjak** [211 C2] (*4 Ibodov;* ⊕ *07.00–18.00; US$12 inc massage*), a women-only bathhouse close to the Kalyon Minar. In both cases you can bathe and/or have a massage, and should expect to go *au naturel*.

A visit to the **House Museum of Faizulla Khodjaev** [209 A2] (*70A Tukay;* \ *224 4188;* ⊕ *09.00–17.00 Mon–Sat*) gives you the chance to see inside one of Bukhara's most spectacular 19th-century houses. It retains its original carved wooden entranceway, wall paintings and separate living areas for male and female members of the family; few such properties remain, and there are probably no others in such good condition.

South of Lyabi Hauz is Bukhara's **Jewish quarter**. Although only a fraction of the city's Jewish population remains (the majority having emigrated to Israel and the US since independence), it is possible to visit the semi-underground **synagogue** [211 F4] and, further out, the **Jewish cemetery**. These wouldn't be of interest to the casual visitor, but those with a passion for Jewish history can ask at the synagogue for more information.

AROUND BUKHARA The outskirts of Bukhara house some other intriguing sites, including a summer palace and a mausoleum to the city's patron saint.

Sitorai Makhi Khosa [209 B1] (⏰ *09.00–17.00 Thu–Tue; US$4*) Just 6km north
of the town centre, this was the summer palace of Bukhara's emirs. Built in 1911 for the last emir, Alim Khan, the three-building compound incorporates elements of both Russian and traditional Bukharan architecture.

The **inner courtyard** was the location for the First Congress of the Bukharan Soviet in 1920 and now houses the slightly dusty **Museum of Applied Arts,** replete with the contents of the emir's bed chamber. Far more interesting, however, are the rooms that surround the courtyard: the emir's bedroom, games room, the mirrored White Hall, and a banqueting hall. These have quite extraordinary mirrored and painted interiors, original chandeliers, and some fine furniture and Chinese porcelain.

There are two other museums in the complex, the **Museum of Costume** and the **Museum of Needlework**, both of which are worth 20 minutes or so of your time. Basic descriptions for some of the exhibits are in English. Check out the *paranja*, a heavy and itchy horse-hair robe akin to a *burqa* that would have been worn by high-class womenfolk, and also the wedding robes. There are some beautiful embroidered boots and hats, and photographs on the walls show how the similar outfits were worn by the emirs. A 1928 photograph shows the emir's unveiled concubines.

The palace compound must once have been the most wonderful garden, shaded beneath hundreds of persimmon and quince trees. Today it is a bit of a wilderness, though still attractive in its way, and you should take the time to wander through to the white harem building and its neighbouring folly, a pair of wooden towers linked by a bridge at the top. The emir used to select his companion for the night by throwing her an apple. The girl had to catch it and then take a bath in donkey's milk before being permitted to enter the royal bedchamber.

Mausoleum of Bakhauddin Naqshbandi (⏰ *09.00–18.00 daily; donations
welcome*) This is just outside the city's northern limits, in the village of Kasri. As Bukhara's unofficial patron saint and the founder of the most important Sufic order in central Asia, the Naqshbandis, it should come as little surprise that his birthplace and tomb is the holiest site in Bukhara.

Naqshbandi's tomb is part of an extensive complex of tombs and shrines. His *mazar*, or shrine, encases a black tombstone, which pilgrims circumnavigate. They used to be able to kiss the shrine as well, but a cordon now prevents them getting that close. The shrine lies in a vast and stunning courtyard with tapered wooden columns and exquisitely painted ceilings. Allow plenty of time to sit here, look up and take in the details.

Within the complex are 20 other graves, including that of Abdullah Khan II, two mosques (one for women and the other for men) and a 16th-century khanagha with a striking, 30m-high dome. Local tradition has it that if you are sick, this is the place to come: those with bad backs should climb above the small pool in the main courtyard, touching their back against its roof, to be cured. If you have any other condition, including an inability to conceive, there is a fallen tree towards the back of the site under which you must wriggle. The saint will then answer your prayer.

The easiest way to reach the site is by taxi, but there are also minibuses going in this direction from the centre of town.

Chor Bakr Necropolis   In the village of Sumitan, 5km or so west of the city, is the Chor Bakr Necropolis, the tombs of four brothers (*chor* meaning four), who were all said to be descendants of the Prophet. The brothers, Imam Sayid Abu Bakr, Ahmed, Fazl and Hamed, were all buried here in the late 10th century, and their graves were later adopted by a sect of Sufi dervishes who believed in the sanctity of the site.

In the mid-16th century Abdullah Khan commissioned a khanagha, mosque and madrassa here, enabling the necropolis to operate as a fully fledged pilgrimage centre, and many local sheikhs, as well as Bukharan khans, were laid to rest in the vicinity. The crumbling streets lined with their mausoleums sprawl out from the central square, largely decaying and forgotten. The gatehouse through which you enter the site, and also the twin façades of the mosque and khanagha, which mirror one another, are in somewhat better repair.

Minibuses from Bukhara to Alat, Jondor and Karakul all stop in Sumitan, though if you expect to be travelling back later in the day you may prefer to go by taxi and to get the driver to wait for you: it's not always an easy place to get back from!

Vabkent Minaret   In the village of Vabkent, 20km northeast of Bukhara, is this 39m-tall , Karakhanid tower, built by Bukhari ad-Din Ayud al-Aziz in 1196. The second-largest minaret in the Bukhara oasis after the Kalyon Minar, it was originally part of a Friday Mosque complex. As per this taller, slightly earlier model, the Vabkent Minaret tapers towards the top and is crowned with a lantern-like shape, the base of which is decorated with stalactites. The trunk of the minaret is divided into eight ornamental bands, each decorated with calligraphy.

Varakhsha   Moving a little further afield, 30km northwest of Bukhara is Varakhsha, founded between the 3rd and 4th centuries BC, which medieval sources described as the biggest city along the Bukhara to Khorezm trade route. It was a well-fortified, important military outpost and an agricultural area, as well as being a major centre of crafts. One of the major towns of the Hephtalite civilisation in the oasis of Bukhara, it was the final retreat for the local kings when the Arab armies advanced. The **Varakhsha Palace**, home to the rulers of Bukhara, was built in the 7th century AD and is situated at the southern fortress wall of Varakhsha. The palace was rebuilt a number of times but was finally abandoned in the 11th century, and now all that remains are ruins. Excavations began in 1937 and were continued in 1947–53, when archaeologists unearthed three halls with an extensive courtyard area. The walls of the hall were highly decorated with exquisite frescoes showing scenes of hunting wild and fantastic animals. The mound is visible today from quite a distance but the excavations comprise only a small area around the citadel. Huge adobe fortifications with arched gateways and high walls may be seen. The site is open air, and has no guardian or entry fees. Varakhsha is on UNESCO's Tentative List for World Heritage status.

If you are travelling in your own vehicle to Varakhsha, it is well worth making a short stop at Chilangu, 20km outside the city limits, to visit the **Hakkim Mullo Mir Khanagha** (*no entry fee but donations welcome*). The best time to visit is on a Friday

The large Djeyran Eco Reserve is situated 40km south of Bukhara, and since the 1970s it has been an important conservation site for the flora, fauna, and landscapes of the southwestern Kyzylkum Desert. The reserve includes a wildlife sanctuary, where injured animals are cared for prior to re-release into the wild, and there is also a respected breeding centre for Persian gazelle, Przewalski's horse the Turkmenian kulan, and the Houbara bustard.

You can reach the reserve easily on a day trip from Bukhara, which is advisable as there is nowhere locally to stay. The best time to visit is in the spring or autumn, when the temperatures are pleasant, there are plenty of flowers, and the wildlife is easier to spot. Binoculars and a camera are advisable, as are hiking boots if you're intending to cover any distance as the going is rough underfoot.

afternoon, when prayers are celebrated and the community joins together for feasting. Providing you are appropriately addressed, you will be welcome to join them.

A *khanagha* is a hostel for dervishes, and they were built to accommodate these wandering ascetics whilst they were on pilgrimage. This particular example was constructed in honour of Sheik al-Islam Emir Hussein Mullo Mir, who died in 1587. The dervishes' cells are arranged around the outside of the central mosque, so that they would have easy access at prayer time, and you can climb to the roof of the building, four storeys up, via a series of staircases within the entrance portal.

Paikend Along the length of the Silk Road were a series of prosperous trading hubs. Although many of these have survived, and you can visit their modern incarnations, others such as Paikend were sacked one time too many, or fell prey to adverse climatic conditions and drought. Excavating the city from the sands is painstaking work, but if you have time, it's fascinating to visit this archaeological site 60km southwest of Bukhara.

In the Sogdian period, when Paikend was at its height, it was the final stop before caravans of merchants entered the Kyzylkum Desert. Traders came here from Afghanistan, China, and India, and they not only traded with one another but also bought high quality glass, pottery, and armour manufactured by Paikend's craftsmen. The city thrived until it was attacked in relatively quick succession by the Arabs and then the Mongols. Besieged, the people were on the verge of starving and had no chance to plant their crops for the coming year, and a subsequent drought necessitated that they abandon Paikend en masse, migrating elsewhere. The wealth amassed in Paikend is evident from the archaeological finds: vast fortifications and watch towers were essential for protecting the city and its inhabitants from invaders; the first pharmacy in central Asia was here; the architecture was on an impressive scale, with one minaret larger even than the Poi Kalyon in Bukhara; and large quantities of documents, jars, and cups have been discovered, too. UNESCO is advising the government on how best to develop Paikend as a tourist destination, though it will be some time before this plan comes to fruition.

GIJDUVAN *Telephone code: 65*

Historically Gijduvan was a cultural, mercantile and religious centre in the region, though today little of this is on show. The city makes its money from cotton production, though there has also been a revival of traditional crafts (particularly ceramics), which are then sold in the tourist centres of Samarkand and Bukhara. It's a pleasant place for a short excursion, especially if you are interested in visiting the many craft workshops.

GETTING THERE AND AWAY Gijduvan is 48km north of Bukhara on the M37 towards Samarkand, so it is best visited as a brief stop *en route* between those two cities. All the **public transport** options between them (pages 207–8) pass through Gijduvan, and it is a small enough town to explore **on foot**.

WHERE TO STAY AND EAT It is recommended that you stay at a hotel or guesthouse in Bukhara (pages 210–13) and visit Gijduvan on a day trip, as there are currently no accommodation options in Gijduvan itself that we can recommend.

Food, fortunately, is a different matter entirely. Gijduvan is famous within Uzbekistan for its cuisine: the shashlik and fried fish are said to be the best in the country, and there are plenty of chaikhanas and cafés where you can indulge.

SHOPPING The finest **ceramics** in Uzbekistan come from Gijduvan, so it would be churlish not to come away with a plate or three. It is best to buy direct from the craftsmen, and we can therefore recommend the **Gijduvan Glazed Ceramics Centre** (*55 Kimsan;* \ *572 7412; www.folkceramic.uz*), which includes a museum of traditional ceramics, a workshop where you can watch the potters at work, and a shop. Director and master potter Abdullo Narzullaev is a sixth-generation potter and learned his craft from his ancestors. He and his family give tours of the workshop in English, French and Russian, and their enthusiasm for their craft is infectious. There is a superb, illustrated article about his work on the Ceramics Centre's website.

OTHER PRACTICALITIES There is no proper hospital in Gijduvan, only a **district health centre** (*5/1 Sharq;* \ *572 5656*). For registration, the **OVIR** is at 35 B Naqshbandi. As ever, there is no ATM here, but money can be withdrawn at the following:

$ **Agro Bank** 1 Edgorov; \ 572 6146; ⊕ 09.00–17.00 Mon–Fri

$ **National Bank of Uzbekistan** 45 B Naqshbandi; \ 572 4633; ⊕ 09.00–18.00 Mon–Fri, 09.00–16.00 Sat

WHAT TO SEE AND DO Other than the ceramic workshops (see above), Gijduvan has two sites of interest to tourists. The third of **Ulug Beg's madrassas** was built here in 1433, and though less impressive than those in Samarkand and Bukhara, it is still an attractive building with a striped minaret by its entranceway, an ubiquitous turquoise dome and a lapis lazuli blue-tiled portico.

Though originally built as a madrassa, in practice it functioned more as a khanagha for those visiting the **Mazar of Abdul Khaliq Gijduvani,** which is contained within the madrassa's courtyard and was the reason why Ulug Beg selected this particular site. Gijduvani was a Sufi saint, an Islamic teacher whose pupils included Bakhauddin Naqshbandi (pages 225–6), and he founded his own Sufi order, the Khodjakhon. The mazar is a simple structure, and unlikely to be of particular interest to non-pilgrims: it is the surrounding buildings you should come to see.

9

Khorezm Province

Khorezm can only exist because it's an oasis, a fortunate strip of fertile land in the Amu Darya delta that is sandwiched between the Karakum and Kyzylkum deserts. The region has at least 57,500 years of known human history, starting with the Mesolithic Keltiminar (5500–3500BC) and moving through Bronze Age and Iron Age cultures to the Scythians, Achaemenids, Sassanids and then, in AD712, the Arab Ummayads. Such fascinating history has left rich pickings for visiting culture vultures: desert fortresses, some 2,500 years old; ancient palaces; royal citadels; and the remains of fire-worship temples.

And then, of course, there's Khiva, the caravan stop turned religious centre turned UNESCO World Heritage Site supposedly founded by Shem, son of Noah. This museum city, frozen in time behind its crenellated, mud-brick walls, seems to contain more historical sites per square metre even than mighty Bukhara. Ignore the distances to get there: it is absolutely not to be missed.

URGENCH *Telephone code: 62*

Konya-Urgench, the historical city, now lies out of reach across the border in Turkmenistan, but its newer incarnation, the Soviet city of Urgench, dismal and concrete though it is, remains significant as the gateway to Khorezm Province and offers things you'd actually want to see.

HISTORY The UNESCO World Heritage site Konya-Urgench (Old Urgench) lies just across the Uzbek–Turkmen border from Urgench. One of the greatest cities on the Silk Road, it was founded during the Achaemenid period and reached its peak in 12th and early 13th centuries, when its only possible rival in the region was Bukhara. Konya-Urgench's fortunes changed suddenly, however: in 1221 Genghis Khan razed the city to the ground and oversaw one of the bloodiest massacres in history. As if this was not bad enough, the Amu Darya then changed its course, leaving the city without water. Life became untenable, and the city's surviving inhabitants were forced to up sticks and move.

The new settlement, situated again on the banks of the Amu Darya, was at first simply a small trading town in the Khanate of Khiva. The the arrival of the Trans-Caspian railway at the end of the 19th century made it viable as an international trading post, however, and during the Soviet era the city was heavily industrialised. The Soviets introduced cotton, motifs of which decorate buildings across Urgench, and this cash crop remains the mainstay of the local economy to the present day.

GETTING THERE AND AWAY Urgench is a long way from anywhere other than Khiva, and so taking a flight or the sleeper train is a sensible option, at least in one direction, if you are likely to be short of time.

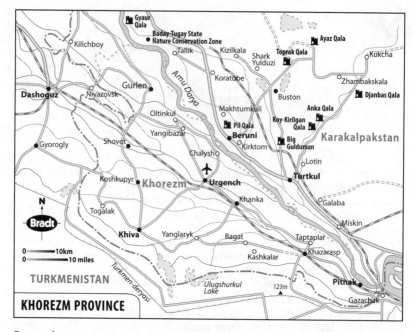

KHOREZM PROVINCE

By road The road between Bukhara and Khiva had been partially dug up at the time of going to print in order (eventually) to make way for a new, multi-lane highway between the two cities. This is a major infrastructure project, however, and very slow going: we first drove the route in 2010 and although some sections are now finished, there is still quite some way to go.

Urgench's **bus station** (✆ 225 5440) is on Al Khorezmi, just north of the train station, and both minibuses and shared taxis congregate here, too. There are cheap buses to Bukhara, Samarkand and Tashkent, but they take significantly longer (Urgench to Tashkent is 25 hours, for example) and are less frequent than the minibuses travelling the same routes, so avoid them unless you are exceptionally strapped for cash. There are regular minibuses to Bukhara (*6hrs; US$10*), and less frequent ones to Samarkand (*9hrs; US$12*) and Tashkent (*18hrs; US$20*), though it may be faster to go to Bukhara and change there.

Shared taxis to Nukus (*2½hrs; US$10*) leave from outside the Olympic Stadium on A Bakhodirkhan. They travel via Beruni, so if there is a shortage of vehicles heading to Nukus, you can always make for Beruni and change there.

Getting to Khiva is more straightforward: there are plenty of options. Shared taxis leave from Al Beruni, close to the main bazaar (*30–40 mins; US$1*); the trolley bus (*1½hrs; US$0.30*) also departs from Al Beruni but one block west of the post office, or you can take a taxi for US$12. If you pick up a taxi from the airport or train station, expect to have to haggle hard to get the correct fare.

By train The train station (✆ 225 6111) is at the southern end of Al Khorezmi. A new train line means it is possible to travel to Samarkand and Tashkent without transiting through Turkmenistan, but if you wish to reach Bukhara you have to change at Navoi or take the new, weekly direct sleeper service (*Bukhara–Urgench Wed; Urgench–Bukhara Thu*).

There are three trains a week in each direction between Tashkent and Urgench. Train No 56/58 (Tashkent–Urgench) departs at 19.30 from Thursday–Tuesday, reaches Samarkand just after midnight, then continues to Urgench, arriving the following afternoon at 13.05. For those of you whose maths is a little rusty, that is 17½ hours. Going the other way, the same number trains depart from Urgench at 15.20 (again there is no service on Wed) reach Samarkand in the early hours of the morning, and finally pull into Tashkent at 10.25. A sleeper ticket starts from 105,122 som, and the cheapest seats onboard are 44,909 som.

Trains north to Nukus and Moscow go less frequently and need to be booked well in advance, as they are invariably oversubscribed. They pass through Turtkul, just east of Urgench. You can make a booking through a local travel agent, or on the Caravanistan website (*www.caravanistan.com*).

By air Given that it is 1,050km from Tashkent to Urgench, many visitors choose to fly, at least in one direction. Urgench's airport (*Al Khorezmi;* ✆ *780 3236;* e *urgench.airport@uzairways.com*) is northeast of the city centre. There are at least two daily flights to Tashkent (*1hr 35mins; US$105*), and occasional flights to Bukhara too, though some of these still route via Tashkent, taking 5 hours in total. It is also possible to fly direct to Moscow (*3hr 50mins; 4 flights a week with S7 or Uzbekistan Airways*) or St Petersburg (*4hr 40mins; 3 flights a week with Aeroflot or Uzbekistan Airways*).

Uzbekistan Airways has a ticketing office in the city centre (*28 Al Khorezmi;* ✆ *226 8860*).

GETTING AROUND Urgench is a relatively large city, but there are a limited number of places you'd want to go, and all of them can be reached by public transport. Minibuses No 3 and No 13 go from the airport and along Al Khorezmi (the main drag), while minibus No 19 links the bazaar and the train station.

You will need to hire a car and driver to reach the Khorezm fortresses, and a 4×4 is preferable for the more remote sites. The tour operators below all keep a list of reputable drivers. The cost will depend on the distance you travel; expect to pay between US$50–80 if you are travelling out from Urgench.

TOURIST INFORMATION AND TOUR OPERATORS Uzbektourism (*2A Al Beruni;* ✆ *226 2627;* e *info@uzbektourism.uz; www.uzbektourism.uz*) and Green Globus (*33 Al Khorezmi;* ✆ *770 5050*) can arrange guided tours of Khiva and the Khorezm forts, as well as making onward travel and hotel bookings. For airline tickets see above. Ayaz Kala Tour (*G Gulom, Buston;* ✆ *(61) 532 4361;* e *ayazkala_tour@mail.ru*) and Turtkul Travel (*Kirkkiz, Turtkul;* ✆ *(61) 221 0707*) are based outside Urgench but specialise in desert fortress tours.

WHERE TO STAY *Map, page 233*
Personally, we don't like staying in Urgench: the accommodation options are uninspiring and generally over-priced. If you can, it is far better to travel straight on to Khiva, where there are many nicer places to choose from.

⌂ Hotel Khorezm Palace (103 rooms)
2 Al Beruni; ✆ 224 9999; e khorezmpalace@mail.ru; www.khorezmpalace.uz. Urgench's most expensive accommodation option is a soulless place aimed at business travellers. It has all the facilities you'd expect, but customer service (& the concept of smiling) appears anathema to them. The travel desk & ATM machines (one each for Visa

& MasterCard customers) may be of some use to non-guests. **$$$$**

⌂ **Hotel Fayz** (37 rooms) 66/1 Al Khorezmi; ☎ 226 2226; e fayzhotel@mail.ru. Comfortable, mid-range hotel with its own restaurant & bar. Rooms are somewhat on the small side, especially if there are 2 of you, but it's clean. Wi-Fi & b/fast inc. **$$$**

⌂ **Hotel Urgench** 27 P Mahmud; ☎ 226 2022. Concrete Soviet block in need of rather more renovation than has so far taken place. Prices start at ridiculous levels but come down quickly if you hold your ground: aim for around US$40 for a twin. The beds are predictably narrow & lumpy. **$$**

⌂ **Komnata Otdikha** Train station, Al Khorezmi. The cheapest option in town is just about bearable if you use your own sleeping bag. Dorm beds only. **$**

✗ WHERE TO EAT AND DRINK *Map, page 233*

If you happen to find somewhere decent to eat in Urgench, please tell us about it. The options we've seen so far are uninspiring in the extreme.

Next to Hotel Urgench is Chaikhana Urgench, which has the usual shashlik and salads. King Burger Chicken, just across the intersection on the other side of Al Khorezmi, has fast food (mostly burgers and fried chicken, unsurprisingly). Look out for the authentic Burger King sign to find the rather less authentic premises.

ENTERTAINMENT If you happen to be stuck in Urgench overnight, for example while waiting for onward transport, your stay may coincide with a performance at the **Ogakhiy Music Theatre of Drama** (*32 Al Khorezmi*; ☎ *226 6264*), one of Uzbekistan's better regional theatres. You will need to pop in, or ask an Uzbek speaker to phone up, to find out what's on, and when.

OTHER PRACTICALITIES

Communications The main post office and telephone and telegraph office (⊕ *09.00–17.00 Mon–Fri*) are both at 1 Al Khorezmi. There are a couple of internet terminals in the same building, too.

Medical Khorezm's Regional Hospital Clinic is at 1 Babajanova (☎ *226 2110*).

Money There are ATMs for Visa and MasterCard holders at the Hotel Khorezm Palace (page 231), and the banks below will change money. The NBU will also arrange a cash advance on foreign debit cards, which is especially useful when the hotel's ATMs are out of order.

$ **Aloka Bank** 23 P Makhmud; ☎ 226 1610; ⊕ 09.00–18.00 Mon–Sat

$ **Hamkor Bank** 24 Mustakillik; ☎ 223 7396; ⊕ 09.00–16.00 Mon–Sat

$ **National Bank of Uzbekistan** 78A Bokhodirkhon; ☎ 226 9050; ⊕ 09.00–18.00 Mon–Fri, 09.00–16.00 Sat

Registration The OVIR is at 28 Al Khorezmi (☎ *227 1840*; ⊕ *09.00–13.00, 14.00–17.00 Mon–Fri*).

WHAT TO SEE AND DO The desert fortresses of ancient Khorezm lie mostly in Karakalpakstan. However, as the majority of visitors will access them from Urgench and Khiva rather than from Nukus, we have listed them here.

The Kyzylkum Desert was not always so dry: as recently as the early centuries AD this was fertile agricultural land, supporting the stable and centralised kingdom

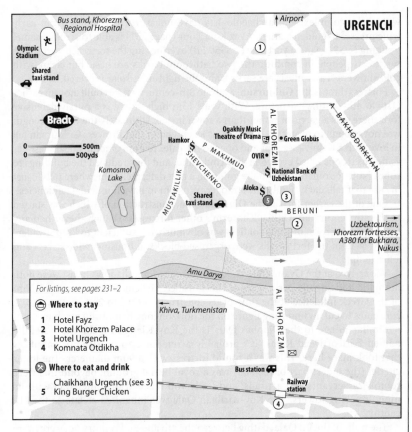

Map labels:

Bus stand, Khorezm Regional Hospital

Airport

URGENCH

Olympic Stadium

Shared taxi stand

N

Bradt

0 — 500m
0 — 500yds

Komosmol Lake

MUSTAKILLIK

SHEVCHENKO

P MAKHMUD

Hamkor

Ogakhiy Music Theatre of Drama

AL KHOREZMI

Green Globus

OVIR

National Bank of Uzbekistan

Aloka

5

3

BERUNI

2

Shared taxi stand

A BAKHODIRKHAN

Uzbektourism, Khorezm fortresses, A380 for Bukhara, Nukus

Amu Darya

Khiva, Turkmenistan

AL KHOREZMI

Bus station

Railway station

4

For listings, see pages 231–2

🏠 **Where to stay**
1 Hotel Fayz
2 Hotel Khorezm Palace
3 Hotel Urgench
4 Komnata Otdikha

✖ **Where to eat and drink**
Chaikhana Urgench (see 3)
5 King Burger Chicken

---

of Khorezm. The area's traditional name, Elliq Qala (the 50 fortresses), gives a stark indication of what lies beneath the desert sands, and UNESCO and local tour companies have worked closely to promote the itinerary they call 'The Golden Ring of Ancient Khorezm'. A detailed, illustrated guide to the main sites has been produced by UNESCO and can be downloaded free from the UNESCO website: search for 'UNESCO Golden Ring Khorezm'.

You will need your own transport to visit the forts as there is quite some distance between them. To explore them properly, and drive between, you will want to schedule not more than three into a day.

Eight major forts remain sufficiently intact to be of interest to the casual visitor. First on the alphabetical list is **Anka Qala**, a 5th-century fort that later became a 12th-century fortified caravanserai built around a courtyard with a well at its centre. The fort is built on a square with double adobe walls, a narrow corridor running between the two. The outer wall, the most important for defence, would originally have been 7–8m high.

Far more impressive, however, is the **Ayaz Qala**, a 'must-see' on every Kyzylkum Desert itinerary. The external walls, built upon a flat hilltop, have survived since at least the 4th century BC, and you can clearly see the scale of the site: the fort's footprint was a remarkable 182m by 152m, and even today sections of wall survive that are 10m high. The Ayaz Qala would once have been a very wealthy place with sophisticated inhabitants. At least ten major structures have been identified within the complex, and archaeologists have unearthed everything from early wine presses to golden statues. Ayaz Kala Tour (page 231) is able to arrange camel trekking (*US$10*) and a yurt stay (*US$50 FB*) overlooking the fort: each yurt sleeps two to six people in comfort. The two bathroom blocks are basic but clean, with cold showers. Tasty meals are served, and the lighting is solar powered.

Fortress three is **Big Guldursun**, a 7th- to 8th-century AD fort built atop an earlier (1st- to 4th-century) structure. With walls 15m high, this was a purely defensive fort: there was a garrison rather than a town inside. Ultimately the fort's strength was not enough to protect it, however, as legend has it that Princess Guldursun fell in love with a Kalmyk warrior and opened the gates to him. Once inside he cast her aside, his troops killed everyone they could find, and they reduced the buildings to ruins. Note to romantics: if you're going on a first date, pick somewhere public just in case that tall, dark, handsome stranger turns out to have homicidal tendencies.

One of the earlier forts is the **Djanbas Qala**, construction of which was started in the 4th century BC. Unlike Khorezm's other fortresses, Djanabs never had any towers; the garrison of 2,000 soldiers was obviously felt sufficient to keep invaders at bay. Within the fort's walls were organised blocks of housing, wide streets and a fire temple.

We arrived at the **Gyaur Qala** late in the day; the long shadows it cast were both dramatic and slightly eerie. One of the so-called Hellenic fortresses on account of the Greek influence at the time of its construction (3rd to 2nd century BC), it continues to cut an imposing figure on the horizon long before you reach it.

Similar in age to the Djanbas Qala is the **Koy-Kirilgan Qala**, the tastefully named Fort of Dead Rams. It's probably a reference to pre-Islamic sacrifices that took place here. This was a round fortress with a 90m diameter. The inner citadel (the oldest part of the site) was a royal burial ground; beyond this were rooms for servants and artisans; and lastly you reached the outer wall with its nine imposing towers. The Koy-Kirilgan Qala was inhabited as late as the 4th century AD.

The walls of the **Pil Qala,** dating between the 4th and 2nd century BC, were more than 6m thick and sloped to make it hard for invaders to attack. It was built by the Afrigids, rulers of Khorezm at the time, roughly on a square and was designed with double walls with a narrow space so that archers could stand between them shooting out at the advancing enemy. We've saved one of the best for last. The **Toprak Qala** covered a site 500m long and, at its peak in the 1st century BC, accommodated a population of 2,500 people. It was both a city fortress and an important religious centre, and the 1ha citadel at its heart was a royal residence: archaeologists have identified a throne room, a fire temple and an armoury. The three main halls were spectacularly decorated with murals of both Greek and Zoroastrian deities, as well as kings and soldiers. The wall paintings are now preserved in the Hermitage collection in St Petersburg.

There is a small, very basic **yurt camp ($$)** next to the car park. From here, it is a steep climb to the top of the site, from where you'll get excellent views across the plain.

KHIVA *Telephone code: 62*

It is rare to come across an entire city that is a museum. Though Bukhara is packed with remarkable sites it is still nonetheless a living, working city. Khiva, however, is more akin to a film set, the local population, rightly or wrongly, sidelined in order to preserve historic buildings and present a manicured scene to tourists.

Whatever you feel about such a policy, Khiva remains one of the greatest cities on the Silk Road: the Ichon Qala in particular is a labyrinth of madrassas and mosques, minarets and trading domes that, at least on the surface of it, look just as they would have done at the end of the 19th century before Soviet town planners, demolition crews and modernist architects got their hands on Uzbekistan. On a cold winter's evening, after the wedding parties have departed and the few tourists are enjoying their supper, you can be entirely alone with the ghosts of the past, wandering the narrow streets and soaking up the atmosphere. Which decade, indeed which century, you care to imagine yourself in is entirely up to you.

HISTORY In October 1997, Khiva celebrated its 2,500th birthday. Archaeological digs in the Ichon Qala during the 1980s and early '90s uncovered a wealth of material as much as 7m below the modern ground level, and the earliest finds from these excavations suggest that the town was first inhabited between the 6th and 5th centuries BC. Legend has it that the city was founded long before this, however, as Shem, son of Noah, is said to have first marked out the city's walls.

Khiva rose in importance and was fortified sometime after the 4th century BC as the Khorezmians attempted to fend off Achaemenid incursions from Iran. A double wall provided physical protection for the city and its inhabitants, and archers were stationed in turrets more than 20m high. The encroaching desert continually eroded these first walls, however, and by the early centuries AD a second wall and citadel had to be constructed. The new walls were between 7–9m thick. This incarnation of the city survived until AD709 when it was razed to rubble by the Arab governor Qutaiba ibn Muslim in his conquest of central Asia.

Khiva became part of the Samanid Empire and the city grew rapidly through the 9th and 10th centuries, becoming a regional economic and cultural hub. It is thought that in the 9th century the city's population may have been as high as 800,000. The city was sacked again by Genghis Khan in 1220–21 but thanks to its reputation for craftsmanship (in particular pottery and tile making), it was able to recover relatively swiftly. The walls of the current Ichon Qala were erected in the 14th century, and Khiva's population again became wealthy, exporting their ceramics and trading all manner of goods along the Silk Road.

In 1505, Khiva was conquered by Mahmoud Sultan on the orders of his brother, Shaybani Khan. When the latter was killed near Merv (now in Turkmenistan) five years later, however, the entire Khorezm state briefly broke away from Shaybanid rule. Military expansionism on both sides during the early 16th century saw numerous battles between the rulers of Khiva and their rivals in Bukhara, even more so after Khiva replaced Gurganj as the capital of Khorezm towards the century's end. Under the rule of Abul Gazi Bahadurhan (1643–64), Khiva became a major cultural centre. The entire population of Gurjanj was forcefully moved to the city, and construction boomed. The rulers funded not only religious buildings but also bathhouses, civic buildings and irrigation canals.

In 1717, Tsar Peter of Russia had sent a 4,000 strong force to Khiva to investigate rumours of Khorezmian gold and a maritime route to India. After an initial warm welcome, they were slaughtered. Prince Bekovich, who led the expedition, was flayed alive in punishment. At the time the Russians could do little to avenge this slight, but they did not forget the insult; in the 19th century they would return with vengeance, and this time they would stay.

Khorezm Province KHIVA 9

235

Two decades later a second force, that of the Iranian Nadir Shah, met with greater success. As he advanced on central Asia in 1740, Khiva and Bukhara initially joined forces in resistance, but Bukhara's rulers then switched sides. Khiva was yet again conquered. As if this wasn't bad enough, plagues and famines followed.

The restoration of Khiva began in the late 18th century. Under the rule of Muhammad Amina-inak (r1752–90), the various tribal factions in the area were united, and each community given a voice in the running of the city. A reformed tax system was introduced, as was a customs service, diplomatic relations with Russia and other neighbouring powers were strengthened, and trade thrived. The wealth of this era is reflected in its architecture: a significant number of the buildings you see within the Ichon Qala today date from the late 18th and early 19th centuries when Muhammad Amina-inak and his descendants ruled.

For centuries Khiva had been famed for its slave market (see box, below), and though the plundering of caravans and abduction of traders may have been lucrative, it eventually brought the Khivans into direct conflict with tsarist Russia. In the winter of 1839 General Perovsky led 5,000 troops across the desert in a bid to rescue 3,000 Russian slaves said to be held within the city's walls. The snows came early, devastating Perovsky's forces and his camel train, and the Russians were forced to admit defeat. It would be a further 35 years before the Russians would eventually enter Khiva and halt the trade of slaves.

To a greater or lesser extent, the Russians were in Khiva to stay. A series of rebellions weakened the khanate and, as it entered the 20th century, Khorezm was a shadow of its former self. Isfandiyar Khan was assassinated in 1918; his successor, Abdullah Khan, abdicated two years later. The Khorezm People's

THE SLAVE TRADE

In the 18th and 19th centuries, the names of Khiva and Bukhara would have simultaneously struck both fear and wonder into the hearts of Silk Road traders. Whilst the cities were deposits of almost unimaginable wealth, and every conceivable good was traded within their bazaars, one of the most lucrative trades was in slaves, and no passing caravan was safe from the slavers' raids. The Russians believed they'd lost in the region of 5,000 nationals into slavery, and though the Great Game was in full flow, even British officers interceded with the khans in a bid to have Russian citizens released.

The Khivan slave market was an interesting example of the free market economy at work. Slaves were traded exactly as if they were livestock, with the finest physical specimens commanding the highest prices. A strong, Russian male would cost you the equivalent of four camels, or two good horses. They were more expensive than either women or other races. When slaves were in ready supply (for example after a battle or particularly successful raid), prices fell. At other times you'd be able to haggle to get a substantial discount. Slaves with deformities, or who had been branded in punishment for a previous escape bid, were already marked down in price.

Slavery was officially outlawed in Bukhara in 1863 and in Khiva shortly afterwards. In reality it persisted, though less openly than before, with the elite maintaining extensive harems and everyone who could afford to do so keeping household staff.

Republic was declared in 1920 and, despite a valiant struggle to reclaim Khiva by 15,000 Basmachis, Khorezm was promoted to a Soviet Republic in 1922 and incorporated into the Uzbek SSR in 1924.

Khiva was proclaimed an open-air museum by the government in 1967 and the Ichon Qala was recognised by UNESCO as a World Heritage Site in December 1990.

GETTING THERE AND AROUND Urgench is the regional transport hub, and so wherever in Uzbekistan you are coming from, you will unfortunately have to route through there (pages 229–34 for details).

From Urgench to Khiva it is just 35km, and by car it takes just 30–40 minutes. You will pay around US$12 for a taxi, and US$2 for a seat in a shared taxi or minivan. You can pick up shared taxis from Al Beruni in Urgench, and they drop you at North Gate in Khiva's Old Town. A new bridge is under construction on the outskirts of Urgench, necessitating a temporary diversion, though roadwork should be complete within the lifespan of this edition

Once in Khiva, you'll explore the Ichon Qala on foot as much of it is pedestrianised and the alleys are too narrow for a car. Much of the Dishon Qala can also be seen on foot, though it is also possible to pick up minibuses (*500 som*) from the bazaar if you want to travel a little further. Local taxis are available to hire; there is no set fare, but you should be able to negotiate a rate of around 3,000 som per hour within the city limits. Longer distances will depend on the mileage.

TOURIST INFORMATION AND TOUR OPERATORS As well as those listed, there is a second information centre inside the Allah Kuli Khan Madrassa, and a helpful travel desk at the Orient Star Hotel.

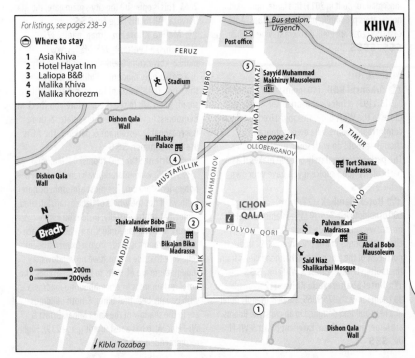

For listings, see pages 238–9

🏠 **Where to stay**
1 Asia Khiva
2 Hotel Hayat Inn
3 Laliopa B&B
4 Malika Khiva
5 Malika Khorezm

KHIVA
Overview

Khorezm Province   KHIVA

9

237

Bek Tour 14 R Majidiy; ☎375 2455; e info@bektour.uz; www.bektour.uz. Professionally run travel agency with its head office in Khiva. In addition to the usual accommodation booking & escorted tours, Bek Tour can also arrange helicopter transfer to the Aral Sea & invitations to attend an Uzbek wedding.

🖪 **Khiva Information Centre** 41 A Boltaev; ☎375 7795; e info@khivamuseum.uz; www.khivamuseum.uz; ⏰ 09.00–18.00 daily. Khiva's main tourist information centre is inside the Ichon Qala, close to the West Gate. It has information about the main sites, sells tickets for dance performances & film showings, & can arrange bilingual guides (*US$30/day*) & tours to the Khorezm fortresses. There are also a couple of internet terminals here.

Zafarbek Travel 28 Tashpulatov; ☎375 8485. Basic escorted tours, guides & reservations.

🏠 **WHERE TO STAY** *Map, page 241, unless otherwise stated*
Almost all of Khiva's hotels are inside the Ichon Qala, putting you right at the heart of the action. There's little reason to stay anywhere else.

Top end
🏠 **Asia Khiva** [map, page 237] (127 rooms) K Yaqubov; ☎375 7683; e asiakhiva@marcopolo.uz; www.asiahotels.uz/en. Modern, functional hotel mostly frequented by tour groups & situated just outside the Ichon Qala's walls. All rooms have AC, there is a large restaurant & a superb outdoor pool to cool down in at the end of a long, hot day. Free Wi-Fi in the lobby. **$$$–$$$$**

🏠 **Hotel Hayat Inn** [map, page 237] (38 rooms) 71 Q Yaqubov; ☎375 7572; e hayat-inn@mail.ru. Built in 2011, this large, upmarket hotel caters predominantly to tour groups. Apts cost US$120 & are ideal if you're staying a while. **$$$–$$$$**

Mid range
🏠 **Arkanchi B&B** (40 rooms) 10 P Mahmud; ☎513 1193; e info@sabir-arkanchi-hotels.uz. Close to the West Gate, this mid-sized hotel has comfortable rooms & its own restaurant, though it could do with some updating. The parking immediately outside makes it a particularly good choice if you have your own vehicle. **$$$**

🏠 **Hotel Islambek** (21 rooms) 60 Toshpulotov; ☎375 3023; e islambekhotel@nm.ru; www.islambekhotel.uz. One of the cheapest options in this price bracket, Islambek is northeast of the Ichon Qala & has good views from the rooftop terrace. B/fast & Wi-Fi inc. **$$$**

🏠 **Hotel Shaherezada Khiva** (12 rooms) 35 Islom Khoja; ☎375 9565. Small & friendly hotel in a new building designed in an old style. Rooms are large, quiet & clean. Excellent b/fast & Wi-Fi inc. **$$$**

🏠 **Malika Kheivak** [map, page 237] (22 rooms) 11 Islom Khoja; ☎375 7610; www.malika-khiva.com. The Malika Hotel Group now has 3 properties in Khiva. Slap bang in the middle of the Ichon Qala, the Malika Kheivak's location is unparalleled. Rooms are immaculately clean & comfortable, but the hotel has a slightly odd atmosphere; it feels a little sterile & empty even when it's not. B/fast & Wi-Fi inc. Also has a decent restaurant (page 239). **$$$**

🏠 **Malika Khiva** (34 rooms) 19A P Kori; ☎375 2665. This is opposite the city's main gate, the Ata Darvoza . All rooms have AC. **$$$**

🏠 **Malika Khorezm** [map, page 237] (32 rooms) 5 Centre; ☎375 5451; www.malika-khiva.com. Malika's second property is in a rather ugly modern building just outside the Ichon Qala. Some of the rooms are a little small, so do ask to see them before you check in. Bedrooms, however, are immaculate, & there is a reasonable restaurant & parking. The AC is useful in summer. **$$$**

✳ 🏠 **Orient Star** (61 rooms) 1 P Mahmud; ☎375 4945; e orientstarkhiva@rambler.ru; www.hotelorientstar.com. The most atmospheric hotel in Khiva, if not the whole of Uzbekistan. Situated, somewhat controversially, inside the 19th-century Muhammad Amin Khan Madrassa, each of its simple rooms is made from a former student's cell. Note that the rooms have no windows, though there are AC units to keep them cool. The hotel restaurant is in a neighbouring madrassa with equally beautiful tiling, & both buildings are in the shadow of the Kalta Minar. B/fast & Wi-Fi inc. Also has a restaurant (page 239). Highly recommended. **$$$**

Budget

🏠 **Meros B&B** (6 rooms) 57 A Boltaev; ☎ 375 7642; e meroskhiva@gmail.com; www.meroskhiva.com. Manager Jaloladdin Matkarimov & his team create a hospitable atmosphere in their beautifully decorated home alongside the city walls. The rooftop terrace offers unobstructed views of the Ichon Qala, & simple, cheap meals are available on request. **$$**

🏠 **Mirzaboshi B&B** 24 Toshpulatov; ☎ 375 2753; e mirzaboshi@inbox.ru. Small, central B&B in the pedestrianised section of the Ichon Qala: bear this in mind if you're carrying a lot of luggage. This family-run place is exceptionally friendly, & the dinners are pretty good, too. Non-guests can book in for dinner (*US$7*). **$$**

🏠 **Laliopa B&B** [map, page 237] (5 rooms) 11A Rahmonov; ☎ 375 4449; e laliopa@mail.ru; www.laliopa.com. Simple rooms in a private house overlooking the Ichon Qala's walls. Dinners (**$$**) are provided on request. Dorm beds US$8. **$–$$**

Shoestring

🏠 **Otabek Guesthouse** (3 rooms) 68 Islam Khoja; ☎ 375 3968. More of a homestay than a guesthouse, Otabek is understandably popular with backpackers & the home cooking is delicious: if you have a choice, request the pumpkin *manti*. Dorm beds only. **$**

✖ **WHERE TO EAT AND DRINK** *Map, page 241, unless otherwise stated*

If anyone opens a really good restaurant in Khiva that stays open out of season, we alone will bring them enough custom to comfortably stay in business. For a city that attracts so many tourists, there are frustratingly few good places to eat. In the winter, that number virtually dwindles to zero.

If you are staying in a hotel or bed and breakfast that can provide evening meals, your best bet will be to eat there. Even if dinner is not advertised, it's still worth putting in a polite request as most places are more than happy to oblige. The home cooking in the bed and breakfasts tends to be particularly good, and you'll get to sit down and chat with the family or other guests. When the electricity is off, prepare to have something cooked solely on the hob.

The following restaurants and cafés are viable alternatives if you don't have the choice of home cooking.

✖ **Kheivak Restaurant** [map, page 237] Malika Kheivak; ◷ high season 18.00–22.00 daily. The Malika Kheivak (page 238) has a small, rather dark restaurant inside & an infinitely preferable patio with a few shaded tables. Uzbek & European dishes, including pizza, which makes a nice change if you've been travelling in Uzbekistan a while. Book at least 2 hours ahead. **$$$**

✖ **Khorezm Art Restaurant** Allah Kuli Khan Madrassa; ☎ 375 7918; ◷ 11.00–23.00 daily. The outdoor patio here has one of the best locations in Khiva, though if it's too cold to stay outside there is an indoor section to the restaurant as well. The Uzbek dishes are tasty enough, if a little on the costly side, but then what you're really paying for is the view. **$$$**

✖ **Matinyaz Divanbegi** Polvon Qori; ◷ 18.00–22.00 daily. Behind the Kalta Minar, this is the restaurant of the Orient Star Hotel (page 238). A converted madrassa (& a separate building to the hotel), it has an impressive exterior & the interior is not bad either. The food can be a little bland. **$$$**

✖ **Yasavul Boshi** Yasavul Boshi Madrassa; ◷ 11.00–21.00 daily. Large restaurant within the renovated madrassa of the same name. You eat at long refectory tables, & the menu includes some pretty good fresh salads, tasty soups & crêpes stuffed with minced mutton. **$$$**

✖ **Bir Gumbaz** P Mahmud; ◷ all year 09.00–18.00 daily. Situated behind the information centre, this stocky, domed structure is home to a pleasant tea house with Wi-Fi. It is possible to get a proper coffee (quite a novelty in Uzbekistan) & also basic snacks. **$$**

✖ **Teahouse Farrukh** Opposite Juma Mosque; ◷ 11.00–18.00 daily. Shady courtyard chaikhana with low tables. Serves Turkish coffee (*7,000 som*), tea & Uzbek snacks. **$$**

SHOPPING Unsurprisingly, there are souvenir shops and stalls everywhere in Khiva, the majority of them selling a fairly similar selection of wooden Qu'ran stands, postcards and hats.

The **Khiva Silk Carpet Workshop** (*P Mahmud; www.khiva.info/khivasilk;* ① *09.00–18.00 Mon–Fri*) is the star shopping attraction, as its story is told in Chris Alexander's excellent book *Carpet Ride to Khiva*. An English-speaking guide is available in high season to talk you through the processes of dyeing and weaving. On the same street you'll also find the **Khiva Suzani Workshop** (① *09.00–18.00 Mon–Fri*), another NGO-backed initiative that produces high-quality silks and other textiles. The *suzani* workshop may be shut in September if the women working there are required to go out and pick cotton.

The bazaar in the Dishon Qala is lively and well stocked. Prices here are significantly cheaper than for goods sold within the Ichon Qala.

OTHER PRACTICALITIES

Communications Khiva has embraced the internet wholeheartedly, and there is no shortage of Wi-Fi spots in hotels and cafés. If you need a computer as well as an internet connection, the information centre (page 238) has several.

Khiva's main post office is north of the North Gate at 23 A Timur (① *09.00–17.00 Mon–Fri*).

Money Khiva no longer has an ATM that accepts foreign cards, and the closest bank offering cash advance for Visa cardholders is the NBU in Urgench (page 232). As the hotels don't take card payments either, you will therefore need to arrive in Khiva with sufficient cash for your stay. The banks below are able to change dollars for Uzbek som, as are some of the larger hotels.

$ **Agro Bank** Dashyk; ✆770 5718; ① 09.00–
17.00 Mon–Fri

$ **National Bank of Uzbekistan** 11 N Kubro;
✆ 375 7081; ① 09.00–18.00 Mon–Fri, 09.00–
16.00 Sat

$ **Xalq Bank** 12 Feruz; ✆375 4288; ① 09.00–
17.00 Mon–Fri

WHAT TO SEE AND DO Khiva's tourist sites are divided between the Ichon Qala (the medieval walled citadel) and the Dishon Qala (the mostly 19th- and early 20th-century outer walled city). Visitors tend to spend most of their time in the former (the so-called 'Museum City'), but the Dishon Qala is not without its own considerable charms.

It is free to wander around both the Ichon Qala and the Dishon Qala and to enter some of the buildings. A single entrance ticket (*US$12*) covers the various small museums, entrance to the mosques, etc, and is available from the booth (① *09.00–18.00 daily*) at the Ata Darvoza (West Gate). One camera permit (*8,000 som*) allows you to take photographs inside all the monuments and is available from the same desk, but there is no need to get a permit if you only want to photograph the exteriors of the buildings. Where additional charges are levied (for example at the Islam Khoja Madrassa), they are mentioned in the text below.

Ichon Qala The heart of the museum, the Ichon Qala seems like a time warp. Listed as a UNESCO World Heritage Site since 1990, it is devoid of cars in its central areas, and with most of the modern infrastructure hidden from view, if you wake up and get out early, or take a walk late in the evening once the crowds

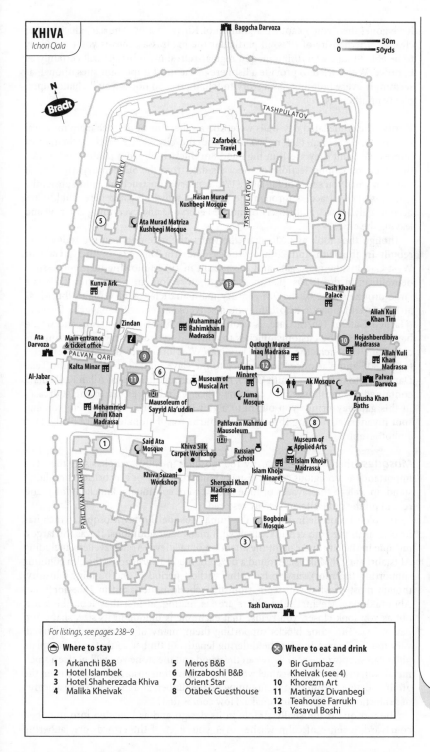

KHIVA
Ichon Qala

Baggcha Darvoza

0 ——— 50m
0 ——— 50yds

N
Bradt

TASHPULATOV

SOLTAYEV

TASHPULATOV

Zafarbek
Travel

Hasan Murad
Kushbegi Mosque

⑤ Ata Murad Matriza
Kushbegi Mosque

②

⑬

Kunya Ark

Tash Khauli
Palace

Allah Kuli
Khan Tim

Zindan

Muhammad
Rahimkhan II
Madrassa

Hojashberdibiya
⑩ Madrassa

Ata
Darvoza

Main entrance
& ticket office

PALVAN QARI

⑨

Qutlugh Murad
Inaq Madrassa

⑫

Allah Kuli
Khan
Madrassa

Kalta Minar

Al-Jabar

⑪

⑥

Museum of
Musical Art

Juma
Minaret

Juma
Mosque

④

Ak Mosque

Palvan
Darvoza

Anusha Khan
Baths

⑦

Mohammed
Amin Khan
Madrassa

Mausoleum of
Sayyid Ala'uddin

Pahlavan Mahmud
Mausoleum

⑧

Museum of
Applied Arts

PAHLAVAN MAHMUD

①

Said Ata
Mosque

Khiva Silk
Carpet Workshop

Russian
School

Islam Khoja
Madrassa

Khiva Suzani
Workshop

Shergazi Khan
Madrassa

Islam Khoja
Minaret

③

Bogbonli
Mosque

Tash Darvoza

For listings, see pages 238–9

🛏 **Where to stay**
1 Arkanchi B&B
2 Hotel Islambek
3 Hotel Shaherezada Khiva
4 Malika Kheivak
5 Meros B&B
6 Mirzaboshi B&B
7 Orient Star
8 Otabek Guesthouse

🍴 **Where to eat and drink**
9   Bir Gumbaz
    Kheivak (see 4)
10 Khorezm Art
11 Matinyaz Divanbegi
12 Teahouse Farrukh
13 Yasavul Boshi

have gone, then you'll capture a glimpse of Khiva in a bygone age, albeit rather cleaner. The density of sites, in particular the madrassas, means you're unlikely to be able to take everything in, and regular refreshment breaks will certainly be in order. We've tried to provide a list here of the most important sites, though as seemingly every building has a story to tell, there's no doubt you'll chance upon plenty of others as well.

Walls The crenellated city walls were Khiva's first line of defence from medieval raiders. Some 2.2km (1.4 miles) surround the city centre, and at their most impressive point they are 10m high and 8m thick. Built from adobe mud bricks, the oldest remaining sections of the walls date from the 5th century AD, though much of what you see is of far later (17th century) construction. Four substantial gateways allowed access through the walls; the sentries posted here would have been heavily armed, and closely monitored everyone and everything entering and leaving the city.

Though they look as historic as the walls, the gateways you see today were rebuilt in the 19th and 20th centuries. The Ata Darvoza (Father's Gate or West Gate) is the main gate and was rebuilt in 1975 following its predecessor's demolition in the 1920s. Just to its right before you enter the Ichon Qala is a large bronze statue of the 9th-century mathematician Muh.ammad ibn Mūsā al-Khwārizmī, born in Khorezm, who discovered algebra. The Baggcha Darvoza (Garden Gate or North Gate) is another 19th-century construction and would have been used by customs officials to collect duty from caravans entering the city from Urgench; the Palvan Darvoza (Warriors' Gate or East Gate) dates from 1806 and was once the entrance to the slave market; and finally the Tash Darvoza (Stone Gate or South Gate), rebuilt during the reign of Allah Kuli Khan, contained a guardhouse and customs office. Climbing either of the staircases in this gateway brings you out onto a viewing platform, from where you can spot invaders advancing through the suburbs (or, fortunately more likely, take a photograph).

Mosques There were once nearly 100 mosques in Khiva, emphasising the city's importance as a religious centre. Usually built from mud or clay bricks, they didn't stand up well to the ravages of time and so were continually knocked down and rebuilt on the same site, or heavily restored.

The oldest mosque in Khiva is the **Juma Mosque** (Friday Mosque), which has its origins in the 10th century, albeit with many later additions. It was the largest mosque in the city and caught the attention of medieval Arab travellers, including Al Istahri and Al Makdisi. Around a dozen of the 213 *karagacha* (the elm columns supporting the roof) survive from this earliest period of the building's history, though most of what you see is from the rebuild undertaken in 1788 for Khan Abdurakhman Mekhtar. The pillars are fascinating: at first they look the same, but as you look closer, you realise that each one is unique in its size, shape and patterning. The stone blocks supporting them, many of which are also carved, vary too, compensating for the differing lengths of timber so that each complete pillar can support the roof. Between the wood and the stone you will notice a small metal cuff, inside which is camel wool. This innovation absorbs humidity from the ground, deters termites from chomping on the timber, and may even give a degree of protection during an earthquake. How cool is that?

The mosque is unusually simple in its design and as you step into the open courtyard, a sense of calm washes over you, even if the crowds are jabbering and hustling outside. The hand-carved pillars and doors and the marble plaque on the south wall detailing the mosque's land holdings are the main attractions, though the mosque also provides access should you wish to climb the Juma Minaret (page 245).

The small, domed **Said Ata Mosque** was built for Yar Muhammad Divan in the 18th century. There is nothing really to see inside.

Restored in 1997, the **Hasan Murad Kushbegi Mosque** dates from 1800 and was the joint endeavour of Kushbegi and his cousin, Shah Niyaz. Kushbegi was the chief of police in Khiva and amassed significant wealth, hence his ability to endow the mosque. The mosque is divided into two parts, an open area for use in summer, and a closed section for winter, and there is a small, whitewashed minaret in the northeastern corner.

The **Bogbonli Mosque** (1809) seems to serve as an unofficial monument to the artisans of Khiva. Funded by two horticulturalist brothers, the mosque is rectangular in shape and is decorated with domes and carved pillars. A stone plaque east of the entrance portico remembers Pakhlavan Quli, the mosque's architect, and engraved on the doors is the name of the woodcarver, Ruz Muhammad.

Perhaps the most beautiful of Khiva's mosques is the **Ata Murad Matriza Kushbegi Mosque**. Built in 1800 and again in the 1830s, its graceful pillars are reminiscent of chopsticks. When a breeze blows through the building you realise how well it is designed for hot weather.

The **Ak Mosque** (White Mosque) was founded in 1657 but the current building dates from 1838–42. The domed hall is surrounded on three sides by an open terrace, and inscriptions name the artisans responsible for the elegant columns: Nur Muhammad, Kalandar and the sons of Adin Kalandar and Sayyid Muhammad. Stop here to admire the finely carved doors and also the diminutive minaret.

Madrassas At the start of the 20th century there were 65 madrassas in Khiva, 54 of them within the city walls. The city was a hotbed for religious education and religious debate, and its wealthier residents bid to outdo each other by building larger, richer and more elaborate madrassas. A selection of the most interesting examples is mentioned here, though there are plenty more you'll find whilst wandering through the streets.

The oldest madrassa in Khiva is the **Hojashberdibiya Madrassa**, parts of which date from 1688. A major rebuild for Allah Kuli Khan in 1834 divided the site in two and the new layout was said to resemble a saddlebag: it was consequently nicknamed *hurjun*, the saddlebag, and this name is still occasionally used today.

The imposing **Shergazi Khan Madrassa** was built by 5,000 Persian slaves captured by Shergazi Khan on a raid at Meshed in 1718. The slaves were promised their freedom once the madrassa was complete, but fearing (probably quite rightly) that he would renege on the deal, they took out their anger on the project manager and murdered him inside the unfinished madrassa in 1720. An inscription over the madrassa's door remembers what purportedly were his final words: 'I accept death at the hands of slaves'. The madrassa's most famous student was the Turkmen poet Makhtum Kuli.

Qutlugh Murad Inaq, an uncle of Allah Kuli Khan, had the madrassa bearing his name constructed between 1804 and 1812 and hoped to be buried beneath its floors. When he died (he was murdered by a rival) outside the city walls, it was thought to be inauspicious to bring the body through one of the gateways, and his family sat scratching their heads. Thinking outside the box, someone suggested the drastic step of demolishing a section of the eastern wall so that the madrassa straddled both the Ichon Qala and the Dishon Qala. The deed was done, and Qutlugh was buried beneath his madrassa's entrance way.

Further demolition was required to accommodate the **Allah Kuli Khan Madrassa** in 1834. Space was at a premium inside the citadel, so the external wall had to be removed to enable the city to expand. Some 99 student cells were constructed (this was an auspicious number), and the building also housed the municipal library, acquisitions for which were funded by profits from the Allah Kuli Khan Tim (page 248). The façade is richly decorated with dark blue, light blue and white majolica tiles.

The largest madrassa in Khiva is the two-storey **Mohammad Amin Khan Madrassa** (1851–53), which now houses the Orient Star Hotel (page 238). Some 250 students once studied here and it was considered a luxurious place to live: student cells had two rooms rather than the usual one, and they looked outward at the world rather than in to the courtyard. The High Muslim Court once had its registry office here, and held sessions in the central courtyard.

Mohammad Amin Khan was one of Khiva's most illustrious rulers, a strong leader who built effective alliances with neighbouring tribes but was also not above beating them bloodily into submission. He commissioned a number of buildings in Khiva including both this madrassa and the Kalta Minar (page 245), but his life and the construction of the minaret were simultaneously cut short in a rather grisly fashion when he was beheaded by a Turkmen horseman. If you wish to climb the Kalta Minar, access is from the northeast corner of this madrassa.

The most fabulous tile work is to be found on the **Muhammad Rakhimkhan II Madrassa**, built in 1871 and restored in 1992, the 150th anniversary of its benefactor's birth. The blue and white majolica is set off by terracotta, and the resultant façade is sumptuous, particularly when viewed in the early evening. Inside you'll find a museum that explores the history of the Khivan Khanate, replete with flags, photographs, armour and robes. In summertime, performances of dance and circus acts occasionally take place in the courtyard in the evenings.

Muhammad Rakhimkhan was himself an intriguing character: he was a fine poet and printed his work on his own printing press under the pseudonym Feruz; he admired Russian culture, smoked cigars and dressed his harem in corsets and crinolines; and when pressure from Russia mounted and he had to cede control to the tsar, he willingly gave up power and joined the army as a major general. He was a man whose rule straddled two markedly different eras and, as the photographs on display in the madrassa's right-hand mosque show, Muhammad Rakhimkhan did a remarkably good job of reconciling them.

The striking turquoise **Islam Khoja Madrassa** (*US$2*) is a surprisingly late construction: it was completed only in 1908. Its founder, Islam Khoja, was grand vizier to the khan and an active educationalist. He introduced several educational reforms, endowed schools and hospitals, and his *pièce de résistance* is this building. Sadly the completion of the project is tied up in tragedy: Islam Khoja was assassinated in 1913 and the madrassa's architect was buried alive by Emir Isfandiyar Khan as a potential witness to the murder.

The 42 rooms of the madrassa now house the Museum of Applied Arts (⏱ *09.00–18.00 daily; US$1.50*). Though the selection of artefacts is not of such high quality as in similar museums in Tashkent and Bukhara, there are still a couple of interesting examples of royal costume, metalwork, leather goods, tiles and carved marble. You won't need long to walk round.

Madrassas are to Khiva as university colleges are to Oxford or Cambridge. As with the colleges, they were higher education institutions endowed by wealthy benefactors where teachers and students lived and worked together.

Endowing a madrassa was an expensive business. In addition to the construction costs for the buildings, benefactors were expected to donate enough land or property to support the students and teachers and to pay for the building's upkeep. The upside for the donor was that as the madrassa bore his name he would have a lasting legacy in the eyes of Khiva's population and, it was hoped, be looked upon favourably when he finally had to account for his good deeds before God.

The curriculum in the madrassas included both secular and religious subjects. Arabic grammar, sharia, and Arabic and Persian literature were taught to the youngest students, who could enter the madrassa at the age of 15; older students also studied logic and law. Classes took place four days a week throughout the year, and students were expected to pass an exam before taking their degree and being given an appropriate job by the khan.

The buildings themselves were divided into public and private areas. Public rooms included the mosque, an audience hall and teaching rooms, and to the rear of the madrassa were typically the students' *hujras* or cells where they slept. In addition to the students and their teachers, the madrassa's community also included an imam, a muezzin to call the residents to prayer, a *mutavalli* (similar to a bursar), cleaners, barbers and water carriers.

Minarets Fourteen minarets have survived in the centre of Khiva. They were constructed so that the muezzin might climb the stairs to call the faithful to prayer five times each day, his voice carrying on the breeze across the city.

The oldest minaret, the **Juma Minaret**, dates from the 10th to the 13th centuries and has distinctive turquoise stripes around its otherwise sand-coloured cylinder. If you have a head for heights (or want a bird's-eye view of the city), you can climb the 81 steps to the top (*US$2*). You can see a lot from 33m up!

Every postcard of Khiva seems to be illustrated with a photo of the **Kalta Minar.** This eye-catching (but rather stumpy) green and turquoise landmark was intended to be the tallest minaret in central Asia: its patron, Muhammad Amin Khan, planned for it to be at least 70m tall, allegedly so that you could see Bukhara from the top. Sadly it was not to be. Muhammad was decapitated by a rogue horseman in 1855 before the minaret was complete and the architect responsible for the project fled.

Rather more graceful looking is the slim **Islam Khoja Minaret** (1910), which adjoins the Islam Khoja Madrassa (page 244). Almost 60m tall, it is just 2m shorter than the Kalyon Minar in Bukhara, but it looks taller due to the tapered shape and the varying widths of the yellow and blue-green stripes. It is possible to climb the 120 steps to the top, where you are following in the footsteps of the city's watchmen. It is said that the minaret was used as a radio tower to summon air support during the 1924 assault on Khiva, though sadly this is probably an urban myth.

Mausoleums The burial places of Sufi holy men were not simply tombs but also pilgrimage places. As pilgrims gave donations as well as prayers, it was possible to build elaborate mausoleums, sometimes centuries after the holy man's death, and so to not only immortalise his memory but also ensure a constant stream of pilgrims (and their money) in the future. Despite the best efforts of the Soviet state to wipe out such practices completely, pilgrims do still occasionally come to the mausoleums to pray, and so you should act in a respectful manner and remove your shoes before entering the burial chambers.

The oldest surviving building in Khiva is the **Mausoleum of Sayyid Ala'uddin**. The earliest part of the mausoleum, the domed burial vault, was built in 1303 and contains a stunning blue and green majolica tile-covered casket. It is thought that the tiles were made in Konya-Urgench (page 229) prior to the city's relocation. Ala'uddin was a holy man from the Naqshbandi order of Sufis (Islamic mystics).

Originally similar in size and style, the **Pahlavan Mahmud Mausoleum** (also known as Palvan Pir) marks the final resting place of Pahlavan Mahmud, a local wrestler, poet and furrier who unexpectedly became a revered saint. The complex was expanded substantially in the 17th and 18th centuries to include a summer mosque, cemetery, reading rooms, kitchen and a decorative portico, and there are 19th-century additions too. A number of significant Khivan figures are buried here including Abdul Gazi Khan (1663), Muhammad Rahim Khan I (1825) and the mother and son of the assassinated Isfandiyar.

You enter the complex through an 18th-century portal that opens out onto a pleasant courtyard framed by a khanagha and *hujras*, the summer mosque and well. Each surface is exquisitely decorated in every imaginable shade of blue, blue-green and turquoise, and a vast blue dome, restored in 1993 after it was brought down by unexpectedly heavy snowfall, looms above it all. Pahlavan Mahmud is buried behind a screen inlaid with ivory, local folk motifs decorating his eternal chamber.

Four other mausoleums, those of the emirs Abdul Gazi Khan, Alla Kuli Khan, Anusha Khan and Mohammad Rahimkhan II are also to be found in the same complex and are worth visiting.

Palaces Khiva's rulers and merchants may have spent vast sums endowing mosques and madrassas, but they also built luxurious, lavishly decorated homes in which they could entertain guests and enjoy themselves. Palaces (and, indeed, smaller houses) were divided into public areas for feasting, hosting guests and doing business, and private, residential areas where the family lived and the harem was kept out of view.

Kunya Ark This fortified palace was built in 1686 by Arangan Khan, son of Anusha Khan. It was a town within a town, with its own defensive walls, mosques and offices, factories and stables, arsenal and mint as well as residential areas. A single gateway in the eastern wall gave access to the complex, which was guarded with copper cannons.

Sadly few of the Ark's original structures remain: when the khans moved into the Tash Khauli (page 247), their former home fell into disrepair, and many of the buildings you see date just from the 19th century. An attractive courtyard is surrounded by the winter and summer mosques, complete with blue and white floral tiles laid out to resemble creeping ivy, and the royal mint, built for Muhammad Rakhimkhan II. The mint holds a collection of coins, medals and bank notes, mostly from the 20th century, and a diorama of a blacksmith's shop.

It's also possible to visit the somewhat gloomy Kurinish Khana (throne room) built by Iltuzar Khan in 1804 to replace the earlier throne room destroyed during the Persian invasion. This was the public audience hall, and the khan's throne, made from wood covered with thin sheets of engraved silver, would have stood beneath the sumptuous painted ceiling. Sadly the throne was taken as booty by the Russian army and is now in the Armoury at the Hermitage Museum in St Petersburg: the one you see if a copy. The emir received his most important visitors here, including the Russian Captain Muraviev, or alternatively inside a yurt erected specially for nomadic guests on the round platform in the middle of the courtyard. The smaller rooms around the throne room would have housed the treasury and valuable manuscripts, and also have given the khan a quiet place to retreat to when required.

Elsewhere in the palace you can visit the Ak Sheikh Bobo Bastion, the Ark's fortified heart, which is the oldest place in Khiva; the foundations here are contemporaneous with the Toprak Fortress in Khorezm. Later in its history the bastion was used as a hermitage, a watchtower and an arsenal.

If you want to climb up onto the walls and ascend the minaret for views across Khiva and thence to the desert (best visible late in the day when the light is not so bright), it is possible to do so. There is a separate charge for this of 4,000 som, payable as you go up.

Tash Khauli Palace This newer palace was commissioned by Allah Kuli Khan in 1830. Construction of the 160-plus rooms took eight years and was undertaken by more than 1,000 slaves; the project's first architect was impaled for daring to suggest (correctly, so it later turned out) that the project may not be completed on time.

The oldest part of the palace is the harem, built around a courtyard. On the southern side of the courtyard are four open areas, one for each wife, and the more elaborate area on the eastern side was the summer living area of the khan himself. You can step inside his sumptuous bed chamber, where his wives and concubines would have presented themselves. The other rooms on the opposite side of the courtyard would have been occupied by the concubines in the summer months. They shared the hall at the far end of the complex in winter. Life as a Khivan concubine was tough. Girls, usually slaves, came into the harem around the age of 12 and, if they were lucky, lived here until about 30. Only wives of the emir were allowed to bear his children, so those concubines unfortunate enough to conceive were subjected to forced abortions, which were often fatal for the concubine, too. If the emir died, all of his concubines were evicted from the harem and resold in the slave market as a son could not inherit his father's wives or concubines.

The blue and white tiles that decorate the harem are absolutely stunning, and the proportions of the courtyard are most unusual. The ceilings are attractively painted. It is thought they were prepared in a workshop and then lifted into place once complete. There is a small Museum of Handicrafts (*entrance included in the Ichon Qala ticket price*) in the harem, which has dusty dioramas and photos, but it's not really worth more than a cursory glance.

A long corridor once linked the harem with the Ishrat Khauli (public court), though visitors are now required to take a more circuitous route. This is where the khan would have received envoys and other guests. As in the Kunya Ark there is space to erect a yurt in the courtyard; the throne room was on the upper floor. In addition to geometric majolica tiles you should also take a look at the calligraphy; the words are taken from the poet Ogahi.

The third courtyard is the Arz Khana (law court). Larger than the Ishrat Khauli, this was where the most important affairs of state took place. Allah Kuli Khan would have presided here for four hours each day and been expected to dispense justice. Defendants would exit the courtyard through one of the two gateways: the first was for those acquitted, the second led to the executioner. The tiles in this courtyard are considered amongst the finest in Khiva. Indeed, they were made by Abdullah the Genius, who was given this particular moniker after completing his work on the palace.

As you leave the Arz Khana, look left to see the emir's carriage. Made in St Petersburg, this was an official gift in 1876 and somehow has survived intact.

During the summer season dinner shows with traditional music and dance take place in the palace courtyard. Details and bookings are available through the information centre (page 238).

Museums Khiva's museums are a mixed bag: indeed many visitors are so focused on the architectural masterpieces that they understandably feel little need to venture inside the small, somewhat dated museums. The pick of the bunch are the Museum of Musical Art and the Museum of Applied Arts (⊕ *09.00–18.00 daily; admission included in the Ichon Qala entrance ticket price*). The former is situated inside the Kazy Kalyan Madrassa and covers the musical traditions of Khorezm, with a number of instruments on show; the latter, in the Islam Khoja Madrassa, has a reasonable collection of regional textiles, metalwork, tiles and carvings, and the Russian School exhibits black-and-white photographs of Khiva and its inhabitants from the first few decades of the 20th century.

Other structures Behind the Ak Mosque are the **Anusha Khan Baths** where, for more than 300 years, the ordinary citizens of Khiva could take a dip. As with their Roman predecessors, these baths had underfloor heating, and the baths themselves were sunk into the ground to conserve as much heat as possible. The baths belonged to the khan and access was prohibited for women, non-Muslims and, probably quite sensibly, anyone with a contagious skin disease.

The cupolas of the **Allah Kuli Khan Tim** (trading dome) link the Ichon Qala with the **Allah Kuli Khan Caravanserai**. Both structures date from the 1830s and would once have been the commercial heartland of the Ichon Qala, selling everything from Siberian furs to Persian carpets, Indian spices to Turkish sweets. The goods these days are a little less exotic, and sadly lean towards overpriced plastic imports from China. Take note of the caravanserai's two-storey design: the upper level would have served as a budget hotel for merchants and enabled them to keep a close eye on their goods at night.

Khiva's most gruesome site is the **zindan**, the city's dungeon. Though less notorious than the zindan in Bukhara's Ark (it's all relative; page 217), prisoners would have been held here before they were sent to the gallows. They were executed into a pit immediately outside the zindan so that those inside could hear the screams and be continually reminded of what ultimately awaited them. The current building dates from 1910 and showcases a range of manacles and torture implements (flailing, beating and stuffing the mouth full of salt were especially popular), as well as artistic but still gruesome paintings of torture and executions.

Dishon Qala The 5.6km (3.5 miles) of city walls of the Dishon Qala were erected in 1842 by Allah Kuli Khan. Unlike the mud bricks of the Ichon Qala, these walls are made of clay mined north of Khiva at Ghovuk Kul. Local legend has it that clay from the same source was also used to build Medina, though there is no scientific or historical evidence to support this claim. Some 200,000 people purportedly worked on the walls' construction (many of them slaves), and there were once ten gateways, though today only three remain. Two of these gates, the **Kosh Darvoza** (Double Gate) and the **Gandimyan Darvoza** (Western Gate), have small domes atop their pillars, and attractively patterned tilework. The Kosh Darvoza is so-called because its forward-thinking architect designed it so that traffic could enter and leave the city simultaneously rather than creating a choke point on the road.

Madrassas Close to the Palvan Darvoza are the **mosque and madrassa of Said Niaz Shalikarbai**, a rice merchant (*shalikar* meaning 'rice grower') who endowed the building in the 1830s. It was completed in 1840. Still in use as a place of worship, it is Khiva's largest mosque after the Juma Mosque and the only place in the city where the muezzin still calls the faithful to prayer. Listen out for his dulcet tones in the early morning and at dusk. The mosque's nine domes shelter worshippers during the cold winter months; in summer they can pray in the courtyard and in the shade of the four-pillared veranda.

There are half-a-dozen or so madrassas in the Dishon Qala, including the beautiful **Tort Shavaz Madrassa** (1885) with its open-sided, columned hall, green chequered minaret and tree-lined garden. Four tombs belonging to Yafandiyar I and three of his generals are also within the complex, and this gives the site its name (*tort shavaz* meaning 'four brave ones'). The Hungarian traveller Armin Vambery stayed in the madrassa's khanagha in 1863, dressed as a wandering dervish to avoid attracting attention. Following his time in central Asia, Vambery published a number of illuminating accounts including *Sketches of Central Asia* (1868) and *Manners in Oriental Countries* (1876). When we were last there, this madrassa was closed for restoration but should reopen during the lifespan of this edition.

Also of note are the **Bikajan Bika Madrassa** (1894), whose construction was halted for seven years following a dispute, believe it or not, over planning permission, and the robust-looking **Palvan Kari Madrassa** (1905), built by a Khivan merchant with profits from his trade with Russia and Turkey.

Mausoleums There are also several noteworthy mausoleums to keep an eye out for. The Abd al Bobo Mausoleum holds the grave of Palvan Ahmad Zamchiy (known as Abd al Bobo), a supposed descendant of Ali and an Islamic missionary in the wake of the Arab invasion. This is also the site of Khiva's original, infamous slave market, though there's little sign of this history now. The Shakalandar Bobo Mausoleum's simple, mud-brick structure remembers the Sufi Sheikh Kalandar Bobo and his two dervish brothers. Muhammad Khan, Muhammad Rakhimkhan II, Isfandiyar, Islam Khoja and a number of royal wives, mothers and children are buried in the much later Sayyid Muhammad Makhiruy Mausoleum; although on the site of an earlier sheikh's tomb, it is, in essence, a 19th-century royal family crypt.

Nurillabay Palace Muhammad Rakhimkhan II began building the vast Nurillabay Palace in 1906 following a visit to St Petersburg. He hoped that the palace, which was intended for his son, would incorporate many of the architectural features he'd seen in Russia. Behind the imposing defensive wall with its towers and buttresses were more than 100 rooms; the cost of construction nearly bankrupted the state. Parquet flooring was delivered from St Petersburg, fireplaces were installed in many of the rooms, and Tsar Nikolai II sent two chandeliers as a gift to mark the palace's completion.

What remains of the palace is languishing in despair, decaying metre by metre with every year that passes. The parts that remain intact, the courtyard, madrassa and reception hall, are largely conserved because of their importance to Soviet history: the last khan, Isfandiyar, was murdered here in 1918; the first people's government was established here in 1920; and the first statue of Lenin in central Asia was raised in the palace's courtyard. He has since been displaced by a modern statue of Mohammad Rakhimkhan II.

AROUND KHIVA

Kibla Tozabag (⊕ *09.00–17.00 daily*) The turn of the century Kibla Tozabag (New South Garden) was the summer residence of Muhammad Rakhimkhan II. Its 0.5ha plot is 2km south of the city centre, and its design incorporates both central Asian and Western features. Though the verandas are open in the traditional style, the palace also has large, European windows made by artisans in St Petersburg, and the front courtyard (there are three in total) is laid out with flowerbeds and a fountain. The buildings are made from fired bricks, in some places decorated with plasterwork and gilt, and the wide wooden doors were carved by German craftsmen. The palace was restored in 1992 to mark the 150th anniversary of its founder's birth, but it's rarely visited by tourists and you may well have the site to yourself.

Chapaev kolkhoz Just 20km east of Khiva, this collective farm has within its grounds the extraordinary 13th-century mausoleum of Sheikh Mukhtar Vali, a Sufi hermit and saint who was a rival of Pahlavan Mahmud (page 246). He is buried alongside his brother-in-law, Sayyid Ata, a follower of Khoja Ahmed Yassaui of Turkestan (now in southern Kazakhstan). The mausoleum complex, which was expanded and restored in 1807, rises 22m above the surrounding landscape and hence is a local landmark. In the past it offered pilgrims a place of refuge from Turkmen slave traders, and though that threat has thankfully now passed, you'll still be invited in for tea.

On the way to the mausoleum, you can stop at Chadra Hauli. This peculiar stepped tower, four storeys high, may at first look like a minaret but was in fact the summer residence of a local merchant. His simple living quarters are perched atop stables and storage rooms, and the caretaker will happily unlock the building for you to look around. Tip him a dollar (or the som equivalent) for his trouble.

10

Republic of Karakalpakstan

This desert province in northwest Uzbekistan is in fact an autonomous republic. It is theoretically sovereign (with the exception of the right to secession), and political decisions impacting upon it are made jointly by the Uzbek government and the Karakalpak legislature in the republic's capital, Nukus.

If you go back 2,000 years, Karakalpakstan was a fertile agricultural region, a far cry from the desert it is today. The indigenous people who lived here, the Karakalpaks, were nomadic herders and fishermen, fishing not only in the rivers but also in the southern parts of the Aral Sea. The area was nominally a part of the Khanate of Khiva, but was ceded to the Russian Empire in the 19th century. The Soviets considered it first as an autonomous part of Kazakhstan, then as an autonomous state within Uzbekistan from 1936 onwards.

Karakalpakstan has a population of 1.7 million, a third of whom are ethnically Karakalpak, a third of whom are Uzbek, and the balance of the population are Kazakh (300,000) and other minorities. There are two reasons to travel out into this Wild West of Uzbekistan: to bear witness to the environmental disaster that is the Aral Sea; and to wonder at how the incredible modern art collection of the Igor Savitsky Museum possibly made it out here.

NUKUS *Telephone code: 61*

Nukus is the provincial capital and therefore also the transport hub of Karakalpakstan. A small, dusty settlement until the 1930s, the planned city grew rapidly after it was chosen as the location for the Soviet Union's Chemical Research Institute. Its remote position made it the ideal terrain for developing and testing chemical weapons.

Today Nukus is a fairly grim and impoverished city of Soviet concrete, visited by few foreigners save NGO workers and environmental campaigners. Oh, and art lovers. For hidden in what is otherwise a desolate cultural wasteland is one of the world's finest collections of early 20th century Russian avant-garde art: the Igor Savitsky Museum.

GETTING THERE AND AWAY Reaching Nukus from almost anywhere in Uzbekistan is a trial; it's an unfortunate fact of life. If you are already in Urgench or Khiva it's feasible to travel by road, otherwise look instead at the rail options and flights.

By road Nukus lies 140km past Urgench on the A380, a 2-hour drive if you're coming by **car**. It's a far shorter drive (40km) across the Turkmen border to Konya-Urgench, though you'll inevitably have time-consuming border formalities to deal with. The border crossing is next to the village of Hojeli, and

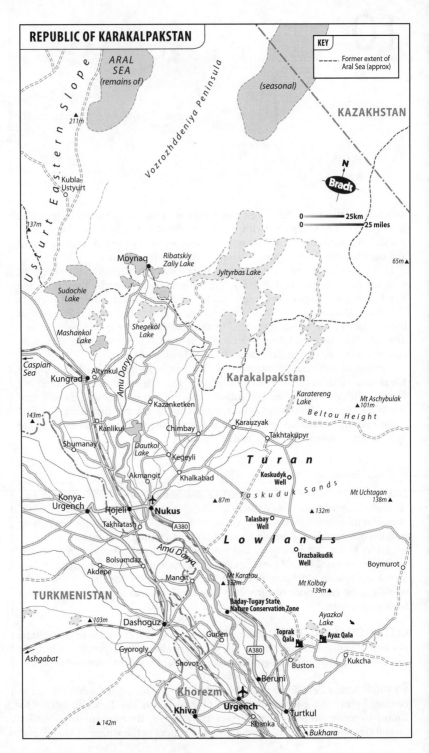

REPUBLIC OF KARAKALPAKSTAN

ARAL
SEA
(remains of)

Vozrozhddeniya Peninsula

(seasonal)

KAZAKHSTAN

KEY
--- Former extent of
Aral Sea (approx)

▲ 211m

Usturt Eastern Slope

Kubla
Ustyurt

▲ 137m

Moynaq

Ribatskiy
Zaliy Lake

Jyltyrbas Lake

▲ 65m

Sudochie
Lake

Shegekol
Lake

Mashankol
Lake

Caspian
Sea

Kungrad

Altynkul

Amu Darya

Karakalpakstan

Kazanketken

Karatereng
Lake

Mt Aschybulak
▲ 101m

Beltou Height

▲ 143m

Kanlikul

Chimbay

Karauzyak

Takhtakupyr

Shumanay

Dautkol
Lake

Kegeyli

T u r a n

Akmangit

Khalkabad

Koskudyk
Well

Taskuduk Sands

Mt Uchtagan
138m ▲

Konya-
Urgench

Hojeli

Nukus

▲ 87m

▲ 132m

Talasbay
Well

L o w l a n d s

Takhiatash

A380

Amu Darya

Bolsumdaz

Urazbaikudik
Well

Boymurot

Akdepe

Mangit

Mt Karatau
▲ 332m

Mt Kolbay
139m ▲

TURKMENISTAN

▲ 103m

Dashoguz

Baday-Tugay State
Nature Conservation Zone

Ayazkol
Lake

Toprak
Qala

Ayaz Qala

Gurlen

Ashgabat

Gyporogly

Shovot

Buston

Kukcha

Khorezm

Beruni

▲ 142m

Khiva

Urgench

Turtkul

Khanka

Bukhara

252

a taxi from Nukus to the border will cost you around US$12. On the Turkmen side, you may be lucky and find a taxi, but otherwise you will need to hitchhike with another motorist going in your direction.

The main bus station is the **Yuzhny Avtovokzal** (South Bus Station), which is on the other side of the tracks from the railway station. From here there are two long-distance buses a day to Bukhara (*8hrs; US$7*), Samarkand (*14hrs; US$10*) and Urgench (*3hrs; US$3*), and more frequent local buses (Nos 1 and 6) to Beruni and Moynaq. **Shared taxis** to Urgench or Khiva via Beruni depart from the same stop (*2½hrs; US$8*).

There are two buses a day to Tashkent. These depart from the **bus stop** outside Hotel Nukus (*4 Lumumba; 22hrs, US$14*).

By train The **railway station** is at the southern end of Dosnazarov. The new line from Nukus to Navoi bypasses Turkmenistan, thus removing the former need for a transit visa, and there are currently two services a week from Nukus to Tashkent (*22hrs; US$22*). Tickets can be purchased at the station or online.

By air There are two or three flights a day to Tashkent with **Uzbekistan Airways** (*1hr 45mins to 2hrs 35mins; from US$92* and onward connections to domestic and international destinations. It is also possible to fly to Moscow with Uzbekistan Airways or **Ural Airlines** (*3 times per week; 3hrs 35mins; from US$172*). The **airport** is northeast of the city, at the northern end of Dosnazarov.

For airline ticketing, you need the **Uzbekistan Airways** office (*43 Pushkin;* ☏ *222 7863;* e *info@uzairways.com*) or **Airservis Nukus** (*1 Saraev;* ☏ *222 1001*).

GETTING AROUND The centre of the city is contained within a square roughly 2km across, and the grid layout means it is easy to get around **on foot**. Most local **minibus** routes run from the bazaar. Bus No 1 goes to the train station, No 34 goes to the South Bus Station, and No 15 runs the length of Dosnazarov from the train station to the airport.

If you prefer to pre-book a taxi, try calling **Taxi Pilot** (☏ *361 5555*) or **Avto Vektor** (☏ *222 0088*). You will need to speak Russian or Uzbek to explain when and where to collect you. A ride within the city limits should not cost more than US$2.

TOURIST INFORMATION/TOUR OPERATORS The following organisations can organise tours of the area.

Ayim Tour 4 K Rzaev; ☏ 222 1100; e jipekhotel@gmail.com; www.ayimtour.com. Karakalpak specialists offering tours of the Khorezm fortresses & the Aral Sea. The same company owns Hotel Jipek Joli & the Karakalpak Aul Cafe.
Bes Qala 29/16 U Yusupov; ☏ 224 5169. Accompanied tours to the Aral Sea.

Sihaya Tours 47 Berdakh; ☏ (93) 920 1217. Guided tours around Nukus, & guides & transport to the Aral Sea.
🅘 Uzbektourism 41 Berdakh; ☏ 222 0203; e info@uzbektourism.uz; www.uzbektourism. uz. State-run travel agent with nationwide offices. Can arrange English-speaking guides, private tours, & bookings for accommodation & onward travel.

WHERE TO STAY AND EAT The food and accommodation options in Nukus have improved significantly in recent years, and though the hotels are not up to international standards, you'll find the below options clean and conveniently located.

Rahnamo Hotel (13 rooms) 2 Karakalpakstan; ☎ 222 4743. Opened in 2010, Nukus's self-professed 4-star hotel is a small establishment with something of the Fawlty Towers about it. Electricity & water can be erratic, but the staff are helpful. It's overpriced for what you get, but the bathrooms are generally clean & the b/fast isn't bad. B/fast & parking inc. **$$$$**

Hotel Jipek Joli (19 rooms) 4 Rzaev; ☎ 222 1100; e Jipek_hotel@gmail.com. The best place to stay in Nukus is owned by Ayim Tour. It's in a good location almost next door to the Savitsky Museum, the staff are helpful, & there is a friendly bar with Wi-Fi downstairs & in the pleasant courtyard garden. There are a few English satellite TV channels. Request one of the slightly more expensive AC rooms in summer. **$$–$$$**

Hotel Nukus (36 rooms) 4 Lumumba; ☎ 222 8941. Partially renovated & in a good location, this hotel shouldn't be so disappointing, but it is. There is a restaurant & bar downstairs but the sullen staff may well put you off your food. Haggle, as out of season you can get a dbl for US$25, a third off the advertised rate. **$$**

Mona Lisa 107 Gharezsislik. This offers something a little different, & does a so-so take on Georgian cuisine. **$$$**

Restaurant Neo 21 Tattabaev. We had a perfectly acceptable meal here, which did fresh shashlik, salads, & beer for 8,000 som. **$$$**

Sheraton 53 Gharezsislik. This is the best restaurant in Nukus & has a menu of good European & Russian dishes & pleasant decor. The toilets are squats only, so be warned. **$$$**

Karakalpak Aul Cafe 4 Rzaev. Decent option, where you can enjoy your plov sitting in a yurt on the patio. **$$–$$$**

ENTERTAINMENT Quite surprisingly for a city that feels completely like it is situated on the face of the moon, there are three theatres in Nukus. They all cater to a local audience with performances in Karakalpak, Russian or Uzbek, but regardless of whether or not you understand the words it can still be a fun experience. You will need to contact the individual theatres to find out what is showing, and when.

Berdakh Karakalpak State Musical Theatre 1 E Alakuz; ☎ 224 0657
Karakalpak State Puppet Theatre 27 22nd Microrayon; ☎ 223 7730

Khodzhaniyazov Youth Theatre 47 Turon; ☎ 222 8457

OTHER PRACTICALITIES

Communications The main **post office** is at 7 Karakalpakstan (⊕ 07.00–19.00 Mon–Fri). The same building houses the **telephone office**, which is open 24/7.

Medical Nukus has a surprisingly large number of hospitals, but the two most useful to visitors in a sticky situation are the **Emergency Hospital** (*100A Dosnazarov;* ☎ *222 9383*) and the **General Hospital** (*110 Dosnazarov;* ☎ *222 8111*). For less severe complaints you should go to **Polyclinic #6** (*1 Ulug Beg;* ☎ *224 4196*).

Money There are no ATMs in Nukus, but you can change money at the following banks, and the NBU can arrange cash advances for Visa card holders.

$ Asaka Bank 2 Karakalpakstan; ☎ 532 5030; ⊕ 09.00–17.00 Mon–Fri. Advances money to MasterCard holders. There is a second, smaller branch at 53A N Abdambetov (☎ 224 2269).

$ Hamkor Bank 135 A Timur; ☎ 222 2309; ⊕ 09.00–16.00 Mon–Fri
$ National Bank of Uzbekistan 52 Gharezsislik; ☎ 780 0020; ⊕ 09.00–18.00 Mon–Fri, 09.00–16.00 Sat. Advances money to Visa cardholders.

Registration The **OVIR** in Nukus is at 56 Berdakh (☎ *222 8615*).

WHAT TO SEE AND DO
Igor Savitsky Museum *(127 Rzaev;* ☎ *222 2526;* e *museum_savitsky@mail.ru; www. savitskycollection.org;* ⊕ *09.00–17.00 Tue–Sun; entrance fee 25,000 som, guided tour 15,000 som, camera permit 120,000 som – please note that smartphone cameras are not permitted)* Like a ruby in the dust, the Igor Savitsky Museum (also known simply as Nukus Museum) holds the world's second-largest collection of Russian avant-garde paintings after the Russian Museum in St Petersburg. It also has one of the largest exhibitions of archaeological finds and folk art anywhere in central Asia. At present, just 15% of the collection is on display, but a major expansion programme has recently begun, and when the two new buildings do open, there will be even more to see.

The museum is divided into five galleries. **Uzbek Art of the 1920s and 1930s** is a comprehensive survey of schools from realism to avant-garde, and the gallery includes the work of both Uzbek artists and foreign artists painting in Uzbekistan. The works show the important interplay of influences from East and West: architecture and decorative arts are drawn from Uzbekistan's Islamic traditions; artists such as Benkov, Koravay and Kashina depict the region's ancient cities; Nikolayev imaginatively blends the techniques of Italian masters and Russian iconography. There are also works of Impressionism, post-Impressionism and Futurism.

IGOR SAVITSKY

Born in Kiev in 1915, Savitsky was an ethnic Russian from Kiev. He was a painter, archaeologist and, most of all, a collector of art and artefacts. He initially trained as an electrician, but in 1950 he joined the Khorezm Archaeological and Ethnographic Expedition with the renowned Russian archaeologist Sergei Tolstov. Savitsky joined up as the expedition's artist, and the trip was to begin a lifelong love affair with Karakalpakstan.

When the dig was complete, Savitsky stayed on in Nukus and began to collect items of anthropological and archaeological interest. He also started buying paintings by Uzbek artists and also a few by Russian artists from the avant-garde school, many of whom had been denounced by the Soviet leadership and were politically and commercially unpopular at home. Savitsky amassed such a large collection that he convinced the authorities of the need for a museum in which to house it all, and the Savitsky Museum was duly opened in 1966 with Savitsky himself as its first curator.

With exhibition space available, and the tacit acceptance of the authorities, Savitsky's acquisitive side was given free rein. Through a network of art dealers, friends and casual acquaintances he bought (or took with the promise of later payment) further works by Russian avant-garde artists including Kliment Redko, Lyubov Popova, Mukhina, Ivan Koudriachov and Robert Falk. These artists were already well-established names but their work was not widely accepted in Russia. It was therefore a buyer's market, and Savitsky seized the opportunity with both hands, albeit at great personal and professional risk. His purchases made during the late 1960s and 1970s form the core of the museum's 90,000 item collection today.

The story of Savitsky, the museum and some of the artists whose work it displays is told in the excellent 2010 film *Desert of Forbidden Art*.

Republic of Karakalpakstan NUKUS

On the top floor is the most famous gallery, is the **20th-century Russian Avant-Garde**, a smorgasbord of post-revolutionary works that narrowly survived Stalin's curtailment of creative freedom and prescription of 'Social Realism' as the only acceptable form of Soviet art in 1932. Art that did not conform with Stalin's ideal was repressed and its artists persecuted.

Savitsky acquired works by persecuted artists (including M Sokolov, the murdered V Komarovskiy, and the Amaravella group) and also paintings by then unknown artists. The works of artists such as R Mazel, P Sokolov, A Sofronova, E Ermilova-Platova and K Red'ko were not recognised, let alone appreciated, by anyone else until the late 1960s.

The **Karakalpakstan Contemporary Art** gallery aims to showcase and develop fine art in Karakalpakstan. Among the artists whose work is exhibited here are several of Savitsky's students: J Kuttymuratov, D Toreniyazov, B Serekeev, A Utegenov and E Joldasov. There are important examples of Karakalpak painting, and also contemporary sculpture based on traditional woodcarving. Here you can also see some of Savitsky's own oils and watercolours: he was a gifted painter in his own right.

The core of the museum (at least in terms of number of items) is the gallery of **Karakalpak Folk Art**. The collection includes more than 70,000 items, many of which were obtained by Savitsky in the 1950s, and it is believed that the relationships and reputation he formed collecting folk art gave him the credibility and network required to later purchase his avant-garde works. The folk art gallery includes a full-size yurt made of wool, leather and wood, pile rugs, flat weaves, embroidery, appliqué work, printed and stitched leather, carved and inlaid wood and traditional jewellery.

Often unfortunately overlooked is the gallery entitled **Archaeology and Ancient Khorezm**. It is here you will find some of the most significant archaeological finds from the various excavations in Khorezm, including from the fortresses. There is some particularly attractive statuary, pots, coins, and ceramic pipes from a medieval sewer system that was in use until 1900.

The **Museum of Historical Studies** has now closed. Part of its collection has been relocated to the Savitsky Museum, and the balance has gone into storage.

House Museum of Amet and Aiymkhan Shamuratovs *(29 N Saraev; \222 3452; ⊕ 09.00–19.00 Tue–Sat)* Husband and wife Amet and Aiymkhan Shamuratovs must have been the darlings of the Karakalpakstan artistic set: he was a leading poet and dramatist, she a beguiling and beautiful actress and performer. In addition to their personal papers and photographs, the museum exhibits costumes from Aiymkhan's numerous theatrical roles and also applied arts from Karakalpakstan, which are displayed within a traditional yurt.

Mizdarkhan and Yusup Ishan If you haven't yet had enough of cemeteries and mausoleums during your tour of Uzbekistan, you can drive 15km west of Nukus on the road towards Konya Urgench, and there you will find two sites of interest, Mizdarkhan, and Yusup Ishan.

Mizdarkhan was once the second largest city in Khorezm. It was founded in the 4th century BC and inhabited for around 1,700 years, when it was destroyed by Timur. Even after the inhabitants fled, the site was still considered sacred, and so local people returned to build mausoleums and small mosques, some of which have survived almost intact. The most impressive of these is the restored 12th–14th century mausoleum of Mazlum Khan Slu. Other mausoleums of note include the

11th century tomb of Caliph Yejereb, and the mausoleum of Shamun Nabi, whose 25m sarcophagus is said to grow another inch each year.

Yusup Ishan was the rival town to Mizdarkhan, and also has a substantially sized cemetery dating back to the medieval period. If you do not have your own transport, you can take a shared taxi from Nukus to the village of Hojeli (*20mins*), then change into a shared taxi heading towards the border, and ride it 3km to Mizdarkhan and Yusup Ishan.

MOYNAQ *Telephone code: 61*

Moynaq (also written Muynaq) is the harbour without a sea. In just 50 years it has gone from being a wealthy fishing port on the edge of the world's fourth-largest inland sea, to a ghost town where skeleton ships lie broken in the desert. The shrinking of the Aral Sea (see box, page 4) is one of the world's greatest manmade environmental disasters, and nowhere is its impact being felt more poignantly than in Moynaq.

GETTING THERE AND AROUND Regular **buses** (*4hrs; US$4*) make the journey back and forth from Nukus's South Bus Station to Moynaq via Kungrad. They're invariably overcrowded. It's faster to take a **shared taxi** (*3hrs; US$10*) to make the journey from Nukus's train station to Kungrad, and then pick up a second shared taxi there.

If you hire a taxi to yourself, it'll cost in the region of US$80 return as relatively few drivers want to make the trip. Most people prefer to visit Moynaq as a day trip rather than staying the night.

A ribbon development less than 2km long, when you get there, you can explore the town **on foot.**

TOUR OPERATORS For guided tours and transport, including helicopter tours out over the sea, you will need to contact a company in Nukus (page 253). Although you will have a superb view, taking a helicopter in Uzbekistan is not advised due to the poor maintenance and safety records of the aircraft used.

WHERE TO STAY AND EAT It is not recommended to stay the night in Moynaq unless you really have to. The only hotel in town is the **Hotel Oybek** (☎ *322 1868;* **$**), which lies 4km north of the centre, tucked behind the police station. It seems clean enough, and there is hot water in the shared bathroom, but the absence of fans (and often electricity) means it's unpleasantly sticky in summer. The hotel can provide dinner if you're desperate, but it's better to bring a picnic from Nukus.

WHAT TO SEE AND DO Coming to Moynaq is, perhaps, what you'd term 'disaster tourism': there are parallels to be drawn with the Polygon or Chernobyl. You come to see where the sea used to be, and the suffering it has left behind. Close to the Hotel Oybek is the **Aral Sea Memorial**, and beneath it the **ships' graveyard**, where various rusting hulks of former fishing vessels have been towed from elsewhere in the desert to create a tourist attraction. There were at one stage many more, but most have now been sold off for their scrap value in a desperate bid to compensate for the loss of income from fishing.

The **Moynaq Museum** (*US$1*) on the main road has photographs of the town in its heyday, as well as fishing nets and cans of long out-of-date fish.

Appendix 1

LANGUAGE

Knowing just phrases of Uzbek and Russian, and being able to read the Cyrillic script will make your life immeasurably easier when travelling in Uzbekistan, especially given that words are often transliterated into Latin with a confusing variety of spellings: variations such as Tashkent and Toshkent are fairly obvious, things get trickier if you're swapping X and Kh or K and Q, or if more than one word or name are combined. Thus, you might see Amin Khan in one place, and Aminxan in another; Muynak is often written Moynoq. You'll have to get used to making some educated guesses.

Though people will always do their best to make themselves understood, English is not widely spoken in Uzbekistan, and you will both help yourself and make a positive impression if you can say a few words. Don't be shy, and don't worry about your pronunciation or grammar. Just go for it.

HELPFUL UZBEK AND RUSSIAN WORDS AND PHRASES In the pronunciation guides for the Russian, capital letters are used to denote syllables that are stressed.

English	Uzbek	Russian
Hello	*As-salomu alaykum*	Здравствуйте (ZDRAHST-ooy-tyeh)
Good-bye	*Salomat bo'ling*	До свидания (da-svee-DA-ee-ya)
How are you?	*Qalay siz?*	Как дела? (kahg dee-LAH?)
Fine, thank you	*Yakshi, rakhmat*	Хорошо, спасибо (khah-rah-HOH spah-SEE-buh)
What is your name?	*Sizning ismingiz nima?*	Как вас зовут? (kahk vahs ah-VOOT?)
My name is …	*Mening ismim …*	Меня зовут … (mee-NYAH ah-VOOT …)
Nice to meet you	*Tanishganimdan hursandman*	Очень приятно (OH-cheen' pree-YAHT-nuh)
Please	*Markhamat*	Пожалуйста (pah-ZHAH-uh-stuh)
Thank you	*Rakhmat*	Спасибо (spuh-SEE-buh)
You're welcome	*Arzimaydi*	Не за что (NYEH-zuh-shtoh)
Yes	*Ha*	Да (dah)
No	*Yok*	Нет (nyeht)
Excuse me	*Kechirasiz*	Извините (eez-vee-NEET-yeh)
Is there someone here who speaks English?	*Inglizcha gapiradiganlar bormi?*	Кто-нибудь здесь говорит по-английски? (KTOH-ee-bood' zdyehs guh-vah-EET pah an-GLEES-kee?)

258

I don't understand	Tushunmadim	Я не понимаю (ya nee puh-ee-MIGH-yoo)
Where is the hotel/restaurant/bank/bus station?	Mehmonhona, restoran, bank, avtobus bekati qaerda?	Где находится гостиница/ресторан / банк / автовокзал? (Gdye nahoditsya gostinitsa / restoran / bank / avtovokzal?)
Where is the toilet?	Hojat'hona qayerda?	Где туалет? (gdyeh too-ah-YEHT?)
Where can we buy ice cream/spices?	Qaerda muzqaymoq/ziravorlar sotib olsa bo'ladi?	Где можно купить мороженое/специи? (Gdye mojna kupit morojenoye/spetsiyi?)
Cumin, Saffron, Cardamon	Zira, za'faron, kashnich	тмин, шафран, кардамон (tmin, shafran, kardamon)
Where can we buy natural silk, cotton fabrics?	Qaerda chin shoyi, chin paxta gazmollarini sotib olsa bo'ladi?	Где можно купить натуральный шелк, хлопчатобумажные ткани? (Gdye mojna kupit naturalniy shelk, hlopchatobumajniye tkaniy?)
How long will it take to reach…?	U yerga borish qancha vaqt oladi?	Как долго продолжается путешествие, чтобы доехать туда?

(Kak dolga prodoljaetsya puteshestviye shtobiy doyehat tuda?)

How long do we have to wait?	Bunga qancha vaqt ketadi?	Как долго нам надо ждать? (Kak dolga nam nada jdat?)
Where can I exchange foreign currency notes?	Pul almashuvi qaerda?	Где можно обменять иностранную валюту? (Gdye mojna obmenyat inostrannuyu valyutu?)
How much does it cost?	Buni narhi qancha?	Сколько стоит? (Skolka stoyit)
It is too expensive	Bu juda qimmat	Это слишком дорого (Eta slishkam doroga)
Do you have this in another size/colour/material?	Sizlarda boshqa razmer/ranglar/material bor mi?	У вас есть это в другом размере? / в другой цвет? / в другом материале? (U vas yest eta v drugom razmerye? / v drugoi tsvyet? / v drugom materialye?)
Please give me the bill	Bizdan qancha?	Счёт, пожалуйста. (Shyot pajalustya.)
I'm sick	Kasaldirman	Я болен (yah-BOH-leen)/ (m)/ (f) Я больна (yah-bahl'-NAH)
Help!	Yordam!	Помогите! (puh-mah-GEE-yeh!)
Where is…?	…qayerda?	Как добраться до_____ ? kahk dah-BRAH-tsuh duh ___?) [lit. How do I get to…?)

LATIN	UZBEK CYRILLIC	IPA (INTERNATIONAL PHONETIC ALPHABET)	ENGLISH SOUND (AS IN)
A a	А а	/a, æ/	ch**ai**
B b	Б б	/b/	**b**at
D d	Д д	/d̪/	**d**en
E e	Е е	/Э э /e/	sl**eigh**
F f	Ф ф	/ɸ/	**f**ish
G g	Г г	/ɡ/	**g**o
H h	Х х	/h/	**h**oe
I i	И и	/i, ɨ/	m**e**
J j	Ж ж	/dʒ/	**j**oke
K k	К к	/k/	**c**old
L l	Л л	/l/	**l**ist
M m	М м	/m/	**m**an
N n	Н н	/n/	**n**ext
O o	О о	/ɒ, o/	h**o**t
P p	П п	/p/	**p**in
Q q	Қ қ	/q/	Ira**q**
R r	Р р	/r/	**r**at
S s	С с	/s/	**s**ick
T t	Т т	/t̪/	**t**oe
U u	У у	/u, y/	z**oo**
V v	В в	/v, w/	**w**est
X x	Х х	/χ/	**kh**an
Y y	Й й	/j/	**y**es
Z z	З з	/z/	**z**ebra
O' o'	Ў ў	/o, ø, ɣ/	w**o**rk
G' g'	Ғ ғ	/ʁ/	**g**uest
Sh sh	Ш ш	/ʃ/	**sh**oe
Ch ch	Ч ч	/tʃ/	**ch**ew
	ʼъ	/ʔ/	(unstressed)
Yo yo	Ё ё	/jo/	**yo**-yo
Yu yu	Ю ю	/ju/	**you**
Ya ya	Я я	/ja/	**ya**wn
Ts ts	Ц ц	/ts/	le**ts**

airport	*tayyorgokh*	аэропорта (ah-ehr-ah-POHR-uh)
bus station	*autobiket*	автовокзала? (ahf-tuh-vah-ZAH-luh)
train station	*temir yul vogzali*	вокзала? (vah-GZAH-luh)
hotel	*mehmonkhona*	гостиницы (gahs-TEE-nee-syh)
left	*chap*	налево (nuh-LYEH-vuh)
right	*ong*	направо (nuh-PRAH-vuh…)

Do you have any rooms?	*Sizga khona bormi?*	У вас есть свободные комнаты? (oo vash YEHST' vah-BOD-nyh-yeh OHM-nuh-tyh)
How much?	*Qancha?*	Сколько (SKOHL'-kuh)
cheap	*arzon*	дорого (DOH-ruh-guh)
expensive	*qimmat*	дёшево (DYOH-shyh-vuh)
The bill, please	*Iltimos, xisob-kitob qiling?*	Счёт пожалуйста (Schyot ah-ZHA-luh-stuh)
menu	*menyu*	меню (men-YOO)
coffee	*qahva*	кофе (KOF-ye)
black tea	*chorniy chai*	черный чай (CHYOR-niy hai)
green tea	*zilloniy chai*	зеленый чай (zee-LYO-niy hai)
milk	*sut*	молоко (ma-la-KOH)
juice	*shira*	сок (sok)
vodka	*vodka*	водка (VOD-kuh)
beer	*pivo*	пиво (PEE-vuh)
wine	*vino*	вино (vee-NOH)
water	*suv*	вода (vuh-DAH)
1	*bir*	один (ah-DEEN)
2	*ikki*	два (dvah)
3	*uch*	три (tree)
4	*to'rt*	четыре (chee-TYH-ree)
5	*besh*	пять (pyaht')
6	*olti*	шесть (shehst')
7	*yetti*	семь (syeem')
8	*sakkiz*	восемь (VOH-seem')
9	*to'qqiz*	девять (DYEH-veet')
10	*o'n*	десять (DYEH-suht')
20	*yigirma*	двадцать (DVAHD-zuht')
100	*yuz*	сто (stoh)
1,000	*ming*	тысяча (TYH-see-chuh)
1,000,000	*million*	миллион (mee-lee-OHN)

Appendix 2

GLOSSARY

Ak White
Apteka Pharmacy
Ark Fortified citadel
ASSR Autonomous Soviet Socialist Republic
Aviakassa Airline ticket office
Avtobus Bus
Avtostantsia Bus stand
Avtovokzal Bus station

Babushka Grandmother or older woman
Bagh Garden
Basmachi Muslim resistance fighters who fought the Bolsheviks
Beg District governor or other wealthy figure
Buz kashi Traditional sport played on horseback with a goat carcass in place of a ball

Caravanserai Ancient hostelry for merchants and their animals
Chai Tea
Chaikhana Café or tea house
Chapan Striped coat, as worn by Afghanistan's President Karzai
Chorsu Crossroads
CIS Commonwealth of Independent States
Cupola Dome

Dacha Holiday home
Dariakhana Pharmacy
Daravaza Gate
Darya River
Dom Building or house

FSB Current incarnation of the KGB
FSU Former Soviet Union

GAI Traffic police
Ganch Alabaster carving
Girikh Star-like motif in tiles or plasterwork
Great Game See box, page 17

Hamman Baths
Harem Female living quarters in a household divided by gender
Hauli Palace
Hauz Pool or reservoir
Hujra Sleeping cell in a madrassa or *khanagha*

Ibn Son of
Ikat Striped silk
IMU Islamic Movement of Uzbekistan
IRP Islamic Renaissance Party
Ismaili Shi'ite sect; followers of the Aga Khan
Iwan Covered veranda with its roof supported by pillars

Jadid 20th-century Islamic reform movement
Juma Friday

Kala Fortress
Kara Black
Kassa Cashier
Khana House or place
Khanagha Hostel for Sufi holy men
Khoja Descendant of Arabian missionaries; gentleman of high status
Kino Cinema
Kishlak Village
Kok Blue
Kolkhoz Collective farm
Kufic Form of stylised Arabic script used in calligraphy
Kum Desert
Kupe Locking railway compartment containing four bunks
Kurgan Burial mound or fort
Kyzyl Red

Laghman Noodle soup
LOI Letter of Invitation

Madrassa Islamic school
Manty Meat-filled steamed dumplings
Marshrutka Minibus
Maydoni Square
Mazar Shrine built around a mausoleum
Mihrab Niche in a mosque that faces
    towards Mecca
Minor Minaret
Mustakillik Independence

Navruz Persian New Year
Non Round, flat bread

Oblast Administrative region
OVIR Office for visas and registration
Oxus Greek name for the Amu Darya River

Piala Handleless teacup
Pishtak Decorative portico
Platskartny Third- or economy-class
    train travel, featuring bunks in open
    compartments
Plov Rice-based dish with meat and carrots
Prospekt Avenue

Rabat Caravanserai
Registan Central square

Samsa Meat-filled pastry
Sayyid Descendant of Prophet Muhammad
Shakhristan Inner part of a citadel
Shashlik Skewered lumps of meat cooked
    over coals
Som Uzbekistan's currency
SSR Soviet Socialist Republic
Sufi Mystic Islamic tradition
Suzani Embroidered fabric, usually used as
    a wall hanging or bedspread

Tash Stone
Teppa Fort
Tim Covered bazaar
TsUM Central department store
Turbaza Soviet holiday camp

Ulitsa Street

Viloyat Province

Zindan Prison

Appendix 3

FURTHER INFORMATION

BOOKS
History and archaeology

Boulnois, Luce *Silk Road: Monks, Warriors and Merchants on the Silk Road* Odyssey Guides, 2012. Detailed history of the people and ideas that spread along the Silk Road. Also available in French.

Francopan, P *The Silk Roads: A New History of the World* Bloomsbury, 2015. A superb reinterpretation of world history, with the Silk Road rather than Europe as its principal focus.

Hiro, Dilip *Inside Central Asia: A Political and Cultural History of Uzbekistan, Turkmenistan, Kazakhstan, Kyrgyzstan, Tajikistan, Turkey, and Iran* Gerald Duckworth & Co Ltd., 2009. A straightforward introduction to the former Soviet Republics of central Asia, and their immediate neighbours.

Hopkirk, Peter *The Great Game: On Secret Service in High Asia* Oxford University Press, 2001. The seminal work on the Great Game. Lively, scholarly and full of all the excitement of a *Boy's Own* adventure.

Soucek, Svat *A History of Inner Asia* Cambridge University Press, 2000. A scholarly account of the history of a complex region.

Tolstov, Sergei *Following the Tracks of Ancient Khorezmian Civilization* UNESCO, 2005. Republished account of the original excavations of the Khorezmian desert fortresses. Translated from the Russian.

Whitfield, Susan *Aurel Stein on the Silk Road* Serindia, 2004. Beautifully illustrated account of Stein's exploration of central Asia and of his archaeological finds.

Wood, Michael *In the Footsteps of Alexander the Great* BBC Books, 2007. A fascinating accompaniment to the television series of the same name.

Post-independence Uzbekistan

Adams, L *The Spectacular State: Culture and National Identity in Uzbekistan* Duke University Press, 2010. An accessible discussion of the creation of a new national identity for Uzbekistan in the 1990s. Incorporates both continuity of Soviet traditions and new, government-led cultural and political ideology.

Murray, C *Murder in Samarkand: A British Ambassador's Controversial Defiance of Tyranny in the War on Terror* Mainstream Publishing, 2007. Murray lays bare the darker side of the War on Terror and the UK and US support for the Uzbekistan government in spite of its disturbing human rights abuses.

Rand, R *Tamerlane's Children: Dispatches from Contemporary Uzbekistan* One World Publications, 2006. Journalist and radio producer Robert Rand draws upon his three years working in Uzbekistan to create this complex picture of a country caught between its history and modernity, unsure of what its cultural and political identity should be.

Central Asian geopolitics

Mullerson, Rein *Central Asia: A Chessboard and Player in the New Great Game* Kegan Paul, 2007. Looks at the geopolitics of the region, with the central Asian republics themselves as players (as against the 19th-century works about the 'Great Game' which tended to regard the region as merely the chessboard across which the 'game' was played out by the great powers).

Whitlock, Monica *Beyond the Oxus: The Central Asians* John Murray, 2003. Vivid account of the last three decades of central Asia's history by the former BBC correspondent to central Asia.

Travellers' accounts

Alexander, C *Carpet Ride to Khiva* Icon Books Ltd, 2010. Fascinating account of the establishment of the UNESCO-backed carpet workshop in Khiva and Alexander's own travels to discover traditional dyes, patterns and techniques. Well written and highly enjoyable.

Burnes, Alexander *Travels in Bokhara* Oxford University Press, 1973. Classic portrait of Bukhara at the height of the Great Game. Fascinating.

Byron, Robert *The Road to Oxiana* Oxford University Press, 2007. The classic traveller's tale of the author's exploration of central Asia in the 1930s.

Krist, Gustav *Alone through the Forbidden Land* Ian Faulkner, 1992. Thrilling account of an Australian POW travelling incognito as a carpet seller in Uzbekistan in the 1930s.

Metcalfe, Daniel *Out of Steppe* Arrow, 2009. Adventurous traveller Metcalfe traverses central Asia in pursuit of distinct ethnic communities disappearing as modernity impinges on their way of life. Features both the Karakalpaks and the Bukharan Jews. A finely written and often moving account.

Omrani, Bijan *Asia Overland: Tales of Travel on the Trans-Siberian and Silk Road* Odyssey Guides, 2010. Beautifully written and heavily illustrated historical travelogue drawing on accounts from Fa Xian to Anton Chekhov, and Marco Polo to Francis Younghusband. Full of humour, *Asia Overland* is an entertaining and informative read for armchair travellers and modern-day explorers alike.

Thubron, Colin *The Lost Heart of Asia* Heinemann, 1994. The author travels through central Asia soon after the emergence of the independent republics. One of a spate of accounts of travels through the region written during this turbulent period. Elegantly written and predominantly focused on Uzbekistan.

Culture, traditions and language

Azimova, N *Uzbek: An Elementary Textbook* Georgetown University Press, 2010. Introductory course to Uzbek that includes a CD with interactive learning exercises.

Harvey, Janet *Traditional Textiles of Central Asia* Thames & Hudson, 1997. Informative introduction to the textiles of the region.

Khakhimov, A *Atlas of Central Asian Artistic Crafts and Trades* Sharq, 1999. The first volume of this series covers Uzbekistan exclusively and has short essays on each craft written by anthropologists and curators. The colour plates are well produced and accompanied by old photographs and maps showing traditional centres for the different crafts.

Visson, L *The Art of Uzbek Cooking* Hippocrene Books, 1999. Authentic recipes for 170 Uzbek dishes, from plov to walnut-stuffed quinces.

Art and architecture

Chuvin, Pierre & Degeorge, Gerard *Samarkand, Bukhara, Khiva* Flammarion, 2003. Heavily illustrated with exquisite photographs, this book is a visual journey through the architectural influences of Uzbekistan's three most famous cities.

Knobluch, Edgar *Monuments of Central Asia: A Guide to the Archaeology, Art and Architecture of Turkestan* I B Tauris, 2001. Scholarly overview of artistic styles and influences.

Lukonin, V & Ivanov, A *Central Asian Art* Parkstone International, 2012. Architectural tour of central Asia focusing primarily on the influence of Persia and China, Buddhism and Islam. Includes well-produced photographs.

O'Kane, Bernard *Studies in Persian Art and Architecture* Columbia University Press, 1996. Collection of academic articles discussing Uzbek art and architecture in the wider context of the Persian-speaking world.

Literature
Aini, S *Bukhara: Reminisces* Progress Books, 1986. English translation of one of Aini's finest works.

Ferdowsi, A *Shahnameh: The Persian Book of Kings* Penguin Classics, 2007. Deluxe, three book set of Ferdowsi's epic. Vividly translated and with fine illustrations.

Tabatabai, S *Rudaki and his Poetry* Leiden University Press, 2010. Scholarly biography of the Samanid poet Rudaki, with discussion of many of his poems.

Thackston,'W (trans) *Baburnama* Modern Library Inc, 2002. The finest English translation of the Chagatai Turkish memoirs of the Mughal emperor Babur.

Natural history
Ayé, R, Schweizer, M & Roth, T *The Birds of Central Asia* Christopher Helm, Bloomsbury, 2012. A useful field guide.

MAGAZINES
Steppe A glossy, annually produced magazine covering the wider central Asian region, with notably strong photography. It is available at specialist bookstores and by subscription. Further information is available at www.steppemagazine.com.

MAPS
Uzbekistan
Uzbekistan 1:1,580,000 ITMB Maps, 2012. New edition in English. Inset city maps of Tashkent and Samarkand.

Uzbekistan 1:1,500,000 Roskartografia, 2001. Large, Cyrillic map. Fergana Valley is shown at a scale of 1:750,000. Inset city map of Tashkent.

Central Asia
Central Asia 1:1,750,000 Gizi Map, 2007. Large, predominantly topographic map with a detailed index of places.

Central Asia 1:1,750,000 Nelles Map, 2011. Combined political and topographical map, including a small city plan of Tashkent.

The colour country map and regionals produced in this book were based on source material supplied by ITMB Publishing (*www.itmb.com*).

WEBSITES
Uzbek government sites
en.mcs.uz Ministry of Culture and Sport.

www.uzbekembassy.org Uzbek Embassy in London.

www.uzbektourism.uz State tourism company site including national tourism strategy and legislation. Limited information on visa requirements.

Travel advice
www.caravanistan.com The most comprehensive online guide to travelling the Silk Road.

www.fco.gov.uk/travel Foreign and Commonwealth Office travel advice.

www.travel.state.gov US State Department travel advice.

www.ukinuzbekistan.fco.gov.uk Website of the British Embassy in Uzbekistan.

News and political analysis

www.bbc.co.uk/uzbek Home of the BBC Uzbek service (in Uzbek).

www.theconwaybulletin.com Independent news sheet covering central Asia and the Caucasus, founded in 2010 by the *Daily Telegraph*'s former central Asia correspondent.

www.eurasianet.org News and analysis covering the central Asian region on a site run by the Open Society Institute.

www.roberts-report.com Analysis of central Asian stories put together by US academic Sean Roberts, an expert on Kazakhstan.

www.timesca.com The Bishkek-based *Times of Central Asia* reports in English on all five central Asian republics, plus Afghanistan.

Culture

www.karakalpak.com Independent, authoritative encyclopaedia on the history and culture of the Karakalpaks.

www.samarkand.info History of the city and its sights, with some practical information.

www.uzbekcuisine.com The definitive guide to Uzbek food and cooking.

www.uzfiles.com An Uzbek YouTube with clips from Uzbek films and tracks from Uzbek singers.

Telephone directories

www.goldenpages.uz
www.yellowpages.uz

Index

Page numbers in **bold** refer to main entries and those in *italics* to maps.

INDEX OF ADVERTISERS